The Limits of
Civic
Activism

Robert Weissberg

The Limits of Civic Activism

Cautionary Tales on the Use of Politics

Transaction Publishers
New Brunswick (U.S.A.) and London (U.K.)

Library of Congress Catalog Number:
ISBN: 0-7658-0261-9
Printed in the United States of America

Library of Congress Cataloging-in-Publication Data

Weissberg, Robert, 1941-
    The limits of civic activism : some cautionary tales on the use of politics /
    Robert Weissberg.
        p. cm.
    Includes bibliographical references and index.
    ISBN: 0-7658-0261-9 (alk. paper)
    1. Political participation—United States.   2. Political activists—
United States.   I. Title.

JK1764. W373 2004
323'.042'0973—dc22   2004058045

Contents

Preface

The Limits of Civic Activism has had a protracted birth. Though I have taught "political participation" for three-plus decades, the urge to put my thoughts down in book form is a recent arrival. No doubt, witnessing the passing parade of student infatuations has slowly engendered a skepticism whose expression can no longer be suppressed. To hear my students energetically defending a medley of momentarily fashionable crusades scarcely conscious of what their passions might bring, let alone conceivable pernicious consequences, has extracted its toll. To doubt their enthusiasm, to gently hint that their confrontation was futile, even counter-productive, suggested a curmudgeonly evil spirit out of touch with a "better world." Attacking motherhood and apple pie would have been safer. Sad to say, the Children's Crusade's spirit lives on though today's Great Evil is likely to be globalization, profit-hungry pharmaceutical companies, the CIA, and others catch-phrase demons about which the anxious-to-join-the-fray combatants know almost zero.

My assigned class readings further exacerbated dissatisfaction. Even reviewing a perfectly humdrum textbook chapter prior to lectures triggered unease, and progressively less classroom time was spent explicating these alleged verities. Once sacred dogma in the Behavioralist Temple was no longer personally believable; the gap between the "standard" disciplinary picture regarding civic engagement and what is patently obvious in daily politics had become nearly unbridgeable, at least to me. I often felt that these assignments transmitted theology, not hard-edged political fact.

To wit, if the professional literature regarding American civic activism were exclusively consulted, the inescapable conclusion is that apathy abounds. The data always reveal that only a smattering of survey respondents do anything more than vote or occasionally heed politics via TV. Worse, it would appear, civic engagement is declining, a fact often attributed to the growing campaign negativity or the imminent collapse of civil society. These dreary figures, then, become the "scientifically demonstrated" reality justifying untold admonitions for "more activism" to "strengthen democracy." Analysis is, predictably, directed toward reversing this insidious apathy. Nobody stops to mention that perhaps political flight constitutes a more adept solution to people's problems or that pestering government is pointless.

By contrast, the political ledger's non-academic side provides irrefutable evidence that society grows ever more politicized. The academy's experts, seemingly, have things backwards—Americans are excessively tinkering with civic life, and notions of limited government now have an antique quality about them. The "noxious politics everywhere" complaint pervades education, law enforcement, commerce, family life, and virtually every other aspect of contemporary society. Even the definition of marriage is now decided politically, not by clergy. Public officials routinely bemoan the fact that any proposal inevitably instigates an avalanche of hostile outpourings, disruptive demonstrations, crackpot science, threats of litigation, and even sabotage. Doubters might recommend building a plutonium-fueled nuclear power plant in California, if verification of this proclivity is needed. Matters once obscurely scientific, e.g., government agency disease classifications, now generate vitriolic pressure. Mass media novelties—"Million person" Washington marches, outlandish, sexually explicit rallies, or conferences on one alleged public malaise or another—are scarcely even noticed by jaded aficionados. I have personally witnessed real-world ideologically charged intrusions in higher education's every corner. Prerogatives once the faculty's sole domain, e.g., curriculum content, is increasingly dictated by legislators hectored by countless activists. To insist that "political activism" is an endangered species is an odd take on a plain-to-see reality.

Scholarship has also grown narrower with age. My "political participation" lectures gradually diverged from the assigned texts to the point where substantive overlap was minimal. My students routinely hear creative items culled from the *Wall Street Journal* or offbeat radical magazines while illustrations drawn from scholarly journals have virtually vanished. I frequently explain how influencing government can be far more ingenious than the hallowed 1950s-style behaviors depicted in the standard disciplinary literature, or that the line between political and non-political is, itself, part of the political struggle. These presentations apparently resonate well with these novices, and seem absolutely essential to a well-rounded portrayal, yet they went unmentioned by scholars formally sketching out the participatory landscape.

Those who might doubt my characterization of this disciplinary thinness might consult the bibliographies in these learned tomes. The range of cited disciplinary journal articles and monographs is staggering. Yet, references to newspaper articles, legislative testimony, and the actual outcropping of political strife (many of which are meticulously compiled in research libraries) are virtually nil. It is as if nothing exists until it surfaces in a professional outlet, and I would guess that if these end-of-book citations were tracked backwards, little of the raw data of politics would infuse these entries, as well. That much of this material is also available on the web or via handy Net search engines can only confirm the professional disregard for actual events. Put bluntly, the study of "political participation" has become the "study of scholarly books and articles about political participation." By comparison, the bibliography offered here overflows with accounts of "real world" events, often coming from what activists themselves say in the midst of the battle.

The Limits of Civic Activism is also a "controversial" book, at least according to some already hearing my views. This is, admittedly, true in the sense that it takes a taboo slant on certain "hot button" issues, notably the civil rights movement's uncertain recent achievements or how gay political mobilization has blood on its hands. But, if we set aside these provocative examples, it is strange to assert that the book's core message—political solutions are never guaranteed and may, occasionally, backfire—affronts decency or is downright loony. If anything, that point would appear banal, and obvious to anyone superficially acquainted with events. As we affix warning labels to cigarettes and liquor, cautions might be prudently appended to appeals for civic engagement. This is hardly "controversial."

Economics offers useful parallels. Imagine if business books were exclusively upbeat—getting rich just entailed investing, any investment, even perpetual motion machines, and nobody could lose. This advice would rightfully be judged half-baked, an invitation to be swindled. Unfortunately, this Pollyanna mentality is pervasive when academics celebrate civic activism: just get involved and you'll win something while apathy is doomed. That political strife is a zero-sum game with endless losers goes unmentioned. As we shall see, casualties litter civic battlefields and participants might have been better off watching TV soap operas.

I suspect, though cannot prove, that this "just get involved" rhetoric emanating from the academy might reflect a thinly disguised political agenda. This is *not* disinterested advice, as a doctor would tell patients to shed some extra pounds. Rather, the counsel is highly selective and the implied objectives are essentially liberal. In this cosmology, fighting corporate greed is commendable; it is unscrupulous to press for free-market pricing that will enrich those taking huge financial risks. It is similarly "good" to advocate greater federal spending for the poor, and conceivably, downright evil to pressure Washington to stop rewarding debilitating sloth. Joining up in a civil right organization is noble; enlisting in the Conservative Citizens Council is deplorable racism. Chapter 1 illustrates that leading participation scholars inevitably highlight *liberal* activism in their examples. Conservatives, it would seem, only battle to repress incontestable claims for justice and stymie economic uplift. This selectivity is no accident, in my estimation.

And while I am admonishing fellow scholars, let me also add my dismay with their irresponsibility when dispensing facile advice. Imploring unsophisticated people seeking betterment to pursue one path versus another imposes tough moral standards. In law, medicine and financial planning, among other professions, expertise is tightly regulated and practitioners are bound by ethical strictures. To insist, without due diligence, "just get involved politically to get relief" is *not* gratuitous, harmless speechmaking. The empirical evidence buttressing this proposition is remarkably slender, and scholars offering panaceas are probably aware of this paucity. Or at least they should be if they read their own literature. In a sense, unless their counsel can demonstrate a reasonable expectation of victory, they are guilty of manipulation or quackery. Sad to say, this easily proclaimed "mobilize to get government to do it" mentality often offers a convenient escape from awkward truths. Not every calamity is solvable. The Promised Land will not appear just over the next hill to the hyper-energetic, regardless of what alleged experts insist. The entire problem is often misconstrued. The initial question should be, "How can we solve a problem, assuming that it is conquerable?" not "How can we galvanize government?" Calling on government to the rescue via citizen pestering is always uncertain, especially for those in dire straits; far more assured is that this entreatment will expand state authority. This Faustian bargain may be a dangerous deal.

Readers of my previous books will recognize some familiar acknowledged characters. The Earhart Foundation again provided valuable financial assistance. The Social Philosophy and Policy Center, Bowling Green State University, Bowling Green, Ohio deserves praise beyond this brief mention. My two summers there made a tough project downright enjoyable. Charles DeWitt, as is his custom, was the perfect research assistant and assembled a masterful index. Stephen Bennett read many inchoate chapters and offered innumerable helpful suggestions. The University of Illinois's Reference Library staff again showered me with uncomplaining kindness and expertise despite my badgering. Delinda Swanson of the Illinois political science department similarly managed various key tasks totally beyond me while keeping a refreshing happy spirit. The Gill Foundation may dispute my skeptical views on gay activism, but they willingly supplied vital data for chapter 8. And, to continue a revered ritual, Erika Gilbert was omnipresent, often with the requisite cup of coffee and a peeled apple. She was the unfailing source of encouragement, understanding and countless other essential amenities. Her skilled midwifery made this book possible.

1

Introduction

The paths to betterment are nearly infinite, and every era has its favorites. Primitive farmers facing catastrophes might sacrifice oxen to their gods or carry magical amulets to ward off evil. More modern prescriptions entailed acquiring the habits of thrift, sobriety, dutifulness, and other Calvinist virtues. Some nineteenth-century pundits celebrated eugenics as the ameliorative solution; others heralded unregulated markets to bring prosperity and personal happiness. A quick tour of today's world assuredly evidences similar variety. Millions heed sacred strictures ever so carefully to guarantee a better position in a future rebirth. Elsewhere, one attains eternal happiness by violent martyrdom against infidels. Rounding out this picture are those stoically accepting their preordained fate as the pathway to happiness.

All this varied counsel aside, if a singular perspective currently pervades American society regarding progress, this is our infatuation with politics. It is but a slight exaggeration to suggest that pressuring government to bestow betterment has grown into a civic religion. Its prophets insist that nearly any obstacle can be conquered via state intervention, and plights once judged quintessentially private now become the objects of grand civic crusades. If schoolchildren leave home hungry, insist that some agency supply meals gratis. If these same children refuse to read, hold public officials accountable for successful literacy programs. When parents worry that their offspring are corrupted by pervasive television violence, the call—true to form—goes out for heightened FCC media supervision. That each of these quandaries—feeding hungry children, eliminating TV violence, and overcoming illiteracy—is remediable privately, perhaps even more effectively, seems scarcely noticed. Embracing state intervention is near reflexive. These examples can be endlessly multiplied.

This hasty call for activism as the grand elixir is not confined to the naïve or the desperate. In 2003, the president of Teachers College at Columbia University implored the parents of failing inner-city school children to force government via litigation and voter mobilization drives to provide a quality education (Levine 2003). Just what these newly animated officials would do to impose progress was conveniently left unsaid. One group of distinguished scholars who have written widely about political activism (e.g., Verba, Schlozman, and Brady 1997) seemingly postulate civic engagement as the *exclusive* mechanism for socio-economic advancement. For them, the have-nots are forever condemned to dire straits since they are out-gunned by the wealthy in getting the attention of those in power. That the poor may have superior non-political options vis-à-vis what the government can provide, or that Washington's programs may be ineffectual or even exacerbate their misfortune, is beyond the pale analytically, though evidence regarding the value of non-government options abounds. One has only to read the local Yellow Pages to see countless for-profit services offering non-government choices, everything from curing substance dependency to education.

The parallels between religious fervor and contemporary political activism are unmistakable. As some creeds envision an all-powerful, all-knowing god, so it is with today's mighty national government. In theological terms, we practice political monotheism—there is only one god, and that is government. Prior to the 1960s this belief was judged excessive, inimical to our limited government tradition, and mockingly dubbed "The Moon and the Ghetto" mentality after the absurd conviction that if Washington could land a man on the moon, they *surely* could rebuild inner cities. Critics rightfully insisted that even if this noble aim were feasible, the practical upshot would be totalitarian excesses. Today this sanguine vision of government's potency grows more respectable despite failed multi-billion-dollar expenditures to alleviate ghetto misery. For true believers, the federal government appears all-powerful: if only Washington was sufficiently pressured, AIDS could be cured, homelessness would vanish, and our environment would return to its pristine state. Even centuries-old atrocities seemingly lost in the mists of history, it is alleged, can be ameliorated by swift intervention.

A disinterested observer might reach the opposite conclusion regarding the helpfulness of political action in contemporary society—

the odds of success are slim, and grow longer by the day. The inherent character of American politics, with its built-in gridlock and multiple veto opportunities, seemingly stacks the outcome towards inertia, not accomplishment. The multiplicity of participants, tens of thousands if only lobbying organizations are counted, means intense competition for finite resources, no matter how worthy the cause. Even defenders of apple pie and motherhood face tough opposition from countless rivals if they pursue a political strategy. Particularly relevant for newcomers, today's politics requires prodigious skills. The United States is not a feudal fiefdom in which desperate peasants can enrich themselves by plundering the manor house. The gap between being active versus being skillfully active is enormous, and blithely disregarded by those counseling, "Just get involved." As in business, ease of entry inevitably means ease of exit, especially for the naïve. There is no reason to suppose that politics offers better odds for success than initiating a fast food restaurant in today's grimly competitive market. Nor, for that matter, can we assume that the demanded policy will, indeed, deliver the expected benefits.

Nowhere is this political activism faith more fervent than among African Americans, especially civil rights leaders. It is the movement's signature. One might surmise that Washington could perform far-reaching wonders if only it wished, especially closing racial gaps. Witness a recent NAACP education pronouncement imploring Washington to half this divide over five years by pushing affirmative action-related programs. That this litigious measure has previously failed to touch achievement disparities and can often be skillfully resisted scarcely cooled enthusiasm for yet more Washington-directed coercive approaches (Henry 2000). The prospect of continued government helplessness or that effort might be more productive elsewhere (e.g., volunteer tutoring programs or even for-profit charter schools) escapes notice—*only* government power will accomplish something. And to put their money where their mouth is, the NAACP spent lavishly to elect Al Gore over Bush in the hope that Gore would continue Washington's expansive civil rights role. When minority high school students, especially blacks, disproportionately failed the Florida Comprehensive Assessment Test in 2003 which was required for a diploma, upset leaders condemned Governor Jeb Bush and threatened litigation plus boycotts of the state's lottery, theme parks, and citrus products. These failures were to be reversed politically, not by greater academic diligence (Canedy 2003; deGale 2003).

A leading African-American politics textbook (Barker, Jones, and Tate 1999: 33) axiomatically declares that racial economic disparities can only be eliminated via political action. When failure is acknowledged (e.g., the 1960s model cities initiative), the possibility that this route may not have been propitious is tersely dismissed (329). Another text (Browning et al. 1997) noted abundant evidence showing the limited impact of past political solutions to the problems facing many urban blacks (277). Then, a section called "What can be done" called for yet *more* political action—alliances with other ethnic groups, city pressures on private industry to hire more blacks, and increased public spending on education targeted for minorities. When "self-help" was mentioned, it was done very briefly (three sentences), with the proviso that black-oriented governments might play an important role in facilitating this "self-help" (297). Ironically, a leading black-oriented *business* publication (*Black Enterprise* 2001) reaffirms this state-centered faith when it stated, "...as we've urged our readers to recognize the direct correlation between the intensity and focus of our political activism and the swiftness and magnitude of our economic advancement." Future efforts, the article continues, should be directed toward building alliances with Hispanic activist groups, not abandoning politics. The message is indisputable: the state does more than just facilitate economic progress; it is the primary source of economic gain. The awkward fact that blacks who have migrated from the Caribbean or Africa out-earn native-born blacks and have lower levels of unemployment despite their near political invisibility goes unmentioned (Fears 2003).

As is true for religious denominations, a sacred creed informs this urge though no formal church codifies and enforces these revelations. Evidently, "everybody now knows" that educational opportunities come to those rallying voters, that economic rewards flow toward those guiding legislation, and tenacious litigation can reduce inequality. Today's formulaic protests, and million man/woman marches punctuated by charismatic speakers often resemble nineteenth-century fire and brimstone revivals where hope overpowers unpleasant reality. Perhaps this unchallenged fervor is predictable since may of today's notable social movements (e.g., opposition to abortion) initially germinated in church-led organizations steeped in the power of faith. Other campaigns, for example, environmentalism, feminism, the battle against globalism, though entirely secular in origin, display a religious-like, almost evangelical, fervor not unlike those nineteenth-century missionaries risking life and limb to Christianize the heathens lest they descend to Hell. To counsel abandoning politics to seek relief elsewhere would probably be deemed heresy, a violation of the sacred creed, not just shoddy advice.

Nevertheless, intriguing parallels aside, what *should* separate religion from political activism is that the latter—at least in principle—rests upon factual analysis. Acknowledging a Supreme Deity is a faith impervious to exterior confirmation. Even creeds depicting real-world events such as the miracle of divine creation are ultimately belief based. One reaffirms faithfulness, not assembles factual documentation to test hypotheses, if sacred dogma is challenged. To insist, however, that marching on City Hall to coerce laggard school superintendents will, in fact, enhance reading and writing performances is scientifically verifiable. That is, if the official responds as directed, do test scores improve? It is infeasible to determine the potency of prayer, but we can marshal facts regarding the efficacy of get-out-the-vote drives.

Knowledge of political participation seems wholly unlike religious doctrine, at least superficially. Storehouses of theorizing and easy-to-follow fact collection instructions abound. One overview (Leighley 1995) offered a 211-item bibliography, and this was admittedly a cursory compilation. A half dozen or more political science books incorporate "Political Participation" in their title, and the subject permeates college courses across innumerable disciplines. Citation-rich texts monotonously catalogue findings as if they were universal scientific Laws. We are confidently told, for example, that the college-educated are more engaged than high-schoolers, that the young are more apathetic than the middle aged, that the rich are more politically embroiled than the poor, and so on and on. The burgeoning "group politics" literature (i.e., African-American Studies, Latino/a Studies, etc.) inevitably reaffirms participation's ameliorative qualities. Here the apathy-activism progression virtually defines group progress, while impassivity is condemned as sinful, if not traitorous to "the cause." Current research, it would seem, largely entails updating hallowed classic truths while reaffirming that political activism is "a good thing."[1]

Unfortunately, the reality as explicated in untold scholarly "political participation" treatises is deficient. This reputed wisdom is, in fact, often far closer to theology than scientifically verified theorems. When pharmaceutical firms tout new drugs, the FDA will rightly insist on detailed proof of worthiness, and this demonstration typically costs millions and takes years. Untold alleged panaceas are judged futile or, occasionally, are banned as toxic despite their admirable scientific pedigrees. Those who dispense this medication are also tightly regulated lest powerful treatments be misapplied. Practitioners operating outside this strict supervision are fittingly condemned as quacks and charlatans. By contrast, those pushing the downtrodden to vote so as to bring personal prosperity need not fear that some FDA-like agency will demand rigorous scientific evidence. Nor, if activist exhortations prove catastrophic, will advisors face costly lawsuits and disgrace; their standing may even rise as a result of their "commitment."

Sad to say, political participation scholarship often rests on uncertain foundations despite what appears to be a scholarly consensus. Insufficiencies color the entire enterprise, beginning with how "political participation" is matter-of-factly defined to its empirical calibration and alleged impact. And these tribulations apply to everything in between, no less. "Objective scholarship," moreover, often has a preachy flavor in its conflation of "is" with "ought," for example, activism's supposed superior power vis-à-vis all rivals to remediate economic shortcomings. That this flawed gospel is relentlessly evangelized to believing acolytes, who then sermonize it as "revealed truth" to the naïve, makes this failing far worse than merely dispensing flawed scholarship.

Why is research far closer to articles of faith than practitioners would admit? No evil plot or malfeasance is relentlessly afoot; explanations are more humdrum. That verities can be glibly repeated without fear of contradiction makes this insufficiency exceedingly comfortable. Social scientists are hardly immune to the herd mentality. If one hears the phrase "Most Americans are politically apathetic" long enough without refutation, it naturally becomes axiomatic by proclamation. Those innumerable conceptual and practical problems bedeviling this disciplinary orthodoxy, for example, separating a purely egotistical craving for publicity from carefully calculated harassment of public officials, can similarly be conveniently avoided without fear of disciplinary rebuke. In other instances, a confined ready-made research agenda permits flight from tough puzzles that defy available analytical techniques. Try getting a "handle" on something as unique as manipulating the public's fear of deadly epidemics to extract government largess. Or falsifying research to advance an ideological agenda. Where do these unique tactics fit into our broader understanding of activism, or are they *sui generis*? Elsewhere, the vexation is more conceptual, for example, assigning the label "political" to behaviors so intricately ambiguous—false hate crime accusations, for instance—that easier topics immediately spring to mind. Why invite exasperation chasing illusive, rare relationships when simple, at-hand government-collected voting data can be profitably milled?

More disturbing, however, is conflating worldly politics with scholarship. Though it is impossible to document this urge conclusively, at least some researchers seemingly advance their ideological disposition under the cover of analyzing "activism." It is as easy as offering college courses in which select crusades are presented as "commendable progress" while relegating opponents to history's dustbin. Now that civic movements of one stripe or another inform the syllabus, lectures are the vehicle to proselytize the researcher's hidden agenda.[2] And, given the liberal ideological coloration of today's social science faculty, it is hard to imagine admonitions for civic engagement to be balanced so as to include rolling back taxes or unburdening industry from ill-advised environmental regulations. In short, what ostensibly passes as recounting scientific inquiry becomes well-dressed agitprop.

This conflation of advocacy with scholarship hardly embarrasses universities proclaiming themselves enlightened guardians of objectivity. The opposite seems more likely. In the summer of 2001 Harvard University, in conjunction with some 180 civil rights groups, sponsored the "Civil Rights Summer" in which twenty-one novices were expertly trained to harass government and, as far as can be determined, all causes were certified liberal (Graff 2001). One student, for example, spent his time critically scrutinizing state achievement testing to uncover bias so as to ensure educational equity, one of twenty such social justice research topics. It is unclear from the brief report whether time was devoted to mastering these test items in addition to exposing their alleged unfairness. Harvard hopes to expand the program and, no doubt, other less prestigious institution—perhaps hoping to gain similar Ford Foundation support— will soon follow suit.

We assign ourselves the task of remediating the multiple inadequacies surrounding "political activism." This is a hard, cold look at a subject so effortlessly glorified in today's society that tough, awkward questions have ceased being asked. Re-directing an entire scholarship mountain range (and its real-world incarnation) a few inches is the ultimate aim. We—hopefully—reinsert a *scientific* perspective into an enterprise quietly inching toward dogma despite superficial signs of "science," for example, an ardor for statistical complexity. Foremost on our agenda is to show that political activism, which is so unthinkingly embraced in today society, is not as axiomatically beneficial as advertised. Matters are far more complex and, more often than not, deeply ambiguous. To be sure, joining the political battle has much to recommend it, but insisting that it necessarily represents *the* superior path, easily surpassing non-political rivals, is excessive. An old pharmacology adage advises that toxicity is in the dosage, and nowhere is this truer than in preaching unrelenting civic engagement. Endless repetition by esteemed academics without any hard evidence is not proof. Engagement occasionally brings disaster, no matter how skillfully directed.

That political activism must be judged by its accomplishment, not its mere existence is our central analytical perspective. Simply put: Does civic mobilization deliver what was desired? And, going a step further, did this achieved outcome bring the expected benefits? After all, the world abounds with examples of success stories turning into nightmares due to unforeseen consequences. Not every lottery winner is happy forever; winning legal job protection may produce eventual unemployment if more flexible labor can be found elsewhere. Economic enterprise offers a useful parallel—one invests time, energy, and money to get richer, though other rewards may also flow from this pursuit, and the resultant wealth may prove more troublesome than past poverty. Note well, goals can be non-material: civic engagement can provide social camaraderie, and that may be its real aim. Inconsequential activism may also perform vital non-obvious services, for example, cementing regime loyalty, or therapeutic release. Still, in the final analysis, we expect activism to produce *something* of value for the activist.

This pay-off question is more than just one more addendum to the existing scholarly literature. It is, fundamentally, the place *to begin* assessing the entire enterprise, much like profit serves as the over-arching yardstick in assessing capitalist ventures though no full business evaluation examines only profit. Just as it would be irrelevant to praise a car manufacturer for its superb vehicles if the firm went bankrupt, so it is pointless to celebrate a futile rally to demand the impractical from those oblivious to the event. Let us confess at the onset—this outcome-oriented approach is exceptionally challenging. A few might insist that it is empirically impossible. Cataloguing a few prominent behaviors is far easier. Political movements hardly issue quarterly, audited balance sheets showing accomplishments; nor do standardized accounting rules permit precise profit or loss calibrations. Most critically, civic engagement lacks a metric of success akin to money in economic activity. Yet, this hardheaded view is absolutely vital given the availability of non-political remedies or even apathy, let alone one tactic versus another. Perhaps parents worried about their children's illiteracy are wasting their time haranguing City Hall. The same hours could be more productively spent reading bedtime stories. Surely it is unwise to offer unsubstantiated cliché-ridden advice to those needing betterment.

This focus differs substantially from how conventional participation studies treat costs and benefits. This literature a priori assumes the superior efficacy of civic action; everything is examined through the lens of what promotes civic engagement versus engendering unproductive apathy (see, for example, Leighley 2001: chs. 1-2). That is, a potential activist balances burdens, e.g., a competing family obligation, against desired pay-offs, e.g., better schools for one's children, and allocates scarce resources accordingly. If apathy is chosen, it is tacitly assumed that the aim—improved schooling, in this example—is abandoned. Normative prescriptions arising from this perspective predictably stress lowering entry costs such as insuring accessible school board meetings or enhancing civic motivation by upping exposure to political stimuli.

What sets our framework apart is conceiving civic engagement as *a* choice among many options that potentially accomplish comparable goals. We postulate that people may pursue near-infinite pathways—civic and otherwise—to accomplishment. One can improve air quality by badgering the EPA, wearing a gasmask, relocating to a cleaner locality, or dozens of other sensible options. This results-oriented perspective implies nothing about discovering authentic motives or judging the wisdom of these ends. Economic analysis, again, is an appropriate parallel—we can ask people their goals or measure behavior against researcher-stipulated standards. Conceivably, some activists may publicly espouse a noble quest like saving the environment while furtively actually seeking self-indulgent therapy; others may happily pursue schemes guaranteed to bring catastrophe, e.g., making energy unaffordable save for the rich by sabotaging power plants. A few befuddled souls may be oblivious to purpose and merely crave excitement. Assessment is possible by accepting face value, assuming a more devious plan, or imposing multiple wholly exterior standards. We certainly cannot insist upon a single evaluative yardstick as superior, whether participant or research imposed.

This hardheaded approach is vital to the normative issues broached earlier—the relentlessness of pushing political engagement sans any demonstrative proof of superior worthiness. Surely it is appropriate for those advised to hector government to request assurance that this pestering is a worthy time-energy investment vis-à-vis non-political alternatives or just watching TV. For engagement devotees to respond, "Yes, that is a fair question, but, frankly, we just don't know the answer regarding the utility of activism" may certify an uncommon honesty, but this does not mitigate the investigator's responsibility. Nor would it be constructive for the researcher to confess, "All I can prove is that those who participate more on a handful of crude measures apparently do better, so this uncertain relationship counsels action." Though nominally research based, this rejoinder is shoddy science. One cannot conclusively link voting turnout with economic gain by just showing a simple correlation. The causal relationship may be entirely opposite—only the economically advantaged can enjoy the luxury of activism, not activism brings riches. The message may even be drearier: if one pursues politics prior to achieving wealth it will be a distraction and only impede economic progress. We submit that *some* calculation on investment return is morally required, and this demands far more than simple-minded associations.

Plan of Analysis

We undertake a long, often frustrating journey into superficially well-settled territory. No doubt, a few readers will ultimately conclude that they knew more prior to beginning this laborious inquest. Chapter 2 delves into the academic theorizing regarding political participation as a general concept, not individual acts such as voting. Problems here abound. For example, once we move beyond terse, dictionary-like definitions, considerable confusion exists regarding what comprises "political activism." Some scholars definitionally exclude violence and anything else subverting democracy, an analytical strategy not even acknowledging terrorism. Theoretical explications also conveniently ignore unsavory behavior often integral to real-world politics, for example, bribery, physical intimidation, and deceit. Are we to reject such behaviors as "non-political" due to their sleazy character? How do we treat those teachers and religious leaders who insist that their proselytizing has "nothing" to do with politics despite clear political ramifications? Are they disingenuous or just naive?

This exegesis is more than the standard academic literature review. Though the activist's agenda and dry academic scholarship may seem light years apart, academy-manufactured lessons have undoubtedly filtered into our common wisdom. Echoes of long past lectures or reading assignments about the government sure-fire positive role in economic uplift are evident in today's boisterous street demonstrations for yet one more program to banish poverty forever. Recall the unwavering optimism infusing books on black politics. That this intervention may make matters worse may well invite rebuke, or worse. As John Maynard Keynes once said, "Madmen in authority, who hear voices in the air, are distilling their frenzy from some academic scribbler of a few years back." At a minimum, we show that the all-too-easily dispensed standard scholarly template for grasping "political activism" is ill equipped to render scientific conclusions regarding its alleged ameliorative impact.

Chapter 3 explores the bewildering variety comprising today's "political participation." We begin by noting that "political participation" entails far more than what is explicated in standard (often dated) scholarly catalogues. As in the evolution of species, new stratagems continuously arise as older methods lose their impact. We highlight some of these more creative ploys (e.g., ideologically driven stock market investing) and dwell on powerful strategies that have outwardly escaped notice among conventional, backward-looking researchers, for example, inserting political messages into popular music. This overflowing abundance raises a perplexing issue—Can a comprehensive cataloguing exercise distill common elements into some quintessential "political participation" indicator? Or, to be pessimistic, is every act so distinctive that formulating some handy global indicator is futile? This debate is vital to calibrate levels of citizen civic engagement.

That aims commonly sought via politics might be profitably pursued via non-political strategies will be considered in chapter 4. As we tirelessly repeat, virtually every goal reachable via civic activism is achievable outside the civic arena, and often more efficiently in a constitutional arrangement mired in gridlock. "Political apathy" scarcely signifies passivity, only a choice of weapons. One might even hire mercenaries or fund international organizations to advance a "private" foreign policy, though foreign affairs is often said to be government's unique responsibility. This "non-political political activism" is especially critical for assessing both engagement levels and proficiency. Conceivably, only the inept or those attracted to quick "magic bullets" gravitate toward public solutions to hard problems. After addressing this quandary abstractly, we undertake a detailed analysis of several possibilities, including how businesses respond to unwanted legal constraints. We shall see that "purely economic" action can be an effective (though occasionally denied) counter-reaction to political pressure. In a phrase, politics is conducted by ostensible non-political means. A business compelled by city authorities to reduce pollution can relocate to a more lenient jurisdiction, bribe inspectors, or buy pollution-producing products elsewhere, all without entering the political fray.[3] These responses can almost invisibly gut statutory victories secured by local environmentalists.

Chapter 5 tackles the qualitative dimension of political activism. This task is commonplace in economics and sports—experts forever rate "the best" mutual funds or the most adroit baseball franchises. Millions are annually spent grading "performance quality" in everything from automobiles to urban ambiance. Sad to say, however, this ratings passion draws negligible attention among scholars depicting civic engagement, though rough judgments are standard among professionals. Washington insiders and savvy journalists undoubtedly know that certain organizations intimidate enemies while others are inept jokes. Here we flesh out this critical subject by examining what goes into "political skill." We also briefly depict some conspicuous political mobilization failures. We conclude that savvy activism can often be best achieved via outsourcing—politics may be no different from medicine where one hires a good doctor versus concocting a home cure.

Chapter 6 lays out the conceptual groundwork for assessing the most challenging of all participation related issues, impact. We offer a brief overview of how scholars have tackled this quandary and their findings. Much of this overview focuses on African-American politics since this "impact literature" is relatively plentiful. Unfortunately, though each study might contribute something of value, and proficiently executed, the collective endeavor is often conceptually haphazard. There is certainly no well-established scientific formula to guide research as one might find textbook standards for calculating company profitability. The upshot is that reaching definite, empirically based conclusions regarding the pay-off of civic activism is extremely challenging. This would be as if drug companies all touted their products relying on impromptu, even opportunistic, research methodology or, more likely, dubious testimonials. We explore several of the difficulties typically ignored in conventional impact studies, for example, determining just what constitutes a "victory" when goals are effortlessly shifted over a campaign to guarantee victory regardless of outcome. These are hardly obscure technical questions given that millions rely on political activism to bring betterment.

Chapter 7 begins a three-chapter case study of the battle against AIDS. The over-arching question is: have these combatants won more than they lost? Analysis begins by establishing a baseline regarding a "fair" allocation of government health care funding. This is hardly straightforward since multiple "objective" allocation standards exist, and all have their ardent champions. That these choices can be matters of life and death for thousands only heightens the political strife. Nevertheless, supposed objective criteria aside, we find that Washington is hardly an "equal opportunity" benefactor when it comes to its generosity—some illnesses, notably AIDS, are disproportionally attended to, and this uneven kindness raises the suspicion that astute political interventions are at work.

Having established AIDS funding as a colossal funding outlier, chapter 8 examines how this might have transpired. We shall see that gay activists, despite public aversion to homosexuality, enjoyed powerful, built-in advantages from the outset. Moreover, their central aim—more government funding to prevent deaths—attracted countless valuable allies. Their successful campaign was often ingenious, and utilized tactics far removed from the standard academic research menu. Within a few years, activists had transformed an illness contracted in unsavory sexual settings into a fashionable cause garnering widespread sympathy. Resources were often brilliantly employed, and this qualitative dimension is all too often ignored in assessing the value of political action—everybody may enjoy the identical right to petition government, but public officials are not obligated to heed every petitioner. Gays were extraordinarily adroit in extracting government money. Powerful lessons exist here for those believing that political mobilization, in and of itself, can perform wonders.

Chapter 9 takes up what most (if not all) participation devotees oddly neglect: the downside. Case studies of fiascos are a business school staple, yet scholarly investigators apparently see little value in such autopsies. Gays not only pressured government for greater research funding, they also mobilized their political clout to sustain the very behaviors contributing to the AIDS epidemic, and thousands consequently died as a result. To invoke that old cliché, political action can be a two-edged sword. More important, despite all their accomplishments, this government-directed strategy still has not brought a cure though medications have extended untold lives. There are also complicated questions here regarding how a "victory" should be defined. Conceivably, a political defense of one's unbridled libido from government interference might have been a triumph to some despite ultimately bringing early death. It is a matter of priorities, and who can set those for others? Chapter 9 ends with a balance sheet-like calculation of the anti-AIDS crusade. This case study is not offered as *the* model of how participation is to be assessed. It is only one of many such possibilities, and may even be among the technically simplest. The momentousness of further demonstrations should give pause to those who glibly insist that civic engagement is the superior pathway.

Our conclusion reflects the twofold nature of this endeavor. We begin by offering advice to the would-be activist based upon our extended case study. This will not be nearly as sanguine as is found in traditional treatments—seeking one's goals politically is not for everyone regardless of what intrinsic satisfaction may be found in civic life. Cause worthiness has little to do with the odds of success. Critically, politics may be a terrible investment for those at the bottom hoping to move up thanks to adroitly pressuring government. Government cannot bestow the very talents needed to extract largess. We then turn toward more analytical issues and set forth multiple unresolved puzzles and invite others to take up these challenges. We confess, moreover, that everything may be unreachable, at least momentarily. For example, how do we establish a benchmark for success and failure in a movement filled with dozens of conflicting aims? Do we measure success by an individual's return on investment, or is the movement itself the appropriate unit of analysis? Can opportunity costs be calculated when political strategies exclude private options? The insertion of opportunity costs also deserves attention—perhaps a political strategy was the most efficient option vis-à-vis alternatives though it ultimately proved only partially successful. Can we do better than informed speculation?

We end by considering the relentless proselytizing infusing the civic activism literature. This is the normative, not scientific, element in our quest and, to be frank, we find these off-the-cuff admonitions troublesome. Possibilities for scholarly quackery abound. Does the arduousness of rendering sound counsel suggest that those imploring civic action be required to justify their admonitions? Perhaps we should draw a lesson from financial advice—anybody can pass along a hot stock tip, but others must pass rigorous exams to be a certified financial analyst. Imagine a world in which those contemplating civic engagement *must* consult with licensed activists before investing time and energy? Meanwhile, others make choices entirely by whim. We also issue warnings about the dangers of reflexive activism. More may be involved than bad investment advice, though that is hardly trivial. Chicanery is always possible when miracles are assured to the unsophisticated (see our discussion of the drug, Kemron, in chapter 9). Finally, and most pernicious, activism may facilitate state control over its citizens. This is no minor quibble judged against traditions of limited government and self-reliance. Those who successfully gain goods and services from government can easily grow dependent on official largess or even just the promise of such betterment. Bountifulness aside, this transformation from citizen to client may be a Faustian bargain even when calculated by the material gains received.

Notes

1.   Like regular exercise and a healthy diet, political participation seems to be a virtue without limit. William Crotty (1991: 4) expressly heralded activism as contributing to political stability, heightening citizen interest and commitment, and, ultimately, promoting a more inclusive and therefore "better" representation. Such paeans suggest that "participation" possesses an exceedingly narrow, reflexive meaning among its academic devotees. Crotty obviously does not have political terrorism, let alone insurrection, in mind.

2.   The ideological flavor infusing scholarship can often be discerned from off-hand exemplars. For example, Conway (2000: 4) broaches the topic of "unconventional" activism in her popular textbook. All the illustrations are about *liberal* activism—advocating a nuclear weapon freeze, ending pollution, and the civil rights movement. The one reference to what might be judged "conservative activism" was repressing lawful 1960s demonstrations (activities that were almost entirely favoring liberal causes). Nothing is said about how these activists often sought to turn these demonstrations into violent confrontations to draw public sympathy. Similarly, Rusk (1976) criticizes conventional research for ignoring civil rights protests or anti-Vietnam War demonstrations. No mention is made of protesting abortion clinics, attending a Klan rally or hounding left-leaning public school teachers. Perhaps these right-wing activities are judged psychological problems, not commendable activism. Norris's (2002: ch. 10) recent, more cross-national analysis is almost entirely devoted to depicting liberal causes such as environmentalism and human rights. Nothing is said about those working for free-market solutions. We note this one-sidedness only to suggest the likely ideological orientation of this enterprise, not to impugn the motives of researchers.

3.   Verba et al. (1995: 40-42) do consider non-political activity in their overview, but—and this is critical—such non-political activities as church attendance are judged important only insofar as they eventually facilitate or enhance more conventional participation. That these acts may be an *alternative* to civic activism is never considered.

2

Disentangling "Political Participation"

Chapter 1 argued that while the scholarly political participation literature is exceedingly bountiful, it offers only the faintest clues regarding civic involvement's utility for conquering our ills. Frequent admonitions "to be active" are wholly unlike scientifically proven medical recommendations. Moreover, to the extent that this counsel is regularly dispensed to betterment seekers, this insufficiency is hardly trivial. Here we delve into this meagerness by examining "political participation" scholarship, that is, investigations treating this concept generally versus zeroing in on a single act such as voting or lobbying. It is here that we find global statements such as, "The wealthier are more active than the poor." We contend that deeply ingrained research habits almost unconsciously redirect inquiry away from difficult assessment and towards unproblematic, and far less consequential subjects. One is reminded of the proverbial police officer encountering the drunk crawling about a lamppost. Asked his purpose, the intoxicated searcher replied, "looking for lost car keys." When further questioned where he had misplaced these keys, the drunk pointed off in the distance. "Why look here, then?" responded the officer? "Because there's more light," he opined.

This corrective effort begins by explicating how leading investigators initially define "political participation." This theory construction component is more complex (and theoretically consequential) than acknowledged. This lexiconic task presupposes an underlying political vision, and congruence between definitions and reality is critical though infrequently explicated. We then move to the multiple conceptual and practical problems embedded in these quite similar formulations.

Defining "Political Participation"

Disentangling "political participation" is daunting and easily avoided altogether as if "everybody knows" the term's meaning. But, the path toward rigorous refurbishment must commence somewhere, and a serviceable departure point can be the perfunctory definitions prefacing soon-to-come empirical excursions. Among the most venerable, oft-cited definitions are:

> Political participation will be defined ...as those actions of private citizens by which they seek to influence or support government and politics. (Milbrath 1981: 198)

> Political participation refers to those activities by private citizens that are more or less directly aimed at influencing the selection of governmental personnel and/or actions they take. (Verba and Nie 1972: 2)

> Participation refers to actions through which ordinary members of a political system influence or attempt to influence outcomes. (Nagel 1987: 1)

> Political participation is action directed explicitly toward influencing the distribution of social goods and social values. (Rosenstone and Hansen 1993: 4)

> By *political* participation we refer simply to activity that has the intent or effect of influencing government actions—either directly by affecting the making or implementation of public policy or indirectly by influencing the selection of people who make those policies. (Verba, Scholzman and Brady 1995: 38, emphasis in original)

Despite the near uniformity of these conceptualizations, all offered in staid "scientific" language, certitude is illusory. The culprit is vagueness, and like "bad" genes at fertilization, this imprecision eventually grows mischievous as research proceeds. Similar phraseology provides only the illusion of exactness. Each of these sound-alike conceptualizations, moreover, subtly facilitates narrow data processing at the expense of broader political understanding. Attentiveness is directed at convenient targets—the lamppost— while ignoring more pressing topics—the keys.

Most plainly, those "activities" comprising "political participation" are only implied, never fully enumerated according to precise rules. These are not physics-like definitions denoting quintessential features. If two experts attempted an exhaustive inventory, catalogues would assuredly diverge. Remarkably, this core fuzziness goes unnoticed and unlamented. Even philosophical inquisitions poring over minute distinctions are frustratingly vague about what, *exactly,* comprises "political participation" (see, for example, Keim 1975;

Braybrooke 1975). Robert J. Pranger's oft-citied *The Eclipse of Citizenship* (1968) includes "participation" in its subtitle, yet bountiful wordplay aside, what "political participation" entails remains unspecified. The single offered example is neighbors meeting to discuss sewer improvement (93). Leighley's (1995) extensive literature overview expressly called for inquiry to encompass more than voting, yet she remained absolutely silent regarding these "other" activities. Norris (2002: xii) observed that today's approach to "political participation" is quite antiquated, but she herself does not venture beyond voting, joining a political party, and a scattering of protest-related activity. The content of these "new" political forms is obviously left to the reader's imagination.

When exemplars are offered, overlap is hardly guaranteed. One state-of-the-art compendium (Verba et al. 1995: 39) explicitly excluded discussing politics or following televised public affairs programs from "political participation" though these acts are matter-of-factly included in other compilations (for example, Nagel 1987: 3). The rationale for banishment went unmentioned. Another definitional inquiry (Parry 1972: 13) expresses doubts whether even voting, that supposedly quintessential political act, deserves to be included as political engagement. Conge's (1988) analysis of usage in several non-U.S. studies concluded that the term's meaning has become so blurred that it is nearly analytically useless. Nor are procedures for including and excluding ever supplied—handiness and familiarity seemingly dictate boundaries. One insightful literature overview nearly a quarter of a century ago opined that demarcation lines often lacked theoretical coherence (Salisbury 1975). Not much has improved since this lament was first uttered. Imagine one physicist defining "matter" as "things like rocks, trees, cats and so forth" while another proposed: "shoes, milk, trees and so on." The conventional definitional strategy, truth be told, resembles fourteenth-century "science" in which the universe consisted of earth, air, fire, and water.

Compounding this vagueness is a backward-looking myopia when exemplars are assembled. Necessarily underlying every "political participation" inquiry is a political mental picture. Analysis cannot proceed without a prior theoretical road map and, furthermore, some significance of what uncovered deeds signify. This vital precondition is seldom acknowledged, and the result is a slapdash inquiry guided by lingering habits. To appreciate a theoretical road map's relevance, envision a New England town meeting-style democracy serving as the prototype in cataloguing political machinations in Stalin's Soviet Union. In the latter, boisterous grumbling about shoddy housing was a momentous political feat risking exile or imprisonment; for New Englanders this lament is barely noteworthy, and certainly irrelevant politically. A Soviet dissenter would thus be "apathetic" by New England standards. The totalitarian and democratic political repertories are as different as Russian and English.

Aligning activism inquiries with specific political practices is deceptively daunting (see Verba, Nie and Kim 1978: ch. 2 for an extended discussion of this comparability). This applies even within apparently alike political arrangements, e.g., "democratic polities." For example, in European democracies, unlike the U.S., judges possess minimal policy discretion and thus cannot impose sweeping policy. Compiling how Germans or Italians sought "to influence the legal process" in culling meaningful participatory acts is therefore largely misdirected. The European promoting liberalized abortion law surely knows that this policy, unlike its U.S. counterpart, is not judicially decided; energies would be better directed toward seeking political party influence. It is here (or perhaps deep within a bureaucracy)—not the courts—where abortion policy materializes. Electoral structure is equally relevant in drawing attentiveness. In the U.S. minor parties play a tangential role, so being a U.S. Natural Law Party mover and shaker is thus more akin to a hobby. The opposite might be true in Israel or Italy where splinter parties, thanks to proportional representation, occasionally exercise undue power.

What type, *a priori*, of political processes do researchers envision when assessing activism? Consider items singled out in several leading studies. Milbrath's 1965 listing is especially notable for its influence on future research. Arrayed from "most difficult" to "least demanding," are:

Holding party and public office.
Running for Office.
Soliciting political funds.
Attending a caucus or strategy meeting.
Becoming an active party member.
Contributing time to a political campaign.
Attending a political meeting or rally.
Giving money to a party or candidate.
Contacting a political leader or official.

Wearing a button or putting a sticker on a car.
Attempting to talk others into voting a certain way.
Initiating a political discussion.
Voting.

Taken together these acts are quite conventional, undoubtedly a reflection of the politically "dull" 1950s and early 1960s. In fact, *Political Participation's* second edition (1977), published some twelve years later, explicitly acknowledged a newly arrived heightened turmoil, particularly the complaints of blacks, students, and women (14). Still, this recognition of unconventional tactics—joining a street demonstration or rioting to attract attention—scarcely altered the underlying theoretical framework. Offering a few haphazard examples of novelties that quickly disappeared from subsequent analysis merely acknowledged—not theoretically incorporated—this turmoil. One might suppose that the academy's favorable endorsement of the black civil rights (and anti-Vietnam war) movement facilitated this superficial homage. Significantly, widespread *resistance* to black demands, for example, disobeying court orders, establishing segregated private academies, or even church bombings, passed absolutely unnoticed despite their consequentiality. Researcher ideology seemingly trumps encompassing theoretical rigor.

Verba and Nie's *Participation in America* (1972) comprises a second seminal work in this conventional genre. Twelve distinct activities were identified (31), and while the precise phraseology differs from Milbrath's compendium (e.g., presidential election voting was distinguished from voting in local contests), the exemplars are nearly identical. *Participation in America* did, however, place a special emphasis on organizational membership (chapter 2). Given that U.S. politics mainly transpires among organized combatants, not isolated individual vs. isolated individual quarrels, this inclusion seemingly added a desirable realism. Unfortunately, including organizational membership only superficially redirected inquiry. Respondents were asked about affiliation with sixteen, researcher-delineated, diffuse association categories (not specific groups)—labor unions, fraternal societies, sports clubs, church-related associations, even hobby groups. Membership itself, independent of purpose, was central. Nor was there any regard to how these assemblages advanced followers' own objectives, let alone the consequences of collective action. Affiliation was behavior. No distinction attended an AFL-CIO member's dues financing Democratic Party voter registration drives versus his or her assisting neighborhood Girl Scouts.

Despite periodic updating of illustrations or ephemeral reference to some current political outcropping, this constrained "political participation" checklist essentially continues onward. Conway's *Political Participation in the United States* (third edition 2000) conveniently illustrates this disciplinary narrowness. As is commonplace in this genre, what comprises "citizen activism" is basically settled by handy example and underscores a handful of election campaign-related activities, for example, attending a party rally or giving money to a candidate, with voting overwhelmingly garnering the most attention. References beyond routine election-related actions are brief asides (e.g., a single anti-Vietnam war terrorist bombing, the repression of 1960s lawful demonstrations). A few pages (83-86) are devoted to sundry (and unspecific) examples of "movement politics"— a farmer's "strike," various civil rights episodes, the anti-Vietnam war movement, and abortion politics. A passing reference is also made to citizen involvement in government consultation mechanisms. The role of interest groups as a conduit for activism likewise receives terse notice (128-131).

When scholars focus on "political participation" among ordinary citizens, election-related activities dominate the compilations. Reference to non-election involvement may occasionally be given, but— critically—these items usually remain outside empirical analysis. No doubt, the sheer variety of these unincorporated activities coupled with survey respondent eccentricity makes empirical integration a severe technical challenge. How is a single respondent hacking a corporate website to protest globalization to be classified? Is a teacher assigning blatant propaganda to unsuspecting college sophomores a "political activist? Yet, to ignore these (and numberless other) possibilities, or to reduce them to intriguing asides, subordinates accuracy to technical convenience. In their totality they may far exceed easier to handle, commonplace acts. Admittedly, no theoretically compelling reason exists to include every odd political venture into analysis, but to justify exclusion solely on convenience hardly honors scientific rigor. Picture Darwin ignoring outlandish creatures since cataloguing endless variety was too arduous.

These participatory creatures lying beyond the electoral arena are hardly obscure. One might even argue that this infatuation with election-related activity displays a naiveté regarding "real-world" politics. It was not that elections are irrelevant; rather, campaign involvement is only one avenue to power, and seldom decisive. Ginsberg and Shefter (1999) put this caution regarding elections sharply: "Over the past three decades, however, politics outside the electoral arena has become the norm, rather than an episodic deviation from the routine pattern of American politics" (18). According to their analysis, today's competing elites cannot triumph only via elections. For one, political parties are incapable of decisively mobilizing their respective supporters. Both Democrats and Republicans chase the same middle- and upper-middle-class constituency so embracing fresh recruits might thus alienate core supporters. Meanwhile, government itself is often divided and inclined toward gridlock, and this renders any one electoral victory less consequential. The upshot, then, is that ballot boxes recede as a coercive instrument. Other stratagems, for example, discrediting opponents though investigations, necessarily move to the forefront. To repeat, electoral politics in all its fullness is not rejected as politically irrelevant; this arena hardly comprises the only game in town and, in many circumstances, is largely irrelevant.

The participatory menu is immense and who can foretell tomorrow's innovations. Going several steps further, some credibly insist that politics is all encompassing, and one's very existence signifies civic engagement. Voting, petitioning government, and similar staples of conventional inquiries are thus trifling outcroppings, far less critical than those habits shoring up society's core structures. From this sweeping perspective, voting Republican versus Democratic is an inconsequential exercise since these choices leave capitalism and economic inequality absolutely untouched. It is society itself that constitutes the real battleground and *every* aspect of a person's existence—family, child-rearing practices, religion, the workplace, and so on— represents authentic political choices insofar as they affect the ultimate distribution of power. *Nothing*—even ostensibly private sexual behavior—lies outside of governance. That a family raises aggressive males and passive females now becomes a politically consequential choice.

Even if the political and non-political were separated, this quandary persists since even the most non-political behavior can be occasional utilized for civic aims. Some 2,500 years ago, Lysistrata, (unsuccessfully) endeavored to convince her Athenian compatriots to withhold sex from men until they ceased their incessant warfare. A few American women were similarly inspired during protests against the Vietnam War when they proclaimed, "Girls say yes to guys who say no" ("no" being refusal to register for the draft). This sex-as-a-weapon theme apparently lives on though more in theatrical form than actual threats. In March of 2003 some 1,000 stage productions of Aristophanes' play were performed nationwide (many with famous actors) to protest a possible war against Iraq (Kelley 2003).

Millions of American daily consciously take political "stands" by buying environmentally safe detergents, avoiding old growth wood products, or boycotting clothing made in overseas sweatshops. Ben and Jerry's ice cream makes "social responsibility" central to its marketing. Other consumers might operate as modern-day vigilantes and boycott businesses antithetical to their ideological views (e.g., refuse to drink Coors beer in light of the Coors family's past association with conservative causes). Is joining a high school Bible reading and prayer club "political participation" if civil authorities seek to suppress these devotional services as "unconstitutional"? Can silent prayers be civil disobedience? Even a cookie sale can be transformed into a weapon. In 2003, several conservative campus organizations ran bake sales protesting affirmative action in which prices reflected the customer's race and ethnicity. White males paid $1.50 for a cookie that a black could buy for twenty-five cents, and this creative ploy generated widespread publicity (Fox News, February 12, 2003).

An especially troubling issue is cataloguing behavior supposedly beyond the democratic pale. This vexation is effortlessly swept aside. With scant exception, today's scholars downplay or exclude activities deemed "undemocratic" altogether. Lester Milbrath's seminal *Political Participation* (1965) proclaimed "The hierarchy [his listing of noteworthy political acts] does not apply to behavior designated to disrupt the normal operation of democratic political processes or to dislodge a regime from office by violent means...."(18). Verba and Nie (1972) likewise confine their exploration to "...ways of influencing politics that are generally recognized as legal and legitimate" (3). This scholarly convention is *never* justified theoretically, nor are the exempted activities specified.[1] Might this reflect the extreme rarity or inconsequentiality of these actions? Or, does Milbrath (and the others honoring this practice) believe that banishment, though theoretically indefensible, commendably promotes democratic governance? Or, might this demarcation merely reflect the impracticality of scrutinizing violence and subversion? Most central to building a sturdy participation theory, does this dismissal render subversive terrorism "non-political"?

This attentiveness to "good" behavior may facilitate data collection, but it certainly subverts knowledge. "Bad" participation is, still, activism and compounding this neglect is the fact that separating "normal" democratic politics from violent rebellion can be nightmarish. Indeed, the differentiation may only be normative, not empirical, and may be ideologically driven. Courts and Department of Justice lawyers long wrestled with whether or not the Communist Party USA was "just another radical group proceeding democratically" versus a treasonous Soviet tool. Were the violence-prone Black Panthers of the 1960s peaceful, FBI-harassed community guardians seeking social justice or apolitical hoodlums manipulating high-sounding rhetoric? Did not the Vietnam anti-war protestors disrupt government? Were they, therefore, "apathetic"? Is abortion clinic bombing or publishing books on scattering anthrax to be classified as "political participation"? Or, again, are these "mere criminal acts"? What about proselytizing an anti-Western Islam? Is this religious devotion definitionally inseparable from "following politics on TV?" All probably qualify as activism if broadly construed, but definition via endless (and at times hypothetical or futuristic) debatable illustration hardly resolves deeper tribulations.

Even more troubling conceptually are illegal (though peaceful) acts to influence political decisions. In less developed nations, "playing politics" via bribery or violent threats may be routine. Pressuring officialdom democratically—no matter how well intentioned—is pointless in these circumstances. The U.S. is hardly immune to such practices either, for example, obtaining gambling licenses in some cities may require *baksheesh* (a bribe). Electoral irregularities, everything from ballot box stuffing to physically intimidating prospective voters, occasionally occurs and may still be locally tolerated. These unsavory acts are inescapable in democratic politics—deviousness attests to electoral consequentiality. Other tactics fall into legal gray areas, for example, for example, spreading malicious tales about a candidate's integrity.

How, then, do we assess a survey respondent confessing, "Sure, I'm politically active—I have twenty legislators on my payroll, and they do as told. If that doesn't work, I just buy voters" If castigated for this lawlessness, our hardheaded respondent reasonably replies, "That's just how politics is conducted here, and playing it by the book is futile." How should this person be classified? Are the researchers' unstated ethical convictions to guide "participation" demarcations? Should definitions try to reflect the ugly "real world" or should they be constructed entirely according to abstract disciplinary (and moral) conventions? Ironically, these politically energetic miscreants are undoubtedly politically influential, but "apathetic" according to the standard yardstick. Collecting this type of information also complicates an already difficult situation. Few wrongdoers might volunteer information about "pressuring government by bribery."

As uncertainty surrounds "the what" in political participation, a troubling haziness likewise infuses the "who" definitional element. Nominally, engaging in a political act, regardless of one's occupation or title, would certify one "a participant." Surprisingly, scholars here diverge. A few (Nagel 1987; Verba et al. 1995) explicitly exclude professionals. Everyone occupying a position of civil authority, from the president downward to local school board members, becomes a non-participant, if this understanding is strictly applied. This surely invites confusion but, more importantly, it evidences the unsettled conceptual cosmology. What if, for example, parents insist on a greater education policy role and, thanks to their pestering, receive advisory board appointments? Or receive fees as independent consultants? Does a salary make these parents "apathetic"? If the gratuity disappeared, would they revert to being "activists"? Do they mysteriously become activists if pursing non-education policy aims? How do we categorize those financially sustained by politically inclined foundations or private advocacy entities, several of which receive taxpayer money? Or, to push the theoretical envelope, what if a foreign government secretly contributes millions to U.S. elections? Are those conduits passing along the funds "activists" or merely dutiful employees? Perplexing examples are easily multiplied especially since few clear lines exist between those inside and outside the official corridors of power.

"Activism" can also exist sans personal awareness. How do we classify union workers or college students obligated to fund organizations advancing explicit political aims? This example is hardly hypothetical, and federal courts have recently protected people against such "coerced" funding. Imagine a student being asked about political contributions, and answering, "I personally don't give a dime, but my mandatory $50 fee goes to dozens of extremists, so put me down as 'radical benefactor.'" What about those erroneously believing that they are funding religious charities to alleviate homelessness when these clergy devote themselves to haranguing City Hall for government-based solutions? It is an open secret that nominally educational or religious foundations are frequently major political players despite IRS regulations forbidding this engagement.

A further waiting-to-happen quandary is the implied motive embedded in these definitions. Activity, understood in prevailing conceptualizations, is assumed to be instrumental (versus being an end-in-itself). A "something" is to be accomplished so we might assume that possessing a non-political motive disqualifies an act as "political." Rosenstone and Hansen (1993), as is typical, conceive political participation as "...action directed explicitly toward influencing the distribution of social goods and social values." Conway's (2000: 3) textbook summary of this literature reiterates this instrumentality characterizing it as an assumption. But, is "to influence the distribution of goods and values" determined from the behavior's intrinsic character or the actor's idiosyncratic aim? And who certifies this end desire one way or the other? The participants themselves? The above-the-fray researcher? A guiding scientific rule is entirely absent here. What if disagreement arises over a behavior's "real" purpose? Are participant justifications to be accepted at face value, or might the investigator probe deeper into the real, perchance murky, unconscious motive?

Consider, for example, those college students pressuring Nike to eliminate overseas "sweatshops" or raise employee wages. What purpose instigates this demand? On its face, this seems like unambiguous political behavior—help the less fortunate. Yet, if the U.S. prohibited sweatshop-tainted imports, what do these students *personally* accomplish? Higher sneaker prices for U.S. consumers? More jobs for American workers? (Even boosting overseas pay would unlikely make U.S. workers price competitive.) But, this last (improbable) gain is hardly beneficial personally since college students are unlikely to ever assemble shoes or have families performing these menial tasks. What if Nike slashed labor costs by firing these exploited workers and automated sneaker production? Or, equally likely, sub-contracted the manufacturing to escape visible responsibility. Would these freshly unemployed Chinese or Koreans benefit? Is a psychological sense of self-fulfillment sans any monetary gain the "real" aim? But what if these Nike workers truly cherished jobs that only looked bad to American college students unfamiliar with even worse employment alternatives? Might these raucous demonstrations be closer to audience participation theater than instrumental political action? Protests can surely bring psychic rewards apart from tangible gain. Conceivably, the deep and dark motive is to burden the U.S. poor with higher clothing costs. This disentanglment of multiple incentives, few of which are evidently political, all but goes unmentioned in these definitions, hardly a minor issue when motive is theoretically integral to making an act "political."

To appreciate just how nightmarish this motivation problem can be, consider the case of Mark Warren Sands, a convicted arsonist (Hibberd 2002). Sands began his arsonist "career" when he felt an urge to burn down a particular house that "annoyed him" in his upscale Phoenix neighborhood. Soon eight houses had been torched, a campaign Sands largely attributed to his desire to prove that he still could create media attention (he was an unemployed public relations executive). Intoxicated by all the publicity, he was soon passing his deeds off as eco-terrorism, even leaving notes such as "U Build—We Burn Agin (sic)" at the site of destroyed homes. In messages to the news media he identified himself as the Coalition to Save the Preserves, a mountain biker organization. A few anti-development types even expressed sympathy. Many Phoenix residents probably believed that this was a politically motivated, anti-development attack, yet the truth was that Sands was just an attention-getting pyromaniac with a flair for publicity, and this publicity was politically tinged. Question: If Sands had never been caught and confessed to his real motives, would this damage still be "political action"?

Inserting the motivation requirement also presupposed that motives are knowable or, even more troublesome, that the *true* cause (or shifting amalgam of inducements) can be accurately ascertained via conventional measurement techniques. Survey-based participation research is particularly ill suited for psychoanalysis. Unfortunately, this is required if our definition mandates establishing motive. Surely people can misrepresent themselves or even feel confused. One might also add to this confusion the compulsion issue. Nagel (1987: 3-4) quite reasonably distinguishes "participation" from "mobilization" (e.g., Soviet-style forced voting). The latter, he argues, is pseudo-participation to the extent that behavior is non-voluntary. This compulsion is not unique to dictatorships— city contract kickbacks disguised as "voluntary campaign donations" do occur in democracies, though illegal. Urban machines long insisted on votes as the price for municipal employment. Perchance coercion can mutate into habit, and these practices psychologically become "voluntary." On the other hand, Nelson (1979: 395-6) in her analysis of participation among the poor in less developed nations accepts such manipulated activism as legitimate since disentangling coerced from non-coerced behavior is nearly impossible. All in all, immense uncertainties regarding this coercion issue are one more time banished.

This elusiveness regarding motives is particularly germane since U.S. politics affords innumerable opportunities to accomplish purely non-political objectives under the guise of civic engagement. A City Hall procession protesting alleged police brutality—patently "political" on its surface—might furnish enjoyable mingling or egotistical TV appearances in addition to furthering bona fide civic aims. Perchance every demonstrator has a unique blend of incitements for their involvement, and these shift day-to-day, moment-to-moment. Voting—the least ambiguous of all political acts—can be performed solely in exchange for a bottle of whiskey or cigarettes, hardly a traditional civic enticement. The bottom line is that these conventional definitions offer scant guidance to distinguish, say, the authentic activist from a shut-in avoiding loneliness via chasing feel-good causes. And present-day conceptualizations certainly offer no assistance regarding, as claimed, distinctions of motive as germane to what is being accomplished. Does it make a difference, according to some scientific standard, if the looter is resisting political repression or just acquisitive?

These distinctions are not academic hair-splitting terminological exercises to elucidate meaningless distinctions. A proper delineation is critical for two reasons. First, if "political activism" is to be grasped as a distinct general concept (not merely a haphazard sample of an almost infinite set of exemplars dependent on the classifier's whim), investigation requires sharp boundaries. When "civic activism" rests entirely on personal intuition, and multiple onlookers each possess unique perspectives, analytical anarchy is inevitable. To reiterate, this delineation is scientifically fundamental, yet sorely neglected when addressing its myriad dimensions. The physical sciences progressed only after elemental concepts were precisely defined—mass or velocity, for example. Where such sharpness was uncertain, for example, in Quantum mechanics, an immense restorative effort ensued. Visualize physics replete with dozens of personalized definitions of "electron"? If this conceptual border regarding participation is cloudy, can we *a priori* assume that what holds for, say, badgering public officials with letters equally holds for campaign contributions? Or, are these two different appearing influence efforts guided by identical principles, just as rocks and feathers are equally controlled by gravity? An "I know it when I see it" or "everybody decides for themselves" strategy may be suitable for casual observations, but impromptu classification hardly advances scientific knowledge. Weekend bird watching differs from ornithology.

This definitional labor is, secondly, politically consequential. Controlling what is included or excluded in "political participation" is itself a momentous political prize. Real-world intrusions exacerbate an already arduous definitional assignment. During the 1960s, for example, classifying urban rioters as despicable "criminal looters" or honoring them as "freedom fighters" was hotly debated and followed ideological fault lines. Is today's Klu Klux Klan a bona fide political organization resisting state racial meddling, or merely some rag-tag demented bigots needing psychological counseling? Is First Amendment protection necessary for homoerotic art displays since its exhibition challenges the commanding heterosexual public (and therefore "political") culture? Soviet dissidents were once classified "insane" (not activists) and dispatched to asylums to cure medically their "irrational" opposition to the Marxist Workers Paradise. With tables now turned, former lunatics are now heroic (political) dissenters. De-legitimizing one's political opponents via labeling behavior a "psychological disturbance" is a time-honored practice. Open-ended definitions assuredly invite such ideologically driven mischief.

Compounding this definitional haziness are today's legal incentives regarding what is, and is not, "political." The U.S. Internal Revenue Service treats political organizations quite differently from those, ostensibly, furthering education, religion, or charity. A church serving as a covert radical assembly risks its tax-exempt status, a major benefit for fund-raising or escaping property taxes. The savvy "minister" might cleverly misrepresent his or her City Hall meddling as "community service" or "educational outreach." The same is true for conservative foundations promoting free market economics—flamboyant politicking invites unwelcome IRS inquiry. No wonder then that some of today's most vibrant political forces eschew the political label. Conversely, First Amendment protection may entice non-political entities to claim, perhaps dubiously, political status. At least some judges would rule that blatant pornography promoted for nothing other than greed might be protected as a constitutionally guaranteed right no different, in principle, from political speech. No doubt, some radicals hoping to subvert the dominant culture might agree with this judgment though for entirely different reasons.

From Definitions to Research Design

Having (imperfectly) disposed of their definitional obligation, the archetype participation study now descriptively ventures forth. Not surprising, given near-identical initial conceptualization plus the exigencies of data collection, empirical treatments traverse roughly similar territory. As noted earlier, core items typically include voting, donating money to candidates/causes, contacting public officials, discussing politics (and similar "attentiveness" indicators), political party work or a small handful of comparable conventional deeds. Indeed, these inquiries can easily be reduced to a "generic participation study." Several key decisions (actually, unreflected mental habits) here are worth scrutinizing.

An especially commonplace—even dominating—approach employs a survey in which sampled respondents report on specific, pre-selected behaviors. The below-the-surface consequences of this formula cannot be exaggerated. The primary question is *not,* "What have you done politically? That invites a plethora of jumbled responses many of which undoubtedly are vague or of uncertain relevance, a serious nuisance requiring time-consuming post-interview coding. The query is the more restricted, "Have you (in some time period) done X? Or Y? Or Z?" If (as likely) a respondent has exceeded the researcher's limited menu, this behavior is "lost" to the compilation. It is the investigator who thusly defines "participation" by select exemplar, and those pursuing unmentioned strategies are misclassified as "apathetic."

As far as can be determined, zero effort is spent independently verifying what campaigning has actually transpired—the reported "yes," "no," or perhaps "how often" define behavior.[2] The study of *behavior* is thus transformed into *reports about behavior*, not observation of deeds within a specified time frame. Absolute honesty and researcher-respondent definitional agreement are assumed, a practice that surely invites error and confusion. This is true even when verification is practical, for example, comparing campaign receipts with alleged donations. Every reported act, moreover, is scored as equal to other similarly labeled acts apart from any contextual details. We shall have more to say regarding this research convention below.

Narrowing inquiry to those acts sufficiently plentiful to permit statistical computation requires that rare or idiosyncratic action, even conduct with momentous consequences, be excluded. Conceivably, these exceedingly uncommon behaviors may be immensely consequential and, taken together apart from their distinctive features, may be quite plentiful. In the civil rights struggle of the 1950s and 1960s, for example, the legal system underwent a sea change thanks to a few thousand relentless activists, pursuing heretofore-unusual tactics, drawn from a population of tens of millions. More recently, only a tiny coterie has instigated state ballot initiatives banning racial preferences, acts of immense consequence. An analogy might be made with small businesses—each is minuscule and distinctive, yet they add hundreds of billions to the economy. Seeking *the* needle in the haystack is daunting, but the haystack may contain a vast multitude of endlessly varied needles.

This prefabricated, researcher-supplied finite list of activities also mechanically projects the past on to the future. For some items—voting, making campaign contributions—this strict continuity is perfectly sensible and facilitates over-time comparisons. To continue our economic metaphors, however, this tactic resembles examining American industry today using 1950s business textbook categories. As in commerce, benefits often accrue to innovators while those sticking with the "tried and true" may decline. Examples of participatory "modernization" abound—creative litigation, funding politically engaged research foundations ("think tanks"), desktop publishing, e-group newsletters, community access cable TV forums, and other innovations once unthinkable or technically unworkable. Recall the anti-affirmative action bake sale eliciting wide press coverage. Public schools in many Southern states are now grappling with what to do about thousands of white students displaying Confederate flags on their clothing—is this "really" resistance to black civil rights? One might even include today's popular music awash in shallow though graphic messages about social injustice or patriotism as a way to influence those who shun traditional political forums. Those still enamored of tactics from the 1960s—protest marches or boycotts—can be likened to merchants believing that a fax number suffices against Web-based competitors.[3]

These time-bound constraints hint at another formidable conceptual problem, namely the variability of "political participation" across political systems. Is our quest strictly parochial—grasping activism in the U.S. here and now—or is the ultimate theoretical goal universal appreciation? The latter aim is more scientifically alluring, but it poses immense obstacles. Obviously, what constituted "serious" activism in the former Soviet Union, for example, a letter to the editor criticizing factory managers, may be judged trivial—even nonpolitical—in the context of U.S. politics (see Hough [1976] for the travails of exporting democratic participation definitions to totalitarian systems). Political action can be remarkably subtle—in some nations merely publicly displaying an antiquated map is a political gesture where national borders remain controversial. Similarly, in less developed nations the true political power is often the military, and thus an Army enlistment begins one's political career. Must we therefore compile a list of participatory equivalencies across varied settings? And conceivably, this dilemma may also apply within the U.S. given local tastes for tolerating politically relevant corruption or violence.

The generic research design recipe then meshes these reported acts with personal and political traits, notably demographic information (age, sex, race, education, etc.) and views on various broad issues as measured by standard off-the-shelf questionnaire items. Environmental "contextual data" (census-like area information) are periodically integrated into this individual portrait. A typical study will report, for example, that the wealthy are more energetic letter writers than the less affluent, or conservatives donate more generously to campaigns. That those sharing certain psychological traits, for example, high political efficacy or identification with a political party, exhibit greater (or lesser) civic engagement, is also a research literature staple.

A point that cannot be over-emphasized is that the analytical unit is almost always the individual's reported act, not the activity. The researcher may speak of collective entities, for example, African Americans, but this entity is a computationally defined category created by pooling survey respondents with identical (researcher-deemed relevant) traits. Even if the term "issue group" (e.g., "liberals") is utilized to depict those sharing a common viewpoint, this denotation derives from researcher-imposed aggregation; category members assuredly lack any physical or organizational interconnection. They might even object to this lumping together. Organized interests (e.g., the NRA's anti-gun regulation advocates) known for especially energetic political involvement escape this survey-based net. Even when a prodigious effort is made to include organization members (e.g., Verba et al. 1995), interviewees are scattered across thousands of such groups. Though an equally ample group-based activism research literature exists (i.e., the study of "movements"), these findings are never closely integrated into this individual-level analysis. One of the most powerful of all citizen influence mechanisms—the interest group or mass movement—is thus inexplicably banished from survey-based investigation. This practice is almost entirely driven by statistical, not theoretical requirements—the usual survey-based inquiry may contain only one or two members of a specific group, and a tiny N renders statistical analysis impossible.

The finished inquiry "product" can be conceived as a grid consisting of randomly sampled individuals and a handful of (investigator) selected political actions. To reduce clutter, separate items are routinely collapsed into a scale ranging from apathy to "high participation." Though this construction can be quite intricate statistically, it essentially awards points for distinct behaviors, with greater weight given to numerically less common acts (usually labeled "more difficult" given their scarcity). Thus, Smith who votes, writes letters, and gives money is classified as "more active" than Jones who merely writes checks to candidates. That is, Smith engages in three acts compared to only one for Jones. That the latter may spend 2,000 hours yearly at fund-raising to collect millions goes unmeasured. This cosmology tacitly favors dilettantism. The scale's metric is, moreover, entirely relative—those classified as "high" are only *more* activist, not full-time activists. Conceivably, "a high-activist" might allocate an hour or two a month forwarding e-mails to public officials or watching a politically flavored talk show.

Political insight necessarily derives from the interplay of within-survey variables. In social science language, pre-selected behaviors are inevitably the dependent variable (what is to be explained), not the independent variable (the variable doing the explaining). Research thus accounts for personal effort expenditures, not outcomes. While results of civic involvement are seldom totally ignored, its discussion is often speculative and clearly secondary. The exigencies of the standard research design once again make themselves felt theoretically—it is exceptionally troublesome to explain an ongoing, typically hazy, collective outcome by aggregating individual traits assessed at a single time point. Imagine, for example, accounting (using standard statistical methods) for government's incessant expansion of subsidized medical insurance for the elderly by a few noisy senior citizen demonstrations years back. Solely for computational convenience it is assumed that impact, like gravity, is a pervasive, uniform force: a vote, letter, or protest demonstration equals any other vote, letter, or protest demonstration.

Having mapped the participatory landscape, our "generic study" occasionally seeks broader implications. A general sameness once more pervades multiple enterprises. Some roughly defined "democratic theory" regularly supplies a theoretical garnish. At this juncture the contemporary researcher's egalitarian perspective often crops up, typically by expressing unease regarding the unequal distribution of activism infecting a less-than-perfect status quo. Strongly implied is that involvement's concentration among society's more affluent poses "a democratic problem" (see, for example, Lijphart 1997 among many others). Note well—the "problem" is not denied access—what the excluded historically sought—but the actual utilization of participatory opportunities to flatten inequalities (for example, Verba et al. 1995: 11 suggests that uneven participation "compromises" democracy). Nor, for that matter, is it acknowledged that potential resources—time, money, energy, statutory rights—are also plentiful, grossly under-utilized or squandered foolishly. The focus is on differences (or "inequalities") in purported behavior. Speculation also often hints that economic resource unevenness itself partially derives from differential engagement—if the destitute seek prosperity, new schools, or improved health care, heightened activism is the superior pathway. For pragmatic advice seekers, the plain-to-see lesson is that individual political mobilization both remedies one's plight and, happy to say, enhances democracy.

Omissions

This (easy-to-execute) research formula's allure cannot be over-emphasized. Disciplinary novices might be incapacitated to resist after repeated exposure to endless cookie-cutter exemplars. As in composing a musical sonata, the basic structure is preordained though variations abound. Unfortunately, what is ignored in these conventional treatments is momentous, far more than what is included. This bountiful literature depicting civic engagement is often but a collection of ephemera. Chapter upon chapter of statistical explication peppered with periodic exhortations only disguises the lacunae. What, then, is slighted?

An obvious place to begin is the mechanical treatment afforded each enumerated participatory act. Each type of behavior—petitioning officialdom, attending a rally—comprises a set of definitionally equivalent undertakings. *Qualitative* differences are, apparently, judged irrelevant: a wasted $5 anonymous donation and a highly consequential $10,000 independent expenditure are *precisely* alike. Forwarding an unread pre-printed letter perfunctorily handled by an intern is likewise equated with a carefully heeded telephone call from a major contributor—both comprise "contacting government." In fact, mailing an incoherent postcard to the wrong legislator months after the communication's subject had vanished is honored as "a political act." "Foolishness" might be a more appropriate label. Participation is thus "democratized" via counting every act equal to every other act. While this counting rule facilitates statistical analysis by avoiding arduous qualitative judgments, it barely captures a political reality deserving better.

At the core of this analytical void is resource utilization *skill*. Only a passing, perfunctory acknowledgement is sometimes, if ever, offered (e.g., Verba et al. 1995: 13).[4] If one reasonably likens civic engagement to other human endeavors, it is self-evident that talent differences are critical. Why else have differential pay for comparable jobs? This topic can be deceptively complex, as we shall eventually discover. Consider how three different citizens might extract political benefits. Larry intensely favors state medical care insurance and for historical reasons, loyally votes Democratic since that party best represents his pro-entitlement views. He also diligently motivates others like himself to the polls. Eventually, for Larry (and his compatriots), this partisanship becomes unthinking habit; abandoning faithfulness becomes inconceivable, and an overpowering sense of dutifulness dictates casting one's ballot. Within today's research cosmology, Larry and his fellow travelers are exemplary— he invariably votes, and choice aligns perfectly with issue stance ("rational" in voting research parlance).

Curly, by contrast, opposes this government medical effort but, unlike Larry, she is crafty, even and slightly devious. She resists being "taken for granted" and periodically threatens to "waste" her vote on minor party candidates if she feels too unattended by the GOP, her "natural" party. Moreover, this "hard-to-get" stratagem is commonplace and artfully coordinated among those holding similar stands. Meanwhile, our third activist—Moe—disdains electioneering altogether and manically builds a colossal fortune from his cream pie business. Flush with profits, he endows a well-heeled Washington-based foundation to finance astute studies advancing his pet health care scheme.

How would the political *proficiency* of these actors be ranked? Connoisseurs of hardheaded practical politics would probably say Moe first, despite his apathy. Though a non-voter, he may forcefully shape the public agenda thanks to his cream pie fortune. If voting alone were assessed, Curly (and her comrades) would be carefully heeded in light of their fickleness. Ironically, Curly scores dismally on the conventional assessment ratings report, and might even be castigated as "irrational" by voting scholars given the occasional vote-issue-stance mismatches and non-voting. Yet, while the consistent and loyal Larry receives accolades from scholarly researchers, his choice is sufficiently "automatic" that he (and his compatriots) can safely be disregarded (at least in the short run). Perhaps a little flattering rhetoric will placate. What is absolutely critical is the (unmeasured) variation in the power to organize and strategically withhold electoral support. Overall, Curly and Moe play politics skillfully (though quite differently) while the Larry and his compatriots remain paralyzed to achieve any advantage. This variousness in dexterity makes an enormous *political* difference, yet it is invisible within the standard, survey-derived activism cataloging. What thus appears as virtuous "activism" in our example is really ineptitude and vice versa.

Success is likewise omitted in the long parade of conventional participation studies. With scant exception, only the expended effort—the letter sent or the donation—is ascertained. Ultimate impact, it will be recalled, is treated almost tangentially in the conventional inquiry. No interviewer asks, "What happened?" Or, better yet, "Did the act yield the expected positive outcome?" And certainly no researcher volunteers to track down what came to pass, particularly for the hundreds of acts uncovered in the typical survey. Where minimal attention is given to repercussions, only the ledger's positive side is scrutinized (see, for example, Rosenstone and Hansen 1993: chapter 8). That this investment could have brought a *net* loss, despite some incidental gain, seems unimaginable. Even hints that political activism *might* exacerbate a calamity seems unspeakable in these conventional accounts though, surely, such failure routinely occurs.

Again imagine assessing political participation from an economic framework. Here the inescapable question would be: what is gained for a given time/energy/resource investment? Surely somebody "investing" in unlucky lottery tickets should not be classified as "an entrepreneur specializing in financial futures" though, superficially, he or she resembles a diligent mutual fund client. Innumerable participants—not just an isolated few—might receive *zero* (or perchance *minus*) from their involvement (other than, perhaps the researcher's admiration). Politics, like finance, overflows with fleece-the-fool scams and counterproductive wild goose chases. For example, in the spring of 2003 the American Knights of the Klu Klux Klan announced that it would hold a rally to support the Augusta National Golf Club's all-male membership policy (it was one of five groups, including Jesse Jackson's Rainbow/PUSH Coalition, seeking parade permits). What would a "successful" Klan rally accomplish? More than likely, it would besmirch the club reputation with atrocious publicity while drawing boisterous hecklers, and for these reason the club has not welcomed the Klan's "assistance" (Associated Press 2003). The key point is that this return cannot *ever* be properly assessed from merely calibrating input or counting up hypothetical plusses. An estimable "high scorer" might waste his or her vote on the Vegetarian Party, contribute to scam organizations, and plead abstruse civic minutia with bored children.

This appraisal entails more than dexterity though skill is certainly pertinent. Where one targets the effort is vital. For example, a modern-day American socialist may be exceedingly able to raise funds or win party leadership positions. He or she also pesters officials with cleverly worded petitions and shrewdly harangues everyone within earshot. Still, what transpires from this resourceful, assiduous application? Has socialism crept closer to fruition due to this astute relentlessness? Hardly. This investment venture, truth be told, mimics buying lottery tickets or a civic hobby. Less proficient effort within the Democratic Party might have produced a substantially larger net profit. Admittedly, assessing precise "return" on a political act may be exceptionally daunting as a research problem, but any grasp of the topic without this ingredient is woefully incomplete.[5]

This likening of participation to the investment of scarce resources illuminates another area of neglect—the value of any act vis-à-vis alternatives. Politics, like all purposeful behaviors, demands choices among vying tactics, and these alternatives often lie outside of politics. This is fundamental, so engaging in one activity—even expertly—versus all others hardly certifies civic capacity. Let us not forget Ricardo's Law of Comparative Advantage. Resources are always finite, so an hour drafting petitions is one hour less than can be devoted to, say, soliciting funds or earning a fortune to create a tax-exempt foundation (recall Moe's stratagem mentioned earlier). The energy expended for assembling a boycott of an uncooperative store might be better invested in establishing a competing business. A well-rounded assessment would therefore ask questions like "Was this the wisest strategy *given available possibilities*?" or even, "What were the opportunity costs for this action?" Disdaining this calculation unwisely assumes that any act is as valuable as any other act. Sad to say, such "obvious" though central questions regarding resource allocation pass unnoticed in standard treatments. Just as a worthy impact is assumed apart from any empirical demonstration, the decision to take a particular step is never judged as one might evaluate one investment versus another.

The familiar activism portrayal also neglects the contentious, *multi-sided* nature of political conflict. One must always ask, "Who is the opposition?" when appraising participation ventures. Politics, like war, is unequivocally a contest with winners and losers, not a collective ritual with everyone advancing shoulder-to-shoulder. This is easily forgotten since opposition might choose to be silent or wait until exuberant activists dissipate their energies. Pursuing an oppositionless cause —demanding prosperity, for example—is hardly politics and accomplishes little beyond passing therapeutic euphoria. Participation can *never* be fully understood if only studied as a collection of singular acts. The equivalent would be describing a tennis match reported exclusively by describing only one player and neglecting the score, to boot. Remarkably, this is what customarily transpires when depicting activism. This disregard is especially consequential since the choice of aim may invite powerful adversaries. Today's researchers never ask respondents, "Who resisted your struggle?" "Did you really expect to win against these odds?" For all we know, participation was utterly ill fated from the get-go. For those heeding the standard academic counsel, battles are seemingly fought against invisible enemies.

Consider, for example, the accomplishments of those who have long pressured government to enact untold anti-racial and age discrimination laws, higher minimum wage requirements, and similar apparent advantages for those at the bottom of the economic ladder. These celebrated victories seemingly prove the power of politics, or at least to those recounting the battles. Nevertheless, these benefits also bring liabilities since these legal requirements raise costs by making these covered workers less desirable compared to unprotected applicants. Employers can fight back though not by mobilizing politically—they can defeat minimum wage laws converting full-time employees into part-timers, or redefining their responsibilities to pay lesser salaries for the same work. Moreover, laws to guard older workers can easily backfire when these workers are fired prior to reaching the protected age (Epstein 2002). Surely, a full account of activism requires double-entry bookkeeping.

A particularly harsh consequence of this inattention is that battle choices are never evaluated. To paraphrase Gertrude Stein, a cause is a cause is a cause. Words like "futile" or "doomed" are absent when depicting participatory efforts. Perhaps the religion-like passions infusing campaigns explains this oversight—no matter how daunting the odds, faith remains unshaken, so why worry about foes? To take an extreme, though hardly fictitious, example, suppose that abolishing all sexual differences in child rearing were one's objective. The "enemy" here is incredibly formidable: social norms, legal prohibitions against state intervention, popular resistance, uncertainty regarding accomplishment, and untold other obstacles. Nevertheless, proposal advocates hurled themselves into the battle, doing everything an impassioned activist could do, and then some. Predictably, all came to naught. What does this quixotic exercise prove? Have we demonstrated that political combat, no matter how pointless and unsuccessful, can mysteriously invigorate democratic self-rule? A less sanguine appraisal is that participation's lure occasionally attracts people incapable of reasonable cost-benefit calculations.

This "what's accomplished?" inquiry points toward another under-appreciated quandary: disentangling political consequentiality from non-political acts. This is the obverse of the "ostensible political being non-political" issue addressed earlier. Action seemingly lacking any political imputation in the most encompassing definition of political can, in some circumstances, be profoundly political, regardless of intentions. Are we to assign the "political" label where behavior, sans any political impulse, has an unambiguous civic impact, motive aside? Recent gun control battles illustrate this situation perfectly. While both sides advance their cause with endless legal machinations, the legislative impetus often comes from murderous shootings involving the mentally deranged. These culprits hardly desire tougher gun laws, probably oppose them, yet this is precisely what their senseless violence generates. And while gun control partisans never desire these incidents, they are—sad to say—more helpful than all the marches, letters, and similar maneuvers. To make a complex situation even more daunting, what if a few deranged culprits secretly—even unconsciously—intended to advance the anti-gun agenda? Would the carnage then become "political," in the sense of analogous to terrorists attacks to provoke political outrage?

Conclusions

This political participation scholarship account has been decidedly negative. That leading scholars have published this research in prestigious outlets further compounds our impertinence. For this faultfinding inclination we are unapologetic. It is not that we find this scholarship inaccurate or ideologically driven. In fact, this research corpus tells us a great deal about political participation, for instance, who votes, attends rallies, or otherwise claims to engage in those activities judged important by investigators. These formulaic studies have, moreover, provided a sturdy set of findings, our discipline's proto-scientific laws.

It is the future that concerns us, and this venerated, easy to follow survey-based formula is absolutely incapable of addressing questions needing resolution. No matter how elaborate the instrument, no matter how many pre-coded items offered, and no matter how incisive the statistical analysis, it is *impossible* to know from these data whether political activism was a worthwhile endeavor or a waste of time. These are hardly trivial omissions. This qualm is not holding a literature accountable for research problems it chooses not to investigate. If that were true our review would be extraneous. What typically transpires, to use the language of advertising, is bait and switch: researchers delve into their data, offer countless correlates of activism, and then—implicitly or explicitly—offer implications about the value of activism for both personal advancement and some vague "democracy." This sequence is a nonsequitur, the equivalent of purporting to scrutinize a business firm without regard to profits. How can one say anything substantial about either individual benefits or democratic vitality from a static opinion poll about possible civic engagement? And this superficial quality is hardly limited to survey-based designs. As chapter 6 will show, even those in-depth studies focusing on group-based activism are woefully incomplete though a step in the right direction by our standards. Put bluntly, political participation scholars are manufacturing a widely embraced cosmology that easily seduces readers to believe far more than has been proven.

The overriding qualm in our collection of complaints is that these ivory tower treatises deny a plain to see reality, especially civic engagement's downside. These inquires are all-too-silent regarding dexterity, the obstacles awaiting would be activists, and, ultimately, success or failure. Recall the drunk and the lamppost tale—a search guided by convenience, not the likely location of the keys. This obliviousness is further compounded by theoretical vagueness and neglect. To the extent that these incomplete (and excessively optimistic) musings filter out into wider society (and they undoubtedly do), deficiencies are consequential, not arcane academic hair-splitting. Guidance seekers should be aware that their options are far greater than what is depicted by the brief survey-based menu, activism is never guaranteed, and private pathways may be more efficacious. Those mulling over civic engagement could immerse themselves in the "political participation" literature for years and emerge clueless regarding their chances of success.

If existing approaches to understanding political participation are so flawed, probably beyond remedial tinkering, how should analysis proceed? The answer is to begin with objectives, not cataloguing handy, familiar activities. The choice to begin with objectives, not input, generates quite different follow-up queries. Instead of the usual "who" and "how much" topics, investigation gravitates toward assessing resources vis-à-vis enemies, legal obstacles, aim practicality, likely utility of tactics, and other indicators of potential or ongoing success. Accomplishment becomes more critical than asking if activists followed a time-honored engagement script. Gone are all the "traditional" design elements such as psychological dispositions and demographic factors unless these have a demonstrable relevance to the enterprise. Either participation brings success or failure, independent of its intrinsic value, its sources or contribution to "democracy." It is no different from judging business performance—can the firm execute a sensible plan, the projected revenues realistic, are key personnel in place, and, critically, is it profitable.

Compared to today's standard political participation treatises, executing this design will not be a tidy enterprise. Immense theoretical and practical problems await us, and solutions cannot be guaranteed. This focus on objectives certainly does not lend itself to statistical neatness, at least not presently. Chapters 7-9 will have an "old-fashioned" descriptive flavor when depicting the war against AIDS. Nevertheless, clear evidence-based judgments are possible, and these "soft" conclusions certainly outshine cataloguing "hard" ephemera. Substantively we shall see—at least in this case study—that outcomes can be exceedingly complicated. Political success can bring death while failed efforts may extend lives. This should be a cautionary tale for those admonishing the apathetic to join the fray.

Notes

1.   This flight from "disruptive" participation is sometimes justified creatively. One major cross-national study (Verba, Nie, and Kim 1978) frankly acknowledged the key political role of violence but defended their exclusion of such behavior from their purview with "…to deal with these would be to write a different book." (1). They then go on to argue that (a) democracy, the focus of their research, is predicated on participation via "normal" channels and (b) the breakdown (perceived or real) of these "normal" channels often engenders violent alternatives. Needless to say, this reasoning is atheoretical, a convenient *ad hoc* rationale for skipping over some exceedingly messy empirical puzzles. Moreover, how would one treat subversive movements *in the service of democratic governance?* Were Eastern European dissidents "apathetic" since they labored to undermine the established Communist regime? What about U.S. civil rights demonstrators in the 1950s and 1960s?

2.   On occasion this verification is done for voting. Here, not unexpectedly, about 20 percent of those claiming to vote did not do so, at least according to official statistics (Bernstein, Chada, and Montjoy 2001).

3.   Fixating on past activities also flows from researcher's desires for over-time continuities. Especially in widely used data sets, comparability offered multiple research and publication opportunities. The possibility that acts change their meaning over time is seldom acknowledged, however (e.g., campaign paraphernalia such as buttons though once common have now become rare).

4.   This perfunctory mention is noteworthy for it reflects on the gap between what is central politically versus what is relevant to research. Though Verba et al. are keenly aware of qualitative differences in activism, this topic vanishes from subsequent analysis. This omission undoubtedly reflects the arduousness of measuring this quality, not its irrelevance. A few sentences later the discussion safely returns to participation measured only by quantity.

5.   To appreciate fully just how quickly the conventional academic analysis flees this impact issue, consider how Verba et al. (1995) address the matter. On page 30 they note that this topic is "…well beyond the scope of this volume…" and cite a handful of studies allegedly "proving" impact. If one were to read these studies, however, civic activism's impact is limited and often unclear. If anything, the cited studies reveal that civic pressure often fails when attacking larger issues, notably socio-economic disparities. A vague reference is also made to an unspecified "vast literature" to bolster this unsubstantiated claim. Yet, it is patently obvious that impact is absolutely central to their thesis that differential participation rates subvert the equitable distribution of democratically decided values.

3

Varieties of Activism

The "real world" of political participation is immensely complicated. "Political act" itself is a murky concept inviting multiple interpretations. Today's potential activist enjoys bountiful opportunities, and nothing presupposes battle plans to honor the humdrum tactics elucidated in academic "political participation" treatments. Activist and academic may profoundly diverge in their visions, let alone influence calculus and available resources, and the once triumphant may now be obsolete. Here we expand the participation canvas typically ignored in conventional compendiums. We briefly depict six such oft-neglected arenas: (1) litigation; (2) disseminating research; (3) shaping popular culture; (4) educational indoctrination; (5) economic investing; and, lastly, (6) violence. These six depicted activities are hardly obscure—novelty derives from their insertion into a typically narrowly defined subject matter. All are consequential and permit ample citizen engagement. This is hardly an exhaustive list, and notably absent are such activities as bribery, manipulating the mass media, or interpretations of crime as political resistance. A full portrait of all possibilities would undoubtedly require a separate book.

Political Litigation

The Founding Fathers envisioned a feeble judiciary. Alexander Hamilton in *The Federalist* No. 78 argued that the magistrates "...will always be the least dangerous to the political rights of the constitution." Judges, he continued, have no influence over the sword or the purse—they have "neither FORCE nor WILL but merely judgment" and depend wholly upon the executive to impose their designs. Nevertheless, in *Marbury v. Madison* (1803) the Supreme Court authorized itself to overrule legislatures and executives. As altercations over slavery and commerce boiled to the surface, the courts quickly entangled themselves in far-ranging quarrels once considered beyond their purview. Judges were now self-anointed political players of the first rank. Within fifty years of the Constitution's ratification, Alexis de Tocqueville, commented, "Scarcely any political questions arise that are not resolved, sooner or later, into a judicial question." Government's prodigious expansion has made this prescient insight ever more applicable. Allegedly, at least for some disgruntled Democrats, five Supreme Court judges, not millions of voters, de facto elected George W. Bush in 2000.

What draws our attention is the court's general policymaking over and above resolving particularly disputes. To decree that Smith wronged Jones, and Jones thus deserves monetary compensation is one thing. It is quite another, however, to pronounce that the *Smith v. Jones* decision applies far-reaching principles. The distinction is momentous, and not all observers welcome this expansion. Alexander Bickel, judicial activism's long-time critic, lamented that "All too many federal judges have been induced to view themselves as holding roving commissions as problem solvers, and as charged with a duty to act when majoritarian institutions do not" (Bickel 1970: 134). Nevertheless, opinions on judicial activism aside, the court's burgeoning political power is indisputable.

Especially to those stymied elsewhere, seeking court decisions to impose sweeping changes is *the* tactic of choice. The African-American civil rights struggle to secure school integration and voting rights can be written as a series of litigations only sporadically punctuated by legislative enactments. On repeated occasions, for example, mandating busing to achieve racial balance, lawsuits successfully produced outcomes with scant statutory grounding. In other instances, for example, employment discrimination, the law's reach, if not very meaning, expanded dramatically via litigation. Paradoxically, efforts to reverse this judicial policymaking have similarly favored lawsuits, not statutes. A parallel though less prominent path has been taken by welfare rights organizations to expand benefits to the indigent. Here, too, judges have rendered expansive decisions, even inviting novel grand principles, on matters such as residency requirements or childcare benefit sufficiency scarcely envisioned by legislators. Judges have also compelled public officials to spend billions to improve school, hospital, and prison conditions.

Achieving judicially created outcomes virtually indistinguishable from legislative enactments is hardly exceptional. Legislatures themselves often explicitly permit intervention or, more typically, enact nebulous laws inviting judicial interpretation. Legal culture shifts have likewise empowered judges—doctrines of mootness, standing to sue, jurisdiction, and ripeness—have waned, and judges have quickly seized intervention opportunities. That plaintiff attorneys can now collect hefty fees from class action lawsuits adds a financial incentive. Meanwhile, the time-honored view that sidestepping litigation best serves the public interest has been gradually replaced by the judicial philosophy emphasizing the court's legitimate policy-making role (Horowitz 1977: ch. 1). And, politically motivated litigation begets yet more litigation, and going backwards is near impossible absent vigorous legislative intervention. For example, *Brown v. Board of Education* (1954) voided a Kansas law permitting public school racial segregation. With the government's other branches paralyzed, this one lawsuits' contrived outcome failed to bring resolution, and a stampede of court cases soon followed addressing the hiring of teachers, school funding, and much more. When faced with inaction elsewhere judges could hardly refuse yet one more school integration suit once the court's door was ajar.

Litigation might even realize goals obtainable via "normal" politicking. Finding a single sympathetic judge and jury out of hundreds of possibilities, not swaying a stubborn legislature, may be the superior tactic given the odds. Prominent examples include gigantic damage awards from out-of-favor industries such as tobacco and firearms. Outright legal prohibition, an exceedingly arduous legislative task, is not being sought. The strategy instead is a war of financial attrition via damage suits that could, conceivably, bankrupt an entire industry on the installment plan. Failing that, the added costs may price tobacco or guns out of the marketplace. The opportunities for private citizens to "play politics" and get rich are enormous. Recently, for example, a Florida jury hit tobacco companies with a $145 billion dollar class action judgment involving private parties. Hundreds of similar suits are still pending. Eventually, tobacco may be unaffordable though, nominally, legal. Meanwhile, a lawsuit—not a statute—instigated by the city of Boston has forced gun manufactures to install trigger locks on newly produced guns. More generally, the mere threat of a colossal jury award, the burden of mount-

ing a defense, and all the unwelcome publicity has proven a powerful weapon to those averse to conventional influence channels.

Even anti-military groups have gravitated toward litigation to
complement their bumper stickers, peace marches, and similar tactics. In the name of defending lizards and antelopes, eco-activists
have brought suit to end training exercises for pilots at the Barry
Goldwater Bombing Range near Phoenix, Arizona. Meanwhile, their
Hawaiian compatriots are seeking the end of live fire training at the
Army's Makua Military Reservation to save the Oahu tree snail and
the endangered Hawaiian hoary bat. Not to be outdone, a gaggle of
witches calling itself "Friends of Gaia" is trying to shut down the
Pinecastle Bombing Range in Florida to shield area bears and save
the gopher tortoises (Malkin 2001).

Litigation is a powerful political tool even if is not victorious or
fails to get one's case before a judge. The mere threat of litigation is
often sufficient. Thanks to fee shifting, a mechanism originally intended to provide lawyers to the destitute, the civil suit loser can be
forced to pay the winner's legal fees. The upshot, then, is that going
to court might add crushing legal bills to damage awards. For example, when Loudoun County, Virginia lost a case dealing with its
attempt to screen out pornography at the local library's internet site,
two law firms submitted bills totaling almost half a million dollars.
Faced with yet more legal fees if this verdict were to be challenged,
appeals were abandoned. Similar threats have been made against
school drug testing policy and drug loitering enforcement (see
www.communityinterest.org). In other words, unless one is willing
to risk a huge legal bill, or is near certain of winning, avoid policies
that might, however remotely, engender further civil litigation.

One especially promising tool in this legal repertoire is filing lawsuits compelling federal agencies to enforce statutory obligations.
Unlike conventional suits, plaintiffs need not demonstrate personal
harm to themselves. Via a judicial ruling, one secures government's
collaboration in one's quest, no small accomplishment.[1] Several key
federal statutes, for example, the Endangered Species Act of 1973,
the Noise Reduction Act, the Clean Air Act, among others, expressly
permit this redress. One example concerns a battle between the U.S.
Fish and Wildlife Service and something called the Fairy Shrimp
Study Group (FSSG). Under U.S. law, the Fish and Wildlife Service
has ninety days to evaluate de-listing requests for anything on its

"endangered species" list. When the FSSG's request to de-list two fairy shrimp species was ignored for two years, the Pacific Legal Foundation, a free-market legal organization representing the FSSG, sued the Fish and Wildlife Service to compel this review. As of April 2001, this dispute was still in litigation. Groups like Defenders of Wildlife, Biodiversity Legal Fund and the Center for Biological Diversity have utilized a far more encompassing pro-environmental litigation strategy to stymie economic development. Here lawsuits are ingeniously filed under the Endangered Species Act to add allegedly endangered species or protect existing ones. In 2001 the Fish and Wildlife Service was contesting some eighty suits on this matter, and an additional ninety were in the works. In short, a Herculean aim—eliminating all economic use of undeveloped land— was being accomplished via shrewd litigation on behalf of plants and animals! Moreover, successful litigation has been an economic windfall for these groups since the losing party—government—must pay court costs (*Wall Street Journal* 2001, A14).

Given litigation's often-colossal costs, the prodigious essential technical expertise, and the usual snail's pace progress, this ploy would appear beyond the ordinary citizen's influence repertory. Not true—legal recourse exists even for the poorest of the poor. Facilitating access are countless organizations, law firms, and untold ambitious attorney ever vigilant for cases to be fought gratis or for a hefty contingency fee. One does not *personally* wage one's legal crusade; the trick is finding sympathetic experts to shoulder these responsibilities. A few telephone calls or pleading letters might thus enlist attorneys by the dozen on one's behalf, a far more efficacious tactic than a one-shot livid missive sent to Congress. If one does not personally require such intervention or lacks legal standing, support via financial contribution to the countless groups providing these services can be equally effective.

Law firms and legal foundations awaiting conscription so as to press their own policy agendas abound. These are widely dispersed geographically, frequently offer 1-800 phone numbers, and increasingly have websites. Among the more prominent libertarian/conservative organizations are the Alliance Defense Fund, Atlantic Legal Foundation, Landmark Legal Foundation, and the Pacific Legal Foundation. Liberal equivalents are the Center for Reproductive Law and Policy, Lambda Legal Defense and Education Fund, the Center for Constitutional Rights, and the Legal Action Center for the Homeless. Complementing these entities are foundations that typically combine more general ideological advocacy with litigation conducted by staff attorneys. Illustrious examples include the Center for Individual Rights, American Center for Law and Justice, Rutherford Institute, the American Civil Liberties Union, Southern Poverty Law Center, People for the American Way, and the Anti Defamation League of B'nai B'rith. To reiterate, it is nearly inconceivable that a litigation-oriented organization cannot be discovered for some cause, regardless of its nature.[2]

Opportunities multiply exponentially when we included law firms doing pro bono work—assistance performed for the "public good." A Federalist Society survey of America's 100 largest law firms (as of 1998) revealed that eighty-eight of these mega firms engaged in pro bono work (hhtp://www.fed-soc.org/probono.htm). These comprise the most prestigious, well-financed, and skilled U.S. law firms, and many subsidize entire departments assisting destitute clients. Similar assistance can be found in virtually every city, and are accessible through state or local bar associations. And what causes attract this big league legal intervention? According to the Federalist Society analysis, assistance generally flows toward liberal objectives: combating AIDS, protecting the environment, advancing homosexual rights, shielding immigrants, ensuring prisoner rights, and protecting abortion access. By contrast, only 31 percent of these large firms admitted to defending causes generally judged free market or conservative.

These legal interventions can have far-ranging ramifications beyond the parties involved. For example, the world-renowned Arnold & Porter firm assisted the National Women's Law Center in the VMI case, litigation concerning the constitutionality of male-only universities (the firm of Shearman & Sterling handled the similar Citadel case). The equally prestigious Covington & Burling defended Sgt. Justin Elzie against dismissal from the Marine Corps on the basis of his homosexuality. Even gay marriages received gratis legal assistance from Davis, Polk & Wardell. Pro bono work also challenged the funding formulae for New York City schools as well as the adequacy of its education. In Portland, Oregon, litigation given without charge secured a $108 million dollar verdict against anti-abortion protestors while in *Edwards v. City of Santa Barbara* Proskauer

Rose lawyers defended the constitutionality of an ordinance protecting abortion clinics.

A notable irony exists here. History clearly shows this approach's immense utility and, as we have documented, it is readily available for practically any cause, regardless of meager resources. Moreover, each year thousands donate to ideologically sympathetic organizations hiring lawyers. Try visualizing African-American civil rights progress, defending abortion or hundreds of other causes without litigation, much of it paid for by sympathetic foundations. Nevertheless, this legal strategy is scarcely—if ever—appended to menus offered by scholars scrutinizing popular participation. Researchers never ask, "Have you sought legal redress by contacting a civic-minded law firm or foundation? Or, do you financially support organizations utilizing litigation for ideological ends?" It is as if the history of civil rights, the quest for legalized abortion, the vigorous enforcement of environmental laws, and untold other crusades heavily reliant on judicial decrees never existed. The upshot, then, is that those who occasionally elect this potent option become "apathetic."

Generating and Disseminating Research

It is a truism that modern society rests upon scientific research, and this applies equally to propelling satellites into orbit or solving urban traffic congestion woes. When would-be presidents compete for the "the savior of education" title favored nostrums inevitably reflect contending studies. While one candidate insists, "studies show the value of smaller classes," another rejoins, "teaching fundamentals has proven most effective." Meanwhile, critics of both embrace evidence proving the family's key role. Debates over crime, poverty, illicit drugs, and teenage pregnancy often resemble academic disputations in their attentiveness to evidentiary rules and causal impact. Environmental clashes—allegations of global warming, air quality, endangered species extinction, the disappearance of forests—are similarly research driven. Does pornography engender anti-women violence? It depends which evidence in credible. It was once said that today's hard-headed businessperson is a "slave" to some long-dead economist; the contemporary version might be that all nostrums rest on some obscure research corpus regarding the problem's true nature and superior solution.

The politics and research connection can be confusing. It might be useful to distinguish politically motivated investigation from absolutely neutral inquiry utilized for partisan ends. Both have political applications despite differing motivation. Consider, for example, medical investigations of AIDS. Laboratory analysis is assuredly objective—researchers dispassionately seek the disorder's causes, how it spreads, possible cures, and so on. Still, even the most hard-edged science can imply radically different prescriptions. Given identical research findings, conservatives might call for quarantining the HIV infected until the disease runs its course; liberals might demand billion-dollar campaigns to develop a non-disruptive cure. Moderates might accentuate sex and drug education. Science supplies ammunition for everyone.

The political use of objective science can be distinguished from politically motivated scientific inquiry. Here, overtly or covertly, one initiates inquiry to buttress policy positions. This is hardly intrinsically nefarious or biased, and may even be executed with only a fuzzy awareness of these hidden ends. Journalists are often unknowing conveyers of ideologically driven findings since they may be unaware of technical details or too pressured to check further (see, especially, Murray, Schwartz, and Lichter 2001). What facilitates this science and politics mix is the immense latitude available in conducting inquiry. Especially in the social sciences, uncovering truth rarely follows prescribed formulas. Options regarding hypothesis formulation, evidence germaneness, the applicable analytical tools, and conclusion generality offer endless permissible leeway. Ideological values can unknowingly intrude at each step. Investigators might twist findings to satisfy sponsors or gain prestigious publication and yet still satisfy scientific standards. That perfectly objective science can yield widely different political prescriptions is bad enough for those seeking a single truth; that dubious science can be passed off as "objective" exacerbates the problem immensely.

Though seldom recognized as such, scientific research—whether scrupulously evenhanded or cravenly biased—constitutes the very building blocks of civic discourse. As Joel Best, put it, "Statistics have a fetish-like power in contemporary discussions about social problems" (Best 2001). It is not unusual to find highly charged debates, for example, global warming, that exist *entirely* over competing scientific studies. The stakes over whose research is embraced as authoritative can be huge. Recall past research linking cigarette smoking to cancer and the subsequent huge legal settlements or the laws emerging from privately conducted auto safety studies. Ironically, growing accounts of scientific fraud attest to the new political importance of research—why risk professional reputation and perhaps criminal punishment if outcomes made no difference?

To appreciate concretely just how scientific research becomes politicized and immensely consequential, consider the debate over Al Gore's *Earth in the Balance*. This is a stridently pro-environmental book deeply alarming those troubled over the planet's impending doom from over-population, famines, depleting essential natural resources, and other calamities. To drive his points home with authority, *Earth in the Balance*'s style is seemingly hard-edged scientific, or at least that's what the average reader would surmise given an occasional highly technical aside. Gore depicts his litany of life or death problems seemingly growing more serious by the day: valuable topsoil disappearing through unchecked erosion, the damage to wildlife from DDT, the illnesses created by the chemical Dioxin, the disappearance of forest, global warming and untold other troubling trends. In one particular section he talks about global warming depriving 10 million residents of Bangladesh of their homes, 60 percent of the present Florida population being relocated (73) and perhaps hundreds of millions of people living in the tropics becoming more susceptible to diseases as a result of migrating germs and viruses (74). Elsewhere he tells of soaring population explosions that may well bring plagues and wars (309).

Critics have accused Gore of partisan advocacy using the prestige of hard science. In a sense, its aim—detractors insist—is conceptually identical to, say, funding pro-environment office-seekers or holding a protest march. Julian Simon (1999: 87-90) in particular asserts that Gore's assertions are typically undocumented, or where referenced, cannot be easily verified, for example, conversations with unspecified bureaucrats. Gore also, according to Simon, shuns overwhelmingly clear (and readily accessible) contrary statistical evidence. Many allegedly toxic chemicals are, in fact, quite safe to humans. Elsewhere, Simon charges, valuable benefits flowing from potentially environmentally disruptive policies are overlooked. Similarly pushed aside are the dire consequences for the poor if draconian measures hamper economic growth. At least according to Simon, Gore skillfully uses the aura of science to promote government's regulatory power. Whether Gore or Simon is the more truthful is *not* the point. We merely illustrate how scientific research is easily politicized. The prestige of science, like money or an army of campaign volunteers, is a potent political weapon.

This political contentiousness is particularly apparent at various "science war" websites. The competition here is to shape public policy by discrediting the enemy's science while praising one's own objectivity. For example, http://junkscience.com is a generally pro-industry, anti-government regulation perspective that dissects alarmist claims ostensibly buttressed by scientific research. It claims to expose how "the-sky-is-falling" assertions are, typically, based on shoddy inquiry, inconclusive data, biased interpretations, or are just flat-out wrong. Their November 2000 bulletin rebutted scares regarding the dangers of generically engineered food, the alleged nicotine and cancer link, the role of man-made pollution in global warming among other politically laden research allegations. This is just one of several websites supposedly skewering alarmist claims. In late 2000, some seventeen free market-oriented think tanks and advocacy groups established www.ClimateSearch.com to make available their views of energy, economic, and environmental issues.

Websites promoting the opposite orientation have also proliferated. At www.earthisland.org are compiled scientific research describing the harmful climatic impact of two-stroke engines plus the warnings about ships and off-road vehicles. The National Resources Defense Council (www.nrdu.org) documents the destructive impact of the 2.7 trillion pounds of animal manure produced in raising food. This site reports an EPA study showing how this waste has polluted some 35,000 miles of rivers as well as the groundwater in dozens of states. The NRDU's site also details the high incidence of spontaneous abortions and other illnesses caused by nitrates seeping into the water supply near animal feedlots.

"Research politics" can be a remarkably open civic arena. "Players" here number in the millions and populate the entire ideological spectrum. At the center are those actually creating the battle's raw materials— the reports issuing from university-based scholars, government analysts, think tank experts, investigative journalists, experts working for private firms and hospitals, and even ordinary citizens with a passion for inquiry. While some of these may be highly technical, for example, professional journals and think tank position papers, others are mass media oriented, for example, journalist accounts infiltrating newspapers and "hard news" TV shows such as *60 Minutes* or *20/20*. A handful may well become enshrined as venerated truth in textbooks, court decisions, and discussion-ending clichés that everyone knows "to be true." No wonder, then, the phrase, "Studies show...." has become ubiquitous and controlling this information has become one of the political arsenal's most potent weapons.

Conservative think tanks have been especially active here, publishing books, journal articles, and technical reports in their aggressive effort to shape the public agenda in such diverse areas as welfare policy, Social Security, de-regulation, privatizing public education, and reducing government spending (see Holcombe 2000 for an excellent overview of foundation impact). According to one compilation, this right-leaning information corpus received some 12,441 media citations in 1996 (Callahan 1999). Liberal organizations are as equally active in disseminating their research. *The Left Guide* (1996) lists some 98 major liberally oriented foundations, and these include such behemoths as the Ford Foundation, Henry J. Kaiser Family Foundation, the MacArthur Foundation, and the Rockefeller Foundation that annually dispense hundreds of millions to generally pro-liberal political organizations.

It is political funding and skill that helps push these findings into public awareness. The most brilliant report sympathetically documenting one's viewpoint will come to naught if consigned to obscurity. Organizations (and government itself) spend millions annually in press releases, conferences, and myriad other publicity tactics to get their messages out. The inner-workings, though not the final product, of this "political activism" may be invisible to the general public. For example, advocacy groups often assign staff members to cultivate close ties to prestige publications like the *New York Times* to insure that favorable research findings receive good press without being labeled propaganda. No doubt, specialists hired by advocacy groups have quietly arranged countless talk show appearances by authors just publishing their research if this research supports the group's aims.

The information technology explosion has greatly assisted this dissemination. The Heartland Institute, for example, a free market

oriented Chicago-based think tank, has (as of October 2002) compiled over 10,000 research reports prepared by several dozen other
free-market policy organizations that are instantly available to citizens, scholars, journalists, and office holders via the Web. In October of 2002 the Heartland's website averaged nearly a million "hits"
a month (*The Heartlander* 2002). The conservative Heritage Foundation now spends about $1 million annually on its Center for Data
Analysis and invites scores of journalists to learn about using government-supplied information in their investigations. Stories utilizing these data have appeared in several widely read newspapers,
and while Heritage (and others) insists that this service is politically
neutral, others are more skeptical (Deane 2002). Desktop publishing allows even tiny organizations to prepare handsome, fact-filled
newsletters to be dispatched by the thousands.

The Net and e-mail have been especially useful to propagating
research favorable to one's cause. Judith Kleinfeld (2001) tells a
remarkable tale of how her web-based rejoinder to a highly publicized report of sex discrimination among MIT faculty zipped around
cyberspace worldwide at virtually no cost to herself or her sponsoring organization. Data on any issue, from almost any slant, is quickly
and freely available via typing in a few key words to a Net search
engine. The government itself is a treasure trove of relevant research ammunition. The site www.firstgov.gov offers some 27 *million* pages of information derived from the government's own 20,000
or so websites. Each agency, including the Supreme Court, offers its
own specialized site. There is scarcely an advocacy group whose
positions papers (and forwarded materials) cannot be accessed in a
few minutes.

Non-experts can readily play politics via science dissemination.
Those advocating, say, banning genetically engineered food, can
bombard thousands of friends and strangers, let alone public officials, with bolstering reports and news stories via faxed photocopies,
e-mail, or simply posting up clippings for public viewing (websites
usually permit easy forwarding). Convenient access to these findings is especially relevant to educators—courses on the environment, for example, might rely entirely on up-to-date, electronically
accessible information. The more ambitious might create
"Frankenfood" Websites or newsletters. With other Web site links
and e-mail lists, this passion becomes a one-person "movement."

Voraciously consuming mass media or print material on this topic might well create an impetus for generating yet more research sympathetic to one's cause. One could imagine, for example, media rushing to uncover yet more bio-engineered food horror stories if encouraged by millions of supportive letters and sky-high TV ratings of shocking exposés. Eventually, the clamor from a terrified public for government regulation will be "everywhere," and officials might view legislation as a no-brainer.

An especially efficient way ordinary citizens can participate in this research "game" is by financially supporting think tanks. These increasingly play key roles in shaping public debate with their never-ending research reports, opinion columns, and issue-oriented conferences. Many have grown quite skilled in intervening directly in government policy-making. While financial assistance often emanates from a handful of wealthy individuals and foundations, a grassroots flavor is nevertheless common. Mass mail solicitations typically request as little as $25, and $50 may "buy" everything from logo coffee mugs to posters. The Citizens for a Sound Economy, an institute closely aligned with corporate America, had some 250,000 individual contributors in 1996 (Callahan 1999: 32). The socially conservative Family Research Council claimed 100,000 affiliated individuals in 1996, and mailed a quarter of a million copies of their *Washington Watch* per month. These figures are hardly exceptional, and comparable groups of all stripes number in the hundreds. Support can also come more indirectly via subscription to think tank-sponsored magazines such as *Reason, Policy Review,* and *Regulation.* This citizen activism will doubtlessly swell as electronic forms of communications make contacting millions of physically separated compatriots virtually cost free.

Shaping Popular Culture

Civic activism champions routinely grumble that Americans favor fluffy lowbrow entertainment over public affairs. This characterization is undeniably true—MTV audiences surely outnumber C-SPAN viewers while "supermarket tabloids" easily outsell "serious" magazines like the *New Republic.* Even during presidential elections, dodging politics is a snap thanks to the TV remote control's instant access to sports, food, shopping, travel, and exotic animals. Avoiding overt political content does not, however, banish politics. These

messages inescapably underlie popular culture without any ostensible "politicking," or even mentioning worldly events. An escapist
entirely devoted to endless *Star Trek* re-runs would still, nevertheless, absorb politically infused ideas. This "trekkie" would almost
certainly now "know" that in seeking Universe domination, the gro-
tesque warlike Klingons are inevitably defeated by the peaceful, eth-
nically diverse and cooperative United Federation of Planets warriors, ably assisted by the hyper-logical half-Vulcun, Mr. Spock. Score
one point for the nice reasonable guys triumphing over ugly impulsive evil—that's the way the universe works.

Popular culture is ubiquitous and is inescapable, even for those
damning its vulgarity. It is embodied in music, art (including car-
toons), TV, radio, the theater, fiction, clothing, billboards, children's
stories, and even sports. For better or worse, it is here where "political reality" often materializes (Coombs 1984: 2). This "reality" is
not always accurate. One detailed analysis of 1980-81 programming
revealed the gross exaggeration of violent crime infusing "normal"
TV life. Murder occurred everywhere and, contrary to statistics, busi-
nessmen (and white wealthy males, to boot) were over-represented
perpetrators. Comparable distortions concern the usefulness of private investigators (grossly exaggerated), the widespread incompe-
tence of police and other government agents, the over-representa-
tion of whites as criminals plus multiple other liberties with hard
statistical evidence (Lichter and Lichter 1993). A more recent probe
into the impact of media accounts found that people severely inflated the dangers of school shooting and the criminal activity of
young minority group members (Tucker 2001).

These ideological messages often infiltrate as barely noticed "bag-
gage." Consumer abundance itself is politically relevant. America's
malls and supermarkets—not meticulous economic studies—probably convinced Soviet visitors that democratic capitalism out-per-
formed totalitarian communism. A robust literature exists extracting
nebulous political content from moneymaking mass entertainment
(e.g., Rowe 1995: ch. 3). It is no accident that anti-Western dictato-
rial regimes energetically ban rock n' roll and TV programs such as
Married With Children that mock traditional authority. Barely anybody ever personally witnesses a murder or watches the subsequent
trial. Everyone can, however, "experience" crime and justice galore
second-hand on *Law and Order*. One compilation reports that by

age fourteen the average American child has "witnessed" some 13,000 murders on TV (cited in Coombs 1984: 7). The immensely popular TV mini-series *Roots*—watched by as many as 130,000,000 at one time—probably shaped public Antebellum slavery images more than hundreds of scholarly treatises. Rowe (1995: 8) reports that, on average, Americans spend 70 percent of their non-working awake time watching TV, or about 7.4 hours per day per household. Even if only a tiny portion of this huge exposure is politically relevant, the impact must be prodigious.

Especially noteworthy is pop culture's role in cementing "American" collective identity, our national "glue" (Trend 1997: 78). The Battle of Yorktown or the Declaration of Independence may be terra incognita to most Americans; a Big Mac or the Green Bay Packers are instantly recognizable, however. If inculcating a common culture is judged irrelevant, a quick tour of the internecine violence in Indonesia, Serbia, Afghanistan, and untold other places should convince doubters. Even religion, perhaps the world's most discordant civic force, is swamped by the commercial culture. The U.S.-born children of immigrants from historically hostile groups, for example, Greeks and Turks, become nationally integrated through a shared appreciation of movies, sports, fashion and all the other pop culture artifacts. This is an enormous, if seldom appreciated, politically relevant accomplishment.

Given mass culture's critical role in shaping "who we are" as a people, "culture war" battles are but civic disputes by tactics that scarcely resemble conventional textbook civic activism. To the extent that all politics rest on cultural foundations, the undermining of culture can ultimately topple the political superstructure. That these are not inconsequential political sideshows is a point that cannot be exaggerated. Marxists have long appreciated this connection and thus paid particular attention to politicizing the arts to educate citizens into socialism. In contemporary society music often inserts politics into entertainment, and skirmishes over song lyrics are often but slight extensions of clashes over gun control laws, censorship, and hate crime statutes.

Consider the storm over the black "rap" celebration of violence as one such "war" example of attacks on the civic status quo. Los Angeles rapper Ice-T's 1992 album, *Body Count,* quickly sold 300,000 copies and included the controversial tune "Cop Killer" in which the lead singer wailed he was "bout to dust some cop off" with a chorus adding "die, pigs, die" (cited in Hershey-Webb 1999). When law enforcement agencies vehemently protested, Time Warner pulled the album and then re-issued it without "Cop Killer." Ice Cube's 1991 album, "Death Warrant" told Korean storeowners "pay attention to the black fist" or "we'll burn your store right down to a crisp." Rap artist Eminem has sold over ten million CDs to youngsters with lyrics glorifying violence against women and homosexuals, a clear affront to legislative efforts in the opposite direction. Theses examples may be exceptionally inflammatory, but such famous artists as Woody Guthrie, Bob Dylan, and Bruce Springsteen have all occasionally praised criminality as a form of inchoate political activism (Hershey-Webb 1999). So-called "punk rock" made famous by groups such as the Sex Pistols, the Clash, and the Jam has likewise spread the adolescent rebellion against "the system" message (Rowe 1995: 41). Innumerable country music tunes intermittently embraced lawlessness, though here the culprits are more mundane: highway tolls, truck weight limits, unfair divorce settlements, and working for Japanese bosses (Rogers and Smith 1999).

On the ideological divide's other side are patriotic songs such as Merle Haggard's big hits, "Okie from Muskogee" and "The Fighting Side of Me." During the Vietnam conflict Sergeant Barry Sadler sang, "The Ballad of the Green Berets" while Kenny Rodgers and the First Edition extolled patriotism in their "Ruby, Don't Take Your Love to Town." Lee Greenwood's "God Bless the USA" was a hit during the Gulf War. A flood of nationalistic ballads with titles like "Our Nation in Song" hit the market n the wake of the September 11 terrorist attack (Matthews and Porter 2001). Charlie Daniel's "This Ain't No Rag, It's a Flag" particularly irked many Muslims and inspired endless talk radio chatter.

Extreme jingoistic sentiments are voiced in what might loosely be labeled "skinhead" or White Power music (opponents prefer "Nazi"). Though hardly a mass media or MTV staple, groups such as Death in June, Strength Through Joy and Sol Invictus often unashamedly and graphically celebrate the white race and xenophobic nationalism to small but energetic followers. These messages clearly contravene the "official" government message of greater racial tolerance and respect for differences.

Popular culture's didactic function is hardly fresh news to governments. Totalitarian regimes have historically managed mass entertainment to manipulate its citizens. In the Soviet Union, for example, every bit of state-subsidized art, from decorative posters glorifying heroic manual labor to pseudo-historical patriotic films such as *Alexander Nevsky*, relentlessly advanced ever-shifting communist ideological agendas. In Nazi Germany abstract art and atonal music were strictly forbidden as politically subversive or degenerate, not just inartistic. During the 1930s American artists under Soviet influence via the Screen Writers Guild often subtly used films to discredit capitalism, for example, always representing landlords as predatory or honest workers as mistreated by profit-driven bosses (Koch 1994). With leftist screenwriters banned and the Cold War at its height during the 1950s, Hollywood now switched to vehement anti-Communism with such releases as *Iron Curtain, I Was a Communist for the FBI*, and *My Son John*. The TV show *The F.B.I.* meanwhile depicted J. Edgar Hoover and his handsome agents as superheroes combating nefarious domestic communists.

Does pop culture have a demonstrable political impact akin to voter registration drives? Though documentation of oft-hidden ideological messages in everything from Aunt Jemima-adorned pancake mix boxes to SimCity2000 (a computer simulation game) is prodigious, the cause and effect relationship is only plausible, not rock solid.[3] Accusations often highlight a single event, for example, whether the lead character's decision in the TV sitcom *Murphy Brown* to bear an out-of-wedlock child—an act filled with civic ramifications if pursued by millions of adolescents—set an unwise precedent. Chicken-and-egg problems abound—have sympathetic treatments of gays on TV's *Ellen* and the Tom Hanks movie, *Philadelphia*, engendered more positive feelings toward homosexuals, or did a newly tolerant atmosphere permit these untraditional kindly portrayals? Literally thousands of studies elucidate the supposed mass media depicted violence-juvenile violence link, yet the subject remains scientifically unsettled. Perhaps *The Deer Hunter,* a movie portraying Russian roulette, attracted the suicidal rather than instigating the twenty-five subsequent deaths from this risky game. Most telling, nobody is forced to absorb any particular message—pacifists are not kidnapped and dragged off to *Rambo*.

Popular culture activism resembles the dissemination research findings pattern. At the core are producers—TV and movie script writers, musicians turning their rage into provocative lyrics, authors churning out damsel-in-distress pulp romances, film executives concocting a fantasized Wild West, and tens of thousands elsewhere crafting people's politically infused "worlds." Song by song, movie by movies, sitcom by sitcom, a political reality—accurate or pure fantasy—emerges. Though mega corporations increasingly dominate the entertainment industry, technological breakthroughs now permit low investment "underground ventures. For example, various small independent record labels—Dischord, Touch & Go, and Jade Tree—have released highly popular, often abrasive and politically charged music. The Kill Rock Stars label, based in Olympia, Washington, specializes in hard-edged songs deploring anti-women violence. These and similar organizations also sponsor well-attended concerts funding progressive causes (Temple 1990). No doubt, millions of attentive youngsters acquire their civic cosmology from this angst-laden, often bizarre music.

Beyond these creators are pop culture gatekeepers: publishers, bookstore executives, TV and radio station programmers, and mall landlords deciding what might be "tastefully" hawked. Though these commercial distributors may scarcely consider themselves enmeshed in the culture wars, their marketing choices can have sweeping ideological ramifications. When a member of the popular country group, the Dixie Chicks, made an anti-President Bush remark during the invasion of Iraq, hundreds of fans destroyed Dixie Chicks CDs and innumerable country music radio stations refused to play their music (Strassel 2003). Even museum curators must decide whether to honor historic masterpieces or defy conventional sensibilities with homoerotic art. Hollywood moguls surely have choices regarding whether to promote patriotic or anti-American action films. And, to repeat a familiar point, the explosion of electronic communications, particularly the Web, now easily affords access to even the most controversial, culturally subversive materials.

Last, but ultimately crucial, are consumers whose marketplace choices ultimately fuel production. We get what we pay for, whether this product upholds or destabilizes civic life. Arguments over anti-police rap music or *Playboy*-like magazines allegedly demeaning women would be pointless without appreciative customers. The logic here is indistinguishable from elections—one votes a preference, though this exercise may pertain to shopping, not a candidate. Both choices are self-inflicted. No legislative enactment demands citizens immerse society in seditious propaganda or, on the other side, blood and guts jingoism. If mall merchants cater to the violent heavy metal or Hip Hop crowd, and one loathes this assault on conventional civic virtues, frequent more tranquil venues. Even couch potatoes can actively join this fray. Let us not forget that *Ellen*, the ABC sitcom that sought to push the boundaries of public acceptability by favorably depicting lesbianism was defeated by falling ratings, not legislation to protect Americans from alleged deviancy.

Educational Proselytizing

If a Martian had visited the U.S. fifty years ago, education would have scarcely drawn notice as a political battleground. "Schooling" largely comprised prosaic administration with only minor civic squabbles over matters like teacher pay. This was especially true for classroom instruction. This inattention did not signify education's apolitical character; legally mandating the Pledge of Allegiance or idolizing the Constitution was inescapably civic indoctrination, and this rationale was surely grasped by educators intent on transforming millions of nineteenth- and early twentieth-century immigrants into patriotic Americans. An entire academic field—political socialization—confirms the centrality of early, school-based civic training. What stilled past waters was a smothering ideological consensus.

Today, by contrast, the education "wars" are intensely vitriolic and encompassing. The once-honored consensus has become unglued. A catalogue of court cases, pressure groups and reformist urges pertaining to education would fill a small library. State legislatures now debate arcane details of college admission standards while bureaucracies galore impose government-enforced rules regarding access for the disabled, classroom racial balances, and untold other procedures once quietly decided by on-site administrators or teachers. Newness aside, however, most conflicts swirling around schools are conceptually often indistinguishable from untold other civic confrontations. Whether additional teachers should be hired versus installing computers to boost student performance is essentially comparable to other budgetary quarrels: each side is but a player seeking to enhance government generosity via the game's standard rules and resources. There are, however, confrontations that diverge profoundly from everyday divide-up-the-riches disputes. These clashes are unique to education, and seldom appear "political" in the term's usual meaning, and are hardly ever money centered.

Instructional content, whether in English or mathematics classes, in kindergarten or universities, is the divisive controversy here. The stakes here are immense. To the extent that today's schoolchildren are tomorrow's citizens, this is the war over national identity. If this characterization seems hyperbolic, consider a future United States if today's grade school pupils (as in some nations) come to believe that armed insurrection was preferable to voting or if laws deserved obedience only when self-serving. Such instruction invites chaos, not orderly democracy. Or, for that matter, try imagining reasonable public debates among illiterate citizens. It is hardly surprising, then, that many radical crusaders, whether from the right or the left, insist that their best long-term hope lies in molding future citizens. Conversely, status quo defenders are passionate about lessons they view as deeply subversive, if not treasonous.

Differences over U.S. and world history instruction—what tomorrow's citizens discover about America as a nation—perfectly illustrates this civic mêlée. These indoctrination opportunities abound. Virtually all students must eventually pass U.S. history courses, and half or so also take world history or a more updated "world events" offering (Sewall 2000). It is here that lessons are taught regarding national heroes and what makes us a great (or terrible) people. Future activism—what is permissible or off-limits—itself may be defined by these encounters. What most adults carry around in their heads about U.S. politics and history for better or worse is undoubtedly traceable to these early encounters.

The textbook is absolutely central to this enterprise. Given that few teachers can challenge its portrayal, this single book (and the numerous accompanying auxiliaries) constitutes an immeasurable prize for reformers intent on transforming Americans. Getting a particular text into a pupil's hands is a major undertaking with ample opportunities for inserting ideological coloration. Superficially, the entire process seems apolitical. On one side are profit-oriented publishers (currently four); on the other side are local school boards, individual schools, teacher groups and, most critically, state bureaucrats devising lists of officially sanctioned statewide adoption choices. Texas, California, Florida, and North Carolina fall into the latter category, and short list inclusion (or the single choice) guarantees huge sales. Even if decision-making is decentralized, acceptance in these four states dictates adoptions more generally (and the books themselves typically reflect mega-market tastes).

Decades back the settled consensus made the publisher-adopter interplay politically uneventful. Even today, if these were still the only participants, bitter civic quarrels would remain exceptional. Profoundly altering today's landscape are untold factions pushing their ideologically colored views as state-sanctioned "official" history. Almost nothing lies beyond these battles (Ravitch [2003] offers an exceptionally detailed account of both right and left censorship efforts). In New Jersey, a fifteen-year battle has been waged over whether students should recite passages from the Declaration of Independence (does the phrase "all men are created equal" offend women and blacks?). Controversy has also involved omitting the Pilgrims, the Founding Fathers, and other traditional icons at the expense of less familiar figures such as Sarah Grimke. Meanwhile, the term "war" was replaced by "conflict" so as to make world events seem less violent (Sorokin 2002). New Jersey's experience is hardly unique.

These engaged "bystanders" occupy all ideological points, but liberals seemingly predominate among the more energetic participants. Meanwhile, to the chagrin of conservatives, older, more traditional textbook approaches are quickly being rejected as excessively Eurocentric, exclusionary, or just "dull." In a nutshell, savvy publishers have learned that catering to aggrieved sizable ethnic groups, feminists and others seeking to re-fashion the existing culture is the surest path to riches. Conservatives may moan and groan, but they seldom offer attractive alternatives and, as we shall note below, largely limit their activities to vetoing objectionable books. There is nothing inherently liberal or conservative, or morally right or wrong, about "capture-the-textbook" campaigns, and radicals would indubitably argue that they are merely replacing a pernicious bias with wholesome truth. The point is that liberals generally reside inside, conservatives on the outside and, conceivably, this could change tomorrow.

The upshot, then, or at least what conservatives insist, is that textbook narratives often resemble propaganda, not objective, traditionally accepted history. This biasing, conservatives continue, is less blatant distortion than selective emphasis and exclusion. For example, the highly popular *Pathways to the Present* overtly caters to African Americans, women and Native Americans, or this is at least what some experts allege (Sewall 2000). Equally notable was its eager race and group-based oppression orientation and near total neglect of the post-World War II-era Soviet challenge to America. Another selective treatment example can be found in the trendy, *The Americans*. Its coverage of the 1920s, for instance, dotes on New York City-based black musicians and authors; by comparison, Herbert Hoover, isolationism, the crash of 1929, and critical technological advances in medicine, electricity, and transportation receive short shrift. The Cold War, a period of enormous historical impact, is chiefly conveyed via recounting relatively minor domestic disputes, for example, the persecution of J. Robert Oppenheimer and McCarthy "witch hunts."

A theme permeating nearly all these books, conservatives grumble, is that American history can best be appreciated as (selected) groups arduously battling for their unquestionably deserved rights. The older theme of gradual, across-the-board national advancement is replaced by recounting past grievances against women, Native Americans, African Americans together with businesses despoiling the environment and exploiting immigrants. One might incorrectly assume from these treatments that U.S. history was one repressive calamity—genocide, cruelty, and unremitting greed—after the next, and only recently, thanks to the Civil Rights movement and feminism, that any progress has transpired. In this context, at least according to *The Americans,* 1950s TV is "an enemy" due to its idealization of white America while omitting poverty, diversity, and the Civil Rights fight against discrimination (Sewall 2000).

Conservatives are hardly quiet in this battle over textbook content, especially in the key Texas market. Here, according to a *New York Times* report (Stille 2002), a coalition of nine conservative groups using volunteer readers and occasionally assisted by the Texas Public Policy Foundation carefully scrutinizes books submitted for possible adoption. Their concerns range from debatable environmentalism, for example, the alleged harm of global warming, to broader assaults on the free enterprise system, patriotism, and democratic governance. Morality-tinged topics like homosexual rights also regularly surface. Like liberally oriented groups, they have had notable successes. In some instances this simply entailed forcing the publisher to delete offending passages, for example, a reference in a history book noting that 50,000 prostitutes worked west of the Mississippi during the late nineteenth century. Several entries had to be extensively revised before being accepted while others were rejected due to their unacceptable alleged pro-liberal bias. Predictably, liberals label conservative successes "censorship."

Activism via education equally applies to teaching, especially at the college level where instructors typically enjoy great leeway. The line between honest instruction and ideological propaganda is, naturally, difficult to establish. A few even insist that *all* pedagogy is political, even science instruction.[4] Precise demarcation lines aside, ample evidence attests to its existence. Marxism's popularity in U.S. universities most conspicuously exemplifies this proselytizing. Lecturing on Karl Marx's ideas or their impact is not what we have in mind. That exposition would hardly qualify as indoctrination.

Rather, activism entails imposing Marxism as an all-encompassing, *superior* (and exclusive) interpretative tool so students, hope the instructor, eventually internalize the Marxist worldview. Now Marxism is not just one possible analytical lens; it is *the* correct interpretation, and education now becomes indoctrination. Ironically, as many observe, Marxism's collapse worldwide has sparked a fervent revival among American academics. For these faithful, the college classroom is the perfect forum to reverse one's fortunes and capture tomorrow's elite (see, for example, Fernández-Morera 1996). Marxist scholars themselves are proud of their academic prominence. Their ideological proclivities are consciously—and often unbeknownst to the innocent— inserted in diverse fields such as history, sociology, political science, economics, anthropology, English, and even the arts (Ollman and Vernoff 1982; 1984). An ample supply of books and journal articles, all published by prestigious presses, are also available to be assigned to reinforcing classroom lectures (see Weissberg 1998: 139). All in all, then, thousands of college students each year are being ideologically tutored in a way radically inimical to a democratic capitalist status quo. Whether or not these Marxist messages bring the intended conversions is irrelevant for our purposes; what is key is that activism is being pursed under the guise of instruction.

Another activism venture often masquerading as "objective instruction" occasionally transpires under the guise of women's studies. Patai and Koerrtge (1994: ch. 4) are two long-time, academically accomplished professors specializing in this field worried that overt indoctrination frequently displaces the dispassionate search for knowledge. In their words, "Women's Studies teachers are deliberately using their classrooms for the recruiting and training of students to be feminist activists" (81). This is not the feminism of sexual equality, the usual characterization of "feminism," but a sweeping ideology stressing inherent sexual incompatibility, if not sexual warfare. Assigned readings are exclusively drawn from this radical perspective, Patai and Koerrtge contend, and opposition to this orthodoxy is scarcely tolerated. A reoccurring exercise is the nurturing of anger and resentment against men (often labeled "getting in touch with one's true self"). Men are relentlessly portrayed as evil oppressors of women, hopelessly inclined toward harassment, rape, abuse, genital mutilation, and degradation. The women as victims theme—abused wives, prostitutes—is ever-present. Society itself, the students are told, is dominated by men for the purpose of subjugating women and, to add insult to injury, rife with racism, classism, homophobia, and similar disorders. To drive these points home even further, courses often require actual involvement in local feminist causes.

Though this "education wars" excursion samples only a minute—and admittedly selective—portion of a vast territory,[5] several general lessons are worth noting. Plainly, pedagogical quarrels entail an extremely frustrating, paradoxical brand of politics. Superficially, politicking here seems highly amenable to conventional formula. Schools—even universities—are readily approachable, and administrators are hardly obscure bureaucrats hidden in distant agencies. A petition from angry parents or taxpayers usually gets attention. That school boards, even state education officials, are typically elected also facilitates responsiveness. In a pinch, voters can always defeat school tax referenda or lobby against the university's state budget. Pedagogical issues, moreover, are seldom incomprehensible. Parents can usually sense if their children are being systematically mis-educated. Even colleges cannot forever hide blatant propagandizing.

Yet, to characterize these battles as mere continuations of humdrum politics is mistaken. Educational proselytizing (whether from the right or left) is not a sport for amateurs heeding the conventional participatory menus. This insulation from the familiar civic repertoire cannot be overstated. America's public education system—whether a kindergarten spelling book or a college curriculum—is a well-protected, fortress-like institution when challenged by ordinary citizens via voting, letter writing, petitioning and so on. Successfully entering its inner sanctums, let alone correctly grasping oft-arcane debates and professional subterfuges, is certainly a demanding, highly specialized job. Conventional tactics, even when fully supported by elected officials, might only annoy, not produce results. Conservatively inclined parents, at least in the short run, are unlikely to banish today's fashionable texts deprecating America's accomplishment in favor of older, more unabashedly patriotic treatments. They are certainly no match for prestigious education professors controlling teacher certification. Ditto for the parents of college students anxious about their children's exposure to Marxism or radical feminism. Students themselves may only be dimly aware of overt indoctrination being passed off as education. That most educators are civil servants, often protected by strong union contracts, or are professors enjoying tenure, greatly limits electoral retribution. All in all, a distraught citizen preferring a more conservative approach can write letters, vote, organize a delegation and do all the other things deemed "political participation" but the odds of success are probably dismal.

One "plays" education politics most deftly from the inside. Those seeking to shape the next generation's political *Weltanschauung* are thus advised to become educators, broadly defined. As a textbook publisher, editor or writer, for example, one might possess ample opportunities to construct what millions of future citizens know about capitalism or the fairness of U.S. elections. School administrators can impose their own views almost unnoticed by outsiders via textbook selection, curriculum choices, for example, multicultural versus traditional, or through hiring sympathetic teachers. Unnoticed, grade-school teacher can impart his or her opinions though such seemingly innocuous exercises as a daily "show and tell" featuring local business polluters. Top university administrators similarly wield great power in favoring one politically tinged academic program over another, while college instructors often enjoy *carte blanche* thanks to academic freedom and tenure. Over a thirty-five-year career, thousands of citizens may thus be exposed to ideological ruminations passed off as factual information. To reiterate, all of these efforts comprise "political activism" though they scarcely resemble the usual election-centered menu.

Politically Investing and Consuming

The phrase "putting money into politics" unquestionably conjures up images of campaign contributions or even bribery. This cash-based stratagem is surely important but it easily obscures alternative, possible more efficacious fiscal approaches. Just as one might donate a thousand to a favorite candidate to promote a cleaner environment, a thousand can be privately invested for the nearly identical civic aim. Allocation merely reflects available options and tactical assessments. In fact, a more circuitous route may be the adroit overall strategy for those lacking substantial resources. To wit, Boeing executives may benefit handsomely from financially supporting George W. Bush's 2000 campaign given his pro-defense spending stance; an ordinary Joe or Jane sharing this national security predilection, however, can probably expect zero personal financial windfalls from their tiny campaign donation. Nevertheless, if Joe and Jane invested the same paltry sum in Boeing stock they can simultaneously accomplish comparable objectives—strengthening national defense—*and* probably keeping their original $100 while securing financial dividends.

Multiple ways exist to "be politically active" via one's pocketbook. Several businesses seek a competitive advantage contributing a portion of their profits to designated political causes. Ben and Jerry's Ice Cream not only guarantees its tasty products to be environmentally correct while behaving in a socially responsible manner toward its employees, but also contributes company profits to various liberal groups. Likewise, Working Assets, a long distance telephone company contributes 1 percent of a person's telephone bill to Amnesty International, Sweatshop Watch, and Greenpeace plus similar left-wing causes (and in a bit of synergy new subscribers once received a free pint of Ben and Jerry Ice Cream per month for a year). On the right there is Sienna Communications, a "Christian Long Distance Company," appealing to potential customers by noting that its competitors fund liberal and homosexual causes. One can now be politically involved while eating ice cream or calling Mom. In January 2001 the Republican Party debated issuing a GOP-branded Visa or Mastercard, a tactic potentially generating millions for the Party as their faithful shopped until they dropped ("GOP Visa Card? Party Study Sees Profit in Affinity" January 17, 2001). Eventually, the lure of connecting shopping and fund-raising won out and the card was issued.

What is generally labeled Socially Responsible Investment funds is this genre's most popular instrument. The Social Investment Forum, a Washington, DC-based SRI fund manager organization, listed at least 175 such funds at the end of 1999 (Scherreik 2000). Though SRI is now fashionable, linking one's social conscience to one's pocketbook actually originated in the 1920s when churches insisted that their retirement accounts exclude firms profiting from gambling, alcohol, and other sinful endeavors (Bell 1999). The strategy's initial modern embodiment was the Pax World Management Fund initiated in 1971 permitting investors opposed to U.S. involvement in Vietnam to avoid financing defense contractors. The 1980s were a watershed period as campus anti-apartheid radicals intensely pressured U.S. businesses to disinvest in South Africa, no small task given the worldwide scope of large corporations. Faced with rambunctious demonstrations and sporadic violence, university endowment fund managers fled from U.S. companies with a South African presence and the "socially responsible" investment portfolio was born.

A cornucopia of investment alternatives exists to advance civic aims while, hopefully, turning a profit. Left-of-center armchair activists enjoy especially bountiful opportunities. Though each venture offers its unique slant, SRI portfolios typically prefer firms that are environmentally conscious, show concern for their employees (e.g., subsidized child-care), embrace diversity, and sponsor community involvement. A prominent "do good" example is the Meyers Pride Value Fund, a Beverly Hills-based fund organized in 1996, that allocates funds exclusively in enterprises adopting anti-discrimination policies to protect gay and lesbian employees. Other "pro-gay" funds include Dreyfus Third Century, Calvert Social Equity and Third Century funds. Especially as the mutual fund market grows over-crowed, niche funds multiply. There is The Cruelty Free Value Fund (only businesses not harming animals) and the Women's Equity Fund (promotes women on boards of directors). Some funds shun U.S. Treasury securities since these fund military budgets (Zweig 1996). For those wanting to assist African businesses, the Sloan Financial Group, a black-owned money management group, offers the African Opportunity Fund. Mainstream Wall Street brokerage firms now provide potential enrichment for liberal reformers. For example, Greenwich Street Advisors, Smith-Barney's in-house money management arm, offers the Concert Social Awareness Fund that screens out companies dealing in tobacco, weapons, and nuclear power (Gill 1997).

Conservatives have likewise created their own investment portfolios though they are far outnumbered by liberal rivals. One might surmise that conservatives are generally less aggravated over pollution, defense spending, and other business practices abhorrent to liberals. Nevertheless, opportunities still exist. Timothy Partners Ltd., a Winter Park, Florida-based fund, shuns companies offering health benefits to same-sex couples, contributes to pro-abortion groups like Planned Parenthood or produces violent or sexually explicit entertainment (Zipser 1998). Independently minded investors embracing strong Christian values can even purchase computer software from the Institute for American Values Investing to assess stocks for their conformity to traditional Christian principles (Gill 1997). The Aquinas Equity Growth fund is available for Catholics wishing to promote Catholic values. Muslims, Christian Scientists, and Mennonites likewise have specialized mutual funds honoring their religion's beliefs (Williamsom 1999). Given that many theological positions on abortion, pornography, alcohol and similar moral issues are simultaneously political quarrels, the pious investor now becomes a full-time do-gooder.

A recent SRI innovation is permitting investors to pursue charitable aims via their portfolio allocations. In the wake of the war in Iraq, the Pax World Fund (with assets of over $1 billion in April of 2003) now permits fund participants to allocate a portion of their capital gains or dividends to assist humanitarian and reconstruction efforts in Iraq. The Calvert Group offers a similar allocation program centered on promoting Middle East peace and global security. Interestingly, and perhaps due to this humanitarian aspect, these SRI funds have recently seen substantial growth while more conventional mutual funds have experienced huge withdrawals (Hayashi 2003).

Though still a relatively small financial marketplace segment, SRI funds have grown explosively, and this trend will undoubtedly continue as affluent "baby boomers" draw closer to retirement. Between November 1977 and November 1999, these funds soared from $1.2 trillion to $2.16 trillion in value, and as of 2000 comprised some 13 percent of all professionally managed money (Scherreik 2000). This strategy is certainly less burdensome than haranguing officials and, unlike, electioneering, it knows no season. The proliferation of flexible retirement accounts plus larger permissible contributions now allows still greater politicking via pension allocation. TIAA-CREEF, a huge pension organization catering to educators, offers its Social Choice Fund ($36.9 million invested as of 9/30/2000), which avoids companies tainted by nuclear energy, alcohol, gambling and tobacco. The Web has, predictably, made ideologically driven savvy investing immensely accessible. Knowledgeable, ideologically sensitive counsel is available at multiple sites.[6] At www.socialfunds.com, for example, potential investors can peruse assorted socially responsible instruments, ask questions via an investor bulletin board, and otherwise collect pertinent information on what benefits their money buys. Greenmoney.com likewise offers advice for the liberal investor. For those who already know what companies embody civic virtue, untold websites provide portfolio management and discount electronic stock trading.

This investing entails far more than merely evincing "support" as one might wear a "Save the Whales" button. Attractiveness of equity offerings has sizeable carrot and stick financial repercussions. Not only will a heightened clamor for stock augment its dollar value, no small consideration for employees with lucrative stock option plans, but executive compensation is often tied to stock performance. This could amount to hundreds of thousands a year in bonuses. Executives of polluting or otherwise unsavory companies might well be personally punished financially, even fired, if their company's stock goes begging. Moreover, a high share price provides financial advantages, for example, affording opportunities to acquire other firms via stock-based purchases. Healthy equity demand is especially critical for new start-ups in offbeat fields since these firms are less able to finance themselves through bank debt. Even companies judged "wholesome" are kept on the straight and narrow via investment choices. For example, in the mid-1990s, The Body Shop, a favorite among the socially conscious, suddenly lost 15 percent of its total value when several environmental misdeeds were exposed in an ethical-investing magazine (Rothchild 1996).

Stock ownership also provides automatic, legally guaranteed access to company policymaking. Rather than lobby the EPA to pressure Exxon-Mobil to cease environmentally dangerous practices, this pestering can be done as an insider. In fact, the irritating stockholder using the annual shareholders meeting as a forum to embarrass top corporate officials before the mass media and other shareholders has become a cliché. At a minimum, stockholders can sue management, an option unavailable to non-stock holders. The more active SRI funds have also cleverly used their proxies together with shareholder resolutions and personal meetings with corporate investor-relations staff to advance their aims (Whittelsey 1999). Politically conscious investment websites reveal a variety of guidelines for vigorous, sophisticated activism. Socialfunds.com, for example, provides step-by-step instructions on sponsoring shareholder resolution (requisite shares the sponsor must own, filing date, length of resolution), tips for contacting corporate management, and advice on enlisting large institutional shareholders support. Shareholdersaction.org provides updated information regarding on-going battles against alleged corporate malfeasance. A recent bulletin featured campaigns against Citigroup's suspected predatory lending, the mêlée over genetically engineered food, and Wal-Mart's selling of sweatshop-made clothing.

The Interfaith Center on Corporate Responsibility (ICCR), a broad-based collation of religious and social justice advocates, has energetically pursued this tactic. Using their shareholder leverage (and moral standing), they have posted notable triumphs over corporate America. In 1999, for instance, ICCR forced Baxter International, the world's foremost health care product manufacturer, to phase out the dangerous chemical polyvinyl chloride in its intravenous products. It also convinced DuPont to abandon its proposed strip mine adjacent to the Okefenokee National Wildlife Refuge. Meanwhile, on the anti-tobacco front, ICCR had previously pressured RJR to discontinue Joe Camel ads, swayed Harley-Davidson to withdraw its name from tobacco advertising, and even won over both Sara Lee Corporation and Kimberly Clark to sell their tobacco subsidiaries.[7] Several major U.S. corporations were also persuaded to cease business in Burma in light of that country's dismal human rights record. Continuing campaigns include banning racist sports logos and realistic toy guns.

SRI investing can be troublesome, however. The obligation to generate decent financial returns often pushes the funds toward firms with debatable track records, for example, Wal-Mart and BP Amoco or those whose commitment is more verbal than tangible (Sheehan

2002). There is also the paradox of investing in "dirty" companies so as to work from within. Is this aiding the enemy or political cleverness? Nor is uncovering unsavory practices always simple since corporations typically deal with hundreds of suppliers, some of whom may violate SRI strictures. For example, Ben and Jerry's ice cream, the alleged paragon of environmental do-goodism once sold a Rainforest Crunch ice cream laced with cigarette butts, glass, rocks and insects due to a (now terminated) supplier's faulty quality control. It similarly boasted that is paper was manufactured without using dioxin though the ice cream itself contained this toxic chemical (Sheehan 2002).

Political Violence

Chapter 2 noted that political violence is conspicuously absent in the "standard" civic engagement menu. If hinted at, references are fleeting, and, more telling, this tactic is always dismissed as analytically irrelevant. One might suppose, according to these experts, that rioting, terrorism, vandalism or anything remotely violating the law only plague Third World nations wracked by civil war. American history, even contemporary civic quarrels and events, tells an entirely different tale, and this story existed long before 9/11. Black agitator H. Rap Brown once mused that violence is as American as cherry pie, and he hardly exaggerated. Those claiming a unique peacefulness to our politics evidently suffer amnesia and, though we may be loath to admit it, violence devotees are hardly dismissible as "un-American." Where Americans are reluctant to use violence, it can be imported into domestic politics from overseas conflicts as the terrible New York City and Washington, DC destruction of September 11, 2001 proved.[8]

Mayhem is an enduring leitmotiv of American politics. The colonial period witnessed one violent eruption after another—periodic slave rebellions, repeated tax riots, pandemonium over elections and—lest we forget—armed anti-British insurrection. Nationhood barely silenced the disorder; industrialization and urbanization replaced whiskey rebellions and tax revolts with something new and different. The Civil War was the deadliest military conflict in U.S. history. Lingering armed battles between the federal government and Mormon settlers once plagued what is now Utah. Hoerder's chronology shows that between 1870 and 1940, some 132 substantial labor disputes occurred, and these—unlike today's uneventful picket lines—typically involved protracted armed worker-police confrontation. Pre-dating the modern African-American civil rights struggle were innumerable race riots. Many lingered for days—even weeks—with prodigious loss of life. The most prominent occurred in 1866, 1867, 1871, 1874, 1900, 1906, 1908, 1917, 1919, 1921, and 1943 (Hoerder 1977). The nineteenth century also had an ample share of immigrant massacres, ongoing wars against Indians, lynchings of blacks, and last—but hardly least—the assassinations of two presidents (Lincoln and Garfield).

Recent decades have hardly seen a slackening of this impulse. Boisterous demonstrations against the Vietnam War during the 1960s and 1970s attracted hundreds of thousands of disgruntled Americans (Skolnick 1969: 32) and these repeatedly turned ugly. Tear gas-infused rallies predictably drew prime-time television coverage, and this heightened exposure both exaggerated their rambunctious character and, it was often alleged, inspired even greater disorderliness among provocateurs. The protestor-police battle during the 1968 Chicago Democratic presidential convention and the shooting of Kent State University students by the National Guard are now enshrined in history textbooks. Anti-war activism eventually escalated to include vandalizing military induction centers and bombings.

The black civil rights struggle turned even more violent. Over the centuries only the forms have altered—early slave rebellions gave way to the Ku Klux Klan cross burnings, lynchings, church bombings, assassinations, police-Black Panthers shoot-outs, and urban riots. The latter, often with thousands of people joining in, have undoubtedly been the most prominent political violence during the last half century. Major urban disturbances largely involving African-Americans afflicted nearly every large city, and while they were most common during the 1960s—occurring in 1964, 1965, 1966, 1967 and 1968—they show no sign of disappearing. One compilation of this era found some *three hundred* separate race-related riots with some eight thousand casualties and fifty thousand arrests (Goldberg 1991: 161). In fact, the 1992 Los Angles riot instigated by the Rodney King beating was among the most tumultuous thus far—$1 billion dollars in estimated damages and fifty-eight people lost their lives. By contrast, the 1967 Detroit riots, generally judged that era's most brutal, cost an estimated $162 million (in 1992 dollars) and killed 34 people (*Business Week* 1992). And these death and dollar figures do not reflect the destruction of job-providing businesses, population migrations from central cities and tax base erosion.

This irrepressible proclivity for violence is well illustrated by the continued incidence of rioting among urban African Americans despite substantial economic and legal progress. In April of 2001, for example, Cincinnati blacks were sufficiently angered by a string of police shootings killing black youngsters that hundreds went on a looting and vandalism rampage injuring sixty people, twenty-five of whom required hospitalization. Though these figures may be tiny given Cincinnati's total population, the widespread media coverage no doubt multiplies impact immeasurably. A similar racially tinged scenario played itself out in Seattle at about the same time. The key ingredients for similar urban upheavals—a sizable disgruntled African-American population and an injurious arrest-related incident—exist nearly everywhere and will hardly disappear.

Politically tinged violence remains endemic despite a booming economy and government's newfound compassion. The FBI (and other government agencies) treats domestic terrorism seriously, and the FBI annually conducts some two-dozen full-scale anti-terrorist investigations. Let us not forget that the September 11, 2001 New York and Washington attacks resulted in over 3,000 people killed and threats to kill even more have become commonplace. The Terrorist Information System monitors some 200,000 individuals and over 3,000 organizations (The Center for National Security Studies, *http://nis.org*). Post 9/11 events will undoubtedly make this anti-terrorism campaign an enduring feature of our political existence.

Direct actions (as European of radicals labeled violence) among zealous environmentalists, or "eco-terrorists" as they are occasionally branded, similarly illustrate political violence's endemic nature. Groups like Earth First! earnestly believe that industrial civilization's destruction can resuscitate the natural environment (Lee 1995). Mere civil disobedience is insufficient, and "monkeywrenching" (as they call sabotage tactics) is the favored approach and this has involved dynamiting power lines, tree spiking and sabotaging ski towers. Though receiving only passing media attention, the impact has been sizeable (victims often remain silent fearing copy cats). Forest executives in Washington State estimate that eco-terrorist attacks cost that state's industry over $2 million per year (cited in Lee 1995). A group calling itself the Earth Liberation Front has, allegedly, done some $40 million in damage against McDonald's restaurants, meatpacking plants, firms developing genetically engineered seeds and other "enemies" of the Earth. The most notable incident was an October 1998 arson attack on a Vail, Colorado, skiing resort expansion causing $12 million in damage. Comparable "eco-terrorist" attacks—the burning of crops, harassing university researchers—have been carried out by animal rights groups. In 1999, for instance, animal rights terrorists attacked research facilities at Western Washington University, the University of California, San Francisco and the University of Minnesota doing extensive damage, even burning effigies of the scientists in one instance (*www.ampef.org/alfhits.htm*). A Eugene, Oregon Chevrolet dealer had thirty SUVs torched by activists who in an anonymous communiqué denounced these vehicles as "[being] at the forefront of this vile, imperialistic culture's caravan toward self-destruction ("S.U.V.'s, Gold, Even Peas Join Eco-Vandals' Hit List" *New York Times*, July 1, 2001, on-line). In 2003 the Animal Liberation Front released a report claiming that it and the Earth Liberation Front had committed some 100 direct illegal acts in 2002. No wonder, then, that the FBI has called both of these groups "a serious terrorist threat" (Berman 2003).

On the ideological divide's other side are the "militia groups" (or the "Patriot movement" to sympathizers). As with eco-terrorists, this is less a single, distinct organized entity than an ever-shifting collection of individuals loathing the central government's mounting, allegedly, illegitimate power. These have names like Posse Comitatus, Aryan Nations, Christian-Patriots Defense League, and Scriptures for America, among others. Leaving aside neo-Nazi, white supremacist, and "skinhead" groups that often share this passionate nationalism, one 1995 account estimated their number at about 200 in thirty-nine states, with about 10,000 to 15,000 members all told (cited in Durham 1996). These organizations revel in a violent aura. Names like Texas Light Infantry, Rocky Mountain Resistance, and Texas Constitutional Militia hardly evoke sissies, and military weapons training, publishing army-style manuals, and publishing inflammatory exposés about imminent foreign invasions of the United States are their staples. To date, save the April 1995 Okalahoma City federal office building bombing that killed 168 innocent people, actual militia violence is largely rhetorical (the other exception might be the 1992 Ruby Ridge stand-off between the Christian Identity group and the FBI in which three people died).

Though it might be tempting (and surely analytically expedient) to relegate violence to obscurity as civic engagement, a full portrayal of "popular participation" is badly served by such neglect. Most plainly, absolute numbers aside, the assembled, cumulative impact can be enormous. The proportion of respondents answering, "yes" to a survey item about urban rioting or sabotaging a logging project is an inappropriate standard. The black civil rights movement achieved an immense, long-lasting public relations triumph when police officers and dogs brutally assailed a small handful of peaceful marchers in Selma, Alabama. The existence of our volunteer army no doubt owes much to raucous student campus demonstrations during the 1960s. When a few thousand raucous globalization opponents trashed Seattle in 1999 to protest a WTO meeting, globalization rocketed into public consciousness. Ditto for "only" a dozen or so 1960s race-related riots involving "only" a tiny portion of the local population. Recall that a miniscule number of school shootings can generated a national panic when given relentless media attention.

More relevant theoretically is *threatened* violence. That matters could easily turn violent, and in ways that are unpredictable, or even unpreventable, is the point. Civic violence is our inescapable sword of Damocles, so mere credibility usually suffices. Who wants to energize "the crazies"? There can be little doubt, for example, that the federal billions for urban assistance was thinly disguised riot prevention though, in reality, these upheavals were relatively infrequent. A tiny handful of abortion clinic bombings and doctor murders have similarly terrified millions. Now, every crank call to an abortion clinic is taken seriously and, conceivably, these terrorists may have had some success in intimidating their foes. The homosexual rights movement was hardly judged violent, yet a few high-profile unruly actions by ACT-UP, for example, disrupting traffic with "die-ins," to protest government inattention to AIDS suddenly made thousands of public officials anxious. What is noteworthy is not that the rioters, abortion clinic bombers, militiamen, AIDS demonstrators, and all the others with an appetite for havoc are but a tiny sliver of the civic landscape. By that quantitative measure they might rightfully be excluded from any engagement compilation. Far more pertinent is the incredible availability of troublemaking options and the support these may garner.

The power of fear, apart from any palpable action, is cleverly illustrated in a campaign conducted by something called the "Conservative Action Foundation" against Gray & Company, a prestigious Washington, DC public relations firm, once employed by the pro-Soviet Angola regime. This tale begins with several CAF members handcuffing themselves to stairwells inside of Gray & Co's fashionably located headquarters. Meanwhile, others distributed flyers in Washington's Red Light district urging calls to Gray & Co's switchboard requesting sexual fantasies. Many unknowing collaborators obliged. The coup de grace was administered when CAF militants dressed in military fatigues conspicuously hung around Gray & Co's building, photographed their clients, and visibly measured the company's building and sidewalks. Within days, after growing media coverage of these attention-getting and vaguely treacherous harassments, a notably edgy Gray & Co dropped the Angola account.[9] Why wait until more serious trouble arrives?

The violently disposed need not be involved personally. Financial support through purchasing subscriptions, books, audio and videotapes, and even memorabilia, let alone outright donations, are obvious, easily hidden, and perfectly respectable methods to secure risk-free benefits. Unearthing these on-the-edge organizations takes minimal effort thanks to modern technology (or even old-fashioned library searching). Simply entering "political terrorism" or "animal rights" into a web search engine quickly locates possibilities by the dozen. The site, www.greenboffin.com provides a gateway to dozens of anarchist-flavored sects in the U.S. and elsewhere. A treasure trove of militia-related links can be found at www.militia-watchdog.org/m1htm3militia. Here one finds some eighty separate militia websites, ninety-three sites for related organizations, ninety-one "neo-secessionist" organizations plus forty-nine links to groups opposing the militia agenda. One might surely disapprove of illegally "liberating" laboratory animals and vandalizing microscopes, but inviting these radicals to campus to speak for a fee subsidizes this anti-science mayhem.

More direct involvement is likewise accessible. These are typically attacks on property, not personal assaults—disabling an opponents' website or putting sand in the gas tanks of scientists engaged in genetic engineering. A seemingly growing tactic is what has been called "information terrorism," using computers to undermine society by disrupting financial institutions, spreading software viruses, or even stealing funds electronically. In fact, during the war in Iraq hacking the enemy's website, including everything from U.S. government military sites to the Arab-language news site run by Al-Jazeera, became quite popular. One estimate put these attacks at between 3,000 and 5,000 per day (Forelle and Golden 2003).

Those intent on annoying the establishment have become quite skilled at provoking police violence before TV cameras (these are now regular major party conventions features). Almost anybody can be a vandal or send life-threatening letters, if they are willing to suffer the legal consequences. Letters claiming to contain the deadly anthrax sent by abortion foes have disrupted hundreds of health clinics, an action costing only a few dollars of postage. Threats may even ingeniously escape technical illegality. When Georgia lawmakers decided to shrink the Confederate Stars and Bars in their state flag, many received plain white envelopes lacking postmarks containing forked-tongued rubber snakes, sometimes with vaguely foreboding messages (Pruitt and Cook 2001). Sad to say, recent terrorist bombings or threats of biological warfare have brought to the surface just how vulnerable we are to political violence.

The ease by which the disgruntled can seriously harass their adversaries might come as a shock to those unfamiliar with the "dark side" of U.S. politics. It is as easy as cherry pie; smashing windows or setting fires does not require genius. The readily available box cutter has proven itself a lethal terrorist device. Access to truly destructive technology is remarkable thanks to our free-speech protections. Respectable bookstores, let alone counter-culture revolutionary outlets, are happy to sell manuals on bomb-making, sabotage and less blatantly illegal ways to cause serious mischief. Would-be revolutionaries have no trouble acquiring handguns or even assault weapons. To appreciate fully this access, be apprised of a book called *The Anarchist Cookbook*, a widely available "how-to-bring-destruction" classic among those with a taste for violence. It has now evolved into a web-based entity readily accessed via a five-minute search. Would-be terrorist can now gain detailed recipes for Thermite bombs, $CO2$ bombs, paint bombs, mailbox bombs, high tech vandalism and, naturally, how to terrorize McDonalds among dozens of similar tips.

Conclusions

This overview should demonstrate the inadequacy of the conventional menu's few election-centered proffered options, and we provide but the proverbial tip of the civic engagement iceberg. Untold other "on-the-edge" possibilities, for example, manipulating broadcast news or subverting the status quo via crime have gone unmentioned. Cliché-like complaints about citizen apathy aside, popular activism is widespread though precise calibration necessarily remains uncertain. The handful momentarily engaging in any singular act may be modest, but the huge array of possibilities insures prodigious engagement. Of critical importance, this abundance appears even more extensive if we include opportunities to support organizations that actually perform "the heavy lifting," for example, those filing the lawsuits or monitoring textbooks.

Our overview suggests tactical fungibility. One citizen agitated over dirty air might file a lawsuit forcing the EPA to impose its regulations; opponents fund a sympathetic think tank challenging EPA data. Others harangue publishers to celebrate environmentalism in high school history courses while pro-growth teachers recommend Julian Simon's treatises to their students as an extra credit assignment. Those too hurried for personal agitation might buy "green" groceries or invest in pro-environment mutual funds. At convention's edge are devotees of more drastic measures—spray painting graffiti on Exxon's corporate headquarters or, on the other side, hacking the Earth First! website. Beyond these are tactics of uncertain legality, for example, attracting media attention with bogus horror stories or even disseminated suspect research.

Option bountifulness indubitably proliferates. Exploding technology, countering enemy responses, and the public's appetite for novelty guarantees evolution. Many stratagems—socially responsible investing, class action lawsuits, communicating ideologically tinged research via the Web—barely existed until recently, if at all. In 2003 the anti-war movement adapted itself to this new reality and took its case online. Two websites—TrueMajority.com and MoveOn.org—sought to mobilize dissenters, and MoveOng.org even raised $300,000 in forty-eight hours to battle a possible war in Iraq (Clemetson 2003). Even the old-fashioned petitioning can be automated. The website NoAttackIraq.org quickly (and cheaply) garnered more than 300,000 "signatures" worldwide, a feat once extremely arduous ("The Professor" 2002).

Less obvious, but more germane theoretically, is that our analysis reveals the absolute futility of distilling some single, handy "essence of political participation" indicator. Though we may properly scrutinize voting, rioting, bankrolling films or passing off propaganda as scientific research as discrete acts, statistically aggregating these activities into a global index imposes an exceedingly unhelpful Procrustean bed. It would be as if a zoologist exclusively sought bears, elk, and pigs in the forest to formulate scientific laws about mammals. To compound the theoretical muddle informing conventional approaches, how are we to treat the contention that political behavior infuses *all* behavior, even child-rearing or friendship, not just what has been deemed "civic"? How can apathy exist for those insisting that the personal is the political?

The conventional sampling model is inappropriate if for no other reason than the universe is unknown; the underlying population may even be eternally indeterminate given contentious definitions of "political" and the inherent fluidity of tactics. Picture an assembly of ideologically disparate participation experts trying to compile a definitive "political acts" compendium from which a sample is to be drawn. Should we add appreciating "rap" music as a "political act" if these tunes castigate police for racist brutality? What about consumers preferring environmentally unsafe products and avoiding Ben and Jerry's Ice Cream due to its objectionable ideological flavor? That behaviors themselves can comprise divergent universes further undermines the sampling approach. The cunning might deny political intent, preferring instead less offending labels like "educational" or "charitable." Looting can be craven economic aggrandizing or, just as reasonably, an ideologically justified protest against economic exploitation, and this classification itself may be a political act.

Where might these unsettling challenges to conventional simplicity lead us, theoretically? The study of particular activist outcroppings, taken one act at a time, is hardly invalidated. An entire lifetime can be fruitfully spent scrutinizing voting or contributing money to candidates. Only when inquiry is directed toward about some undifferentiated "political participation" does analysis go astray. It is the disjuncture between the coarse, conventional scholarly approach and

the infinitely more complex reality that concerns us. It is in this facile substitution—a few handy outcroppings indexing an immense
phenomenon that is so mischievous. Original theoretical sin, if one
prefers theological allusions. The alternative, as we initially broached
in chapter 1, is to re-focus analysis away from singular, researcher-
specified acts to concentrate on objectives—where one seeks to go.
Put concretely, rather than ask, for example, what an environmentalist does to advance his or her objectives, we inquire: Does this
crusader succeed? With this in mind, we now turn to the possibility
that achieving civic goals may best be accomplished by disdaining
civic engagement altogether.

Notes

1. Recourse to legal compulsion is more complex than suggested here, and competing
    doctrines often govern. Nevertheless, both Congress and the Supreme Court have
    generally accepted these suits. These legal nuances are depicted more fully in Brisbin
    (1989).
2. Ideology is not always decisive here. Many partisan groups often defend "enemies"
    since principles can transcend momentary ideological positions. The ACLU, for
    example, though generally liberal has periodically protected conservatives on the
    free speech issue.
3. The fervor, sans any scientific evidence, behind many of these claims can be re-
    markable. One review of advertisements (Kern-Foxworth 1999) speaks of the
    "devastating psychological effect" on the self-esteem and aspirations of various
    minority groups by stereotypes such as the Frito Bandito. She further insist that
    these advertising images have laid the foundations for slavery, Jim Crow and Propo-
    sition 209, banning racial preferences in California state policy. From these perspec-
    tives, selling Aunt Jemima pancake mix can be likened to a hate crime.
4. The blending of politics and mathematics can go well beyond using politically
    flavored examples. There are those who would insist, for example, that the very
    nature of higher mathematics, even when abstractly formulated, is rife with sexism
    and, thus, to teach existing mathematics perpetuates male domination (see Gross
    and Levitt 1994: 113-117 for this argument).
5. Educational indoctrination is not limited to one ideological position. Examples from
    the Right equally abound, and many liberal observers would insist that American
    education in general favors the Right, so these leftish exemplars are prominent only
    due to their rarity. More conspicuous examples of conservative proselytizing might
    be found in private, religiously oriented schools and numerous college courses on
    such subjects as free-market economics and classical philosophy.
6. The sophistication of SRI investing, especially in comparison to more publicized
    attention-getting ploys, cannot be exaggerated. A visit to the website www. kld.com
    provides a massive bibliography of professionally written books and essays plus
    listings of firms specializing in SRI. Several offer detailed tips for those choosing
    this avenue.
7. It should be noted, however, that these political pressures are sometimes reversed
    by financial realities. While activists initially had success in getting state pension

funds to divest themselves of tobacco stocks, the lure of increased value coupled with the need for revenue sometimes forced states such as Kentucky and Maryland to re-purchase these "bad" stocks (Palmeri: 2001).

8. Equally relevant are violent attacks on Americans overseas. On April 18, 1983 the assault on the U.S. embassy in Lebanon killed sixteen Americans and in October 23 of the same year, terrorists killed 241 U.S. servicemen at their barracks. Plots against American tourists are apparently commonplace thought most are thwarted.

9. This account comes from a mimeographed "how to" paper called "Civil Disobedience: The New Buzzword for the Conservative Political Activist" and issued by a group calling itself the Conservative Action Foundation.

4

Politics by Other Means

Political activism is quite correctly treated instrumentally—re-sources are invested to accomplish tangible goals. Objectives can vary from the narrowly selfish to some lofty collective attainment, but a *something* is always sought. Always implicit is that civic engagement is the preferable means regardless of what is sought. To accomplish objectives thus *necessarily* demands civic involvement. This state-centered supposition powerfully directs subsequent inquiry to choices among political tactics. Analyzing voting, for example, thus becomes explaining turnout variability and, within that, selecting one candidate versus another. Viable non-political rivals thus remain beyond theoretical attentiveness. Those on the civic sidelines are thus "apathetic."

Political disengagement hardly implies passivity. Few goals customarily pursued via pressuring government cannot be secured nonpolitically. A strident environmentalist frustrated by bureaucratic lethargy might, for example, buy his or her own water purification equipment, relocate to a cleaner locality among multiple other "do-it-yourself" responses versus investing yet more effort cajoling the EPA. Microsoft co-founder Paul Allen tapped his fortune to establish a private foundation that has, among other things, purchased 600 acres of Washington State virgin woodlands to forestall development. Other wealthy dot-comers have likewise funded private preservation efforts, including businesses marketing energy saving devices rather than directly lobby government (Carlton 2000). Environmental mission accomplished, though, technically, not one finger was lifted politically.

Substitutability is even feasible in foreign affairs, the one policy area generally judged government's exclusive domain. It is estimated that some 50 percent of the World Bank's projects to assist less developed nations involve non-government organizations (NGOs). In fact, Western aid donors are increasingly relying on private, not government-run assistance efforts (Onishi 2002). One recent compilation reports that assistance from foundations, religious groups, universities, and private individuals amounted to some $34 billion compared to the government's $10 billion foreign aid commitment. An even easier "do-it-yourself" solution is to personally send money to those overseas—in 2000 some $18 billion was thus transferred from people in the U.S. to those abroad (Adelman, 2002). Without exaggeration, as the array of political tactics is enormous, the private options ledger is even grander.

Some General Arguments for Non-Political Responses

Abandoning politics in favor of more private solutions is a pragmatic choice, not a matter of principle, and can only be justified on a case-by-case basis. Overall, however, several reasons recommend private responses versus entering the public fray. Shortness of time often counsels forsaking civic action given that our fragmented, decentralized system may require years (if not decades) before progress appears. This is especially true if change is sought via marching through the courts or enacting fresh legislation. As the British economist John Maynard Keynes quipped, in the long run we'll all be dead, so time-pressed supplicants can take scant comfort assisting future generations.

Personal solutions can, by contrast, be nearly immediate and, as an added bonus, action can be fine-tuned personally. Since the 1960s, for example, many American cities have experienced soaring crime seemingly immune to political resolutions. Revising the criminal code or electing get-tough judges offers scant security to those in peril. By contrast, private recourse—installing burglar alarms, buying Rottweiller guard dogs, hiring bodyguards or traveling only by taxis—might sharply reduce victimization odds. Renting in a gated community will undoubtedly outshine attending one more anti-crime rally.

Non-political solutions can also be cheaper. That political effectiveness can be costly in our sprawling gridlock-disposed system is beyond dispute. Minimal civic strategies, for example, sending $50 a year to multiple causes, can quickly add up before any return on investment accrues and there can be substantial opportunity costs.

To wit, for a frustrated would-be gun owner altering one's state's highly restrictive firearms laws would surely be an expensive (and arduous) endeavor. Better to visit a permissive jurisdiction or attend gun shows where gun laws are more lenient. The classic cost-effective personalized solution to daunting political obstacles is bribery. Though illegal and morally reprehensible, pay-offs are often highly efficient vis-à-vis politicking. Indeed, unrealistically draconian laws typically make corruption perfectly rational given the impossibility of compliance. Why should an exasperated contractor spend years laboring to reverse burdensome outdated building codes when a few hundred dollars slipped to a housing inspector instantly accomplishes the task?

Escaping obligations entailed by collective actions is a further comparable privatization benefit. Oscar Wilde quipped that socialism would never work—it demanded too many evenings. Political mobilization entails accepting compromises, haggling over petty details, dealing with disagreeable compatriots, and untold other endemic liabilities. This is especially likely as quests expand and participants grow more heterogeneous. Movements haranguing officialdom routinely squander untold hours simply sustaining organization life, for example, raising funds and deliberating policy, apart from pursuing substantive agendas. An individualistic approach can, however, deftly avoid these onerous responsibilities: one simply pursues aims as one sees fit apart from outsider meddling. One does not have to be a billionaire like Paul Allen to improve the environment. Just pester neighbors to recycle, buy environmentally friendly products, avoid unnecessary driving, or otherwise take matters into one's own hands. To be sure, this is certainly not entirely an "either/or" choice, but such individualistic behavior guarantees at least *some* progress versus the uncertain outcome of political mobilization.

"Private politics" flexibility cannot be exaggerated. While public policy always applies generally, and thus may be imperfect personally, privately fashioned solutions can satisfy the most idiosyncratic needs. This is vital given that public agendas may reflect only a tiny sliver of one's desires. Consider, for example, providing better education for poor children having to attend terrible schools. Curing this problem is a Herculean, if not insurmountable, political task and any accomplishment would be a bundle of compromises. Undoubtedly for these reasons, private foundations have now circumvented politics altogether by simply paying private school tuitions. In 1998, for example, The Center for Educational Reform estimated that various private firms and foundations were sponsoring some 17,000 students in private schools. Since this money is given at the benefactor's discretion, it is unencumbered by the usual political pressures from teachers unions, public school bureaucracies, and countless other political interests let alone the legal morass of co-mingling taxpayer money with religious instruction (Shales 1998). What is notable here is that such personal intervention is commonplace, and should properly be judged a substitute for political action, not abandoning intervention altogether. The choice is between tactics, one of which entails badgering the government, not apathy versus activism, and what makes this private pathway so alluring is that it can reflect one's aims *exactly*. Why settle for third-best choices or be exasperated by office-seeker indifference?

Channeling one's energies into philanthropic endeavors similarly offers opportunities to creatively accomplish aims pursued by government but without the occasional odious constraints. Civic engagement scholars seem oblivious to the sheer number and variety here.[1] According to Center on Nonprofits and Philanthropy data, there were 648 *thousand* public charities in 1998; among these, for example, were 24,703 health-related charities (excluding hospitals) and over 76,000 providing various human services. These figures do *not* include myriad churches and other religious organizations that offer programs comparable to what is provided by public bureaucracies. In 2002, Americans donated some $242 billion to private charities, a figure that has remained steady (when adjusted for inflation) despite a recent cooling of the economy (Strom 2003).

These private sector entities offer a far more inventive "parallel universe" to government across innumerable domains, and a quick phone book search will surely uncover multiple sympathetic local groups. Instead of lobbying Congress to boost Medicare coverage, volunteer at a senior citizens center or donate magazines to nearby nursing homes. Not only does this "participation" have an almost immediate positive impact, it provides options usually impermissible in bureaucratically administered assistance efforts. As a private citizen one might, for example, lead a Bible study discussion or sponsor lectures by radical speakers, problematic activities if taxpayer financed. When existent opportunities are lacking they can be readily created sans pleading to public officials. Invite the Salvation Army or Alcoholics Anonymous to town to address growing public drunkenness in lieu of demanding "more government" anti-alcoholism spending.

Effort might also be directed towards securing corporate and foundational support for one's cause. Again, the choice is between pressuring government as opposed to inveighing non-public entities to assist in comparable ends. Corporate charities is huge. In 1995, for example, private corporations awarded some $179 million dollars to various ethnic/racial group endeavors, especially education. Notable contributors included Exxon ($6.6 million), General Mills ($6.1 million) and Coca-Cola ($5.3 million). Corporations and corporate foundations gave $12.19 billion to various charitable in 2002 (Strom 2003). The Bradley Foundation has generously funded Milwaukee's highly regarded school voucher program. The Robert Wood Johnson Foundation annually awards millions in grants to further health care, often directed towards assisting minorities. The Ford and Rockefeller Foundations rival government agencies in their budgets and pursuit of worthwhile public aims. Given the abundance of these programs and their attentiveness to nearly every ill imaginable, "working" the private sector might easily outshine elbowing one's way into the public trough, especially if one seeks novel, adaptable approaches.

Going outside government channels may also be simpler. This is not to say that private resolution is straightforward; rather, when judged against legislative roadblocks, administration red tape, and all else required when pursuing aims via the public sector, "homemade" solutions are child's play. Take assisting the homeless, an issue of immense complicatedness given a city's arcane zoning regulations, loitering ordinances, restrictions on how public money is spent and other formidable impediments. Program guidelines could keep lawyers busy for months before anything is built. Nevertheless, this bureaucratic Gordian knot might be cut privately by personal intervention. Modest pooled efforts could rent space where the homeless can daily safely congregate, receive donated food, and even learn about jobs and health care benefits. Compare this straightforward effort with arcane legal debates over counselor qualifications, budgetary allocations, and similar hard-to-follow quarrels that inevitably bedevil public solutions.

Individualistic resolutions also typically attract less opposition, let alone notoriety. Stealthiness permits untold possibilities denied to those locked into public strategies. Consider the emotionally charged abortion debate. Reshaping public policy—one way or another—inescapably generates firestorms. Imagine the backlash over demanding mandatory public school programs promoting abstinence or, on the other side, portraying abortion as acceptable birth control in heath textbooks? By contrast, unobtrusively handing out flyers off school grounds, placing discreet ads in media outlets favored by teens or sending a check to Planned Parenthood will likely inspire fewer counter-mobilizations. These are all First Amendment-protected activities, to boot, that require zero official authorization.

An especially attractive benefit is the ease with which formidable objectionable policies can be circumvented. Victory is thus achieved in a "hopeless cause" by avoiding politics altogether or even illegality. A recent illustration concerns how insurance companies are resisting potentially hugely expensive claims to treat mental illness (Carnahan 2002). Given both legal obligations to offer such treatment plus a powerful mental health lobby (and public sympathy) insisting on insurance payments, insurance company obligations appear inescapable. Nevertheless, using such perfectly legal tactics as higher co-payments and far tougher "utilization reviews," insurance companies have reduced claims. Instead of challenging this difficult-to-reverse law, would-be claimants are discouraged via endless red tape and bureaucratic scrutiny. "Free medical care" is now transformed, happily for the insurers, into an exceedingly unpleasant experience, often avoided altogether.

"Non-political" strategies might be particularly inviting if enforcement is lax or the consequences of defiance are bearable. Millions customarily violate speeding laws rather than petitioning government to up limits, a bleak endeavor given honored national safety concerns. Chronic speeders install radar detectors, avoid heavily patrolled roads, or just accept fines as a "speeding license." Escaping detested laws, versus organized efforts at repeal, is particularly ubiquitous with regulating morality. Laws criminalizing gambling, drug use, prostitution, alcohol, and untold other irrepressible human vices are commonly defeated by subterfuge, not adroit lobbying. Why try to decriminalize prostitution against formidable odds (and probable damage to one's reputation) if these services can be insured by paying a small premium required to ward off police inter- ference? Perhaps only stubborn, cost-insensitive activist devotees seek repealing loathsome morality statutes when personal escape is handy.

Put more formally, private solutions often nimbly avoid the zero- sum battles so endemic to civic strife, even if enemies do take no- tice. If those fighting AIDS want to establish their own hospice or counseling program, not pressure government for a slice of the bud- get, they need not defeat other disease warriors. Who can argue against spending one's *own* time and money for a cause, even for debatable aims? The significance of escaping zero-sum conflict can- not be exaggerated. Entering public arenas, no matter how noble the aim, *inescapably* draws opposition, if only for budgetary reasons. By contrast, these wary opponents are probably indifferent, or per- haps even allies, if competition is forsaken. Heart disease charities could willingly provide assistance to those concerned over AIDS, provided the public treasury is spared.

Finally, and least obvious but hardly trivial, taking matters into one's own hands may well engender the personal efficacy often cel- ebrated by civic participation fans. Idealized communities rising up to wrest control away from impersonal forces versus self-centered egoism is *not* the relevant comparison. Formulated in stark either/or terms, private solution recourse certainly appears inferior. We agree, moreover, that society bereft of civic life, an atomized world of all against all, hardly appeals. Nevertheless, accomplishing something versus Quixotic forays to gain unsure rewards against difficult foes is an equally, if not more so, appropriate standard. From this instru- mental perspective, achieving objectives, even if modest and per- sonal, outranks failures at fulfilling abstract collective obligations, or, a bird in hand is worth a thousand promised government-sup- plied birds.

Recourse to Non-Political Solutions: Specifics

Analysis has only briefly illustrated certain non-political pos- sibilities. We now examine in greater detail three specific policy areas where private solutions often outshine efforts to mobilize government intervention yet equally permit effective private reso- lution: tax reduction, education, and defeating civil rights regu- lations.

Reducing Taxes

It is sometimes said that only death and taxes are certain. This adage is only partly true—taxes can be avoided, or at least minimized. In fact, tax dodging doubtless began with the very first levy, and as extraction has grown more sophisticated, escape routes have likewise evolved. As Charles Adams (1998) has depicted, the United States is founded upon tax avoidance, and this inclination lingers on. The Boston Tea Party, the Stamp Tax uproar, the Whiskey Rebellion, even the Civil War (with its high tariffs to protect Northern industry), all centered on hated levies. This is not entirely ancient history. Vietnam War opponents often refused to pay that portion of their income taxes financing the war effort (and anti-militarism by tax resistance via the National War Tax Resistance Coordinating Committee—www.nwtrcc.org—continues on). On July 13, 2001 an angry crowd of 200 protestors chanting "No new taxes" descended on the statehouse in Nashville, Tennessee to rally against a proposed state income tax. Lawmakers were accosted and several windows were broken (*Health Care News* 2001). Yet further on the periphery (though by no means trivial) are the "tax protestor" movement, an amalgam of crusaders with names like "Christian Patriot Association" that deny the government's taxing authority and concoct phony churches and non-existent banks.

Anti-tax advocates have achieved notable successes in recent decades via the electoral route, for example, California's 1978 Proposition 13 that capped local property taxes (and subsequent Proposition 4 restraining local government expenditures) and Massachusetts' comparable 1980 proposition 2 ½ (these state crusades are reviewed more fully in Smith 1998). Their most prominent recent success, of course, has been the Bush-instigated $1.3 trillion cut in levies over ten years. Meanwhile, and less openly, armies of well-paid lobbyists manipulate the tax code to insulate corporations and the super rich from the tax collector's rapacious reach. For those unable to launch ballot initiatives or afford well-connected professional advocates to create personalized loopholes, organizations such as Tax Free America, the National Taxpayers Union, and the Howard Jarvis Taxpayer Foundation, among others, will press this fight.

Still, these remarkable political successes and energetic organizations aside, relief via one-slow-step-at-a-time political activism hardly suffices for millions unsatisfied by uncertain government reprieves.

There also have been several high-profile ballot box anti-tax failures. Nor can the self-designated overburdened usually afford professional advocates to exploit today's fiendishly bewildering 15,000 page tax code or plead for special legislative treatment. Just monitoring code changes—some 9,500 since 1986—is beyond ordinary citizens. For these discontented ordinary souls, alas, shrinking Uncle Sam's take via legislation or protest rallies is scarcely feasible. Fortunately for these sufferers, but unhappily for the IRS, "customized" solutions are practical. Do-it-yourself opportunities abound, and nearly all of these adaptations, even those clearly illegal, routinely (but not always) escape notice. For the average taxpayer it is better to award oneself a quick personal tax cut.

Though estimating avoidance is a momentous task since few tax evaders openly confess their deeds, there is little doubt regarding its pervasiveness. In addition, the line separating tax avoidance—perfectly legal—and tax cheating—clearly illegal—is often disputed, even among tax court judges. Washington itself is hesitant to reveal the scope of tax dodging (and cheating), lest admission encourage others. Nevertheless, the guessed figures are substantial. Barlett and Steele (2000: 3) offer the minimum figure of $300 billion a year in total tax fraud, and this excludes potential tax revenue not forthcoming from drugs, prostitution, and other overtly illegal industries. One secret IRS report estimates that outright corporate cheating (not just clever legal interpretations) cost the government between $14 to $18 billion in 2000 (Johnston 2003) Nor does this figure reflect the millions of slightly questionable tax calculations, for example, unrealistically high valuations of worn clothing given to Good Will and liberally deducted as a charitable donation. The National Center for Policy Analysis applying the federal government's own figures has estimated tax evasion solely on the personal income tax. Specifically, businesses in 1998 paid out some $6,087.7 billion in wages while $5,389.3 of this showed up on tax returns—a gap of $695.4 billion in "missing income." That is, some 11.4 percent of all personal income was neither reported nor taxed in 1998. If these earnings were taxed at the usual rates, some $145 billion in foregone revenue from just this one form of taxation would be collected. An estimate of escaped estate taxes put the figure at $4.2 billion in 2000, and further added that gifts (which are taxed if they then exceeded $10,000) were severely underestimated (Johnston 2000).

The rise of filers claiming zero taxes also points toward extensive evasion. Between 1990 and 1997 returns reporting nil tax liability rose at a much faster rate than all returns filed (Barlett and Steele 2000). Even more eye-catching are those who refuse to file income taxes forms altogether despite indications of income, let alone pay any tax. The IRS keeps mum about this discomforting data, but in 1991—the last year when such information was released—this figure was 6.5 million people, and 74,000 of them had, allegedly, reportable incomes of $100,000 or more (Barlett and Steele 2000: 13). In 2002 the IRS filed extensive documents in the Tampa Federal District Court claiming that at least 150,000 Americans had filed bogus tax returns the previous year, offering such "explanations" as "taxes are voluntary" or that a slavery reparations tax credit reduced taxes to zero. Significantly, many of these bizarre ruses were bought from promoters who shamelessly hawk their schemes on radio talk shows, the Internet, lectures and elsewhere despite IRS efforts to close them down (Johnston 2002e).

Reducing Uncle Sam's bite need not involve subterfuge and, in fact, Congress has traditionally *encouraged* legitimate tax avoidance to promote praiseworthy aims. It takes some effort and planning, however. The generous deductions afforded home ownership (both mortgage interest and property taxes) converts one's residence into a tax shelter. Family foundations are now widespread and legally minimize estate taxes. A proliferation of officially authorized retirement devices—various Individual Retirement Accounts (IRAs)—now permit substantial shielding of current income, all up and up. Investors have traditionally bought tax-free municipal bonds (now conveniently sold as share funds) to escape every penny of tax. It was no coincidence that a May 21, 2001 *U.S. News and World Report* advertisement (anticipating the Bush tax reduction) for Franklin Templeton Investments rhetorically asked, "Why Wait for Congress to Enact a Tax Break? You're Entitled to One Now."

Reducing can be as uncomplicated as knowing where to shop given variable tax levies. Want an expensive diamond ring or watch? Purchase it in Oregon, which has zero sales tax. Boosting taxes often results in counter reactions since excessive tax rates offer new avoidance incentives. When New York State and New York City sharply hiked cigarette taxes, sales at some eighty-five Indian reservation-based smoke shops (all legally exempted from taxes) skyrocketed. Now smokers, or their friends, could drive, call or contact via the net these Indian-owned businesses and buy—without any limit—cigarette cartons at about half price. This shopping is absolutely legal provided the items are not resold. This consumer tactic costs the state an estimated $24 million a month in lost revenue (Reeves 2002).

An inviting personalized anti-tax stratagem is often dubbed the "cash economy." Though precise figures are elusive, economists generally agree that "off-the-books" labor is widespread across innumerable business sectors (Tucker 1991). One reported 2002 IRS estimate put the figure at $160 billion in lost revenue due to people working "off-the-books" (Johnston 2002c). A study by the Economic Roundtable, a Los Angeles research group, issued in 2002 found that off-the-books employment was soaring in Los Angeles while the legitimate sector was stagnating. Using various payroll records, it was estimated that this sector comprised between 9 percent and 29 percent of the total local economy and might cost California about $1.1 billion a year in lost revenue. Ominously, this growth has occurred despite California's special task force to combat this escape via various legal and economic enforcement efforts (Cleeland 2002).

The "cash economy" is hardly limited to low-paid immigrants or neighborhood baby-sitters. Plumbers and electricians, even CPAs and freelance computer consultants, among untold other independent trades people, sometimes charge less if paid in hard cash, a transaction benefiting both seller and buyer. Neighborhood cash-based ventures—beauty shops, daycare facilities, convenience stores, household cleaning services, Mom and Pop-owned restaurants—offer exceptional opportunities to avoid taxes given the near-impossibility of establishing exact income plus less stringent record keeping regulations. There are also elaborate bartering arrangements escaping taxation since money never officially changes hands. Entire industries, for example, gypsy cabs, traveling jewelry stores run out of suitcases, are invisible according to government records. A similar anonymity hides the "collectables" industry—everything from sports cards to antique silver changes hands unbeknownst to the IRS. Small manufacturing, notably the apparel industry, is famously virtually tax-free since larger firms frequently sub-contract tiny shops far too miniscule to attract bureaucratic notice.

The internationalization of business coupled with electronic communications has also permitted major U.S. corporations to cut their tax obligations dramatically. A February 18, 2002 *New York Times* article recounts how such well-known American companies as Stanley Works (makers of Stanley tools), Ingersoll-Rand, Global Crossings, and Cooper Industries have shifted their nominal corporate offices to Bermuda and thus cut taxes dramatically (Johnston 2002a). Tyco Industries, for example, claimed that it saved over $400 million in 2001 by moving from New Hampshire to Bermuda. Stanley estimated its yearly savings at $30 million a year, an amount (no doubt) far in excess of the costs associated with this move (companies need not even have any physical presence in Bermuda—just an agent to handle some paperwork). Clearly, why pay lobbyists millions for an uncertain outcome versus a sure-fire cheap solution.

For ordinary people fervently hunting tax reduction, self-employment offers appealing prospects, even for those regularly employed. Judging from the gap between overall economic growth and reported receipts, tax dodging here has mushroomed dramatically (Barlett and Steele 2000: 45). Joulfaian and Rider (1998) analyzing the IRS's own data show that those filing Schedule C (individual proprietorships) and Schedule F (farmers) substantially underreport income and tax liability compared to wage earners. According to the Commerce Department, a farmer's true income is 136 percent higher than claimed (Bartlett 2001). Profits from partnerships (a business form favored by the wealthy) also tempt those attempting to avoid taxes since the IRS does not generally match these tax filings with individual income tax reports. It is estimated that between $9 and $64 billion in tax revenue are lost annually due to this under-reporting (Johnston 2002c).

Meanwhile, according to the IRS, those who informally work for cash report less than 20 percent of their earnings (Novack 2001). Not only can the self-employed hide earnings, more importantly, deductible expenses can be aggressively maximized. A home office permits everything from utility bills to lawn care to be written off. Inflated travel and entertainment expenses have long been favorites here. Who can say, exactly, what constitutes a business "necessity"? It is hardly illegal for, say, an attorney to visit Florida in January to attend a bankruptcy law seminar at a lush resort and deduct the trip's full cost. Disentangling purely personal expenses for automobiles, home furnishings, telephone calls, and so on from legitimate occupational expenses is often impracticable. Entrepreneurs such as Sanford Botkin, an ex-IRS agent, grow rich teaching the self-employed to deduct virtually every nickel as a "business expense" (*Newsweek* 2001). If one's occupation inhibits self-employment, hobbies such as horse breeding or refinishing antiques can be reclassified as "businesses" so paper losses (e.g., asset depreciation) offset regular income.

As income burgeons, tax reduction schemes predictably grow more attractive. Most are feasible with minimal expert assistance, so solidly middle-class people can now avail themselves of ploys once reserved for the rich. According to a March 5, 2000 *Los Angeles Times* story, a perfectly legal loophole is for the self-employed to hire one's own children. Now, parental income is shifted to offspring enjoying much lower tax brackets, and all the customary employee taxes are foregone if the business is parent owned. A 2001 *Newsweek* account told of one Denver marketing consultant who pays her six-year-old daughter to answer the phone and clean her home office (McGinn 2001: 42). Another popular ploy is fixing up and selling homes provided they have been lived in for at least two of the last five years. Because profit (up to $250,000 per transaction) derives from selling one's residence, not conventional asset transactions, the tax code awards substantial benefits. Home-based businesses, in addition to the generous deductible expenses already noted, further permits taking an allowance for car travel associated with one's work. These are only current highlights, and new avoidance schemes appear regularly. All in all, provided one can satisfy modest IRS rules regarding business legitimacy, clever bookkeeping can dramatically lower tax bills, all legally.

If we move beyond legitimate escape routes into grayer or even outright illegal scams, possibilities explode. Critically, these ventures are accessible to ordinary people, even the poor, and while they require some industriousness, they are more straightforward than, say, hiring lobbyists to manipulate tax codes. The earned income tax credit (EITC), a popular 1970s anti-poverty measure to encourage the destitute to seek work over welfare, has grown especially mischievous. Now, the qualified impoverished parent can receive tax credits as refunds or offsets against other taxes (the maximum in 1998 was $3,756). The 1990s economic boom notwithstanding, the EITC has seemingly become a popular cash cow though of dubious legality. Between 1990 and 1997, families claiming the EITC increased some 56 percent; returns requesting a refund check climbed 78 percent. In fact, the total in EITC refunds paid out by the IRS soared from $5 billion to $25 billion despite scant indication of economic conditions triggering this needed relief. Inadvertent IRS generosity is not difficult to fathom. For one, for-profit tax advisors gladly counsel poor people on maximizing refunds for a share of the "profits." More telling, and this applies to untold other dodges, deviousness is too inviting to resist. Children can be "borrowed," just invented, and checking non-existent paperwork would severely over-extend IRS organizational capacity (Barlett and Steele 2000: 24-28).[2] Even if crackdowns were feasible, the public backlash against depriving the poor of their modest windfalls (while simultaneously ignoring abuses among the rich) would be immense.

The stock market boom of the late 1990s provided the more affluent a totally uncomplicated method to minimize tax bites. Stock sale profits are fully taxable capital gains and equity sales are reported to the IRS. But, and this is a huge "but," the government lacks any legal way of establishing purchase price. This figure is taxpayer supplied, and while it exists in the broker's records, it is the filer's obligation to behave honestly. Given wide stock price fluctuations, it is a no-brainer to substitute higher cost prices and thus artificially reduce capital gains. This ploy is hardly hypothetical. That stock transaction capital gains have grossly lagged behind market advancements and trading activity suggests that this creative—and unambiguously illegal—accounting is pervasive (Barlett and Steele 2000: 41-43).

Of all the schemes available to potential tax avoiders, perhaps none offers greater promise than offshore secret bank accounts. Though once confined to international embezzlers and insecure despots, it has recently become "democratized." Again, it is difficult to put precise numbers on the ruses. One IRS inference put the total cost to the U.S. Treasury at some $70 billion a year in lost revenue (Novack 2001). A 2002 guess for individuals alone was $40 billion in tax revenue forgone (Dooren and Anderson 2002). Note well, this activity seldom involves drug smuggling, laundering pay-offs or any of the other nefarious acts one associates with gangsters traveling with suitcases packed with $100 dollar bills. Users are more likely to be professionals or independent business people shielding assets from lawsuits, ruinous divorce settlements, or other unwelcome claims. There is nothing intrinsically illegal about these accounts; misdeeds come from hiding initial earnings or investment income generated by these accounts. And since these offshore assets are explicitly designed for concealment, even from the prying IRS, they naturally also attract those illegally fleeing taxation.[3] Just how much taxable income is hidden away overseas is shadowy, but given that total offshore assets have been reasonably guessed to be in the neighborhood of $5 *trillion*, the possibilities are enormous (Silverstein 2000).

Several features of this industry are worth mentioning. First, access to mysterious offshore tax heavens such as those in Somoa, Vanuata, Tonga, and Nauru is virtually effortless. In fact, according to the Organization for Economic Cooperation and Development, there were some thirty-three documented tax havens (Cloud 2001). Financial advisors facilitating transfers are ubiquitous; many reside in high-income areas and vigorously advertise their services. One firm, Research Press, Inc., conducts a nationwide business selling its guides to tax havens, trusts, and ways to remain abroad forever. Another savvy promoter, Offshore Outlook Inc., issues a steady stream of newsletters and brochures on wealth preservation to anybody who can subscribe. For the exceptionally curious, "Shorex, the International Money Show," is an annual London event featuring the industry's who's whos. For those anxious about unfamiliar firms handling their assets, U.S. financial heavyweights such as Citibank, Goldman Sachs, Morgan Trust Company, and Chase Manhattan (among others) have entered this lucrative business lest the upstarts steal all the profits.

The modern electronic economy has, predictably, democratized evasion. Even Switzerland's venerable MFC Merchant Bank has gone after the more pedestrian cyber customer instead of exclusively relying on aristocratic old wealth. Subscribing to incriminating newsletters, confessing one's plans to strangers, or visiting exotic places with satchels of cash is now obsolete. Typing in "tax avoidance" into a net search engine will promptly generate an electronic supermarket of offshore financial services. Fighting excessive taxation now only requires filing out a credit card application. In some nations—the Cayman Islands and Austria—supplying a name is unnecessary. The available service array is staggering. Offshore Secrets, a web-based company, can provide anonymous bank accounts, diplomatic passports; even obtaining new citizenship or a foreign drivers license is possible. The Unitrust Capital Corp site supplies a detailed fee schedule for nearly any imaginable financial transaction. Need a private Panamanian chartered foundation—that will cost $1,390, though professionals receive a 50 percent discount. A numbered offshore bank account here costs a mere $300.

No less important, electronic banking permits the safe, and virtually undetected encrypted shifting of funds from the U.S. to these hidden accounts, using reputable U.S. banks as transfer agents, if desired (and these encryption devices daily grow more powerful). To insure additional protection, offshore advisory firms often provide advanced computer networks so secreted funds can be quickly reallocated across countries into numbered accounts should subterfuges attract unwelcome curiosity. On Monday assets sit in Belize, by Tuesday they can migrate to Bermuda and on Wednesday they suddenly appear in Costa Rica, and the owner never leaves his or her home computer! That each of these (and several other) nations imposes stringent laws protecting account secrecy minimizes eventual detection. Only if overwhelming evidence of illicit activity exists can secrecy be breeched, and this is frequently unachievable. IRS agents suspicious of your Cook Island dealings must *personally* travel to the Cook Islands (a former New Zealand territory) and appeal to Cook Island courts since foreign judicial orders are invalid. Don't trust computers or are computer phobic? No problem—elaborate secretive mail drops can render the paper trail nearly untraceable. (Other companies offer a comparable e-mail message service to obscure the initial sender.)

The invulnerability of these offshore accounts was made plain in U.S. Treasury report that noted that of some 21,000 corporations registered in the Netherlands Antilles in 2000, only about 300 filed the required U.S. Treasury reports. In Panama, the ratio is even worse—340 reports filed of an estimated 372,000 registered corporations, and the overwhelming majority of these are believed to be American owned (McKinnon 2001).

Nor is it necessary to visit exotic lands to tap concealed assets. A favorite contrivance is a standard-looking credit or debit card issued by secretive financial services (they display innocuous identifiers like "Baltic Bank'). Having a name on the card is optional since transactions are executed via numerical codes. The IRS itself estimates that between one and two million American possess these cards (Johnston 2002a). Thanks to the worldwide credit card acceptors and ATM network, a superficially normal appearance is possible (so-called "smart cards" with imbedded cash have also become popular).[4] Now the tax avoider and over-burdened taxpayer are indistinguishable save the absence of mailed monthly credit card statements for the former. Moreover, as credit card limits increase, they can even be used to pay for such "big ticket" items as college tuition and fine art, let alone daily groceries. If currency is needed, ATMs supply it. Everything is deducted from the offshore accounts, so unlike the revealing paper trail left by U.S.-based plastic, luxurious lifestyles can be kept beyond prying eyes. Meanwhile, suspicion-arousing exotic cars and yachts can be suitably registered to shadowy foreign entities whose generic name obscures actual ownership (Johnston 2002f). Best of all, if arrested or sued, there are "no assets" to confiscate.

Significantly, it is generally becoming *easier* to escape government monitoring, government enforcement threats aside. One would think that with all the fresh evasion chances and the personal wealth explosion, Washington would launch a *jihad* against tax cheats. Not true. Between 1990 and 1998 the IRS reduced staff by 16 percent. Congress has even joined the anti-IRS bandwagon, insisting on a "Taxpayer's Bill of Rights" with seventy-two specific provisions and rights further complicating enforcement (agents guilty of harassment are now easily dismissed and "harassment" is generously defined). When tough anti-cheater measures are enacted, they are typically soon reversed or quietly de-funded. Meanwhile, the IRS is further pushed toward becoming a service-oriented agency and less a feared extractive entity. Agents too vigilant currently risk their careers (Barlett and Steele 2000: chapter 4). More telling is the sharp decline in audits, a justifiably feared weapon that undoubtedly kept many taxpayers honest. Despite mounting tales of tax cheating, Congress has tightly restricted the IRS's audit capacity and many of the most qualified have left in the last five years. By its own admission, the IRS is short some 29,000 auditors (Johnston 2003). Critically, audits among the self-employed reporting gross receipts over $100,000—a category rife with abuse—have been cut 55 percent between 1988 and 1999. Not surprisingly, money collected by tough enforcement actions has fallen 13 percent since 1996 while seizures and liens are down even more dramatically (Novack 2001). In November of 2002, Charles O. Rossotti, the IRS commissioner, resigned in frustration, complaining that paltry IRS resources severely limited the battle against tax cheats, especially the wealthy (Johnston 2002g).

A parallel weakening of tax-enforcement has been occurring at the state level despite the 2002 economic downturn that would counsel *greater* revenue collection vigor (Johnston 2002d). Iowa, for example, has cut 200 of the more than 500 jobs at the state's tax agency while budgetary shortfalls in Minnesota, Nebraska, and Wisconsin have pushed tax collectors into more clerical positions. More telling, most states have failed to utilize IRS-supplied tax data to collar those under-reporting income to state agencies despite offers of nearly free assistance.

The peculiar nature of this situation is illustrated in a *Wall Street Journal* headline: "U.S. to Crack Down on Violations of Laws on Offshore Bank Accounts." (Simpson 2002). The thrust of the story, contrary to the impression generated by the headline, was that enforcement continues to be minimal. For example, the Treasury estimates that only about 20 percent of those with offshore accounts above $10,000 bother to report these accounts as required by law (about one million do not). In 1999 and 2000 not a single U.S. taxpayer was charged with hiding such an account, and between 1996 and 1998, a mere nine were indicted. The agency especially designed for this task—the Financial Crimes Enforcement Network— has only passed on twelve referrals to the IRS since 1993 that resulted in two fines and four letters of warning. The Treasury attributed this laxity to offshore bank secrecy and the complexity of uncovering illegality. The story concludes that the Treasury promised, "to do more," especially post-September 11, but it is unlikely that this effort will inconvenience many other than those who might be involved in terrorism.

Our analysis offers a tempting clue why Americans gripe about excessive taxation yet major reductions draw tepid support. The era of Proposition 13 certainly seems forgotten. This ambivalence was apparent in the lukewarm reception received by George W. Bush's tax-cutting plan. Democratic opponents hardly embraced it or offered rival schemes, and doubters scarcely suffered grievous electoral consequences. A tough legislative battle also ensued. This oddity may well reflect personal accommodation—nearly everyone can utilize "homemade" escape routes without ever venturing into the political fray. Why join the National Taxpayer's Union if thousands can be cut from one's 1040 by under-reporting freelance consulting fees or exaggerating charitable deductions? Why spend hours campaigning for anti-tax candidates when opportunities exist for re-selling old furniture as "antiques" at flea markets sans tax record keeping? Better to insert five minutes of "business" into a scrumptious meal and deduct the full amount and thus cut the true cost in half. These bountiful opportunities undoubtedly make political battles poor investments, at least for many.

Improving Education

At least superficially, U.S. primary and secondary education resembles the classic state-controlled monopoly. Legally, *every* aspect of a child's schooling is state dictated, even if transpiring beyond government's immediate physical supervision. Short of disappearing into the hills, parents must acquiesce to rules regulating mandated curricula, "school year" definitions, and countless other requirements. Not even children's health and nutrition might escape officialdom's grasp (e.g., legally mandated vaccinations). Where the bureaucracy's long reach ends, judges now issue commands regarding classroom racial mixes, prohibitions against religious observances, access for the disabled, even science textbook content. Recent trends are harbingers of yet more state intrusion as teachers supplement parental training on matters such as sexual morality.

If one accepts as final this government-centered early education vision, a political redress strategy seems preordained. A quick scan of today's classroom battles confirms this seek-relief-via-government inclination popularity. Conservatives demand that government impose stringent testing standards, a return to basics, and instructing traditional morality. Liberals meanwhile fervently petition government to impose multicultural awareness, tolerance, bilingual instruction, and so on. All frustrated sects have their noisy grass roots organizations and Washington lobbyists. Nevertheless, dissimilarity aside, these combatants reflexively accept government's central educative responsibility as a matter of faith. If Dick and Jane cannot read, demand the local Board of Education hire effective teachers. If the principal refuses graduation day prayers, sue. In sum, government "gives" education, so to improve schooling, harass government.

Reality, fortunately, encompasses more than overcoming stifling monopolies. Fighting the tax code offers a parallel: one need not reverse Congress, let alone crush teacher unions or demand the local school superintendent restore traditional pedagogy, to succeed. The place to begin is to acknowledge U.S. primary and secondary school diversity. In 1997-98 there were 14,427 public school districts with a little over 90,000 primary and secondary schools (NCES, Local Universe Agency Survey, online). Given local finance and academic preference variation, options flourish. Not every taste can be fulfilled via the public sector but choices remain ample without lifting a political finger. Within the same geographical area, one finds institutions accentuating traditional academics and schools pushing sports; some schools impose tough discipline while others ignore transgressions; a few gladly assist disabled students while others supply minimal facilities, and on and on. Urban school districts frequently make available dedicated centers for those with artistic or science talent, an approach followed at the primary level with specialized "magnet schools." According to one 1994 government survey, intra-district public school choice availability ranged from a high of 47 percent in the West to a low of 13 percent in the Northeast, and the tend here appears upward (National Center for Educational Statistics, "Use of School Choice" www.nces.gov/pubs/95742r.html). If one includes differences across states, the range of possibilities is far greater.

Deciding where to live can be critical since residency controls schooling options: vote educational desires with one's feet (or moving van), not the ballot box or campaign contribution. A 1993 national survey found that a quarter of all children in urban areas attended schools actually chosen by parents, not administrators (NCES 1995). This tactic is hardly restrictive and, arguably, it is probably *the* single most popular remedy for terrible schooling, regardless of how defined.[5] "Better schools" has become a cliché in explaining residential mobility and, as we show below when describing "white flight," dissatisfaction has instigated huge migrations. Even among those economically or occupationally restricted, residential choices *always* exist provided instruction is a priority.

The ease of uncovering the "right" school, regardless of pedagogical content, makes this "non-political" approach especially alluring. Compared to, say, demanding Creationism or radical multiculturalism, migratory habits are invisible. Who will protest the sport-minded relocating to a village celebrated for championship football teams? States and localities routinely issue school-by-school report cards detailing test score performance, student body ethnic mix, and other potentially relevant data. Reputations can be gleaned from real estate brokers or business people. Educational disasters or accomplishments are seldom secret. Nor is one forbidden to visit schools personally to inquire about, say, advanced placement courses, teacher certification, Internet connections, or basketball coaching. Compare this detective work with navigating legislative obstacles to reform bureaucratic catastrophes.

Moving beyond the public sphere, choices multiply. It is here that parents can find attractive alternatives, even options that would *never* be permitted in the public sector since non-public schools enjoy wider pedagogical latitude vis-à-vis their public rivals. Parental financial involvement also encourages consumer responsiveness rare in the public sector: if parents want French language tutoring, they can buy it. Though the private primary and secondary education sector's exact size is uncertain, it is indisputably large. A fall 1997 federal government estimate puts the total number of non-government schools at 27,402 with a little over 5 million students. By contrast, the National Private School Association Group's database puts the school count at 130,000 with 13.6 million students (National Private School Association Group, www.npsag.com/database.html). One might surmise that discrepancies exist over what, exactly, comprises a "school," and not every administrator enthusiastically cooperates with Washington's curiosity.

Statistical divergences aside, wide-ranging options permeate society, are often reasonably affordable, and appear demand driven— if enough people express the need, somebody will build it. If one hankers for military-style discipline, one website lists some twenty-six U.S. high school military academies offering coed and same-sex programs. Meanwhile, anti-militarists might avail themselves of places renowned for so-called progressive views such as Vermont's Putney School. A different website details multiple therapeutic schools for the emotionally troubled or those with learning disabilities (www.strugglingteens.com/therapy.html). There are private schools specializing in the physically disabled, the sports-minded and even the theatrically inclined. Renowned expensive "Waspy" academies, the likes of Phillips Exeter or Lake Forest Academy also await to serve elites (and these always award scholarships to less wealthy students). To a surprising extent, objectives so fervently sought by education activists, e.g., inculcating traditional morality, *already* currently exist though, to be sure, not necessarily in the precise form or location desired. Ample financial assistance is also available for the poor to attend any of these hundreds of schools. One organization in particular, Children First America, in 2001 has coordinated the efforts of some 100 private foundations to fund scholarships to 100,000 low-income children (www. childrenfirstamerica.org). The upshot, then, the quest frequently entails unearthing the right school, less pressuring government to create it *de novo*.

Among private schools, Catholic Church affiliated institutions are the most common. In the academic year 2000-2001, according to the National Catholic Education Association, there were 8,146 Catholic K-12 affiliated schools with nearly 2.7 million students. Stereotypes aside, few are decaying urban buildings administered by nuns sternly instilling the Baltimore Catechism into frightened ruddy-faced youngsters. Some are, indeed, time-honored parish-centered institutions serving local Catholic populations, but others draw from an extensive diocese, and can resemble private academies though traditional teaching approaches still dominate. Religious orders supply less than 7 percent of all teachers. In 2000-01, according to a NCEA, 1,570 Catholic elementary schools served rural areas while 919 were located in the inner city.[6] Pedagogical philosophy depends on the religious order running the school and local needs. They can be single sex (almost always exclusively at the secondary level), coed and, occasionally, offer specialized education in fields like foreign languages. San Francisco, for example, has nine Catholic elementary schools, one of which offers extensive Chinese language instruction while another specializes in French (Coulson 1999: 264).

These schools are far more accessible than popular impressions might suggest. Catholic schools are hardly restrictive, and admission is usually immediate (only 44 percent maintain waiting lists). Moreover, since admission criteria vary from school-to-school, rejection at one place need not mean refusal elsewhere. One in five will also admit students expelled from public schools for disciplinary or academic reasons (data cited in Coulson 1999: 268). Equally relevant, due to local control, policies regarding admitting non-parishioners fluctuate greatly, as do subsidy policies for those unable to afford tuition. The average primary school tuition in 2000-01 was $1,787 (high school tuition was $4,100) but some 81 percent of all grade school pupils received scholarship aid. Nationally, in 2000-01, 13.6 percent of all enrollees were non-Catholic (National Catholic Education Association, 2001). Many effective inner-city schools serving the African-American community are Catholic institutions, though few of the pupils are themselves Catholic, or can afford the full tuition (blacks made up 8.2 percent of all elementary students, nationally, Hispanics another 11 percent in Catholic schools).

Paralleling Catholic education are schools run by other religious denominations, the most common being "Christian Schools." This label covers a multitude of pedagogical/doctrinal approaches. Some, like those belonging to the Association of Classical & Christian Schools, stress Old and New Testament Scriptures; others concentrate more on values than religious texts. Home Study International (www.his.edu) offers a Christian-oriented home study courses by mail ranging from Kindergarten through college. Much depends on geographical concentration and community religious traditions. For example, numerous "Protestant Reformed" schools serve sections of Michigan and Iowa settled by Dutch immigrants who brought the Reformed movement with them from Holland over a century ago.

Not unexpectedly given the voluntary nature of information collection, statistics here are often approximations. The government's Center for Educational Statistics puts the 1997-98 figure for "Conservative Christian" schools at 4,978 with 737,000 students. By contrast, the Association of Christian Schools claims a 2001 U.S. membership of nearly 5,300 schools with approximately one million students. What is clear, however, is the obvious accessibility of these alternatives and, since they accentuate pedagogical content over expensive infrastructure like computer labs, their budgets are quite modest (a situation further enhanced by the low pay many teachers willingly take).[7] Regardless of locality, they dot the landscape and, critically, several Websites describe varied Christian school offerings. And, as was true for Catholic schools, though hardly bargain basement priced, Christian schools are middle class accessible (and subsidies are sometimes available for less well-off families). The Christian Schools International, a group of some 380 U.S. schools, lists average regional tuition figures for its members from a low of $2,781 to a high of $3,926.

The movement toward non-public institutions embodying Jewish religious teachings has recently been especially energetic. Growth here is in addition to supplemental temple-run Sunday school or thrice-a-week afternoon religious training. These full-time institutions range from traditional Orthodox yeshivas devoted to Talmudic interpretation to more modern academies lecturing on Jewish values and history. According to one estimate, some forty new Jewish high schools have opened since the early 1990s, and by the end of the nineties, approximately 190,000 students were enrolled in some 650 Jewish-run primary and secondary schools. Some experts expect enrollments to soar even further, as many Jewish parents become uneasy over intermarriage and assimilation. Though commonly centered in areas of large Jewish populations, for example, New York City, and Los Angeles, they also thrive in areas seldom associated with extensive Jewish communities, for example, Mississippi, Oklahoma, and Iowa (Beinart 1999). Once again, the Web offers several sites listing these schools, often with accompanying websites and e-mail addresses.

What is particularly telling about burgeoning Jewish-centered education is its origin in *private* efforts, not government intervention. One organization in particular, the Partnership for Excellence in Jewish Education, has created an $18 million fund to establish twenty-five new Jewish schools nationwide by matching funds raised by community-based organizations. Interestingly, this organization comprises a mere twelve high-profile philanthropists each annually pledging $300,000 for five years (Cohen, nd). This generosity supplements already remarkable levels of financial support provided Jewish education by established charities such as the United Jewish Appeal and local synagogue donations. Though Jewish education, like Christian instruction, is not capital intensive, this munificence has made Jewish learning possible for thousands of children otherwise unable to afford the $5,000 to $6,000 primary school fees, let alone the $10,000 per year high school tuitions.

Less prominent has been the African-American recourse to non-public schools to accomplish their special goals. In the mid-1990s, for example, black parents dissatisfied with Atlanta's public system helped found three new independent schools (a fourth already existed). Even with just four institutions, options were formidable, though all sought to enforce stronger discipline while building scholastic achievement rooted in strong cultural and religious commitments. Baptist parents could elect the Greenforest Christian Academy; Nation of Islam admirers could send their children to the Islamic Clara Mahammed School; meanwhile Piaget and Rousseau fans had the Freedom Academy (a long-standing independent school catering to African-Americans was also available). These were hardly elite, exclusive institutions given that over half of these enrollees came from families with annual incomes below $30,000 (http://horizon.unc.edu/287/1996/abstracts/Martin_abs2.asp).

Creating a private academy hardly exhausts the possibilities for black parents disdaining public options. Home schooling, a subject that will be explored in greater detail below, is especially promising for those preferring non-mainstream pedagogy. A *Washington Times* story (Sorokin 2003) estimated that some 85,000 black children are now being home schooled, often to impart strong moral and black cultural values absent in local public schools. Another guess put the figure at 120,000, a near five-fold increase over 1997 that seems closely related to the growth of a suburban black middle class (Jonsson 2003). One website describes such options as Akebulan Homeschooling, a curriculum imparting an African consciousness and appreciation for African culture. The Afrocentric Homeschoolers Association makes available resources and a gateway to like-minded parents. Though tiny in number, these innovative approaches make a key point: African Americans aggrieved over the educational status quo are not wholly dependent on political solutions. Recall that Christian schools can thrive with a handful of students and low-paid teachers in rent-free donated spaces. Admittedly, establishing a private school or teaching at home is far more arduous than painlessly enrolling children in public school, but—and this is critical—this do-it-yourself "private" tactic may well outshine contentious political pathways.[8]

At the "customized" education's extreme end lies the home school movement. Figures here are imprecise but home schooling's burgeoning popularity is beyond doubt. A 1999 government household survey put the figure at 850,000 children or 1.7 percent of all school- age children (School Reform News, 2001). A larger estimate—between 1.7 and 2 million—is offered by the National Home

Education Research Institute, a home schooling group (www.nheri.org). What was once an obscure corner to the education world is quickly becoming a major, though only faintly visible, industry. Several magazines including one devoted to legal issues (*Court Report)* cover this movement from the inside. One might speculate that at least part of this attractiveness is its low cost vis-à-vis any rival—a 1997 estimate put the average home schooling at $546 per child, hardly surprising since both labor and facilities are "free" (www.homeschooltoday.com/articls/ongoing/8step.htm).

Of the utmost importance, it is legal in all states though differences do exist in statutory requirements, paperwork, and bureaucratic supervision. Where obstacles surface, an organizational network is readily available to smooth the transition. The national Home School Legal Defense Association closely follows regulations both nationally and state by state. Every state also has multiple advocacy groups serving specific clienteles. Alabama, for example, has five such groups, all with websites and e-mail addresses, two of which are explicitly Christian oriented, and one Catholic. National organizations supply inexpensive "How to" books and, if that is insufficient, guidance can be obtained personally at countless monthly home school fairs and conventions, all Web listed (www.homeschooltoday.com).

The diverse pedagogical resources available to parents make this approach especially enticing. The www.homeschooltoday.com site handily lists venders offering everything from advanced mathematics lessons to the latest in high-tech Christian-oriented material. African-American parents choosing this route can tap into the resources of the National Black Home Educators Resource Association via www.christianity.com/nbhera. Even tutorials teaching computer programming to ten-year-olds can also be purchased (www.innovatus.com). The site, www.home-school.com, recommends information on home school driver education, history, and home school class rings among myriad other possibilities. If readily available library and bookstore resources are included, the do-it-yourself option menu is truly gigantic. Clearly, for hundreds of thousands of parents, even private school variety cannot possibly outshine what can be accomplished one-to-one. Politically, the non-trivial dividend of escaping confrontations with professional educators is particularly noteworthy. Why spend hours arguing about, say, phonic versus whole word spelling, if victory can be gained without expending political capital? Home school parents often glowingly recount educating children likely to fall between the cracks elsewhere. On typical anecdote told of how instruction was carefully fine-tuned to overcome shyness, math phobia and hyper-activity (www.homeschooltoday.com/articls/ongoing/8step.htm). Another commonplace story concerns exceptionally bright children whose boredom with conventional school caused discipline tribulations.

Complementing the home school approach are diverse "for-profit" education endeavors expressly designed to remedy public school deficiencies. These are not the "contract" institutions such as the well-known Edison Schools that run deteriorating public schools. Rather, these offer specialized services for children outside of the classroom on a fee basis. If Dick cannot read or Jane cannot spell, and home schooling is impractical, just consult the Yellow Pages (under "tutoring") and hire a specialist to overcome the school's failure. Again, contentious politics is effortlessly avoided via the economic market. What is remarkable about this industry is its pervasiveness and explosive growth. One brokerage firm recommends it to be an attractive investment given mounting dissatisfaction with publicly run schools.[9]

The options list here is enormous, and for-profit education suited to specific local needs can be found nearly everywhere. Parents seeking academic advantages for their youngsters can avail themselves of everything from Montessori schools to educationally oriented facilities such as KinderCare. The Toledo, Ohio Yellow pages, for example, devotes four and a half pages to early private education centers. While all provide basic custodial care, a few stress their attentiveness to computer skills, music and creative movement, science programs and religious training. Sylvan Learning Centers, Inc., a publicly traded company with some 840 North American centers, makes available private coaching at all levels, including reading, mathematics (basic to pre-calculus), writing and study skills. What is especially striking about Sylvan is that it finely tunes instruction to individual student needs, a benefit seldom obtainable in the public sector. Kaplan, Inc., purveyors of the famous Stanley H. Kaplan tutorials for standardized tests, has now evolved into a virtual private educational supermarket complete with specific tutoring and after-school programs in regular academic subjects. Needless to say, these proprietary institutions possess a powerful incentive to succeed—profit.

Less visible, though hardly less consequential, than these well-known corporate entities are the so-called "cram schools" that are especially popular in localities with high Asian concentrations. They have names like "Ivy Prep" or "Harvard Academy" and provide intense after-school academic instruction, usually at cheaper prices than their corporate competitors. Significantly for our purposes, their growing fame has led to many non-Asians sending their children to these academies, including many black and Hispanic children otherwise mired in dreadful inner-city schools (Luo 2003). One such account tells of how a black mother living in Manhattan's Harlem sends her son via subway to a cram school in Queens for rigorous study in English, science and math, and with dramatic positive results (Maxwell 2003).

At the extreme end of this drift away from public facilities are newly emerging "cyber schools." These owe their existence to many state laws permitting schooling outside a pupil's immediate neighborhood and are often hybrids, drawing funds from both the public school and private, for-profit firms. As of 2002, only some 50,000 students were enrolled in these schools, communicating with their teachers via e-mail, telephone or chat rooms. Nevertheless, this number is sure to grow as technology develops and school districts seek cheaper ways to serve specialized student populations, notably high achievers bored with humdrum lessons (Tomsho 2002). Private firm such as Sylvan Ventures and K12 have even established various state-based "Connections Academies" or "Virtual Academies" for primary school students (Morris 2003).

This burgeoning choice illustrates a key principle, namely, civic victories can eliminate incentives for future activism. Why continue cajoling government for relief when private solutions are handier? A superb illustration concerns charter schools (and home schooling). To wit, when during the late 1980s states began authorizing charter schools (state-funded schools enjoying sizeable pedagogical autonomy), immense opportunities became available to parents dissatisfied with public education. One simply signed Junior up, an act identical to past public school enrollment. By 2003 some 600,000 children were attending more than 2,700 charter schools in 39 states plus the District of Columbia (Tomsho 2003). Significantly, these varied arrangement were especially attractive to minority and low-income students (Nelson et. al. 2000). The June 27, 2002 Supreme Court ruling upholding the use of publicly funded vouchers for religiously run schools will undoubtedly enhance non-government-run options.

Unhappy educational customers can also rely on support organization, for-profit franchisers, and several wealthy individuals (including the Walton family of Wal-Mart fame) anxious to assist. As with purely private academies, survival is market driven. Those Lansing, Michigan parents who want a top-quality academic Afrocentric education for their children can send them to Sankofa Shule without having to badger public officials. The existence of idiosyncratic Sankofa Shule (which substitutes African rituals for U.S. national holidays) suggests staggering possibilities. Critically, unlike up-scale private school, the out-of-pocket cost for parents can be zero or close to it when privately subsidized. Charter schools now exist for the academically disadvantaged, those with a bent for the performing arts, those hankering after stern discipline and morality and even students combining high school with fast food industry jobs, among untold other options (*US News* 1998).

Analysis here offers a key clue why popular dissatisfaction with public education has failed to develop into a burning Holy Crusade: multiple non-political options soften the outcry for government rescues. Even under the most inhospitable circumstances, dissatisfied parents can compensate for public education's deficiencies—just sell the TV, read library books aloud, buy educational toys, or otherwise take matters into one's hands. And these possibilities proliferate as eager businesses enter the education market. In sum, educational politics, as the cure for educational deficiencies, is not pre-ordained. To be sure, our argument scarcely renders politics irrelevant. The overarching civic framework remains critical; private alternatives depicted here survive at government discretion. Home schooling, charter schools and Sylvan Learning Centers all could be abolished tomorrow, and politics would then, necessarily, return to the forefront. The point is merely that given these non-pubic opportunities, retreating from civic activism can be prudent.

Overcoming Civil Rights Laws

The African-American quest for equality has been one of the modern era's landmark political accomplishments. This triumph, often marked with violence and great personal sacrifice, scarcely needs retelling. Hundreds of laws and judicial principles, all backed up with special enforcement agencies, now demand racial equality across virtually every aspect of one's existence. Whether it is housing rentals or securing home mortgages, applying for employment or voting, government is vigorously committed to eliminating racial discrimination. No respectable party or group advocates racial segregation, "white-only" elections, or otherwise seeks to restore second-class citizenship for blacks. Racial conflict, to be sure, remains divisive, often intensely, for example, facilitating black access to higher education without unfairly excluding whites. Nevertheless, civil rights legislation, especially the commitment to equal opportunity and access, has become part of the rock-solid national legal consensus.

This overwhelming public agreement does not signify, however, that conflict has ceased. A more encompassing account would be that disagreement has evolved, gone underground, and remains largely muted in public. Guerrilla warfare might be the more apt label. That barely anybody openly seeks to repeal the 1964 Civil Rights Act, which extensively banned racial discrimination, does not mean that its integrationist strictures are heeded. Ditto for the endless court rulings mandating public school integration: even parents accepting integration in principle do not always cheerfully choose racially balanced schools. Indeed, civil rights advocates periodically insist that, outward appearances notwithstanding, progress has been slight beyond cosmetic changes since the "bad old days" when white racism constituted official policy. In a nutshell, opposing black civil rights can take a private pathway.

Given powerful public pressures to reaffirm racial equality, uncovering this concealed resistance is formidable—it is typically denied altogether or disguised. Even tax-cheats may be more forthcoming. It occasionally exists as veiled "informal" tactics; in other instances, it can only be imperfectly inferred from behavior. Consider, for example, "challenging" the Community Reinvestment Act of 1977 and the Fair Housing Amendments Act of 1988 (among many others) banning racial discrimination in housing transactions. Nominally, these are tough, eagerly enforced laws with substantial penalties. Nevertheless, below-the-radar avoidance is possible. A recent *New York Times* story tells of New York City white neighborhood where houses were never openly listed for sale (Herszenhorn 2001). Information was shared entirely by word-of-mouth with other whites, and thus undetectable to civil rights enforcement agencies.

This tactic's frequency is impossible to estimate, but it well may be commonplace nationally given the continuance of widespread residential racial homogeneity. In fact, subverting all these fair housing laws is fairly straightforward. Knowledgeable realtors may prosper in some localities *only* by catering to these exclusionary preferences—those showing houses to unwelcome prospective buyers never receive future "for sale" listings. With no advertising, let alone acknowledgment of property being on the market, claiming racial bias is nearly impossible (and note well, this tactic applies to any ethnic or racial group, not just whites excluding blacks).

Exurbia's explosive growth, as central cities turn increasingly black and Hispanic, further firms this "non-political" solution to civil rights legislation. The 2000 census reveals that of the 157 counties that grew by 40 percent or more during the 1990s, two-thirds were at least 80 percent white and a third were 90 percent white. While Atlanta, Georgia, has seen its African American population soar, four of the fastest growing U.S. counties are in Georgia, and all are overwhelmingly white. Whites fleeing polyglot California have fueled much of the growth in Nevada, Idaho, Utah, and other inter-mountain states. This pattern is widespread, especially in urban areas, and the voluntary nature of this migration makes it totally legal and unstoppable (Tilove 2001).

The arsenal of subversive tactics to maintain racial separateness is surprisingly large, though—again—seldom candidly acknowledged. Such racially neutral housing policies as zoning, minimum lot size, access to public transportation, covenants dealing with architectural style, among untold other provisions, might exclude African Americans (who generally cannot afford expensive housing) by inflating purchase prices or otherwise making it unattractive to potential black buyers. Other perfectly bona fide arrangements such as classifying apartment buildings as a cooperative permit sellers a wider discretion in selecting occupants.[10] Poor black (and white) shoppers will be discouraged if malls are inaccessible from public transportation or levy parking fees. Restaurant and bar proprietors often shape clienteles by fine-tuning background music, pricing, décor, and menu selection, all of which cannot be legally interpreted as racial "discrimination" though this may be the unexpressed (and fervently denied) purpose. A wily supermarket anxious to filter its customer base can readily do so via inventory or selective pricing.

These mechanisms barely scratch the surface and, fundamentally, all are perfectly legal and well within the realm of respectable business practices, regardless of their racial intent or impact. Even the toughest anti-discrimination law is silent regarding barroom jukeboxes or liquor selection.

Of all the potential mechanism to undermine civil rights law intent, physical location is undoubtedly the most efficient. One "solves" potential race-related troubles by fleeing them, a device beyond challenge given our venerated freedom to live wherever we please. Consider an employer navigating the thicket of employment-based regulations prohibiting racial discrimination. According to the U.S. Equal Opportunity Commission, racial discrimination can occur in hiring or firing, pay scales, job classification, job advertisements, recruitment, testing, use of company facilities, fringe benefits, retirement pay, among multiple other factors (www.eeoc.gov/facts/quanda.html). These formal rules only begin race-related constraints, and hold even if the actual bias violates company policy or is unintentional.

Given the murkiness of "equality" in these litigation-prone matters, even innocuous seeming acts, e.g., advertising jobs in newspapers favored by whites, may bring costly racial discrimination suits. And how does one legally define a "racially hostile work environment"? A seemingly innocuous calendar picture could, conceivably, instigate a complaint from a hypersensitive employee. Equally important, plaintiffs have free access to government attorneys, or as is increasingly common, can hire private lawyers entirely on a contingent fee basis. Racial discrimination litigation figures can run to the hundreds of millions as such blue chip companies as Texaco, Delta Airlines, Xerox, Microsoft, and Coca Cola have discovered (and suits are frequently settled out-of-court though still are costly). Even the totally innocent must pay for "discrimination-proofing" the workplace, for example, hiring expert compliance monitors or holding periodic racism awareness seminars. That only a tiny handful of workers among thousands assert partiality counts for naught—individual damage awards can still be momentous. For smaller or financially weak companies even litigation successes can bring ruinous legal fees. The indisputable upshot, then, is that hiring "protected" minorities involves considerable financial risk, possible terrible publicity and workplace disruption.

Though "smoking gun" statistical evidence of avoiding racially tinged employer-employee strife is lacking, a credible, though often anecdotal, circumstantial case exists. One evidentiary tidbit is the sizeable flight of companies away from concentrations of African Americans to the rapidly growing inter-mountain region. As Brad Bertock, president of a firm promoting high-tech business in Utah frankly put it, "One thing people do not want to worry about is race relations. Companies think that if they go to a neighborhood where everyone is like me, it makes it easier. It takes away from stress." Another expert on this migration admitted, "it [relocating to exurbia] is a move to remove as far as possible from the inner-city poor areas" (quoted in Kotkin 1996). In many instances, terms like "no crime," and "good schools" are the polite code words for "no blacks."

Business-oriented publications like the *Wall Street Journal* routinely tell of firms gladly relocating to areas far removed from "ethnic diversity" though the "race angle" is never overt. One such account told how cities such as Boise, Idaho, Provo, Utah, and Fort Collins, Colorado, had job growth patterns well in excess of national averages. In the early 1990s, for example, at least a dozen California companies shifted operations to Fort Collins, and this increase continues unabated (Gavin 2001). An April 10, 2000 *Wall Street Journal* story recounted how one Philadelphia-based travel company originally transferred a few jobs to North Dakota to assist draught-stricken farmers, but was soon so impressed with local workers that forty part-timers quickly grew to over 1,000 full-time employees. Repeatedly the firm's owner raves about the good work habits of these new employees in contrast to labor problems (such as chronic absenteeism) back east and has tried to entice other companies to follow his lead (Carey 2000). Notable other top-flight corporations—Citicorp Bank, U.S. Healthcare, Unisys, United Airlines among untold others—have migrated to sparsely populated states once considered economic Siberia. The common thread in this migration is "quality of life," not state-supplied economic incentives— superior schools, low crime, cheap housing and, most of all, workforce quality. This shift contrasts sharply with the meager job creation successes of government-sponsored incentive-rich inner city "Empowerment Zones." Here, with scant exception, lavish tax breaks and other tangible rewards have failed to bring jobs (see Weissberg, 1999: ch 6 for details on these fiascos).

The location of Japanese U.S. automobile factories—it is often alleged—further illustrates this tactic. One 1989 statistical study reported selected factory sites (and other company policies) minimized the job opportunities available for blacks. At the Marysville, Ohio Honda plant, for example, blacks comprised a mere 2.8 percent of the workforce. At Nissan's Smyrna, Tennessee facility, 14 percent of the workers were black, and this figure is typical for other Japanese owned factories. By contrast, the figure at newly built U.S.-owned factories was 25.4 percent (Cole and Deskins 1988). When Illinois fervently sought Mitsubishi's new plant, the firm finally selected Bloomington-Normal, a prosperous area with a relatively small percentage of African Americans versus nearby Danville or Decatur, rust belt cities of high unemployment and high concentrations of blacks.

Today's global economy makes this flight solution exceedingly tempting. Quick and cheap international transportation means that even manufacturing jobs can be thousands of miles away in localities absolutely free of discrimination lawsuits or protest marches led by Jesse Jackson, and with low-cost wages, to boot. Many U.S. corporation now outsource service clerical work that was once the mainstay of central city offices. General Electric, for example, uses computers connected via telephone to handle its customer claims processing, credit evaluation, research and countless other tasks worldwide. A retail customer asking about a warranty might be speaking to someone in India and never know it (Lavin 2002).

Of all the exemplars possible to illustrate "voting with one's feet" to subvert civil rights legislation, the "white flight" from government-mandated public school racial integration is the most observable. This is an immensely complex tale, but the gist of it is as follows. Until the 1954 *Brown v. Board of Education* decision, state-required racial segregation was legal in the U.S. (though generally rare nationally outside of the south). In a 1955 follow-up case, the Court ordered school integration "with all deliberate speed," but nearly a decade of inaction followed. Of critical importance, this desegregation effort focused on eliminating the remnants of state-enforced segregation, not integrating schools that were "naturally" segregated due to residential homogeneity.

The status quo lay undisturbed until the 1960s when judges finally confronted this de facto segregation. Case by case, but especially in the key ruling of *Swann v. Charlotte-Mecklenburg Board of Education* (1971), the courts sought to finish off segregation regardless of parental—white or black—preferences. The mandated measures were commonly draconian and nearly irreversible given federal judges' lifetime tenure and legislative reluctance to intervene. Compulsory busing away from neighborhood schools, the reassignment of teachers, the required hiring of minority faculty, plus opening and closing schools themselves were all widely judicially imposed and malingering officials faced heavy fines. On occasion, judges themselves administered schools and levied additional taxes to fund their integration designs. Classroom procedures, e.g., ability groupings, disciplinary standards, were sometimes modified to avoid any hint of differential treatment (Armor 1995: introduction, ch. 1). A sea change now occurred in American primary and secondary education.

Early resistance by abolishing public schools altogether or other political attempts to curb judicial authority failed miserably. What did prove successful for integration opponents was a massive exodus from forced integration. Though social scientists were initially skeptical about white flight (believing that defiance would recede once inter-racial contacts multiplied), the link between compulsory school integration and sharply declining white enrollments became incontrovertible. James Coleman and associates scrutinized enrollment trends in sixty-seven of the largest central school districts between 1968 and 1973 and found significant out-migration of whites to the suburbs (cited in Armor 1995: 176). Another examination of 1,200 school districts reported that any type of interracial contact engendered white flight (cited in Armor 1995: 177). The incidence of white "no shows" following court ordered integration was particularly dramatic. In four analyzed cities, between 42 percent and 57 percent of white students compelled to attend predominantly black schools simply failed to arrive when school commenced (cited in Armor 1995: 179). By 1990 the white enrollment in Atlanta's public schools had fallen to less than 10 percent while in Dallas it was 18 percent and this "blackening" of urban public education is hardly extreme (Armor 1995: 72). Particularly striking is the pattern's ubiquity and persistence. Charles T. Clotfelter's (2001) detailed statistical investigations found that white flight still continues and is unrelated to district size or metropolitan area population. Put bluntly, judicial orders aside, if one does not want integrated school, don't go to court or try to elect sympathetic leaders; just move.

Conclusions

Analysis offers a simple point in immense detail: goals achievable via civic engagement are also obtainable non-politically. This is a practical, not principled, conclusion. Mechanically counseling one pathway versus another is futile, and our guidance could change tomorrow. Newfound IRS vigor or cracking down on suspect charter schools could easily remobilize the now apathetic toward 100 percent civic solutions. Our exemplars are also constrained—it is obviously risky to anchor theory entirely on three case studies, though taxes, schooling, and civil rights are hardly atypical issues. Over and above remarking on this substitutability, what can we add?

Most clearly, a free market, consumer-driven and reasonably prosperous economy makes seeking non-political avenues eminently reasonable, if not preferable. Rather than hurl oneself into vexing, time-consuming civic battles of uncertain outcome, the prudent takes matters into their own hands. This pathway will, moreover, expand as private resources proliferate and market entrepreneurs meet burgeoning needs. Thus understood, abandoning politics is less a rejection of the public realm than a calculating adjustment necessary to accomplish tangible aims. Whether this individualized strategy, indeed, out-performs public routes can only be answered empirically, on a case-by-case basis. The proof is in the pudding; little Johnny, the classroom dunce, might fail miserably at Sylvan, too. Conceivably, those shunning politics will fall short—harassing the school board might via a letter-writing campaign have been the superior pathway.

Critics might insist, nonetheless, that the foregoing view is more suitable for the rich and serious neglects political power's remediation for the less affluent. No principled rejoinder to this criticism is possible, especially when advanced by those blindly enamored of government's remedial power. Certain facts do, however, caution against this all-to-easy class bias argument. First, to the extent that modern politics requires resources, and resources are often roughly convertible, politics may be an unwise investment for those with the fewest resources. Even for the poor, batting City Hall is not cost-free. Nor is politics necessarily cheaper for the impoverished vis-à-vis private options. Hours parading for better housing might be more productively allocated to acquiring a trade or learning to read. The latter two alternatives can surely boost earnings and thereby make better living accommodations more obtainable. Dangers also lurk for those fixating on single solutions regardless of circumstances. What scientific law proclaims the inherent advantage of political remedies for the destitute? (Or for the rich, too.) Have untold case studies or statistical data demonstrated this "fact"? Plainly, this politics-is-always-superior supposition survives as unsupported faith among activism aficionados.

A reoccurring theme particularly relevant for poor people is conquering obstacles by relocating. This response applied equally to avoiding taxes, improving education and escaping civil rights laws. Happily, it is difficult to imagine any detested situation in which flight cannot outshine political action. Nothing ideological or racial inheres in this tactic. Millions of southern blacks once "defeated" Jim Crow by migrating northward decades before the civil rights movement (just as whites "defeated" unwelcome court-mandated school integration). Excessive taxation has been checked by the ever-present threat of the wealthy running off to more amiable settings. Crime-infested cities yearly lose population as people seek safety elsewhere (and this may be the cheapest solution for poor people unable to afford expensive private security). If the U.S. really becomes insufferable, one can immigrate overseas. This is hardly hypothetical though the process is usually the reverse—political refugees flock to the US. Exodus is never cost-free, but especially for those at the bottom, history shows it to be potent weapon.

The preceding analysis is particularly helpful for explaining why decades of increasing education and wealth do not mitigate apathy. The *opposite* tendency is more plausible: as prosperity daily affords more personalized options, incentives for exclusively seeking political relief shrink. The total menu is now much larger. Civic engagement is most appealing when non-political alternatives are scarce, as in socialist or totalitarian settings. A corollary might be that this bountifulness also encourages outsourcing public activism. Those with decent jobs should heed Ricardo's Law of Comparative Advantage—pay professionals $100 a year versus personally spending fifty hours politicking.

The role of rising education coupled with burgeoning technology also deserves mention in the context of this paradox. The savvy can now easily uncover solutions via the Net outside of the standard civic *carte du jour*. This was dramatically illustrated by our foray into education—those despondent with public schooling easily find innumerable alternatives requiring zero civic engagement. The Net was also useful for avoiding taxes. No doubt, the impending broadband revolution will yet further propel civic avoidance. We already are witnessing this shift in health care despite far louder cries for greater government helpfulness. Today's sophisticated consumer can rummage around the web for diagnoses and low-cost prescription medications (occasionally without a medical exam or prescription) all the while avoiding ponderous bureaucracies. Several providers now offer reasonably priced medical "second opinions" on-line and thus permit consumers to avoid endless private and government red tape. Who know what the future foretells—send one's vital signs electronically to a Bermuda clinic and receive the medicine the next day via FedEx from a pharmacy based in Turkey?

From our perspective, capitalist entrepreneurs and government are rivals. When government falters, ample discretionary income attracts profiteers offering superior rivals to political action. If schools satisfied parents, Sylvan Learning Centers would be superfluous. Nor would offshore banks thrive if taxes were minimal. Put in economic terms, citizens buy goods and services privately rather than seek shoddy merchandise from government. This is no different from the Post Office-UPS rivalry. Even if the service levels are comparable, the private sector offers an immense advantage—access is usually easier, hardly an accident since the marketplace rewards convenience. Compared to reforming a lax criminal justice system, reducing one's personal crime risk is a no-brainer. Just consult the Yellow Pages or go on-line and audition the quick-to-appear problem solvers. One might surmise, moreover, that as with public schools, public hospitals, and the like, the pursuit of aims via the public sector might be the choice of last resort, save, of course, among those indiscriminately venerating civic activism.

No conflict exists between private versus public solutions. They can often be artfully combined, as we have just suggested—political action permits subsequent private solutions. This possibility was dramatically illustrated in a *Wall Street Journal* story telling how home-schools have brilliantly mobilized to resist Congressional meddling (Golden 2000). The chair of the House Committee on Education and the Workforce ironically called home-schoolers Capitol Hill's most effective lobby despite their tiny numbers and avoidance of civic-based solutions. These parents are also far *more* active in traditional politics—writing letters, organizing boycotts, and funding election campaigns, and the like—than those with children in public schools. These activists via skilled, coordinated conventional political efforts have crushed objectionable policies such as mandatory testing. In other words, a full understanding of "activism" would assess the public-private mix, not just the ledger's public side.

Our last lesson is a cautionary note. This proliferation of choices, including all the political options depicted in the previous chapter, daily makes strategy selection more arduous. Wrestling with multiple political options is daunting enough; when private alternatives are added to this array, the situation resembles bewildering hypermarket shopping in the extreme. This proliferation will not necessarily benefit everyone equally. Those already skilled at navigating life's complexities will probably enhance their already notable advantage. Just imagine an unsophisticated parent choosing among dozens of schooling options for a troubled child, let alone numberless private sector lures? Ditto for hundreds of tax avoidance schemes. Alas, this perplexed parent cannot conveniently turn to a *Consumer Report*-like guidebook for sage advice. Subsequent chapters will return to this deceptively difficult issue.

Notes

1. Modern participation scholars also seriously neglect how private charities once conquered problems that now seem amenable only to government solutions. An excellent account of these successes is provided in Magnet (2000).
2. The claiming of dependents for tax purposes offers a revealing insight into taxpayer honesty. Prior to 1987, no Social Security numbers were required to make a claim. When this requirement was instituted, some 7 million children mysteriously vanished (reported in Kristof 1995).
3. It is also important to note that illegality, in and of itself, need not make an offshore account vulnerable to government seizure. A government investigation of possible money laundering can only be instigated if seven specific crimes are suspected, for example, drug sales, bank fraud or extortion, and other reprehensive activities such as stock manipulation do *not* meet this test.
4. Recent events hint, however, that this favorite device may be at risk. In October of 2001 a federal judge issued a summons requiring MasterCard and American Express to release all their records of Americans with accounts in the Bahamas, Cayman Islands, Antigua, and Barbados. Whether or not this order will be upheld, or be of any consequence to habitual evaders, remains an unsettled question. More on the IRS's recent efforts to challenge this rampaging avoidance can be found in Novack (2001)

5. The 1993 study found no significant differences in whether the school was chosen or assigned. What did differ were reasons for choice—poorer parents were more inclined to have convenience over academics though this difference was modest.
6. This is probably a euphemism for African-American since the data also list 2,177 urban schools as a separate category.
7. A visit to the Protestant Reformed Christian Schools (www.prca.org) will show this bare-bones quality. Most have fewer than ten teachers for sixty or fewer pupils across eight or nine grades. One school—the Free Christian School, employs two teachers for nine students in grades K though 9!
8. Compare this under-the-radar approache to what has transpired in Detroit where Afrocentric pedagogy has been inserted into twenty-one *public* schools. Here, predictably, bitter controversy abounds and there have been shootings, supposedly instigated by this conflict. Even those sympathetic to emphasizing students' African heritage have been outspokenly opposed (http://detnews.com/menu/stories/45050/htm).
9. Lips (2000) reviews a Merrill Lynch & Co. report that foresees a 13 percent growth rate, an expansion that compares quite favorably with other industries. At present, the for-profit sector is a mere 10 percent of all education spending, but, according to Merrill Lynch, the continuing demands of a knowledge-driven economy will inevitably create a larger market for firms that can promise effective training.
10. In the New York City co-op market, for example, getting "board approval" is a mysterious process that requires more than financial resources. Prospective tenants can be rejected given their occupation, notoriety, unconventional life-style or traits such as religion. Legally challenging rejection is exceedingly difficult.

5

Skilled Activism

We possess a rich quantitative picture of "political participation." We know how many people of varying traits vote, the incidence of campaign contributions and even the volume of congressional mail, among innumerable other facts. Scholarship, by contrast, is notably silent on its *qualitative* side though academics do occasionally mention "skill" or "expertise" as indispensable resources. In fact, terms like "stupidity" and "blunder" seem notably absent from scholarly portrayals. Yet it is obvious that acumen is as critical as the sheer volume of clamor—it is absurd to count a thinly attended rag tag gathering as identical to imposing black tie dinners inundating office seekers with campaign contributions though participants in both, technically, can be said to be "attending a political event." The 2000 presidential election sadly demonstrated that dutiful citizens might show up to cast votes but their heartfelt efforts may come to naught if befuddled by ballot mechanics.

Political activism portraits almost never appraise the skills of participants. The inevitable awkwardness of faultfinding assessments partially explains this neglect. Condemning apathy is relatively inoffensive compared to labeling activists bunglers dreadfully administering high-sounding crusades. These harsh remarks may be judged disrespectful, regardless of their accuracy, and might invite retribution. Prudence often dictates accentuating virtues when rendering judgments— inept organizations might instead be celebrated for their "fervent ideological commitment."

This unwillingness to judge dexterity is further compounded by the task's great difficulty. Compared to, say, rating the women's movement, ranking movies or mutual funds is a snap.[1] Even something as straightforward as how to calibrate voting proficiency still remains unresolved. Especially discouraging is that competence measurements can rarely be made prior to outcome. For example, countless well-attended, attention-getting rallies denouncing possible U.S. military intervention in Iraq occurred in March 2003. By the standard of attracting media exposure to these popular, well-scripted anti-war outpourings, they were a resounding tour de force. They certainly far outnumbered pro-war rallies. Was this adept activism? Judged by the ultimate outcome—the U.S. did launch military action against Iraq—they failed miserably despite their tactical brilliance, and holding even more anti-war events after hostilities commenced scarcely slowed the pursuit of total military victory. Yet, activists might plausibly insist that opposition may prevent future military ventures.

Overlooking dexterity is a momentous omission and inserting ability into analysis may cast the all-too-familiar "more activism equals greater benefits" claim in an entirely new light. Failure may have zero to do with apathy: *the inept application of available resources, not lethargy, may explain disappointment.* Under such circumstances, improving skills first, not just turning up the volume would be wiser advice. And if requisite talents cannot be mastered, one might encourage eschewing politics altogether rather than continue the failures—additional schooling might be more productive for economic advancement than yet one more maladroit street demonstration.

Given the incredible intricacies of political action (recall chapter 3's brief sampling) and the varied idiosyncrasies across ever-changing situations, qualitatively judging untold crusades à la *Consumer's Reports* automobile ratings is unreachable. Note well, it is formulating a *general framework* regarding wise political investing that is so challenging, not specific, situational assessments. Our quest only highlights certain issues in political activism's qualitative side, it does not provide encompassing ratings standards. We begin by considering the link between skill and the political system since civic aptitude is not a fixed, universal trait, and much depends upon circumstances. We then outline the arduousness of skilled activism, occasionally contrasting it with economic proficiency. Our purpose is less to discourage those about to take the plunge than to counsel against unrealistic expectations. We further consider certain strategies and benchmarks useful for assessing dexterity, and end with some possible shortcuts for those bewildered when contemplating independent strategies.

The Fluid Nature of Political Acumen

If the "game" of politics were uniformly conducted as one might play basketball, determining the necessary capacities for superior performance would be straightforward. Obviously, politics is not only "played" quite differently in diverse settings, but shifting circumstances inevitably make today's deft ploys obsolete. A savvy nineteenth-century urban party boss magically transported to the twenty-first century would discover that his once valuable skills at employing recent immigrants readily marched off to the voting booth almost worthless in today's media oriented, more vigilantly administered politics. Moreover, those who perform inadequately under existing conditions possess a powerful motivation to alter the playing field—photogenic candidates with appalling oratory skills surely welcomed TV where their messages could be advanced sans a single public-speaking engagement.

The catalogue of required proficiencies typically varies as battles develop. For example, in the environmental movement's early stages getting favorable publicity regarding pollution was vital. Those who could publicize the dangers of DDT, contaminated water, and similar alleged disasters were thus key players. As public awareness grew the baton was passed to experts supplying the hard scientific research and those navigating legislative hurdles. With tough environmental laws now the status quo, the campaign becomes more bureaucratic and defensive. Feeding environmental horror stories to the mass media during the early days did not require a huge war chest. Today, skilled fund-raising is absolutely critical to support professional policy analysts monitoring the EPA's performance.

Sufficiency applies to far more than narrow technical skills. It all depends on circumstances—almost anything can be relevant. Drafting a letter to a legislator does, after all, require being able to write cogently and follow instructions regarding where and when to send the missive. Not everyone wishing to pressure government can organize their finances to free up $50 in annual dues to support professional advocates. It is perhaps no accident that in our service-oriented entrepreneurial economy a business now exists to assist those so befuddled that they are unable to organize a credible rally. For around $50 to $175 an hour a firm now exists that will arrange competently performed White House demonstrations for just about any client. This service even has its own website: www.whitehouseprotests.com (*USA Today* 2001).

Nevertheless, the bountifulness of potentially relevant civic skills aside, it is clear that present immensely complicated, slow-moving U.S. political arrangements put a premium on more intellectually demanding capabilities. Moreover, accomplishment may involve dozens of diverse interests locked in endless negotiations so perseverance is vital. The amount of technical material to be mastered even for the simplest endeavor is enormous. The graduation day speech image of outraged good-hearted citizens spontaneously being energized to accomplish instant political victory against evil forces is almost always folklore fantasy. To be sure, even the most inarticulate can riot and pelt the police with bottles to express displeasure with law enforcement. But, moving from that single episodic undemanding action to instituting the desired policies (assuming that remedies exists) requires far greater proficiency. Try formulating police recruiting standards that cull out those prone to excessive violence.

Perplexities Awaiting Future Activists

Admonitions for greater involvement are oddly silent about the potential pitfalls awaiting those embracing political solutions. It is tacitly assumed that once energized, participants will (somehow) navigate the awaiting obstacles. To appreciate just how formidable this journey can be, consider the divergence between pursuing civic aims and daily economic behavior. For one, government regulations galore insure minimal marketplace quality. Dangerous products and schemes do occasionally slip though, but untold agencies serve as watchdogs, and harmed consumers enjoy ample legal recourse against fraud. Non-governmental experts, e.g., newspaper advice columnists, shopping guides, further assist consumers to avoid lemons. Woe to the pharmaceutical company that sells dangerous medications—this would be a bonanza for the sensationalist mass media and ambitious lawyers.

By contrast, political charlatans escape government supervision regarding their chicanery unless they act illegally, and even then, a certain amount of malfeasance is tolerated. No statute prevents demagogues from fleecing naïve supporters by promising castles-in-the-sky schemes. While federal regulators would ban dishonest business claims or even jail chronic deceivers, the First Amendment vigorously *protects* political sects regardless of foolishness. Nor are activist leaders constrained by ethical codes akin to the strictures limiting doctors or lawyers. Imagine suing a leader of one's organization who squandered millions wildly demanding absolutely free government-supplied medical care without raising taxes? "Political malpractice" is not a crime regardless of how ruinous the impact.

Compare the information available to would-be political recruits versus financial investing. Professional advice regarding the latter overflows at bookstores, the Net, free seminars, and at thousands of neighborhood investment firms and banks anxiously soliciting clients. While this industry has its share of swindlers, and nothing prohibits inept amateurs from hawking dubious tips, financial advise-giving is tightly regulated to insure substantial competence. Licensed stockbrokers, Certified Financial Planners and others in this industry must pass multiple grueling examinations before plying their trade. The industry itself monitors performances, and this information is readily available at zero cost to potential users. If anything, it requires effort *not* to receive informed counsel when building a retirement account, purchasing stocks, or buying a house.

Compared to those seriously seeking financial advice, "how to" books are unlikely to be helpful. To be sure, these guides do exist—notable examples would include *How to Win in Washington* (Wittenberg and Wittenberg 1994), *The Activist's Handbook* (Shaw 1996), and *A Citizen's Guide to Politics in America* (Rubin 2000) plus several others. They offer upbeat accounts of ordinary people mobilizing to take on the establishment. The drawback is that their counsel, while undoubtedly sound, is far too general. For example, *The Activist's Handbook* (Shaw 1996) offers a first-hand account of several actual successful battles involving San Francisco's poor, and concludes that formulating a clever strategy is fundamental. Yet, just how specific strategy is to be developed in myriad circumstances is never explicated—it is just the leader's responsibility to execute this formidable task. The importance of keeping followers abreast of events is likewise reiterated, but this is far easier said then done in a world where political apathy is pervasive. Sad to say, this advice is little more than a collection of vacuous admonitions than a useful how-to manual.

Consumer choices are also relatively structured vis-à-vis political options. A supermarket offers immense variety, but within each product category, selection is constrained. Catsup shoppers can only choose among a few proven brands and sizes, and debacles are ex-

tremely unlikely. Those seeking new consumer protection legislation by contrast confront a bedazzlement of opportunities, some of
which may initially appear irrelevant though, in fact, may be quite
pertinent (e.g., opponents of government regulations). And evaluating these multiple alternatives—as we noted above—can be exasperating compared to visiting neighborhood groceries. Consumer
behavior also tends to be routine and thus amenable to learning—if
a novel catsup brand tastes terrible, just revert to reliable Heinz. Political engagement, by contrast, tends to be episodic and less structured with the outcomes beyond immediate experience, at least for
those habitually on the sidelines. Would-be activists seldom enjoy
the luxury of daily comparison-shopping excursions necessary to
correct mistakes.

There are also different standards regarding "customer satisfaction" when political aims are pursued. Expectations about what politics is immediately supposed to produce are often far lower than
when buying merchandise. Paying fifty dollars for a defective car
muffler would probably be totally unacceptable and trigger a demand for an on-the-spot refund. By contrast, the identical sum yearly
given to those advocating some whimsical high-minded scheme may
be a tolerable self-indulgence, even providing a sense of self-satis-
faction. Decades might pass before futility sinks in and requesting a
refund is unthinkable. Market discipline is virtually unknown in much
of grassroots politics since typically nothing tangible is directly provided by the transaction. Normally sensible people need not worry
about losing their day jobs when chasing ephemera

The hyper-fragmented, decentralized nature of American politics
further complicates matters. Literally thousands of governments,
regulatory boards, semi-independent agencies, and commissions can
have their finger in the policymaking pie and this intervention varies across issues. Just tracking existing policy is a full-time job. Even
among sophisticated professionals, the varied mixtures of local, state,
and national administrative supervision makes exerting effective
influence a challenge. Further add the intertwining of legislative and
judicial control (which is seldom unified in purpose) and navigating
this divergent landscape becomes even more confusing. If this were
insufficient, try deciphering the arcane, highly technical language
informing government policymaking. Savvy involvement obviously
demands extraordinary diligence.

To appreciate the complicatedness of converting "being involved politically" into *proficient* engagement, consider the options faced by the economically disadvantaged when instructed that civic mobilization comprises the superior pathway for uplift. To recall chapter 3's encompassing option menu, everything from smashing windows of predatory merchants to investment clubs rewarding socially conscious firms might be pursued. A website or newsletter depicting local misery to catch the media's attention is also feasible. Nor is a potential activist confined to any single ideological viewpoint—even free market champions insist that their deregulations nostrums will conquer poverty, and this choice cannot be tersely dismissed. What about non-political entities like churches or social groups that can be re-directed toward civic causes or serve as rivals to government intervention? Maybe the church should establish a low-cost cooperative grocery rather than spend hours inveighing for government crackdowns on predatory merchants? After enlisting, is an occasional gift and reliance on professional judgment sufficient, or is personal intervention indispensable? Might this meddling disrupt? How is this participatory role to be decided? Does it depend on time available to activists or the qualifications of professionals? How much money and other resources does the organization genuinely need? As with a collapsing stock, when should an activist "bail out" of politics altogether and pursue aims elsewhere or non-politically?

Those counseling "activism" seldom appreciate the thorny policy alternatives awaiting those anxious to enlist, regardless of tactical choices. Even zealots cannot investigate every credible option and pursue a multi-front campaign, so narrowness is essential to avoid desultory wastefulness. To express solidarity with everyone and everything to "end to poverty" hardly comprises brilliance. What, for example, might be the *most* fruitful vehicle to end indigence for those attracted to government intervention? Should better schooling be demanded in light of the schooling-income connection? If so, which of dozens of alleged educational reforms, for example, vouchers, job training, mandatory pupil testing, more stress on basic skills, upgrading teacher preparation, should one demand from officialdom? Or, as other experts advise, are family assistance programs key since poverty and single-parent homes are linked? Which family assistance policy—early childcare intervention, food stamps, subsidized housing, among untold others—is primary, or is some judicious combination vital? What about tax breaks for businesses to re-relocate in high unemployment areas? Should government be pressured to combat crime and drugs since these impede economic progress? Abundant other possibilities (including violent ones) could also be added to this potential remedy compendium and, critically, each requires different political stratagems depending on fluid circumstances.

The very permeability of U.S. politics puts a premium on flexible astuteness. The openness that permits one newcomer entry *also* facilitates involvement of new enemies or at least rivals for the same potential clients. As in Newtonian physics, action begets action in the opposite direction. A sudden influx of the indigent badgering government will doubtless bring counter-mobilizations among those threatened by tax increases as well as new sympathizers anxious to get on the bandwagon. What has permitted liberal civil rights groups seeking state intervention on behalf of African Americans to flourish has also facilitated the creation of Black Americans for Family Values, Center for New Black Leadership, and Brotherhood Organization for a New Destiny (a religious organization focusing on black family issues) opposing government-centered solutions. An African American contemplating jumping into the fray fifty years ago had it far easier. He or she had a mere three or four notable organizations to select from. Today, this potential recruit might spend hundreds of hours "auditioning" innumerable claimants seeking his or her backing. And propagation is unstoppable as the clamor for civic engagement grows louder and modern technology reduces market entry costs.

One feature of the confusing civic landscape deserves special mention—discerning an organization's true purpose from its name. Trademark-protected brands solve this problem in consumer economics. Hunt's catsup cannot legally rename itself "Hinetz" to lure unsuspecting shoppers preferring Heinz. In politics, however, seductive (if not deceptive) labeling is permissible to attract the unwary and, plausibly, signifies skill, not illegality. Nor do "truth in labeling" laws compel political organizations to describe their agendas or finances candidly—the wealthy can cleverly incorporate themselves as "Friends of the Poor." Imposing legal transparency standards would surely be judged inappropriate, surely impractical, if not unconstitutional.

Consider two environmental organizations, the National Wilderness Institute (NWI) and the National Wildlife Federation (NWF).

Despite sound-alike names, they offer sharply opposing solutions—the NWI endorses private stewardship while the NWF is more government intervention oriented. Similarly, how is one to surmise that Physicians for Social Responsibility is anti-gun while Doctors for Responsible Gun Ownership is pro-gun? Other groups from all points on the ideological spectrum are so generically labeled or bedecked in glittering generalities that discerning their true intent requires tedious research. What does "educational reform" or "fair taxation" really mean to the casual political shopper? How can honest organizations be separated from shrewdly branded frauds? With thousands of groups freely using alluring catch phrases, some potential enlistees will inevitably be befuddled or even inadvertently support their enemies.

In short, compared to consumer economics, shopping the "civic marketplace" can be exasperating, and little presupposes that these impediments are surmountable. The First Amendment also forbids government intervention to prevent foolishness save the most extreme instances (e.g., converting campaign contributions into personal funds). If life prior to strict consumer protection legislation foretells what might happen with sudden influxes of the less sophisticated seeking political remedies, pessimism only deepens. Widespread gullibility, a hankering for impracticable or perilous solutions is unavoidable, not unlike the days when snake oil elixirs seduced innocents. If Ph.D.'s have difficulty untangling myriad educational reforms, how are novices to resist frauds or hopeless quests resting on ambiguous evidence? One can only wonder, then, why those who counsel engagement remain so optimistic, especially regarding the likelihood of success among those challenged by the less demanding economic marketplace.

From Obstacles to Savvy Politicking

Though we have insisted that effective engagement is frustratingly complicated, it is by no means impossible—in fact, countless people earn handsome livelihoods producing stellar results. Nevertheless, the sheer variability of political battles and varied combatants precludes elucidating easy-to-follow formulae guaranteed to work under widely varied circumstances. Alas, *The Complete Idiots Guide to Political Power* is probably not on the horizon. At best we can offer certain general considerations conducive to victory, factors that hardly insure astute success though disregarding them surely invites defeat. Many choices will seem rather obvious to those following political conflicts but, truth be told, they are often ignored.

Goals are the obvious place to begin—what, *exactly*, is to be accomplished? This is no trifling issue since one must pick specific battles and establish priorities in any quest. A feasibility checklist seems almost self-evident. Aims should be legally achievable, should not demand impossible-to-assemble resources, have some chance of succeeding against foreseeable resistance and, ultimately, will likely deliver the desired benefits. Specificity of objective is also an asset—triumphs are far more likely to come to those focusing narrowly (e.g., centrally registering firearms) versus waging a broad, multi-front war (e.g., combating violent crime). Defending the status quo is also an advantage given the constitutional proclivity toward gridlock. It is pointless to pursue quixotic objectives requiring wholesale legal upheavals. As the old adage goes, politics is the art of the possible. No doubt, thousands of well-established lobbyists and causes fulfill these minimal requirements if only because financial supporters refuse to chase utopias.

Knowing what is feasible under existing political conditions is part of this equation—Should one settle for a half a loaf or a quarter of a loaf? Consider, for example, the tactics of those who oppose abortion. This is an exceedingly difficult quest given that this right rests on judge-made law that has withstood repeated challenges and is thus difficult to overturn directly. Public support for abortion is also quite substantial. For opponents of abortion, a direct assault on *Roe v. Wade* is probably futile, so it may better to nibble at the edges if reversing the clock is one's goal. That understood, beginning in the 1990s many within the anti-abortion movement lowered their sights and instead sought state legislative limits, not outright bans, a far more pragmatic approach though still short of the ultimate goal. For example, abortion foes pushed legislations that permitted abortion only to save a mother's life and this restriction has made some headway though still firmly resisted by pro-abortion forces. Anti-abortion activists heeding poll data also redirected their efforts away from converting hardcore opponents and instead focused on those holding ambivalent views (Salhotz 1990).

The ability to select aims *astutely* cannot be exaggerated. As our example of tackling poverty briefly illustrated, activists always face myriad options in pursuing general goals. Consider legalizing marijuana. What is the shrewdest pathway? Surely boisterous street demonstrations to "repeal all prohibitions" will fail given widespread opposition though these may be psychologically gratifying. Working to pass sweeping state initiatives (as has been done several times in California) is also probably doomed given the legal supremacy of federal anti-drug laws. A far more intelligent aim is to work for decriminalizing (though not totally legalizing) personal uses of small amounts, a policy that succeeded in places like Oregon where being caught with tiny quantities is now equivalent to receiving a parking ticket. A bird-in-hand campaign here may well outshine a more grandiose crusade.

Language can be critical since the "wrong" terminology needlessly exacerbates the quest. At a minimum, one wants to secure social acceptability and gain the moral high ground. It is no accident that abortion proponents speak in terms of a "woman's right to choose" versus, say, conveniently terminating accidental pregnancies. Chapter 8's depiction of the highly successful battle for increased government AIDS funding will show that many gay rights organizations wisely downplayed their sexuality—they created the Human Rights Campaign, not People for Homosexuality. Gays also went to great lengths to avoid anything suggestive of offbeat sexual practices. The battle was over "saving lives," not sustaining sexual abandon featuring rampant anal intercourse. Nomenclature can be decisive in fundraising—who wants to write checks for causes promoting unsavory or illegal behavior?

Assessing enemies is also fundamental, and amateurs often mistakenly minimize this element since their aims appear so laudable. After all, who can argue against world peace or cleaner air? Such disregard invites failure—political disputes always have opposing combatants. Obviously, any proposal that requires spending public money will automatically draw resistance from anti-tax forces (including elected officials anxious about tax hikes) plus existing public funding recipients jealously guarding their turf. Politics is a method for dividing *scarce* resources, and the supply of praiseworthy causes *always* far exceeds public generosity. "It is a wonderful proposal, and I'm sure it would be most beneficial, but we can't afford it" is a rejoinder not easily dismissed. Even purely symbolic, cost-free requests will usually generate opposition if it is of any con-

sequence or might prove to be a future embarrassment. Political careers can be made or lost over such non-financial issues as displaying Confederate symbols on state flags. Below-the-radar resistance
is easily overlooked. Nearly invisible tax resistance will be threatened against those pushing the government to wildly expand social
welfare, regardless of how many decent people are falling into in
dire straits. Recall the stealthy nature of opposition to black civil
rights depicted in chapter 3.

Balancing this appreciation of likely enemies is counting up potential supporters, and not every worthy endeavor attracts allies. This
is especially important for campaigns in which majorities must be
fashioned across innumerable settings. If, for example, the objective calls for budgetary increases, who will also benefit from this
fresh public treasury largess? This need not be immediately apparent. Untold school reforms remain highly popular despite their unsure effectiveness since they attract countless partners anxious to
join the lucrative bandwagon. Parents seeking smaller classes, for
example, gain immediate support from powerful teachers unions,
politically well-connected building construction contractors, school
equipment firms, plus countless others who will profit from this particular fix. The 1960s "War on Poverty" prevailed against doubters
when it created a sprawling constituency of beneficiaries located in
nearly every congressional district. Even as failures mounted, economic incentives sustained the effort. On the other side of the coin,
as chapter 7 will show, those battling certain diseases with soaring
death tolls often fail to attract friends willing to pry loose government backing.

Nevertheless, such down-to-earth, "be modest" guidance is valuable only to a point. The opposite pathway *sometimes* works. American history abounds with victorious campaigns that rejected this pragmatic counsel. If everything were dictated by "reasonableness," slavery might still exist while women and African Americans would be
unable to vote. The accomplished civil rights movement undoubtedly appeared unpromising when it commenced, and a 1920s *Consumer Reports*-like assessment of the NAACP might have concluded,
"Totally unpromising, separation of the races is natural and irreversible, and only fanatics want racial integration—better try making
progress elsewhere or just forget about it." Similarly, when environmentalism first attracted notoriety in the early 1960s many savvy

observers probably dismissed it as hopeless kookiness. Transformations can require decades, so bleak prospects or momentary setbacks need not confirm wastefulness. Today's activists striving toward eliminating pervasive gender inequality might resemble those 1970s investment visionaries cannily buying Microsoft or Intel before their value soared.

Though abstractly formulating sensible, manageable objectives is unproblematic, this can become troublesome in the heat of battle. Displacement all too easily afflicts even the most admirable causes, particularly when primary quests are problematical and time consuming. To appreciate this seductiveness even among the sophisticated, consider a 1992 situation involving Stanford University students, surely among the smartest of the smart. In the wake of an all-white jury rendering an innocent verdict for the white police officers who beat Rodney King (who is black), students organized a demonstrations centering on inner-city poverty and despair. When 1,000 angry protestors marched into downtown Palo Alto, several businesses closed for the day fearing violence (quite reasonable in light of events elsewhere). Copeland's, a sporting goods store, took the extra precaution of quickly boarding up its windows. One demonstration leader then fervently denounced Copeland's precautions as "a huge insult" to the Stanford community and demanded a boycott (Sacks and Thiel 1998: 180). A rally against inner-city conditions thus became directed against a hyper-cautious merchant catering to upscale shoppers. Needless to say, the link between this boycott, the King beating, and inner-city poverty (the rally's ostensible theme) is murky, at best.

What invites pseudo accomplishment is that substitutes are often virtually indistinguishable from genuine political advancement and, at least in some instances, absolutely integral to (eventually) accomplishing the end goal. "Doing something" regardless of its ultimate value may also be convenient and satisfy psychologically needs for measurable accomplishment without the sought-after benefits. Leaderships desire to retain their positions regardless of solid successes further makes this replacement alluring. Political organizations often need to justify patron support and so ineffective organizations seeking donations might boast of well-attended rallies, barrages of mail directed to legislatures or similar visible, readily counted behaviors. Always implied—but rarely proven—is that this bustle must "somehow" breed clout. If all else fails, assert that this mighty struggle intimidates potential enemies or that circumstances would be ten times worse if nothing were done.

Yet, separating distractions from core missions can be complicated. Politics is not economics where a single, agreed upon book-keeping standard (namely profit) exists. While a business promoting unpopular merchandise will likely go bankrupt and this certifies ineptitude, those Stanford students hassling Copeland's cannot automatically be judged "inexpert." Nothing about civic engagement dictates that goals must be instrumental, realistic, or sensible; self-indulgent goals may be just as bona fide as ameliorating poverty. On a more practical level, perhaps boycotting Copeland's was a necessary precondition for subsequent, more tangibly oriented behavior (e.g., building membership), and in this context, was an adroitly executed act. Or, its true purpose was not publicly known or otherwise admitted.

Closely linked to aims are the tactics selected to pursue these objectives. Again, this linking of ends and means would hardly appear to be rocket science. Knowledgeable calculations would target the appropriate decisions-makers, the best ways to exert influence, how enemies are to be overcome, timing, and the multitude of other details familiar to experienced practitioners. Reasonable people might disagree on particulars, and much will depend on unique circumstances, but certain tactics can only be characterized as incompetent. For example, while the link between raising aample campaign funds and victory is axiomatic, misguided solicitations from troublesome donors, even if financially successful, can be the kiss of death. The botched 2002 reelection campaign of Rep. Cynthia McKinney (D-GA) well demonstrated this point. Specifically, in the wake of 9/11, she made a determined high-profile effort to solicit funds from Muslim organizations and individual Muslim donors, some with shady, controversial reputations for ties to terrorism. Given that House incumbents are overwhelmingly reelected, and more mundane funding sources were readily available, this novel, risky outreach was hardly preordained, particularly since scarcely any of her constituents were Muslims or favored pro-Muslim policies. McKinney's admitted coziness with pro-Palestinian groups also provoked out-of-state Jewish donors who generously assisted her Democratic primary opponent. In the end, her misguided fund-raising backfired and cost McKinney her job despite all the money it brought in.

The importance of selecting the best, not just any tactic, among multiple options cannot be exaggerated. Consider, for example, the situation in the late 1950s when racial segregation of public facilities in the South was the law. How could these practices be overcome, especially given the historic powerlessness of African Americans and their economic vulnerability? Possible responses ranged from the violent (e.g., arson, rioting), to more peaceful routes such as petitioning government to overturn these Jim Crow laws. The tactic wisely chosen was the then obscure peaceful "sit-in" in which black college students politely requested service at a lunch counter, and when denied service, simply refused to leave. The immediate (and predictable) reaction was that frenzied, ill-mannered whites verbally abused well-dressed, courteous and self-restrained students. Civil rights leaders also insured that these dramatic one-sided confrontations were widely and sympathetically publicized. An outpouring of national support for integrating public facilities soon ensued, and in 1964 a national civil rights law was enacted. It is no exaggeration to label this tactic as innovative and brilliant. One can only imagine if, for example, these protestors had dressed in outlandish costumes and instead abused the waitresses when denied service.

It is also true, however, that yesterday's stellar ploys may grow inappropriate as enemies grow resistant, threats that were once intimidating grow irrelevant. The continued reliance on lawsuits by civil rights groups to achieve educational equality well illustrates this possible obsolescence. Beginning in the 1930s, litigation proved vital in gradually undermining the legal basis of racially segregated education—after all, judges certainly had the power to overturn Jim Crow laws, so seeking judicial relief made perfect tactical sense. By the 1970s, dozens of rulings had accomplished this legal revolution and judges further ordered school districts to expand school budgets or bus students to overcome past inequities. Similar court-based strategies gained voting rights and access to public accommodations. Litigation obviously was an investment strategy with an exceptionally high rate of return. Nevertheless, despite these courtroom victories, black students generally lagged behind whites academically regardless of school racial mix, lavish compensatory funding, or myriad other court-ordered interventions.

How might equality-of-results advocates now proceed? Should litigation be continued in light of past accomplishments? Or should fresh strategies be undertaken, for example, lobbying for vouchers or even abandoning politics altogether by organizing library trips? In this context of myriad rival means, consider the potential usefulness of a proposed Seattle, Washington NAACP branch lawsuit against the Seattle Public Schools to compel (on 14th Amendment grounds) local administrators to bridge both learning and classroom discipline gaps (Denn 2001). Now, if the suit was successful and disparities persisted, teachers and administrators risked judge-administered fines or other punishments. Is this threatened litigation a sensible continuation of a proven asset deployment strategy? This choice is consequential since going to court is expensive, time-consuming, and entails substantial opportunity costs.

Though the future can never be foreseen entirely, it seems unlikely that judges can legally coerce teachers to close learning discrepancies that have resisted countless past (and quite costly) efforts. This tactic assumes (debatably) that schools could perform successfully if they "had to" under judicial supervision. It is further presumed that these academic disparities are entirely school controlled versus lying beyond the reach of education. This legal tactic is also fraught with potential pitfalls. Would teachers giving lower grades to African Americans be fined or jailed for violating judicial orders? What if this dilemma were "solved" by lowering the achievement scores of whites? Would this constitute a "success"? And this Seattle NAACP approach is commonplace nationally as civil rights groups continue to underscore judicial intervention to achieve academic gains.

An example of proficient adaptation comes from the religious fundamentalist movement that first surfaced during the 1980s. Despite its initial notoriety (including the emergence of such high-profile leaders as Pat Robertson) plus attracting many conservative Christian followers, by the early 1990s it had bogged down politically. Worse, its strident pious rhetoric often made it a liability when endorsing candidates. Movement leaders then discovered from surveys that the issues they had repeatedly stressed, namely the hot button topics of abortion, homosexuality, and school prayer resonated poorly among both the general public and born-again evangelicals. The movement's message was then re-directed away from vague, emotion-tinged religious fundamentalism and toward specific "safe" policies, for example, reducing taxes to give families more spending money and reducing crime, that would promote a more family-positive environment (Reed 1993). The upshot of this refocus was a rebirth as conservative Christians shed theirs fanatical "extremist" image and entered mainstream politics. By 2000 the movement was playing a major role in the Republican Party.

The alignment between tactics and resources is obviously critical. Simply put, an absolutely brilliantly scheme may come to naught unless participants possess the requisite capacities. An environmental group trying to convince government of its views *must* master the arcane science necessary to make plausible arguments to experts. Without this knack, activists are unlikely to rise above being a dismissible nuisance. Similarly, if a campaign is to be a long one, enlistees should have the requisite patience, or at least be able to hire those who will fight this protracted struggle. Political conflict abounds with examples of people whose appetites outstripped their resources, and this mismatch would have been obvious had this quest been a business seeking a bank loan.

What may seem like petty tactical details can be deceptive, and participants may not be able to fulfill their responsibilities regardless of their enthusiasm. "Minor" details can turn out to be major—recall how many Floridians "lost" their vote in 2000 when those mobilizing voters failed to explain the mechanics of the infamous "Butterfly" ballot. Consider generating publicity, one of the most basic and essential political skills. There are countless ways to attract attention—issuing press releases, holding a newsworthy event, securing celebrity endorsements, and so on. What makes matters difficult is that innumerable rivals are simultaneously competing for the same limelight to pierce clutter facing an overwhelmed public. Even with a fairly specific cause, there are multiple outlets for one's enthusiasm. Skilled political operatives thus know how to draft an eye-catching press release or cultivate close relationships with reporters and editors. They also must appreciate the intricacies of the mass media and how this knowledge can be best utilized (e.g., supply information before, not after, story deadlines), and insure factual accuracy.

Those effortlessly preaching "get involved" seldom appreciate the prodigious skill required for even the simplest *successful* political event. One experienced professional recently outlined the requirements necessary for a small—300-400 people—fund-raiser. She said that one must begin about eight weeks prior to the event, and that it entails approximately 100 necessary steps to be executed in the proper sequence to ensure a profit. These included formulating a budget, inviting appealing speakers, renting hotel rooms, recruiting volunteers for various duties, arranging transportation for invitees, drafting press releases, garnering sponsors, monitoring flight schedules for speakers, sending out thank-you notes, and multiple other tasks to be executed adroitly (Meeks 2003). Messing up at any one stage can spell disaster, and dozens of such events may be required to raise sufficient funds. And, of course, ample funding still does not guarantee victory.

The plethora of political strategies outlined in chapter 4 offers an immense menu, and these choices can be especially valuable to those lacking in-place conventional resources. Not every battle need be fought via the tried and true strategy, if that playing field is disadvantageous. As in "real" war, politics sometimes permits "guerilla" tactics. The hopelessly disorganized need not attempt to choreograph lavish banquets or build enduring national organizations. Recall how partisans of difficult-to-achieve, long-term social change (e.g., feminists) have shifted their efforts into stealth-like education efforts such as Women's Studies courses, re-focusing high school civics textbooks, and similar efforts to mold the views of future generations. Such politicking is undoubtedly a more efficient tactic than, say, badgering legislators with e-mails or holding marches demanding sweeping gender equality. As we also noted in chapter 4, Marxists (and others) have long believed that major upheavals first required altering the underlying culture, and this endeavor may entail such innocuous routes as ideologically shading movie scripts and surreptitiously inserting radical messages in popular music.

On occasion doing nothing may outshine behaving incompetently. Consider a post 9/11 rally held in Brooklyn, NY during 2002 by local people of Arab ancestry (Miniter 2002). Its nominal purpose was to show support for the Palestinian cause against Israel in the hope of redirecting U.S. foreign policy, a tough though not impossible sell given the well-recognized influence of the pro-Israel interests (recall how African Americans during the 1950s still managed to gain popular sympathy despite being a virtually powerless minority). What happened here, however, was a "successful" animated turnout that undoubtedly undermined the rally's nominal objective. Signs were deliberately (and needlessly) provocative, for example, displaying a Star of David (the symbol for Judaism) equaling the Nazi swastika. Another placard said, "Declare Jahad [sic]." Some participants hailed Yasser Arafat, a generally reviled figure in the U.S., as a hero, and characterized Israel as equivalent to South Africa under apartheid. Participants distributed outlandish anti-Semitic conspiratorial literature. Some demonstrators openly blamed Israel for the 9/11 attacks and insisted that the evidence against Osama Bin Laden was "circumstantial." The reporter covering the event generally characterized it as more a pro-terrorism rally than an estimable (though futile) effort to shift U.S. foreign policy. Of course, from the prospective of just enumerating activist behavior without factoring in proficiency, this event is indistinguishable from its opposite.

Shortcut Mechanisms

Our political adeptness account has so far stressed obstacles awaiting individuals about to take the plunge. Nevertheless, the prospects for savvy engagement are not quite so dismal as we have suggested. As in economic activity, personal expertise is often uncalled for when choosing wisely, even when time and knowledge are limited. Shortcuts can reduce—though do not eliminate—many of our depicted obstacles. As one might shop in stores with well-deserved reputations for price and quality, a sensible activist may rationally rely on others to navigate these formidable obstacles.[2]

Working through a major political party is one practical alternative to this bewildering cacophony. For the discouraged "do-it-yourselfer, " this may be the classic, ready-made solution. In an instant, one gains access to ample in-place resources, including access to money and policy expertise that would demand years of hard work to produce independently. Parties also provide invaluable free training in fund-raising, event staging, election law, and other skills. Critically, party influence often translates into power *within* government, a claim that few independent groups—let alone ordinary citizens—can make. Local Democratic and Republican party branches are commonplace, and they typically welcome any and all willing to enlist, including those who may reject some party views. This entrée may require nothing more than looking up addresses in a telephone directory, calling, and then appearing at the next meeting.

This relatively cheap option is particularly attractive to beginners with scant funds or clout.

Even if the party may not initially favor one's position, working from within to sway opinions is a time-honored, not terribly difficult practice. During the 1960s those opposing the Vietnam conflict "captured" countless Democratic state and local organizations by virtue of just arriving on the scene and shouldering responsibilities. Activists successfully pushed their agenda into national prominence though the favored candidate, George McGovern, ultimately lost his bid for the presidency in 1972. Since the 1970s, pro-abortion supporters have insistently transformed the Democratic Party into one of its staunchest advocates and being pro-choice has become the non-negotiable litmus test for potential nationally oriented Democratic candidates. In neither instance did the Democratic Party initially hold a view on these two issues.

Recent political history attests to this party-centered strategy versus a more entrepreneurial, re-invent-the-wheel outsider approach. We have already noted that the Republican Party has increasingly become the home to many fundamentalist Christians, a group initially inclined during the early 1980s to develop their own and now defunct (and largely ineffectual) Moral Majority. Judged by GOP electoral success and the newfound power of evangelicals, this "work-from-within" alliance greatly benefited both sides. Much of the notable influence of African Americans in securing countless government benefits flows from their role as a core Democratic voting constituency, while pro-Israel Jewish groups have likewise become central to Democratic (and more recently, Republican) strategy. Chapter 8 will show that gays are following this time-honored mechanism to gain considerable political influence.

Supporting a preexisting organization that has already solved the quandaries that await clueless novices goes one step further in this strategy. This is particularly relevant for those favoring relatively narrow aims unlikely to generate broad-based followings. There is scarcely a national or local issue that has not attracted the attention of organizations advancing nearly every ideological viewpoint. One compilation in 1995 found some 7,400 national associations with headquarters in Washington, DC. While many represent corporations and business associations, many are geared to ordinary citizens who scarcely realize that they are formally represented in Washington. These include such the YMCA, Parent Teachers Associations, the Boy Scouts, and countless health and religion-oriented charities (Segal 1995). Though many of these groups may seem entirely non-political, they still may pursue political goals. The myriad groups representing disease sufferers (e.g., the American Lung Association, National Kidney Foundation) are often powerful advocates of millions of people needing government health assistance.

These policy-oriented groups can immediately supply off-the-shelf analysis, legal advice, legislative updates, and in-place networks of fellow supports, and nearly everything else necessary to become a formidable participant. Comparable organizations thrive in state capitals and many cities while nationally based groups may assist in creating state or city branches. In the business world this is the equivalent of getting a McDonald's franchise versus developing one's own unique formula for a profitable fast food restaurant. Chapter 3 has already highlighted several attractive options—prestigious law firms taking on pro bono clients and think tanks happy to help ordinary citizens so as to advance their own ideological agendas.

Today's "information explosion" greatly facilitates this search for organizational assistance. A public library visit would undoubtedly supply several compendiums of these advocacy groups. Among these might be *Political Marketplace USA* (Kurian and Schultz 1999), *Washington Information Director 2002-2003* (2003), *Encyclopedia of Associations* (Hedblad 2003) *The Left Guide* (1996) and *The Right Guide* (2000) among multiple others. These typically provide thumbnail descriptions, addresses, e-mail contacts, and other details useful for finding a match. Many reference books are also organized geographically. The Web is also an obvious choice in finding professional allies, and entering in a few key policy terms to a search engine such as Google can provide a useful starting point.

To illustrate this abundance, imagine that one were pro-choice on the abortion issue and believed that more could be done to secure this view. A glance at *The Left Guide* (1996) would show some forty-three listed groups, and while many of them are state branches of national organizations, the menu is still considerable. Varied entries include Abortion Rights Mobilization, Catholics for Free Choice, CHOICE, National Abortion Federation, Population Council, the Pro-Choice Resource Center, among others. Judged by size, type of advocacy, resources, and almost any other criteria, this lists comprises a virtual supermarket of options (abortion opponents can be similarly found in *The Right Guide*). Going on to the Net will provide additional possibilities and these listing sometimes include up-to-date announcements regarding events and various political battles.

Advocacy organizations sometimes also offer various hands-on training seminars that stress the usual nuts-and-bolts elements of civic engagement, everything from how to organize non-violent demonstrations to savvy ways to contact public officials. These generally come with an ideological slant, and may require fees and travel expenses, but this off-the-shelf instruction will undoubtedly outshine starting from scratch or even consulting "how-to" books though there can be no assurances that lessons will prove 100 percent effective. Again, the Net offers superb opportunities to find these resources. The Leadership Institute, a conservative group, holds activist schools teaching such subjects as using direct mail, running fund-raisers and how to recruit volunteers (www.LeadershipInstitute.org) while a trip to www.casagordita.com/tools.htm (accessed via "political activism training" on Google) provides countless educational opportunities for those on the left ranging from promoting vegetarianism to working for peace and social justice. African Americans can upgrade their skills through The Training Institute for Leadership Enrichment, sponsored by Black Women Organized for Political Action (www.bwopa.org).

The Net also offers immensely valuable advice for those inclined toward more independent action. Rooting through what might be generated by using "lobbying, Washington DC" or a comparable phrase, will be various sites offering concrete advice to would-be activists. At www.serviceleader.org one finds a cornucopia of links that offer detailed lobbying advice. Particularly useful are compilations of federal tax laws regulating lobbying, sources of professional legal advice, and how to preserve a group's charitable tax status while still engaging in politicking. The link to www.igc.org offers suggestions on such topics as group fund-raising and tactics. Multiple links also detail how the net itself can be utilized for political purposes.

An even more focused approach is to hire professionals to fight one's battles for a fee. In a matter of weeks one acquires insider experience and instantaneous access that would otherwise require major efforts to assemble independently. An added advantage in going this route is that past efficacy can be realistically assessed. The very fact that the firm continues to hold clients strongly implies effectiveness, and if still uncertain, and one can always ask for tangible proof of worthiness before payment (and past clients might be contacted, too). While nothing can be guaranteed, this is nevertheless a far cry from heeding some self-appointed community activist whose assurances of benefits-to-come are little more than glittering rhetoric.

These specialists exist wherever governments are to be found and can champion virtually any agenda, or at least offer advice that amateurs might heed. In 1999 there were some 20,512 registered lobbyists plying their trade in Washington (Stout 1999). The 2002 District of Columbia Yellow Pages listed some 140 lobbying firms and 278 firms specializing in public relations. Navigating this plethora can seem overwhelming but shortcuts readily exist. Policy-oriented organizations will certainly know favorably disposed professional lobbyists and the cost of their services. Digging into websites can be productive. An online search would, for example, uncover Capital Advantage (capitaladvantage.com) that offers such services as consulting, political training, information about Congress, and on-line advocacy tools. At Governmental and Political Associates Consortium (www.gpac.net) one finds a full-service organization employing former government employees to help navigate the Washington maze.

The web is particularly useful for finding policy allies among these options. For example, a Google search using various phrases with "lobbying" in it would find a site—www.opensecrets.org—that offers a lobbyist database useful for zeroing in on those professionals representing specific policy organizations. Going from "Ideology/ Single Issue" to "Abortion Policy/Pro-choice" brings up several policy groups and the amount each has spent on lobbying. Clicking on Center for Reproductive Law and Policy we find that they employed two firms—Burgess Consulting plus Griffin, Johnson et al. Even the names of the actual lobbyists are provided.

To appreciate the value of this "rent an expert" tactic, consider the acumen of the Choctaw Indians, an 8,800-member tribe. As with many other long-neglected and impoverished Native American groups, multiple alternatives are available to move up the economic ladder via politics. They could, conceivably, follow in the footsteps of African Americans and organize boisterous demonstrations to publicize their plight, organize get-out-the vote drives, or even threaten to disrupt government. Their choice of weapons, however, has been a quite "insider" strategy of generous election campaign contributions ($8.6 million since 1993) and paid lobbyists to protect their grant of sovereign immunity that allows them to run their highly lucrative Silver Star Resort and Casino on the Mississippi River. In 2000-01 they spent $20 million on lobbying, most of which has gone to Jack Abramoff, a top Republican fund-raiser. This below-the-radar approach has proven exceptionally lucrative—federal agencies over a five-year period have lavished some $245 million in aid to the tribe despite their gambling enterprise generating over $100 *million* in annual profits! The tribe even bought a $4.5 million private jet. Stealthy language in obscure legislation has also exempted the Choctaws from all sorts of unwanted federal regulation that adds even more to the bottom line (VandeHei 2000).

Though this account strongly argues in favor of professional outsourcing, this stratagem remains limited. It is an improvement over independently reinventing the wheel, but it cannot be applied to every situation, and still requires considerable dexterity. Helpful information may be readily available but this accessibility is irrelevant if would-be participants lack the motivation, cannot raise the requisite funds, or are befuddled by the choices. Even working through political parties—the most straightforward option—as one's weapon of choice can be quite demanding. After all, meetings must be attended, compatriots mobilized and policy choices coordinated. Financially supporting advocacy organizations or professional experts can also be tricky—there will always be charlatans ready to fleece the gullible. Further, recall our discussion of how organizations can be distracted from their ostensible aims, and how busy-work can be substituted for genuine accomplishment. And not every organization can be trusted to spend donations wisely, and personal corruption is hardly unknown. Even professionally trained doctors and lawyers are not above exploiting clients. All in all, yet one more time we must offer cautions about the link between activism and proficient activism.

Conclusions

Being skilled politically—versus just joining the fray—is exceptionally tricky, far more arduous than day-to-day economic decision-making. Nor is imparting this skill a straightforward task. Rank amateurs can boycott a store that abuses customers to "fight exploitation." Far greater expertise is demanded to guide government's remediation of this unfairness, and unless this difficult-to-formulate advice is supplied, activism may exacerbate conditions—neighborhood businesses may flee rather than operate at a loss if activists insist upon lower prices. There is no guarantee that those drawn to a boisterous Saturday rally will show a similar zest to participate in dense policy discussions come Monday.

Calibrating this expertise is also exceedingly complicated over and above saying that those who succeed are, by definition, capable. Success may also be decades away, so repeated failures are not the last word. This insufficiency is no small impediment for those anxious to invest their time and money wisely. There certainly is no clear-cut textbook formula, and details are forever changing, especially as new enemies join the fray. The awaiting research agenda is substantial; much of our analysis, though sensible, has been ad hoc and illustrative with minimal theory building. If one draws comparisons to how today's business enterprises are appraised, qualitative judgments regarding civic engagement are rather primitive, comparable, perhaps, to the era before double-entry bookkeeping.

Acknowledging these shortcomings does not, however, justify abandoning the task altogether. Rough and ready verdicts are feasible and, more important, necessary. Surely it is arguable whether suing school officials to close racial gaps in educational attainment efficiently utilizes scarce resources. The menu of potentially superior possibilities overflows, for example, using funds otherwise paid to lawyers to hire private tutors. Only if this litigation has some other non-evident goal in mind, for example, publicizing discrimination, might we deem this effort worthwhile but this hidden purpose seems improbable. Ironically, ballpark assessments are undoubtedly commonplace though they may be muted—surely thoughtful participants must have raised qualms about proceeding via litigation versus alternative remedies. It is difficult to believe that this single option outshone all rivals.

It cannot be repeated too often; the dangers in assuming that would-be activists might behave skillfully if only better informed. This optimism invites disappointment, especially when applied to the disadvantaged hoping to leverage political activism to overcome formidable tribulations. Hapless consumers everyday act unwisely though relevant information is readily available. It is unreasonable to anticipate that academic dropouts or those beleaguered by exacting jobs can be transformed when taught dexterous political action. Disgruntled parents delving into "uncomplicated" local school politics must master myriad statutory requirements, public finance, personnel policy, inter-governmental regulations, and untold other pertinent education issues if they are to rise to the level of *capable* participants. Surrounding City Hall to insist on "better schools" and then doing nothing more is not adroit politics no matter how deafening the cries.

The merit of collective, professionally directed intervention is our most sensible advice. The advantages of task specialization and outsourcing are well known in economic behavior, and these principles can also be productively applied to civic life. Our brief tour of shortcuts demonstrated that established organizations, from political parties to lobbyist groups, offer an immense menu of potentially useful options. Make no mistake, individuals acting sporadically *can* be adroit players, but very seldom by being entirely on their own when beginning afresh. It is pointless to struggle at lobbying elusive officials when experienced experts can be hired. Similarly, why attempt to disentangle arcane government regulations when a policy organization might already perform similar services? In sum, those about to put their faith in do-it-yourself political solutions should be forewarned about lurking dangers if tangible results are of the utmost importance.

Notes

1.   Technically this is not true since *Fortune* magazine does periodically rate Washington's top twenty-five lobbyists. Washington insiders make these ratings and only include high-profile organizations with substantial budgets. The results vary by year, but the "Power 25" is predictable, for example, the National Rifle Association, Association of Trial Lawyers, and the AFL-CIO. Unfortunately for the average citizen, however, only a tiny faction of all possible organizations are listed and its focus on success excludes charlatans to be avoided. Birnbaum (2001) explains how these rating were compiled.
2.   We admit that some analysts, for example, Verba, Schlozman, and Brady (1997) take a dim view of paid professionals replacing citizen amateurs. This view, in our estimation, places the intrinsic value of activism ahead of actual accomplishment, a trade-off that at least some would be willing to accept. For those who put a favorable outcome before direct participation, however, the hiring of professionals is a far superior approach.

6

Assessing Impact:
Theoretical and Conceptual Issues

Having examined political activism's qualitative side we now lay the conceptual groundwork for a forthcoming case study assessing pay-offs. Ironically, the accomplishment record appears self-evident, hardly in need of scholarly confirmation, at least for activist disciples. Surely that the wealthy are more engaged in civic affairs than the poor strongly implies—if not proves—a benefit link. That well-connected corporation insiders regularly extract immense government largess further (ostensibly) confirms this relationship. More generally, if engagement fails to deliver, why do sensible people by the millions annually spend untold hours in grassroots politicking? Can so many people be that foolish or improvident? Who can deny that women and, more recently, gays have secured extraordinary progress via political pressure? What about the environmental movement's plain-to-see accomplishments? Thus depicted, the potential gains from civic engagement seem undeniable.

Reality is less conclusive, and those rhapsodizing about this mighty pathway conveniently slight contrary evidence. Participating hardly guarantees victory, and "involvement" concerns accomplishment, not just any impact. A disinterested observer might even argue that repeated failure, not recurring success, is to be expected when trying to extract benefits from a constitutional arrangement famous for inertia. Moreover, defeats are intrinsic to political action so periodic triumphs prove little regarding overall effectiveness. That a gambler occasionally wins big hardly establishes that betting begets wealth. Momentary gains may mask net losses or unpleasant side effects. Environmentalists proud of ending Artic oil exploration should appreciate that these restrictions bring detested higher consumer prices to themselves and hardships to the impoverished elderly relying on cheap energy. Activism is seldom a positive sum contest—anti-tax advocates must suffer when government acquiesces to a new program. Many crusades are studies in relentless defeat. When did a U.S. socialist party last triumph despite thousands of diligent supporters? Political gains can be almost invisibly undermined—tax opponents quietly work "off the books" or ship money offshore to defeat extractive-minded legislatures.

For practical reasons having to do with a robust research literature, our analysis heavily draws from black politics. Note well, though we uncover less-than-claimed success here, this exercise does not dispute the activist contribution to the civil rights agenda. Attention then turns to four theoretical quandaries bedeviling impact assessment: determining causality, calibrating activism productivity, the multiplicity of complex goals sought, and certifying final victory. These tribulations doubtless require decades of careful scrutiny and final verdicts cannot be done by either proclamation. Nightmares await those embracing glib answers.

Uncovering the Impact of Political Activism: Past Approaches

African Americans (or at least most black leaders) have long accentuated civic mobilization as the superior, if not exclusive solution across multiple policy areas. If net positive influence is to be demonstrated anywhere, black politics should be the most preeminent illustration. Two impact-related questions are central: first, can blacks elect fellow blacks, a central African-American mobilization theme; second, and far more critical, does electoral achievement translate into anything beyond racial pride or cosmetic change?

The first query—organizing to gain political office—appears straightforward though the answer is less sanguine than it initially appears. On the upbeat side, since the 1960s African-American voting participation rates have increased substantially and now nearly match those of whites. In the 1996 presidential election, blacks trailed whites by a mere 5.5 percent in turnout, a gap less than half of what transpired in the 1960s. This white-black disparity has also noticeably fallen in off-year elections and registration, an especially significant pattern given the absence of media hype attending these key activities. During the 2000 presidential election, the black share of the vote in the electorally important states of Florida, Tennessee, and Missouri saw dramatic increases, and high turnout elsewhere often tipped the balance to Democratic candidates in statewide races (the *American Enterprise* 2001). Corresponding surges in other election-related activities have paralleled voting. Black churches have emerged as electioneering hotbeds providing registration volunteers, and rides to polling places, among other essential services to boost turnout. Voting cohesion has also been vital—overwhelmingly Democratic or favoring the black candidate in Democratic primaries. This solidity, coupled with high turnout, makes the black vote's net contribution far higher than if support were widely scattered.

A striking upswing in black office holding is plain to see. When the Voting Rights Act became law in 1965, fewer than 500 African Americans held elected office (Williams 1982). By 1970, this figure had reached 1,469 and ten years later it soared to 4,912 (cited in Williams 1982). By 2001, there were some 9,101 elected black officials all told in the U.S. Particularly outstanding was increased House of Representatives membership—up from a tiny handful in the 1960s and 1970s to thirty-nine by 2001 (Bositis 2001). Municipalities saw the most prominent gains—as of May 2001 there were 478 black mayors throughout the U.S., a number sufficient to justify a permanent national organization. America's largest cities—San Francisco, Philadelphia, Dallas, Cleveland, Atlanta, New Orleans, and Detroit among several others—all had black chief executives in 2001. Our three most populous cities—New York City, Los Angeles, and Chicago—were likewise African-American led in recent times. That these triumphs sporadically occurred in cities having few blacks accentuates this accomplishment. Willie Brown, San Francisco's two-term mayor, gained election though blacks comprise just over 10 percent of the city's population. Columbus, Ohio, Minneapolis, Denver, and Dallas demonstrate a similar success pattern.

Do these upbeat numbers demonstrate voter mobilization payoff? Resolution is more complicated than highlighting sporadic election victories. The total context of U.S. electoral politics must also be considered—the applicable measure might be proportionality, not raw numbers. Judged by this standard, African-American advancement is less impressive, even a failure in light of the centrality of electioneering. Specifically, black office holders comprise a mere 1.7 percent of all office holders, not the 12 percent that would come from exact proportionality (Whirter 2000), and nothing foretells an upcoming major increase in electoral advancement necessary to reach statistical equivalence. Today's figures may well be the high water mark, especially given the obstacles to galvanizing the apathetic and lack of African-American population growth. Nor will the post-1970s "blackening" of many urban areas that facilitated black successes likely continue elsewhere. Conceivably, the faster growing Hispanic population, many of whom reside in areas with current black office holders, will soon demand these black-held offices for themselves. Gains may also be temporary—voters sporadically replace black incumbents with non-blacks while black officials can succumb to term limits.

More serious negative news is the continuing disappointment when blacks seek statewide or national office requiring substantial non-black support.[1] To be sure, an occasional black lieutenant governor or state attorney is elected, but top of the ticket success remains elusive. The plain-to-see-fact is that black office holders generally owe their position to preexisting black majorities or, for numerous legislators, federal government-imposed gerrymandering of district boundaries creating so-called majority-minority districts. Absent repeated Justice Department intervention, many of today's black incumbents would be private citizens. Even where black officials represent a largely non-white district, success partially rests on Hispanics or other minorities being legally unable to vote, a condition portending future black decline as these immigrants gain access to the ballot (see, for example, Lubin 1997: 87 on this interrelationship). Evidence also exists that once Hispanics do become a significant electoral factor many will disdain black candidates as rivals for the same benefits (Williams 2003). Mayors Willie Brown (San Francisco) and Sharon Belton (Minneapolis) and other deft coalition builders may be exceptional, not the rule. Black U.S. senators are virtually unknown, and the most recent example, Illinois' Carole Moseley-Braun, benefited from an unusual fractured three-way Democratic primary, and served only a single term before being defeated by a conservative Republican. Black governors have likewise been scarce (only one, Douglas Wilder in Virginia), as are black judges serving on statewide courts.

Nevertheless, black office holders are sufficiently plentiful and this raises the question whether these achievements assist African Americans. What evidence exists for positive effect? Government employment is assuredly an observable reward deliverable by electoral success, and one especially relevant to African Americans given economic circumstances. This is the so-called "spoils system"—to the victor goes the spoils (jobs) whether a lowly toll road collector job or a mighty police commissioner. Empirical studies of this victory-jobs relationship generally show a mixed influence of African-American electoral success. Predictably, abundant black municipal employment is closely associated with black election accession where African Americans far outnumber other racial or ethnic groups (Eisinger 1982). That is, Gary, Indiana and East St. Louis, Illinois, and other largely black cities choose black leaders who, in turn, hire blacks across the board to serve black residents. Though hardly trivial, this relationship does reflect clout.

What about gaining municipal jobs when in the minority? Evidence here varies, and is often murky given unique circumstances (e.g., government structure, local personalities) and the severe impediments to disentangling intertwined causal factors. Eisinger's (1982) analysis drew from two years during the 1970s and reported little impact due to electing black city council members. Having a black chief executive did, however, produce modest positive outcomes through energetic affirmative action hiring. More encouraging for activists are Dye and Rennick's (1981) analyses of forty-two cities with populations greater than 25,000. Here electing blacks to the city council did generate employment gains, including higher administrative positions. Confirmations of this city council's role (apart from having a black mayor) also come from studies by Mladenka (1989) and Kerr and Mladenka (1994). These (and comparable) studies all reiterate that population size is absolutely critical—African Americans are less likely to land municipal jobs when black officials govern a largely white city. Clearly, talent pool size may outshine politics in filling city positions.

The "black power" and municipal jobs link can get bewildering as additional factors are taken into consideration and the data are statistically manipulated. In Santoro's (1995) analysis of 100 cities with over 100,000 in population in 1986, the presence of black mayors or black city councilors had no direct impact on the presence of comprehensive affirmative action plans (a vital factor in black employment). What apparently mattered—again—was the percent of the city's black population plus civil rights organization vitality.

The role of intermediary factors in this equation is further demonstrated by a study of ten California cities where blacks comprised a significant population element (Browning, Marshall and Tabb 1984). Gaining entrance to decision-making—being a "player" versus a bystander—was critical here over and above raw numbers. When this occurred, more blacks were appointed to various commissions, cities hired more minority contractors, police review boards were established along with similar initiatives desired by African-American residents. Joyce's (1997) analysis of black advancement in New York City's versus Chicago's civil service confirms that numbers must be combined with deft politicking to achieve tangible victories. A similar rapid transformation from bystanders to key players occurred in Atlanta when Maynard Jackson was elected as the city's first black mayor in 1973. Within five years of his election, the black percent of the city's workforce went from 38.1 percent to 55.6 percent and, most notably, the black share of professional positions climbed from 15.2 percent to 42.2 percent (Bayor 2001).

A more indirect measure of the black electoral clout-municipal employment link focuses more on the general role of blacks in city politics. That is, votes for competing whites may be sufficiently decisive to bring city jobs as a reward for electoral fidelity. An example of this indirect influence concerns black municipal employment in New York City since the 1960s when blacks first emerged politically. Between the early 1960s and 1990, the black proportion of the municipal work force soared from 21 percent to 35 percent (and blacks in 1990 made up about 28 percent of the city's population). These jobs further encompassed all levels, including managerial ones, not just menial positions such as sanitation worker (Waldinger 1992a, 1992b cited in Fainstein and Fainstein 1996).

In fact, government employment has generally grown indispensable to blacks, a situation reflecting both mushrooming political activism and the absence of private sector opportunities. Between 1972/3 and 1990, the black proportion of the government work force at all levels (excluding postal employees) rose from 14 percent to 17 percent. By comparison, only 9 percent of the private sector workforce in 1990 was African American and, significantly, the wage gap was greater in the private than public sector. This migration into government jobs has been essential for the creation of the black middle class, a trend seemingly growing with time (Fainstein and Fainstein 1996).

What about the policy impact? Does black accession to power bring better schools, safer streets, and untold other government-supplied amenities? The "before-after" format in which local services rendered to blacks are examined following black political empowerment is one especially useful approach to uncovering possible impacts. Several studies of Green County, Alabama, a county evolving from white to black dominated in a mere six years, clearly confirmed the policy value of capturing political office (Coombs et al. 1977; Perry 1980). Blacks now became more willing to contact local officials regarding grievances, law enforcement became less abusive, and reports of police brutality declined post election success. The local atmosphere regarding race relations also improved and, most notably, the federal government suddenly showered the county with improved health initiatives, newly constructed public works facilities and various social welfare projects aimed at the indigent. Private sector progress (as well as public school desegregation) was, however, virtually nil. Attempts to attract private industry to Green County likewise came up empty.

But, if one thrives by the vote, one can also suffer by the vote. When Washington's largess dried up in the mid-1970s, public sector jobs for poorer blacks largely disappeared though middle-class positions did remain. Significantly, the civil rights activists initially instrumental in securing these benefits were themselves ousted in the mid-1980s by a bi-racial coalition of better-educated citizens upset over bureaucratic bumbling and cronyism. Even a major revenue producing project (a racetrack) once hailed as a great accomplishment of black political clout soon symbolized the ineptitude of early reformers (Edds 1987: ch. 9). Overall, the new political power's principle benefit was to trigger federal assistance, not transform local conditions outside of the physical legacy of the public works projects, and even then, the benefits were fleeting.[2]

Keech (1968) offers a case study of two small cities in the 1960s when African Americans first flexed their political muscle. Durham, North Carolina and Tuskegee, Alabama both saw material benefits for blacks expand as blacks mobilized though outcomes varied by local circumstances. Law enforcement relations improved (including court proceedings) in both instances, and blacks gained entrance to varied commissions and boards necessary to gain better municipal services. In Tuskegee, political empowerment brought freshly paved streets, upgraded garbage service, and improved recreational facilities that were at least officially racially integrated (some comparable Durham efforts fell short but this largely reflected the direct personal costs these amenities required). And, unlike Green County, progress in Durham also occurred outside of government with the passage of anti-discrimination laws and an upsurge in private sector employment. All in all, gains were tangible and highly visible though, on the ledger's other side, enduring economic and social inequality remained untouched and these shifts often flowed from threats of federal action, not political pressure by local activists.

The last "before-after" design example is Button's (1989) study of six Florida communities that spanned the earliest days of the civil rights era to the mid-1980s, a period when black civil rights were an uncontestable fact. Button reports a fairly substantial range of outcomes over this period. In some communities political power arrived fairly early; in others this required decades. Equally relevant, civic relations between whites and blacks shifted over time across myriad patterns ranging from black apathy to bi-racial cooperation to black domination. Plainly, like rain after a storm, civic influence follows the peculiar indigenous contours that reflect history, economic resources, and all else that distinguishes one locality from the next. Still, variations aside, all communities moved forward in black participation in civic affairs, and the civil rights movement was indispensable to this progress. Predictably, gaining key offices was especially notable where blacks enjoyed the numerical edge.

More relevant for day-to-day life, these political shifts brought upgraded municipal services—adequate police and fire protection, regularly maintained paved streets, better parks and recreation, increased city employment (especially police and fire personnel) and multiple other government-supplied amenities. This improvement was especially beneficial given the second-class service traditionally received by African Americans and their relative greater reliance on public services. To be sure, not every outreach evolved as intended (e.g., nominally integrated recreational areas often remained segregated in practice) and low maintenance budgets periodically reduced the value of neighborhood parks. Problems also occurred with shifting city personal into black neighborhoods versus constructing capital-intensive facilities.

Nevertheless, a by now familiar pattern emerges when moving beyond basic tangible gains. Progress in the private sector was less notable though mixed—integration is more common in movie theaters than restaurants. Much of this also reflected economic factors—the unemployed can hardly be expected to join posh country clubs. Of pivotal importance, however, was the minor progress in private employment beyond traditional menial positions. Again, this undoubtedly at least partially reflects the difficulty of imposing rapid changes quickly versus overt discrimination—gaining professional education takes years, and sudden job vacancies cannot create skilled workers. Even so, after combining all these pluses and minuses, only modest socio-economic advancement transpired. Decades after the first successful political challenges, blacks still remained at the bottom economically (and many still remained impoverished) though black-white wage gaps had diminished and a black middle class had emerged. To repeat, tangible gains were real and enduring, but racial equality remained far distant.

A different analytical approach to assessing impact examines budgetary allocations. An early example is Keller's (1978) analysis of over-time spending patterns of six large cities in various race-related categories (e.g., public welfare, policing, housing) that varied by whether the city had a white or black mayor. On the whole, the data fail to reveal any clear-cut impact of black mayors. Delving beneath these budgets shows that mayors typically addressed local conditions more or less independently of their race. For example, in Gary, Indiana the black mayor sharply upped police protection spending, a fact largely explainable by prior neglect. In Newark, New Jersey, by contrast, a black mayor ignored this issue given the city's already burdensome debt. A similar idiosyncratic pattern held for welfare spending—fiscal resources over and above race and pressing competing obligations made the mayor's race virtually irrelevant. At best, black chief executives might have different policy preferences than their white counterparts, but these seldom translated into discernable action.

Karnig and Welch (1980) offer a comparable though more detailed analysis of 264 cities with populations above 25,000. Expenditures in various categories of special relevance to blacks, for example, police and fire protection, health care housing, street maintenance, and so on, are tracked as black representation fluctuated over a six-year period. The outcomes were mixed. Overall expenditure levels did rise and, most notably, social welfare-related outlays expanded as part of the overall budget. On the other hand, protective service and various amenity expenditures remained steady. Especially relevant to calibrating effect, observed racial factor impacts diminished once such mitigating factors as per capita income or the precise distribution of political power were statistically held constant. Even more disconcerting for those hoping for positive impacts, gains in one benefit (e.g., more generous social services) were generally "paid for" by cuts in other useful amenities. This last finding is hardly surprising—no mayor or city council, black or white, can overcome the economic constraints bedeviling all public money-based efforts to uplift the poor.

Additional evidence downplaying the role of the black mayor (together with black city council members) in redirecting city services to areas most relevant to African Americans comes from the work of Robert A. Brown (nd). When city expenditures on public welfare and housing plus community development are examined from 1972 to 1988 for all cities with over 50,000 residents (about 380 cities), Brown finds that black mayors were associated with heightened spending for housing and community development but not with social welfare. But, significantly, white mayors likewise raised housing and community development outlays during this same period though not at the high levels enacted by black leaders. Moreover, all mayors, regardless of race, respond to the economic conditions afflicting their constituents though outreach details noticeably depended upon local conditions. All in all, non-black leaders are unlikely to diverge greatly from their African-American counterparts when facing similar needs.

Given decades of documented experience, what's the overall verdict regarding a black mayor's impact? Case studies drawn from twenty-one cities (Browning, Rogers, and Tabb 1997) reiterated a familiar theme—gains do occur in municipal employment and better police treatment. Beyond these limited accomplishments, however, progress was modest. As to whether the civil rights movement achieved its broader goals, notably, economic equality, the authors unequivocally answer, "no." They even hint that matters may deteriorate as whites and white-run businesses abandon black-controlled cities, the growing difficulty of creating effective multi-ethnic governing coalitions, and the occasional willingness of middle-class blacks to abandon those below.

A recent sympathetic retrospective account of high-profile black mayors reaffirms our earlier cautions (Colburn and Adler 2001). Though each personality and venue has its own flavor, certain common themes are unmistakable. On the ledger's positive side, all left civic legacies by expanding black city employment, opening the doors (and contracts) of government to the once excluded, and provided countless improvements in municipal services and facilities to black constituents. The movement of African Americans into well-paying positions such as school principal or fire captain also built a flourishing middle class (and providing goods and services to the these newly affluent consumers doubtless generated other decent non-public opportunities). Diminished racial polarization and hostility was also an apparent dividend. Particularly where whites remained a sizable population bloc, the old fear that the city "would go to hell in a hand basket" following black victories was now dismissable.

These office holders did *not*, however, produce the hoped-for economic transformation. The evidence here is absolutely unavoidable as grim economic "de-industrialization" and demographic trends beginning in the 1960s have not altogether relented. For millions of blacks at the bottom of the socio-economic ladder, life has barely improved by electing one of their own. Nor have the changes instituted by black mayors, especially hiring black top administrators and securing Washington, DC assistance, been cause for future hopefulness. In some instances (e.g., New York City and Chicago), minimal progress might be attributable to the shortness of the black mayor's incumbency. Yet visits to Atlanta, Los Angeles, New Orleans, and similar cities that had black mayors for years (decades in some instances) still evidence widespread violent crime, drug abuse, dilapidated housing, educational insufficiency and all the other familiar "urban" pathologies in black neighborhoods. Residents of black-dominated cities like Detroit, East St. Louis, Newark, New Jersey, Gary, Indiana, and many others are almost permanently dependent on state and federal aid despite almost four decades of nearly top-to-bottom black administration.

What explanations for this disappointment do investigators offer? Interestingly, the likelihood that far-reaching socio-economic uplift was unreachable via civic mobilization goes unnoticed. Apparently, the chance to transform urban life just slipped away owing to a multitude of unfortunate—though implicitly surmountable—circumstances. Accounting for failure typically emphasizes obstruction from reactionary white politicians, tightfisted downtown corporations, hostile state officials, the emergence of rival ethnic coalitions, or squabbles among African Americans themselves. If these impediments were insufficient, add ostensibly irreversible business decline, periodic corruption scandals exposed by white-run newspapers, or accidental fiascos such as ineptly handled neighborhood violence. Remarkably, fixed features of U.S. pluralistic politics—the necessity of brokering coalitions, the dispersion of private economic power, and multiple legal checks on political authority—are often viewed as impediments *imposed* by enemies of far-reaching black progress.[3]

Does this picture shift if we go beyond traditional election-centered engagement and look at more disruptive, even violence-related activities? This is a vexing and, to be frank, politically awkward question. The link between periodic black riots, crime, and other threatening disruptive behavior is often indirect and may be undetectable via conventional research designs. Still, more than a few commentators plausibly allege that government entitlements and social welfare generosity (e.g., the Great Society, Model Cities, Youth Corps, Empowerment Zones, etc.) is explainable *only* as an effort to "cool" impending urban violence. That these programs typically persist despite modest success of ostensible aims would further confirm this ulterior "keep the peace" motive. Black activists, moreover, are not above raising the specter of violence and public officials must undoubtedly see a "peace" and a cornucopia of material enticements connection. The awkwardness derives from candidly acknowledging an arrangement bordering on extortion. This "gun to the head" motive is rarely easily admitted in public.

That being said, does black violence itself (or via threats) produce rewards comparable to those resulting from voting or office holding? Button's (1977) examination of forty randomly selected cities that experienced rioting in 1967 that varied by degree of violence is one of the few forays into this field. Impact was measured by assessing pre-and post-riot changes in a wide range of government remediation efforts. This was then supplemented by case studies of two riot-inflicted cities. Overall, and hardly surprising, HUD,

HEW, and multiple other federal agencies quickly poured millions of dollars into riot torn cities and a new term soon entered the political dictionary—"poverty warrior." This benevolence included everything from beefed-up law enforcement to prevent further mayhem to subsidized housing, summer jobs for unemployed teenagers, and incentives to encourage private businesses to hire ghetto residents. If the rioters intended to catch government's eye, they certainly succeeded, and within a remarkably brief time. Button further argues (ch. 5) that these upheavals finally made government (and whites) aware of the terrible conditions African Americans faced daily, plus the need for quick action to avert impending future disasters.

Kelly and Snyder (1980) correlate non-white income, unemployment rates and various occupational data with racial violence in more than 400 cities between 1960 and 1970. To factor out general trends during this period, cities were divided according to whether they had direct riot experience or not (other possible contaminating factors such as political structure were similarly held constant statistically). Violence was also measured by both incidence and severity (e.g., number of people killed). Overall, the authors report that rioting and black economic advances were minimally, if at all, associated. Nor was there any evidence that rioting assisted blacks to secure a higher occupational status.

These analyses make a critical though rarely articulated point: securing government largess is only the first step, not the desired pay-off. Countless well-intended job training programs are worthless unless enrollees seize the opportunity. No Washington intervention, especially hurriedly built ones to address intractable problems, is guaranteed and initial failures are normal. If pupils refuse to attend newly created classes, the only beneficiaries will be teachers paid to lecture to empty chairs. If these two studies are true more generally, rioting is best conceived as an attention-getting mechanism to stimulate government action, not the definitive solution to enduring black dilemmas.

How is this documentation of occasional, often everyday improvements, to be squared with the avid black enthusiasm for political enlistment action as the great transformer? Or, to be a bit speculative, and formulate the disjuncture in financial investment return language, one body of evidence suggests a small though respectable return of, say, 6 percent while other devotees insist that a whopping 20 percent or more per annum is more accurate. One possible rejoinder challenges scholarship as underplaying activist accomplishment—the 6 percent (or even 20 percent) estimate omits huge dividends. To wit, these microanalyses, though factually correct, miss the bigger portrait far more favorable to participation efficacy. Arguably, momentous progress is so discernable, so historically lucid, that it scarcely needs documentation. Why dwell on how untold boycotts and demonstrations ended Jim Crow laws or overcame racially biased business practices? Even those with a fleeting knowledge of history appreciate the NAACP's battle to eliminate racist laws and segregated public facilities. Surely all the 1950s and 1960s turmoil was responsible for myriad civil rights laws, government set-asides, human rights commissions, anti-discrimination enforcement agencies, and untold other official interventions benefiting African Americans. Does anybody seriously doubt that plain-to-see steps forward would have materialized if blacks remained apathetic? How can the newly created black middle class or burgeoning college enrollments be explained outside of political pressure? Millions of blacks owe their betterment to affirmative action or equal opportunity laws, policies that directly flowed from black political insistence.

Though this buoyant view is the official civil rights orthodoxy, it hardly comprises a discussion-ending scientific fact. That civil rights activism preceded a particular policy does not automatically certify cause and effect. Black activism may be integral to this accomplishment story, but it is not the only—or even overwhelming—ingredient. At least some economists wrestling with this influence flow contend that recent black prosperity *cannot* be accounted for by political mobilization (Donohue and Heckman 1989). Perhaps already improving economic circumstances encouraged blacks to seek even greater gains, and these newfound opportunities then engender yet more activism, but the two phenomena were substantially independent.

Contrary evidence and alternative interpretations can be overlooked but they cannot be unthinkingly refuted. Much depends on how victories are measured. Consider activist claims of post-1960s socio-economic advancement. Most generally, energetic political activism no matter how successful in generating government programs has *not* abolished multiple racial discrepancies, modest absolute improvement aside. Sizable black-white gaps in income, educational attainment, and overall quality of life still (notably health care and criminal victimization) remain. Data on violent crime, drug use, teenage illegitimacy, and other societal attainment markers, suggest that conditions may have *deteriorated* since black-instigated government intervention commenced (Murray [1984] documents this deterioration). It is one thing to ban racial segregation legally, quite another to end it in practice, and the U.S. may as be racially separated as it was four decades back. That well over one hundred billion dollars has been extracted from government for Head Start, college scholarships and similar politically imposed expensive educational uplifts are beside the point students skip classes or disdain academic achievement (these data are presented in Thernstrom and Thernstrom 2003: ch. 11). If all the marches and protests for "economic justice" were as efficacious as intimated, how can the lingering black urban underclass that has resisted decades of ameliorative efforts be explained? Recall how black mayors failed to solve these deeply rooted problems even when blacks totally dominated local politics. Ironically, today's persistent mobilizations to sustain affirmative action and other mechanisms favoring blacks in competitive economic situation attests to the *failure* of past activist nostrums, not their success.

Even if activism did produce benefits, it still may have been a relatively poor investment given opportunity costs. Hours consumed demanding new educational programs might have been better allocated to homework. One clue regarding the efficacy of non-political alternatives comes from a recent study comparing U.S. blacks to recent immigrants from the Caribbean and Africa who generally shun political activism (Fears 2003). These newcomer groups have substantially higher family incomes than native-born blacks, average more years of schooling, and lower unemployment levels.

A far more candid squaring of these contrary assessments is to acknowledge that grains of truth may be scattered everywhere. Black activism might, as advertised, be the mighty engine of progress, but heartfelt belief does not rest on scientific knowledge. It *must* be verified, as one must validate the power of a newly formulated medication. On the ledger's empirical analysis side, despite their methodological diversity and ingenuity, existing studies are theoretically *in*adequate to provide conclusive answers. These investigations taken together are frustrating—agreement on basic measures or how to unravel statistical complexities is almost entirely lacking. At best, the present literature consists of first-cut efforts, not unlike sixteenth-century chemistry experiments sufficing with crude approximations and rudimentary theories. The bottom line, then, is that the jury remains undecided on the glowing rhetoric versus the less appreciative (but still substantial) scholarly findings. Moreover, even a few dozen scholarly snapshots cannot possibly capture this vast panorama, and the list of potentially relevant factors required for a conclusive judgment remains barely touched. And, most critically, this calibrating impact insufficiency is a general problem, not one limited to assessing the value of black activism. If anything, we know far more about this phenomenon than any other. Thus formulated, the message is clear: much fundamental labor remains to be done, and this means calibrating impact generally, not just black activism in particular.

Analytical Issues in Return on Political Investment

Disentangling Causality

Establishing causality—if I do A, B will follow—is absolutely central to securing gains via politics. Surely one wishes to act consequentially. Though determining causality bedevils experts, the good news is that its principles are clear. To simplify a knotty subject, we can infer (though not absolutely prove) that A caused B if three conditions are all satisfied. First, A precedes B, not occurs after or simultaneously with B: increased jobs for blacks occurred *after* the election of a black mayor. Second, the supposed cause and effect must co-vary systematically. If a hundred election campaigns all sought the identical policy goal, the causality argument is strengthened if the election triumph generally succeeded (or failed). A random pattern of outcomes argues against causality though activists might rightfully herald occasional victories. Finally, to connect black election victory and employment causally requires eliminating all other relationship possibilities. *Only* election brought the jobs. Conceivably, shifting populations, rising black education attainment and untold other factors had independently led to swelling municipal employment among African Americans long before the election. In these circumstances, a new leader at City Hall only apparently produced the outcome when, in fact, it truly resulted from other, less visible trends.

These requirements are demonstrated only with great difficulty since political conflicts rarely (if ever) lend themselves to scientific, physics-like laboratory experiments.[4] We cannot insert political placebos or create alternative universes to assess what happened if the civil rights movement never existed. Moreover, similar-appearing political acts are seldom precisely identical, and unique elements can vex establishing the regularity essential for systematic inquiry. This uncertainty is also an awkward embarrassment to those preaching activism's benefits. Imagine if drug manufactures claimed that their pills cured disease though were unable to prove their case scientifically. Their recommendation would be rightfully dismissed as quackery. To appreciate these complexities, let us consider each of these requirements in greater detail.

Of the three conditions, the first—the time sequence—appears easiest to ascertain though this, too, is seldom clear-cut. That A comes before B can often be witnessed when observing discrete actions and subsequent government responses. To wit, the farm lobby decides in January that farmers need a tax break. In February, the lobby group hires a tax specialist to pressure Congress throughout the spring. In October, Congress enacts the tax cut, the farm group celebrates their feat, and this causal element seems satisfied. The chicken- and-egg dilemma still persists, however. Conceivably, some members of Congress facing reelection had eyed farmers for donations. Sensing that a tax cut was legislatively possible, they slyly approached the farm lobbyist months before January and hinted that tax reduction could be arranged if only the campaign donations were forthcoming. Thus galvanized, money poured into Congress and Congress ultimately delivered. Scientifically speaking, however, it was Congress itself that caused the tax break with the farm organization merely acting as an intermediary. In other words, B caused A, not the opposite.

This time-ordering messiness is perennially illustrated in the relationship between money and electoral success. Again, impact looks superficially straightforward: winners far outspend losers, so money causes victory. Nevertheless, it is equally plausible that likely winners will usually attract greater contributions since backing winners outshines contributing to those doomed from the outset who cannot deliver anything—reelection causes bigger donations, not the reverse. Multiple possibilities exist—money may have initially caused a victory in 1994 (A causes B) and this established success generated bountiful contributions in 1996 and 1998 (B causes A). In other words, money is *both* a cause and an effect, and this can vary across candidates and circumstances.

This chicken-and-egg time problem can become a nightmare. Consider the connection between rising black political election success and the racial and economic changes in many U.S. cities commencing in the 1960s. In several instances (e.g., Cleveland) initial black victories occurred when African Americans constituted a sizable though still less than a population majority. In a few years, however, swelling black in-migration coupled with whites moving to the suburbs expanded the black share of the total vote. Cities like Newark, Atlanta and Detroit now had black majorities, while elsewhere (e.g., New Orleans, Baltimore, Cleveland, and St. Louis) blacks voting as a bloc could effectively veto a citywide office seeker. And as we saw, these numbers were quickly converted into wide-ranging political successes. Paralleling this urban racial shift was a sharp economic decline ("de-industrialization") within cities. This was especially true for manufacturing jobs, long the mainstay of urban blacks, circumstances making municipal employment all the more valuable as an alternative. If that were insufficient to stress city government, many new arrivals were quite poor and immediately burdened already overwhelmed social service and school systems (these urban woes are depicted in greater detail in Adler [2001]).

These ingredients can interact in varied ways and deciding what came first, second, or last is no easy matter. Perhaps white preferences for suburban living was the original cause of black municipal job gains since this population shift opened both jobs and set the stage for subsequent black political triumphs. The reverse might possibly be true—whites fled in response to mounting taxes or due to their aversion to black empowerment. Conceivably, white flight and black political success occurred roughly simultaneously, both resulting from southern blacks relocating northward. Did economic woes mobilize black voters to elect one of their own to secure new jobs or, alternatively, did this municipal accomplishment exacerbate economic declines by overburdening the tax base to finance soaring city employment? These (and other) rival sequences must be disentangled empirically, no small feat given that everything is occurring during the same period.

A second major concern is B's absence despite A. Technically, with no impact there can be no cause: the school daycare rally resulted in zero, and this showed the futility of it all. All the same, a counter (and certainly credible) interpretation is that B has yet to arrive. When the difficultly of realizing political goals is factored into this equation (as is commonplace in U.S. politics), the B portion may reasonably take decades. Consider recent agitation for slavery reparation, a seemingly futile quest. Still, a final decision may be premature. Perhaps fifty years or longer must pass before success transpires, a figure comparable to how long it required the government to compensate Japanese-Americans interned during World War II. Recall that efforts to defeat state imposed segregation required more than a century following the Civil War! Indeed, those efforts to redirect American culture depicted in chapter 3, for example, influencing school textbooks, are knowingly directed toward effects visible only when today's analysts have retired.

A particularly difficult analytical conundrum might be called the unmoved mover: B happens without A yet A is truly the force instigating B. An organization may be so dominant (based upon past outcomes) that it dictates policy without actually acting. To wit, Congress might expand Medicare "voluntarily" rather than battle dreaded, easily galvanized senior citizen lobbies committed to regular increases. The American Association of Retired Persons (AARP) thus (apparently) prevails by "doing nothing." Threats may even go unvoiced—everybody dreads just angering these associations. This invisible impact might follow a learning curve—after several punishing encounters, desired behaviors occur autonomously, or so it might seem to a naive observer. To compound matters, the A of this causal relationship transpired decades back and applied to other issues with different legislators.

Non-linear variation is also troublesome. To say that A and B change together does not necessarily mean that the two elements co-vary indefinitely by equal amounts. In some circumstances A may truly cause B but as the situation changes, this relationship evolves or disappears altogether. Campaign spending may garner votes but heightened fiscal bountifulness might bring diminishing results until each additional dollar spent is meaningless. Put in dollar terms, going from nothing to $100,000 may produce 10,000 new votes; going from five to ten million may yield no change—a ceiling has been reached. Spending widely deemed "excessive" might lose votes, too. Unfortunately from the analytical standpoint, a study that commenced when the campaign was already awash in funds would erroneously conclude that "money made no difference." Again, everything depends on circumstances, not scientific principles.

Ceiling affects and diminishing returns are commonplace—boycotts, protest marches, letter writing campaigns, and many similar stock-in-trade tactics may grow ineffectual as they evolve into ritualistic gestures. Limits also exist regarding what can be extracted. At some point government is paralyzed or just lacks the resources, so continued pressure is inconsequential—success in getting a black mayor to hire more African Americans may be successful initially, but the same pressure will likely be less successful as available municipal positions grow fewer in number. The opposite pattern can also occur—the impact grows disproportionately with use. Recall that socially responsible investing has evolved from being a trivial to a politically important weapon.

Diving deeper into murky conceptual waters, inaction might bring forth a corresponding inaction, a set of casual circumstances that defies empirical research though participants may readily grasp its true nature. No prudent president would ever nominate an openly segregationist federal judge and risk unleashing an unnecessary, embarrassing confrontation. Clearly, civil rights organizations can shape (cause) judicial appointments, and may have overtly acted in the past, but in current circumstances, mobilization is unnecessary. In other words, certain actions decades back "caused" today's nonevent. Statistical detail aside, existing research methodology is baffled when confronting this pattern. Which particular acts spanning several decades explain today's inaction? How could today's "doing nothing" be measured scientifically? Imagine correlating various inactions with each other?

An especially difficult covariation predicament concerns which particular B to attach to A. No doubt, even the most minor act has multiple future ramifications, and when dozens of such events are considered, these consequences must exceed thousands. Given data bountifulness, it is statistically *inevitable* that some effects will systematically be connected with some events. Uncovering causality in such circumstances has far more to do with numerical odds and information sufficiency, not necessarily genuine impact. A hundred rallies demanding after-school daycare have numberless effects, and we might find, for example, that in 75 percent of the cases a committee was formed to explore this possibility. This specific event (i.e., creating a committee), to repeat, was only one of hundreds (maybe millions) of rally-generated outcomes, and may not even have been an initial priority. Disappointed activists might insist that seeming failure only demonstrated data insufficiency so collecting more information would prove impact. Eventually, "some" effect will emerge though it might arrive years after the triggering event. Chance alone virtually *guarantees* uncovering proof of worthiness.

The real impact calculation nightmare occurs when we face a single incident producing momentous repercussions across decades, most of which now seem unconnected to the original event. In 1955, for instance, the modern-day civil rights movement had its innocuous beginning when a black women, Rosa Parks, refused to surrender her seat to a white person on a Birmingham, Alabama, bus. The resulting 381-day bus company boycott (organized by a then little known Martin Luther King, Jr.) was a success, and quickly inspired countless other direct actions that, in turn, brought a sea change in American law and race relations. Did this single boycott cause civil rights legislation, anti-poverty programs, and untold other policies potentially helpful to African Americans? Going yet one step further, can we now say that boycotting segregated businesses will *cause* African-American betterment since this happened before? Or, might a skeptic also claim that this one action, though effective in desegregating local bus service, had millions of consequences, so it is unwise to attribute these to what transpired in Birmingham in 1955.

The third causality requirement—no other factors produced B—is undoubtedly the most challenging to satisfy since the potential rivals to A are virtually infinite. Particularly when we move beyond specific acts aimed at narrow goals within a constricted time frame, the possibility that factors beyond activism caused the outcomes is quite credible. That the advancement of African Americans, women, and others embracing the political route may have resulted from society-wide economic forces beyond group influence, not pressuring government, has already been mentioned. Specifically, anti-discrimination laws or affirmative action programs were superfluous thanks to society-wide prosperity. A fuller accounting for progress might also include changes in immigration, birth rates, migration, and shifting cultural norms as explanatory factors. Whether one reason is superior to another is irrelevant and none may be accurate; the important point is that multiple plausible rivals *always* exist, and each has to be considered before reaching a conclusion.

Success (or failure) may reflect more the very structure of politics, not specific actions. Groups trying to safeguard the status quo, whether preserving a law or sustaining a broad policy such as protecting free speech, particularly benefit from the existing gridlock-inducing arrangements. They win, so to speak, because they can scarcely lose. Consider, for example, those American activists who on December 2, 2001 marched on behalf of free trade, globalization, rule of law, liberty, the profit principle, and free speech (*Wall Street Journal* 2001). No doubt, at day's end they could honestly announce that capitalism had been sustained. A skeptic however might insist that this march was the equivalent of primitive people making sacrifices to prevent the sun from disappearing during the winter solstice. Other interests might benefit from well-established statutory-required "rules of the game." Victories "just happen" with scarcely any effort. For example, the two major parties easily defeat minor parties thanks to our plurality-based election system. This built-in advantage can be reversed (though with enormous effort), but to assert that Democrats and Republicans somehow *cause* their partisan preeminence grossly exaggerates. The real causal agents here may be deeply ingrained legal inertia (created decades before), well beyond daily conflict.

The argument here is not that politics and claimed benefits may be unconnected (though that remains possible). Nor do we aver that the matter is beyond resolution, though that too may be periodically true. The key question is the relative contribution of a specific political activism versus other factors in untold combination, and the answer can vary from zero to 100 percent. Resolution is inescapably empirical; it cannot be decreed by activist boasts or reaffirmed as faith. To complicate matters yet further, unraveling everything grows more arduous as we move away from specific, highly structured situations and shift toward grand efforts. Lobbying the city council for a traffic light lends itself well to assessing causes; a comparable effort to achieve "social justice" invites endless conceptual and technical quandaries if impact is to be *correctly* calibrated. This is *not* to say that pursing grand schemes is pointless or doomed to failure and therefore efforts should be spent elsewhere. "Social justice" may well be achieved. The relevant lesson is that such investments rarely permit straightforward measurement.

No doubt, some activists may acknowledge the indeterminacy of their efforts but still take a position akin to Pascal's Wager—civic engagement's impact is hopelessly uncertain, but it remains worthy since in *might* prove efficacious. Or, to repeat an old folk saying, nothing ventured, nothing gained. Reality is a bit more complex as we shall now see when we consider political activism in terms of *net* gains.

The Productivity of Political Activism

A sophisticated financial investor never just asks, "Can this venture make money?" Gains are to be maximized, and this involves complicated calculations well beyond inquiring whether any riches will be forthcoming. Somebody contemplating buying a McDonald's franchise would certainly inquire about the rate of return—5 percent, 8 percent, or 10 percent—on his or her multi-million dollar investment with a downward adjustment for time-consuming training and long hours. A prudent prospective franchise owner would then calculate this risky, effort-intense, flipping burger return versus buying absolutely secure U.S. Treasury notes. Another potential investor might disregard yearly income in favor of long-term appreciation—today's million-dollar McDonald's could be worth two million in five years, a 20 percent annual gain. Meanwhile, yet another potential investor believes that rampant inflation will wipe out future investment profits and instead pursues immediate luxurious consumption. All seek gain, and each will assuredly secure some benefit, yet each calculates their potential profits and losses in radically different ways.

A comparable calculus applies to civic involvement though it is seldom executed with this sophistication. Calculations typically assess *absolute* positive gains independent of any costs, drawbacks, or even larger gains from alternative investment strategies. To take a simple hypothetical example, parents contemplating rallying for after-school day care just desire subsidized babysitting. From this single aim framework even a risky, low-yield effort is worthwhile since even failure brings no net loss outside of potential incidental costs, for example, missed favorite TV shows. That this program appears "free" given diffused fiscal burden might only add to its allure. Furthermore, since only a single victory out of multiple tries could be decisive, relentless activism is justifiable á la winning the big lottery by daily buying tickets.

A more hardheaded scrutiny would be more attentive to net (not absolute) gains from a possible victory. This investigation would assuredly paint a different picture. Participants should realize that allocating funds to school daycare will redirect money away from other (perhaps more desirable) educational benefits if revenue is fixed. After all, staffing and supplies must come from somewhere. Even if federal grants supplied the money "for nothing," inescapable administrative and opportunity costs still remain—newly imposed teacher responsibilities could detract from consulting with parents or grading homework. Other "hidden" costs might include having one's children exposed to unruly peers or walking home after dark. Overall, in the context of the school's primary mission, the newly won daycare addition might be a net educational *loss* regardless of how much appreciated by harried parents.

Opportunity costs also must be considered—comparable efforts might be directed toward securing better qualified teachers or regular skill testing, both of which might yield benefits outshining daycare. Rival options are virtually unlimited and each brings its own rewards and risks. Pressuring school officials for smaller classes might, for example, entail twice the uncertainty in outcome as demanding after-school programs, but the educational yield might be five times greater. But, on the other hand, if participants lacked the resources to secure smaller classes, this less productive daycare option may still constitute the best available choice. Everything must be calculated on a case-by-case basis.

Non-political options should also be added: endless hours lobbying bureaucrats might be more effectively allocated to earning money making commercial daycare affordable (especially given political action's uncertain pay-off). Meanwhile, all the meetings dedicated to pressuring officials could have been spent raising private funds for new school equipment. Participants could even collectively redirect their energies to establishing a cooperative, parent-run childcare program. Relocating to a school district that currently provides after-school daycare is yet another non-political possibility. Absolutely nothing warrants exclusively traveling the political pathway, so pay-offs depend entirely on personal, situationally determined calculations.

To continue the economic parallel, a savvy activist would likely diversify rather than pursue one option exclusively. Multiple political and non-political options might be sought simultaneously to minimize failure. Instead of myriad confrontations with school administrators, do this once or twice and spend the rest of the time on a part-time job. Alternatively, if one avenue appeared to be a dead end, fresh possibilities would be explored. Should all this politicking seem unpromising, the fallback might be an entirely private solution requiring nominal energy, for example, altering work schedules to reduce needed after-school daycare.

The upshot might be that any single endeavor yields a small benefit (and fails altogether), but taken as a whole, the quest succeeded, eventually. Unfortunately for social science, this judicious adaptive strategy typically escapes notice in the typical one-shot research design. It is a major undertaking to collect often-idiosyncratic information about many separate acts, over time, directed toward ever shifting aims. This is a survey research nightmare. If the rally was the exclusive object of research inquiry, the highly misleading conclusion might be that parents briefly tried it, school officials were unresponsive, and the parents quickly lapsed into deplorable apathy.

This exercise should demonstrate that treating absolute benefits as the final measure of impact success without subtracting losses is bizarre bookkeeping, and only loads the dice for those heralding the value of civic engagement. No commercial enterprise could ever survive with this one-side-of-the-ledger accounting methodology. The potential real-world consequences of this lopsided counsel are obvious. Those parents winning their cherished after-school program conceivably lost more than they gained if this "victory" meant budget cuts elsewhere or enhanced opportunities foregone. Meanwhile, compatriots who "dropped out" from this quest may be the authentic winners despite being castigated for civic lethargy. These "apathetics" quickly realized that this campaign would make things worse (even if "free") so they left town rather than see local schools neglect their primary purpose. Meanwhile, other parents stayed put but shunned rallies and instead used their time to tutor their children.

Murky Political Activism Gains

In principle, the aim of political participation is to secure some political objective. Recall chapter 2's sound-alike definitions regarding the essence of civic activism. Milbrath (1981) spoke of "influencing or supporting government policies" while Rosenstone and Hansen (1993: 4) stipulated, "influencing the distribution of social goods and services" were typical in their policy focus. This underlying civic motivation is always *inferred* from the overt behavior, seldom measured independently. Voters are assumed to be voting to achieve civic aims, not visiting the polling place to get a breath of fresh air. If this voter were interviewed, inquiries focus on what determined his or her vote and similar politically centered inquiries. The research agenda typically excludes non-political factors drawing the voter to the polling place.

Political action's instrumental value most clearly applies to professionals seeking short-term tangible goals. This instrumentality is less clear, however, when we move beyond these salaried professionals. Political action, regardless of outward behavior or claims regarding ultimate purpose, affords multiple occasions to satisfy non-civic aims. Perhaps Ku Klux Klaners just enjoy exotic costumes or notoriety, and altering race-relations policy, the ostensible purpose of their rallies, is mainly incidental. Even the most carefully directed street demonstration offers conviviality, and this side benefit may outweigh what is nominally sought. We are not insisting that non-professional political activism is rife with non-political aims though this may occasionally be true. The key point is that *some* of this engagement *is* so directed, and that its establishment is an empirical matter, and cannot be settled *a priori* by an imposed research classification scheme.

To disentangle political from non-political aims is absolutely vital in calibrating pay-offs from political action. Exclusively using a political yardstick is not mandatory, and contemporary political activism seemingly has little to do with tangible civic pay-offs. Politics is not the economic marketplace where only the efficient survive and the inept go bankrupt; pressures may push activists in the opposite direction. Doomed-from-the-outset crusades may be attractive *because* of their hopeless idealism and murky, never-to-be-verified accomplishment (e.g, bringing about nebulous "social change").

Meanwhile, these efforts as chapter 5 noted, like endangered species, are legally protected against government suppression, assuming that officials care about such quixotic movements. We also reside in a culture venerating fair political competition, so while defeating rivals is acceptable, it is impermissible to obliterate them by force, so they may linger on forever.

To appreciate how ostensible "politics" affords ample opportunities to pursue aims largely divorced from tangible policymaking, consider the recent anti-globalization movement. At least superficially, it appears to be a paradigmatic example of citizens energized to accomplish concrete political ends—diminish the mounting influence of multinational corporations (the McDonaldization of the world) and Western domination of less developed nations through the International Monetary Fund, the World Bank, and similar centralized institutions. Judged by event turnout and the immense publicity, the Direct Action Network, the Anarchist Marching Band and the Ruckus Society among untold other movement participants might be proud of their efforts. This movement has certainly pushed globalization into public consciousness and caused endless inconvenience as officials meet in secret to hide from rowdy demonstrators.

Is this genuine instrumental politics? Probably not, though certain outward appearances might say otherwise. This movement might be better depicted as street theater built around certain attention-getting themes superficially having to do with "policy." Most plainly, noisy commotions are hardly likely to disrupt World Bank interventions. Far more likely is that meetings will be rescheduled in calmer locations. Desperately poor nations will still accept IMF loans despite protestors performing a Buddhist Circle dance while bystanders beat the communal drum in downtown Washington, DC (Foer 2000). The worldwide economic penetration of Philip Morris, Pizza Hut, and comparable multinationals is impervious to street puppeteers and musicians. It is hard to imagine smokers in Ghana forgoing Marlboros or indigenous Thai entrepreneurs forgoing riches selling brand-name pizza owing to vivid murals in Seattle.

The tip-off that this movement is essentially self-indulgent, not instrumental politics is the bizarre participant behavior. Admittedly, taking on giant multinationals is vexing, but these tactical choices strongly insinuate that "having outrageous (and perfectly safe) fun" outshines genuine accomplishment. What is to be concretely realized when three topless women parade down Washington's Pennsylvania Avenue with magic marker slogans on their backs telling bystanders to "smash the state"? Will public opinion be won over when outlandishly dressed protestors smash Starbucks windows and vandalize newspaper boxes? Can bystanders decipher puzzling slogans like "Spank the bank" or puppet shows offering esoteric ideological messages? Even those anti-globalization protesters disinclined toward violence nevertheless seem drawn to this movement by its "fun" and opportunities for creative artistic self-expression. No doubt, a "success" here has far more to do with personal enjoyment than evicting Kentucky Fried Chicken from China.

An important message resides here for assessing impact: no single evaluative hierarchy can exist regarding what activism is supposed to accomplish. Theoretically, *any* goal, from the tangible to the purely psychological, can *legitimately* be satisfied via political activity. Even personal self-destruction is possible—just make sure the suicide note contains a political message. Should those publicity-seeking anti-globalization anarchists be interrogated about their motives before experts can render alleged activism judgments? Consider two people attending a civil rights demonstration. Abbott attends to supports the African-American cause and believes that a large turnout insures publicity. His behavior is purely instrumental—to promote black civil rights. By contrast, Costello cares zero about black civil rights but enjoys stirring assemblies, and is there entirely for that personal reason. Though Costello will surely add to the multitude and thus make for greater notoriety (the rally's political aim), this is irrelevant. Psychologically she is politically apathetic despite her attendance though, measured by overt behavior, both Abbott and Costello are political insofar as their presence will have a political impact.

Further assume that Costello got what she sought, namely an exciting time and encountering old friends. Score one for the value of "political activism"—the sought aim (conviviality) happens. Abbott, by contrast, was gravely disappointed. His presence scarcely added much, and the media ultimately ignored the miniscule gathering. Other attendees shared this dismal assessment—Abbott (and others) failed in their mission. Score one negative outcome for participation. The message is that success may greatly depend on aim, not what is objectively accomplished.

If almost anything can be deemed a "success" by those involved, even if delusional and made retroactively, how can we have failures? In principle, Abbott could instantly alter his aims and insist that he really wanted some conviviality, or this once far secondary benefit far outweighed the loss from his original, more overtly political aim. Maybe those "unsuccessful" parents seeking after-school daycare just enjoy hassling school administrators and "success" would end this pleasurable endeavor. The possibilities are infinite, so why even bother with assessing the net benefits of political activism when defeat can be so effortlessly transformed into accomplishment? Indeed, as we have hinted at before, some activists might genuinely treasure hopelessness believing that success would bring unwelcome idleness. Others might honestly prefer accomplishment but quietly acknowledge that continued failure supplies a paycheck or psychological fulfillment. This perspective places a deceptively heavy burden on research, but as we shall see in subsequent chapters, this obstacle is not insurmountable.

Ambivalent Triumphs

It goes without saying that politics is a series of battles. Less obvious, but no less true, is that a single skirmish is seldom conclusive though it may help fundraising or boost a sense of accomplishment among foot soldiers. The most irrefutable-appearing coup can eventually be reversed, so scoring a single positive outcome as a war-ending victory is almost always premature, a sure invitation to future failure. The stealthy nature of counterattacks further complicates matters. Chapter 4's accounts of non-political resistance to school integration illustrated below-the-radar maneuvers in detail.

The substitution of means for ends can easily bedevil the naïve. Women seeking equal pay for equal work might substitute a new law itself, not the desired economic outcome, as to what certifies success. Efforts might even move backwards until the original goal fades from memory—securing a parade permit to hold a rally for equal pay becomes Armageddon! Such Pyrrhic victories breed shame. If a glittering statute itself sufficiently satisfies advocates, rendering it ineffectual is a snap—just assign responsibility to an unsympathetic agency or minimize non-compliance penalties. Yet, when all is said and done, these shortsighted activists believe they have won it all (and their opponents would certainly publicly agree!).

Unraveling *net* gains from total positive accomplishment, especially given the reluctance of activists to admit their follies, is a troubling task. The creation of black majority House districts in southern states offers a perfect and highly consequential example. To condense a story full of twists and turns, African Americans had long expressed displeasure regarding the paltry number of black office holders, especially representatives from the south where blacks are relatively numerous. The often-scattered distribution of rural blacks and the majority-based nature of the U.S. electoral system posed major barriers (and this was further compounded by white unwillingness to elect blacks). Nevertheless, beginning in the 1980s the Justice Department, enthusiastically backed by civil rights groups, using sections 3 and 5 of the Voting Rights Act, pressured southern states to redraw district boundaries to create black voting majorities. The historic aim of access to the ballot now gave way to maximizing the election of African Americans to represent other African Americans.

The task's primary instrument was to reconfigure districts to maximize black voters without blatantly violating Supreme Court gerrymandering edicts (a few majority Latino districts were similarly created). By all accounts, this was a well-designed, cleverly executed campaign in which distinct boundaries wandered through neighborhoods, down highways, and otherwise picked up scattered potential black voters. Advocates even utilized high-tech computerized mapmaking programs coupled with detailed census data to gain every microscopic advantage. This well-orchestrated struggle plainly paid off in the 1992 congressional election: twelve new southern blacks joined the three previously elected. Black representation from the old Confederacy instantly quadrupled and these beneficiaries held on despite ongoing legal challenges.

Was this surge in black House members an authentic African Americans victory? Superficially the answer seems decidedly "yes" given the plain-to-see numbers and resultant pleasure of civil rights leaders. Add the well-paid, prestigious positions both inside and outside of Congress. A less visible, but still plausible, benefit is that this change will encourage bi-racial cooperation (Cannon 1999 stresses this advantage). Conceivably, black constituent requests might now receive better House member service, and Cannon's (1999: ch. 4) analysis does indeed find these black legislators to be more attentive to their African-American constituents as reflected in hiring multiracial staffs, locating offices in black areas, and otherwise "reaching out" beyond what comparable white legislators offered.

Going beyond these statistics to larger consequences makes the verdict less clear-cut. The evidence does suggest a heavy price for these victories (Hill 1995). Though the exact details are debatable, shifting black Democrats into majority-minority districts indisputably helped create areas with yet larger white majorities, and many of these congressional districts now shifted to the Republican column—nine seats from these southern states in 1992. Overall, between the late 1980s and the post-racial gerrymandering election of 1996, the Republican share of southern House seats improved from 34 percent to 57 percent. One might further add that these district reconfigurations to benefit African Americans helped drive white Democrats towards the Republican Party, a fact of no small relevance in presidential and Senate elections.

This Republican House control post-1992, albeit by slim margins, is of the utmost political importance. Thanks to a handful of Republican triumphs where Democrats once prevailed, every committee and sub-committee chair is a Republican, as are all committee majorities, no small matter in a legislative body dominated by committee decision-making. The policy ramifications of this shift cannot be exaggerated for it affects everything from what bills receive floor consideration to parliamentary rulings from the Republican speaker of the house. The House Black Caucus may have gained new members, but several senior black legislators (e.g., Charles Rangel [D-NY]), have been blocked from assuming key committee chairmanships while other black legislators often find themselves out-voted by a Republican majority.

What about policy benefits to blacks who finally have a fellow African American representing them? Are things noticeably better than under a white Democrat? This is an exceptionally difficult empirical question, and past investigations unfortunately offer no straightforward answer if only because their analyses draw on diverse historical periods and policy benefit indicators. Pre-civil rights era data show that a sizable black population in a district resulted in less attention to black interests, hardly surprising given the exclusion of black voters (Cameron, Epstein, and O'Halloran [1996] carefully review these divergent findings). Nevertheless, technical impediments and ambiguities aside, the contemporary evidence fails to reveal clear, consistent policy benefits associated with the racially driven strategy. In their study using an index of fourteen House bills of special importance to blacks (e.g., greater funding for early education), Cameron, Epstein, and O'Halloran conclude that pooling black voters together to virtually guarantee an election of a black did *not* maximize African-American representation, at least as reflected in roll call votes. Their analysis suggests that if policy, not physical, representation were the main objective, black voters outside the south should be equally distributed in House districts while within the south, districts should be drawn to include as many blacks as possible just short of a majority. In other words, political influence and black office holders are somewhat contradictory goals and require trade-offs.

This trade-off is put into a larger political context by the work of Lubin (1997). Following the theorizing of others, he distinguishes majority-minority districts (MMD) from "influence districts," that is, areas where blacks comprise about 40 percent of the population. Only on rare occasions can blacks electorally prevail in the latter circumstances, but according to Lubin (1997: ch. 5), substantial black presence effectively pushes elected whites in the pro-black liberal direction. Though blacks infrequently elect a fellow black, they undoubtedly veto the election of a conservative Democrat and absolutely prohibit a Republican from serving.

Most critically for our purposes, going from about 40 percent to well past the 50 percent required to assure election of a black adds little to liberal policy representation. These new black representatives may be exceptionally racially liberal compared to white Democratic predecessors, but this extremity counts for naught in a majority-based legislative body. Fiery speeches and introducing beyond-the-edge legislative proposals may bring psychic rewards back home, but they are empty—if not counterproductive—policymaking gestures. Moreover, unless the partisan distribution of seats remains unchanged (highly unlikely), pushing the district into the "safe for black victory" yields a net *loss* for African-American goals. To wit, blacks get a legislator marginally more pro-black, an uncertain legislative advantage, but the Republican elected from the district from which the blacks were "removed" is likely to be quite conservative (this possibility is, in fact, demonstrated by Overby and Cosgrove [1996] using House roll call data).

Ironically, these black victories may have largely been unnecessary from a purely instrumental perspective. Whitby and Gilliam's (1991) pre-1992 election analysis reported that southern white Democrats had steadily moved toward racial liberalism as district blacks registered and voted. This responsiveness was especially discernable among younger representatives who entered Congress when the civil rights revolution was an accepted fact. They clearly grasped that future careers depended on racial accommodation. Meanwhile, the steady aging of "old-time" racially conservative Democrats made them a diminishing force in southern politics, and by the 1980s many had retired or died. Herring's (1990) analysis of Alabama, Georgia, and Louisiana state legislators during 1980 similarly finds that white office holders gradually accommodated black constituency needs on varied economic and social issues as the black district size grew. The message is clear: burgeoning black votes count in influencing those in power, but having black versus white Democrats is hardly decisive for policy representation.[5]

Yet one more wrinkle in tallying up gains and losses concerns what African Americans themselves preferred. Relying on a 1996 survey of African Americans, Tate (2003) finds a decidedly odd collection of views. On the one hand, clear majorities reject this idea of concentrating black voters to maximize blacks in Congress. Yet, when the question is posed in terms of altering (unspecified) elections rules to facilitate black representation, 60 percent embrace this proposal. Compounding this ambiguity, sizable numbers shifted their positions on majority-minority districts when various counter-arguments were presented. The bottom line is that these data can be used to demonstrate almost *any* majority preference, so *any* outcome is a certified "victory."

These complicated analyses of racial gerrymandering hardly exhaust the tallying of winners and losers given disjunctures between public and private views. Politics need not resemble sports where wining is unambiguous. Murkiness abounds. For example, as a matter of principled support for color-blind society, conservative Republicans typically overtly opposed black majority districts as breeding Balkanization. Yet some of these very same partisans privately acquiesced to this manipulation since it contributed to a Republican House majority. Untold Democrats were similarly of divided minds and offered evasive or contradictory pronouncements. Savvy southern white Democratic incumbents grasped that these new "black" districts might end their careers yet, given their dependence on black votes, they could scarcely openly oppose "better black representation." Civil rights leaders themselves were not immune to the catch-22 of helping fellow black office seekers yet fearing ghettoization and a Republican House majority.[6] The ironic bottom line, then, was that regardless of outcome, *everyone* could simultaneously be both a winner and a loser depending on a person's "real" goal.

An even more cloudy quandary concerns how African-American legislators respond to immigration issues. Purely as an economic issue it might be argued that boosting immigration, particularly from Mexico, hurts many blacks by lowering their wages and otherwise diminishing their standard of living (e.g., greater competition for housing). Yet, members of the Congressional Black Caucus (CBC) have been among the most supportive of opening the doors to these immigrants plus assisting those already here with amnesty, worker protection, and other benefits. Might this pro-immigration espousal be based on the expectation that these immigrants will eventually become political allies? Or is the motivation humanitarian? All in all, separating a victory from a defeat is a formidable task (see Guzzardi 2003 for the record on immigration).

The final possibility bedeviling certifying a "victory" concerns when hoped-for outcomes go terribly wrong, a situation commonplace with exotic consumer purchases—the long-fantasized luxury yacht becomes a dreaded liability as unexpected maintenance costs soar. A particularly intriguing example of this pattern comes from the unintended consequences of pressuring cities to hire additional black police officers (and in some instances, firefighters as well). Recall that this aim was always judged positively. Adding additional African-American police also had a special urgency in largely black cities given lingering tensions and periodic brutal police-civilian encounters. Securing these positions would not only show that African Americans had "arrived" politically, it was also expected that black police officers would outperform whites in dealing with fellow African Americans and thereby reduce crime. Black officers knew black neighborhoods, were more attuned to cultural disputes and, perhaps most imperative, would show greater savvy in avoiding riot-instigating confrontations.

Still, these attractive reasons aside, increasing black representation on the police force proved to be troublesome. The main obstacle were civil service qualifications that covered everything from physical attributes (height, stamina, etc.) and, most relevant for potential black recruits, performance on standardized-type tests assessing reading, reasoning, writing, and comparable cognitive abilities. Repeatedly, blacks disproportionally failed these entry-level tests, a fact activists attributed to the cultural biases of the tests. The upshot was a medley of pressures from community activists, civil rights organizations threatening litigation, and, most importantly, the Justice Department to reformulate recruitment standards to minimize disparate racial impact. These pressures largely succeeded, and police departments altered hiring criteria by substituting other credentials (e.g., a history of community service), racially norming test scores, or, in a few instances, eliminating cognitive criteria altogether or lowering the pass cutoff point. In other instances (e.g., Chicago) activists focused on promotion and here court decrees were occasionally secured to guarantee career advancement based upon race or ethnicity. In any case, yielding to these pressures hundreds of blacks soon joined police departments and, in a few cities, black officers were hired and/or promoted.

What was the community benefit of these heralded successes? The positive side is again self-evident: untold blacks (plus women and other racial/ethnic minorities) gained jobs they would not have otherwise attained given previous test-taking failures. One might also add the credit-taking election benefits that accrued to officials advocating this policy. Beyond this good news, however, the picture is bleaker. According to Lott's (2000) detailed (and admittedly often approximate) statistical analysis of crime data from cities legally pressured to add black police officers, a generally *higher* crime rate soon followed. Put bluntly, these new hires, regardless of race, lacked the essential job skills and this deficiency was hardly abstract. Significantly, cities with the largest black populations experienced the greatest jump. This directly contradicts the argument that black law enforcement is better suited to patrolling black neighborhoods. Lott further calculates the concrete costs of this substitution of lower-qualified black officers for average scoring whites. Between 1987 and 1990 this preferential policy was associated with an additional 1,145 murders and over 37,000 aggravated assaults (263). Although the evidence suggests a decline in certain crimes (e.g., far fewer motor vehicle thefts) on the whole the verdict is that the hiring of black police failed to lessen crime and probably made matters worse.

This intricate statistical portrait is further confirmed by anecdotal tales of law enforcement troubles when cops lack elementary writing skills, regardless of notable talents elsewhere. In Washington, DC, for example, the shortage of qualified police force candidates during the 1980s resulted in many barely literate new recruits. This shoddy paperwork and inaccuracies resulted in botched prosecutions and countless criminals going free, no small matter in a city wracked by crime (Carlson 1993). Washington, DC's experience is hardly exceptional. Systematic studies of comparable private sector outcomes reveal that those hired using lower cognitive-based standards under-perform, show higher job turnover, and are far more likely to cause disciplinary problems (Murray and Herrnstein 1994: 497). To repeat, such hiring does have its positive values, but the costs remain high, and this bottom line is vital when assessing political activism. African Americans may fully appreciate more blacks on the local police force, but they are more likely to "pay" for this benefit with higher crime rates.

The drawbacks resulting from political "victories" can often be barely discernable and thus, again, encourage overstating the plus side of the ledger.[7] Consider, for example, the subtle impact of the 1991 Civil Rights Act that sought to assist African Americans and women in gaining employment in fields where they tended to be under-represented. The act's aim is to help by easing racial or ethnic discrimination claims and upping the potential damage awards for uncovered discrimination. The actual impact was quite different though far from obvious, a predictable outcome since the act made these hires potentially quite expensive. For one, the number of "protected workers" hired sharply slowed after the act's passage—why bring on board somebody who can easily sue if fired? Second, the safest legal way to fire a "protected worker" was via mass lay-offs, and this increasingly became a crude tool to escape potential litigation. Finally, and perhaps most unfortunate for novices, employers rationally avoided risky hires when it came to blacks and women. Hiring sure bets to reduce the likely litigation over dissmissals made far more sense. The upshot, then, is a constricting of opportunity for those trying to move to gain an economic foothold, the very category that the act was intended to assist (Oyer and Schaffer 2003).

Conclusions

When all is said and done, what useful analytical lessons can be extracted regarding calibrating political activism's impact? The challenging nature of this task is irrefutably the first lesson. It is not that demonstrations regarding influence are lacking. Studies of newly elected black mayors boosting minority employment or social service spending (and similar inquires) abound. It is connecting these first-step accomplishments to some terminal, unambiguously beneficial goal that is so daunting. That a black-run city hall hires 100 more African Americans does *not* confirm the utility of political solutions to far-ranging problems outside of the jobs given to these grateful new employees (and there is certainly no guarantee that these positions bring satisfaction to recipients).

Moreover, yesterday's rewarding accomplishment can be today's debacle—when Carl Stokes became Cleveland's first black mayor, one of his proudest accomplishments was the massive public housing expansion for African Americans. Within a few decades, however, these and similar "accomplishments" had become acknowledged catastrophes and their physical destruction is now celebrated as progress. The moral of this tale is that participation's alleged benefits cannot be separated from policy impact. Policy analysis and measuring participation are thus inevitably joined. One must ask, "What happened, and was this a beneficial outcome?" To examine only input makes the improbable assumption that any outcome is as useful as any other, a process akin to conducting a business divorced from profit.

Particularly lacking in this summation of activism's net benefits is engagement's *marginal* utility. Both experts and activists themselves apparently judge dividends as fixed: if today's protests end "colored only" drinking fountains, tomorrow they will bring equal educational attainment. This approach is patently imprudent—calculating marginal return is vital in business and daily humdrum decision-making. A firm discovering that advertising boosts revenue will not mindlessly quadruple the ad budget given diminishing returns of new expenditures. Political activism often seems immune to this logic. It is clearly insufficient for investigators to link black election gains to public employment opportunities with the implication that Nirvana is just around the corner. The entire voting-reward relationship likely becomes flat or even negative after a point, so the savvy activists should start investing elsewhere.

These inadequacies offer a pressing research agenda to social scientists. Given that activist goals are usually (and sometimes more efficiently) achievable via non-political means (see chapter 4) the calculus regarding yields should be in activist hands *before* they undertake their crusade. The researcher's responsibility is inescapable. Why should church parishioners be counseled to allocate countless hours and millions of dollars electing black House members if this investment is likely to be a net loss? Surely squandering valuable assets imposes opportunity costs. That such vital preliminary information is often ambivalent and rests on unsettled technical choices further makes the case for better guidance. If ordinary stock investors exclusively depended on such vacuous "advice," only professionals or greedy fools might play the market.

A second warning is that assessing investment returns entails more than an economics-style cost-benefit analysis of tangible policies. Politics is not commerce where pay-offs must be dollar driven and psychological rewards are secondary. Attending to this non-material dimension is, unfortunately, exceedingly rare in this literature. To ignore emotional needs, even if objectively "irrational," leaves much unexplained. Our black politics overview suggests that objectives regularly seemed *primarily* psychological, though this conclusion is entirely inferential. How else is one to account for black leaders insisting that semi-literate black police officers be hired or relentlessly defending majority-minority legislative districts long after the negative impacts of both plans are unmistakable? Surely these advocates do not prefer more crime or GOP domination; other aims were evidently pursued. Yet, and this point is beyond contention, there is nothing inappropriate or inherently dishonest about chasing castles in the sky. Who can certify that tangible aims outweigh momentary euphoria when politicking? After all, is not happiness the object of everything, and who can impose their values on others?

A third lesson concerns going beyond global, shorthand certifications of victory. Deciding *exactly* who emerges victorious is not as simple as typically alleged. It is unrealistic to speak of "benefits to blacks" (or any other category of participants) as if everyone with these traits equally shared winning or losing. That even members of a supposedly benefited group often diverge on the outcome's usefulness should be kept in mind. Examples repeatedly show the pervasiveness of mixed outcomes despite contrary rhetoric; even disasters bring benefits to some. Creating majority-minority House districts may assist dreaded Republican House control but countless previously excluded African Americans gain prestigious office. A capable "political accountant" would summarize these outcomes (including the advantage for racially conservative whites and blacks) into a comprehensive balance sheet.

The inherently cloudy nature of "victories" is a point that cannot be repeated too often, even if we could decide which side won. Bestowing the label "great triumph" on an outcome is easy and typically requires just honoring scholarly conventions. Consider the widespread (and totally accepted) custom among researchers of treating expanding welfare services as a success for black politicking (or the tightening of eligibility as a defeat). Facile consensus aside, the advantage for blacks of expansive welfare spending is, however, hardly incontrovertible. To the extent that adding black workers to administer this putative generosity occurs, and that these positions outshine any employment alternatives, expanding welfare seems a net gain. But, is this newly won entitlement progress up the socioeconomic ladder for recipients? Or might this erstwhile generosity just engender a pernicious dependency culture, an appalling condition outweighing momentary cash rewards. Surprisingly, researchers *never* ask welfare recipients if this condition is preferred over economic independence. Conceivably, being on welfare may be disliked though accepted, not "a victory." Taking a broader perspective, might this expensive policy also detract from other, more valuable government services? There are honest, hardheaded differences of opinion on all these issues. To repeat, sorting out assets from liabilities cannot be done by fiat though this may be a great convenience for conducting research. Even the most innocuous, helpful looking assistance may eventually turn out to be a poisoned gift.

What is absolutely vital, then, is to develop a system for assessing impact, just as accountants have multiple detailed formulae for judging business performance. When a thick *Modern Principles of Political Accounting* finally arrives and is applied, experts will be able to tell potential activists just how their cause is performing and whether, indeed, additional investment makes any sense. Alas, until that long-awaited day arrives, we are much closer to the blind leading the blind.

Notes

1. This picture is even grimmer if we consider House elections. According to one compilation (Cannon 1999: 10), of 6667 House elections between 1966 and 1996, only thirty-two were won by blacks, and eleven of these were by one congressman—Ron Dellums (D-CA) who represented a highly unusual and extremely radical constituency.

2. Button (1982) also examines how newly elected black officials in Florida sought to secure national government assistance. Needless to say, even if wildly successful (and it was not), this get-the-money-elsewhere strategy is an uncertain method to translate political influence into material gain. It is obviously dependent on the generosity of others, and this could quickly change as political fortunes shift and revenue dries up.

3. This "rediscovery" of system-imposed constraints in 2001 is a monument to the durable triumph of hope over reality. A quarter century ago, Levine's (1974) excellent analysis of then-pioneering black mayors shows just why less-than-grand outcomes were virtually inescapable save under unusual circumstances (and other urban politics accounts confirm this pessimistic judgment though not explicitly focusing on race). Again, those preaching activism's bountifulness seem disengaged from hardhearted reality or at least shunned well-balanced accounts of urban politics.

4. We say "rarely" since impact, even in difficult situations can be assessed via the experimental techniques that have proven invaluable in the physical sciences. For example, during the height of the movement against the war in Vietnam, Humphreys (1965) assessed the impact of an anti-war petition signed by 100 faculty members placed in a local newspaper. Calling town residents and assessing their reactions to the advertisement determined impact. This technique is clearly limited, but if does convert hopeless speculation regarding a political act into at least some scientific knowledge. Similar experiments might be feasible, and their sum total might offer a much broader impact picture.

5. Studies of the relationship between percentage of blacks in a district and legislator behavior are a cottage industry, and results predictably vary by research details. The evidence usually shows that black enfranchisement does push white Democrats toward racial liberalism and this transformation typically comes from changing personnel, not ideological conversion of the Old Guard. An excellent overview of these findings is presented in Bullock (1981).

6. Getting to the bottom of who really favored what is challenging. I personally served as an expert witness in one districting case (*Shaw v. Reno*) and private, off-the-record conversations with some of the legal principals revealed extensive gamesmanship. Public and private positions did not always agree. Some of this conflict is depicted in Cannon (1999: Introduction).

7. Perhaps the murkiest negative impact of civil rights victories concerns de-industrialization and the movement of jobs overseas. For years many blacks relied on decent- paying industrial jobs and in the 1990s many U.S. firms shuttered their domestic factories and moved production to China, Mexico, Thailand, and elsewhere. The ostensible reason was always lower labor costs, not race-related issues. Yet, these anti-discrimination laws do comprise an element of "labor cost." That many of these abandoned factories were in areas with high African-American concentrations hints that race was, indeed, a factor. One thus has to read between the lines when these grim tales of de-industrialization appear. A 2003 *New York Times* article called, "Blacks Lose Better Jobs Faster as Middle-Class Work Drops" illustrates the shadowy, awkward phenomena (Uchitelle 2003).

7

Assessing Impact: Establishing Baselines

Calculating return on political participation is immensely complicated. Politics is not like business where profit is preeminent and well-defined accounting formulae dictate its calculation. Theoretical guidelines barely exist and past ad hoc efforts offer scant assistance for future endeavors. Nevertheless, it is insufficient to say "too laborious" and just continue cataloguing activism divorced from impact. The next three chapters move a few steps toward linking investment with outcome by focusing on federal government health care policy, more specifically, why one disease receives near-frantic government attention while others, perhaps equal candidates for consideration, relatively languish. This chapter argues that AIDS (Acquired Immune Deficiency Syndrome) activists have won mighty political victories vis-à-vis rival claimants as measured by government financial commitment. After briefly outlining the emergence of AIDS, we discuss how "a fair share" of funds might be allocated to diseases more or less objectively. These "fair shares" provide the critical statistical baseline indispensable to calculate political impact. Chapter 8 explains how this federal generosity came into being via civic engagement. But, recounting these triumphs scarcely announces the war's end. Politics produce victories *and* defeats, and a full accounting requires examining both sides of the ledger. Chapter 9 addresses this downside, and we shall see that activist commemorations may be a bit premature.

The Great Federal Government Health Care Honey Pot

The federal government spends lavishly on health care and this generosity will doubtlessly rise. Office seekers habitually offer "a health care solution," and millions undoubtedly suffer from infirmaries that arguably could receive government assistance. This munificence is highly popular—countless polls since the 1960s report overwhelming majorities approving greater federal largess (Shapiro and Young 1986). In 1999 total public health programs cost taxpayers nearly $550 billion, with the federal government picking up 70 percent of this bill (*US Statistical Abstract* 2001, table 120). Nevertheless, Washington cannot be a medical emergency department rushing to every 911 call. Even the most pro-health legislature cannot satisfy all commendable desires or respond to every cry of impending calamity, and more is involved than sharp elbows when Congress annually carves up the budget.

For one, not every physical (or mental) problem is a "certified disease" demanding government intervention. Certain well-recognized conditions (e.g., cancer, tuberculosis) easily fulfill this inclusionary standard. Just obtaining the desired funding is the task here, not gaining a seat at the negotiation table. This criterion is forever fluid, however. Alcoholism was historically judged a weakness of will, not a medical disorder, and remediation entailed acquiring healthier habits, drinking tea instead (being a teetotaler) or religious devotion to forbear temptation, not government-sponsored rescues. Today alcoholism is a government research and treatment priority. This shift from a purely private matter to one requiring government intervention is commonplace. The opposite pathway may occur, though rarely—witness homosexuality's evolution from a criminalized vice to a treatable sickness to, according to today's medical standard, a preference well beyond government eradication efforts.

Delving into pathological antecedents further sows complexity since the link between funding and wellness is often murky. To wit, a disease can often be expeditiously treated prior to the disorder erupting. Consider heart disease, a pervasive killer consuming enormous public and private resources. How can this malady be prudently tackled? Prevention is typically highly efficacious—education regarding proper diet, encouraging regular exercise, and, conceivably, taxing unwholesome fatty foods. Should we therefore shift drug research and expensive medical technology funding into anti-obesity informational campaigns though this tactic offers scant assistance to today's sufferers? Is preventing future coronary-related deaths morally and financially comparable to keeping alive those who've already suffered heart attacks?

On the other side of the coin, government nutritional programs (e.g., Food Stamps, subsidized school lunches) are not labeled "healthcare" though are occasionally defended for their long-term well-being benefits (and these efforts might, contrary to intent, promote disease-causing obesity). Policies as far removed immigration have medical consequences—newcomers occasionally overburden hospitals while others serve as doctors and nurses in resource-starved localities. At the very edge of this treat-the-sources-not-the-symptoms perspective are those claiming that countless maladies result from capitalism or economic inequality, not germs or inadequate doctoring, so cures necessitate major socio-economic transformations. One AIDS analysis saw it as an out-of-control pandemic mired in racism, sexism, and classism plus discrimination against those with unconventional sexual preferences (Theodoulou 1996: 2).

A parallel quandary concerns disease-centered approaches versus concentrating on basic science. For example, fighting cancer entails basic biology only distantly related to cancer. This dualism is reflected in the National Institute of Health's organizational structure—a disease-centered National Cancer Institute coexists with a far more encompassing National Human Genome Research Institute (which focuses on cancer genetics). Choices here comprise a serious potential dilemma and can easily disguise long-term goals. A disease-centered arrangement is especially politically inviting since it provides a supporting constituency (the ill, their families, and specialized professionals), and both legislators and voters immediately grasp objectives. By contrast, backing pure science, even if eventually relevant to cures, is less attractive politically since it lacks a natural constituency (outside of scientists themselves) and may seem too abstract.

The division between purely private medical problems and those properly warranting public attention adds additional complexity. While some afflictions are self-evidently public (deadly communicable diseases such as Ebola), others are plausibly wholly private. Are myopia or eczema conditions demanding federal attentiveness, or are they purely personal? What about migraine headaches, PMS, and similar excruciating conditions that are economically costly though hardly life threatening? Should marital counseling be publicly subsidized since broken families breed innumerable pathologies, some medical in character?

Traditional morality is also relevant—does self-inflicted illness deserve public assistance? Strict moralists might withhold government dieting assistance to the obese (regardless of the fitness benefits) since overeating is typically volitional. By contrast, those blamelessly undernourished (e.g., infants) do deserve help. This self-infliction criterion may, however, shift. Drug abuse and numberless other personal "bad behavior" disorders demonstrate how private vices can be pushed to become major (and expensive) *public* health crises.

Should medical conditions be dismissed as a public problem if primarily a vanity or quality of life disorder? Sexual dysfunction, physical flaws, phobic reactions, and minor allergies are all troublesome conditions that fall into this category. Must taxpayers subsidize plastic surgery to "correct" a perfectly functional but otherwise "too big" nose if that nose brings debilitating mental illness? That the private firms routinely meet these needs (e.g., Viagra) again suggests the non-inevitability of public intercession. Still, in light of history, it is almost inevitable that private remedies currently available to the wealthier will eventually be demanded from the U.S. Treasury. Plausibly, decent sex (provided at Washington's expense) might ultimately encourage better physical health via weight reduction or regular exercise, and thus reduce costly ailments such as diabetes.

Finally, the definition of "good health" is quite malleable. A century ago many elderly suffered from arthritis, osteoporosis, impaired memory, and additional debilitating states comprising "old age." These were perceived as natural, inescapable steps in the aging process, less treatable maladies requiring costly public intervention. Today, of course, these age-related infirmaries instigate billion-dollar research campaigns, much of it publicly funded.

The inescapable message is that securing health-related public funding is never automatic and certainly not a guaranteed right.[1] Anguish, in and of itself cannot guarantee access to the U.S. Treasury, and AIDS is no exception. A recent *Wall Street Journal* story tells that an estimated 32,000 Americans die each year due to aneurysms, a ballooning of a blood vessel. Though this number is twice the deaths from AIDS, and well beyond many more notable killers (e.g., cervical cancer), and these deaths could easily and cheaply be prevented by prior scanning, it has drawn miniscule government funding. It is not that these lives are unimportant; rather, these 32,000 victims are not a "natural" political constituency and many aneurysms go undetected (Burton 2003). Going even further, it has been carefully documented that inadequate regular exercise is closely associated with cardiovascular disease, colon cancer, non-insulin dependent diabetes, osteoporosis and various mental health disorders, and here the deadliness far, far exceeds AIDS mortality (U.S. Department of Health and Human Services, 1996: ch. 4). Nevertheless, the demand for zealous government involvement (e.g., publicly subsidized health clubs) has yet to arrive. The moral is clear: AIDS activists (or those with comparable conditions) must convince officialdom of a bona fide medical catastrophe that *should* be treated at public expense versus a self-inflicted risk or a regrettable but inescapable fact of life. Even more daunting, this uncertain and likely expensive eradication campaign must commence immediately, and outshine wars on far deadlier killers where many victims were absolutely innocent versus self-inflicted illness. Lastly, those morally conservative Americans who view AIDS sufferers as getting what they deserve from illegal drug use or, in the case of gays, dangerous (and sometimes illegal) promiscuity in unsavory venues must be overcome, or at least neutralized. In other words, mobilizing government to conquer AIDS is hardly pre-determined.

The AIDS Epidemic

Unlike most illnesses receiving public funding, AIDS surfaced abruptly though evidence suggests a longer, undiagnosed history. Its multiple symptoms in divergent populations initially baffled medical experts. The first documented outbreak occurred in 1979, but went unrecognized as such since the outward cause of death was a lung blockage with *Pneumocystis carninii* (PC), tiny protozoa, an illness familiar to experts. This death was also initially linked to Africa, not the U.S. or Europe. The earliest ominous sign of something entirely new surfaced in 1980 when U.S. doctors encountered a handful of deadly Kaposi's Sarcoma (KS) cases among young gay males, a relatively rare, benign cancer as a rule striking elderly Jewish and Italian men. Still, though KS cases among gay males multiplied, the outbreak was hardly a disquieting epidemic, especially since mysterious maladies periodically happen and then inexplicably vanish.

The official inkling of something more serious occurred in 1981 when a Center for Disease Control (CDC) researcher detected a sudden upturn in pentamidine prescriptions originating from New York City to treat *Pneumocystis carninii*. That pentamidine is normally approved for chemotherapy patients with weakened immunity systems, not pneumonia, raised eyebrows. Fresh KS and PC cases were soon reported in New York, Los Angeles, and San Francisco both among gay men and intravenous drug users. A few hemophiliacs receiving blood transfusions also unpredictably became ill. By the middle of 1981 louder alarms were being sounded, but health experts remained baffled regarding underlying causes. On July 4, 1981, the CDC officially announced the peculiar, and seeming perplexing, outbreak of KS in its weekly report (a total of twenty-six patients, mainly in New York City) plus ten cases of PC among gay men.

By late 1981 a few observant doctors and public health experts realized that something serious was spreading and research began in earnest. The term "gay plague" now appeared. To condense a riveting tale, unraveling AIDS entailed a colossal scientific effort, with frequent false leads, often overcoming major challenges and paltry funding, but by 1985 the basic infection process seems plausibly clear, though some well-regarded researchers remain skeptical. Essentially, AIDS results from a virus—the human immunodeficiency virus, or HIV—transmitted via bodily fluids (semen, blood, on needles) and can lay dormant up to five years. This bodily fluid aspect explains its odd prevalence among male homosexuals, intravenous drug users, and hemophiliacs (who periodically receive blood transfusions). HIV is a fragile organism, so multiple transmission efforts are often necessary to produce infections. Once activated, however, HIV annihilates the body's natural immunity system so death results from other illnesses (such as KS), not, technically, the virus itself. How the AIDS virus arrived in the U.S. still remains controversial, and its impact varies by geography and ethnicity, but its lethalness is absolutely unquestioned.

This deadliness can be seen in Figure 7.1 depicting mortality among those aged 25-44, a generally healthy age cohort. By the mid-1990s, AIDS had quickly risen to be the principal killer among *all* people this age though by the late 1990s its devastation had receded. The role of gay men in this epidemic is revealed in figure 7.2 that presents all types of AIDS-related deaths, by source. From the earliest data (1985 and prior) gay males are always the most decimated category, drug users second. All others, including heterosexuals, are less affected, and if gays were left untouched, AIDS would probably still be an obscure illness.[2] Only by the late 1990s did deaths decline significantly though numbers remain substantial. Overall, through 2000, the official total AIDS-related death toll for gay men was 235,000 with another 32,400 deaths among homosexual men who were also intravenous drug users (CDC http://cdec.gov/hiv/stats/hasrsupp81/table5.htm).

Figure 7.1
Death Rates per 100,000 Population from Leading Causes of Death among Persons 25-44 Years Old, United States, 1987-2000

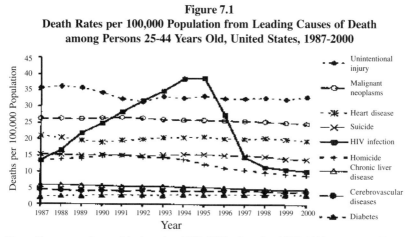

Note: For comparison with data for 1999-2000, data for 1987-1998 were modified to appear as if based on ICD-10 rules for selecting the underlying cause of death instead of ICD-9.
Source: National Center for Health Statistics National Vital Statistics System.

Figure 7.2
Estimated[1] Adult/Adolescent Deaths Among Women with AIDS, by Risk Exposure[2] and Half-Year of Death, United States

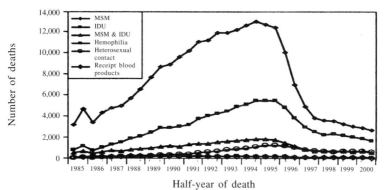

Half-year of death
[1]Data are adjusted for delays in the reporting of deaths and the redistribution of cases initially reported without risk information.
[2]Excludes approximately 1960 cases with other or unknown risk exposures, see technical notes.

Winning the Battle to Conquer AIDS

On July 9, 1999, The Senate Subcommittee on Labor, Health, and Human Services, and Education and Related Agencies held hearings in San Francisco regarding funding AIDS research and services. Though this sub-committee was Republican controlled, and was operating in an atmosphere where containing soaring medical expenses had become a public concern, the hearing's overall tone reassured AIDS activists. Senator Arlen Specter's (R-PA) opening remarks recounted the grimness of AIDS: in eighteen years since the disease was first recognized, 690,000 Americans were reported to have AIDS, with some 410,000 resultant deaths. He acknowledged that while federal funding had been generous, going from $3.3 million in 1982 to $4.1 billion at that moment, it was still insufficient despite a declining death rate. The purpose of the hearings, said Specter, was to develop a public awareness to sustain high funding levels in the face of mandated shrinking budgets. Specter's call for even more federal financial commitment was soon echoed by a parade of witnesses, public officials, health care officials, and citizen activists (even the 1998 Miss America), nearly all of them recounting their own efforts to establish anti-AIDS programs. *Nobody* testified against greater funding.

This "do more, and do it soon" atmosphere was hardly unique to San Francisco and high-profile AIDS sympathizers. Poll data confirm an unmistakable popular consensus regarding defeating this malady and, significantly, this enthusiasm cooled only slightly as actual funding soared. The University of Michigan's National Election Study (NES) poll conducted in 1992 when AIDS appeared to be surging out of control found that 61 percent favored greater government spending. By 1996, again according to the University of Michigan's NES study, the "increases" category drew 56 percent, with 33 percent saying "keep the same" and 10 percent saying "decrease" (less than .5 percent volunteered "eliminate altogether"). By 2000, when AIDS spending *had been* sharply increased, 51 percent wanted still more with only a relative handful favoring cutbacks according to this Michigan survey. Similarly, a May 2001 survey funded by the Henry J. Keiser Family Foundation reported that 55 percent agreed that "too little" federal money was being spent on AIDS (5 percent said "too much"), 86 percent said that the federal government's fight against AIDS was "very important" while 83 percent endorsed support to discover an anti-HIV vaccine. This enthusiasm even persisted when other diseases were mentioned. A 1994 NBC News/Wall Street Journal poll found that 45 percent said that government AIDS spending was insufficient relative to fighting cancer and heart disease, two far deadlier illnesses (a 1992 Gallup poll with the same question reported that 59 percent said that it was *more* important to fight AIDS than cancer and heart disease).

In short, AIDS activists have won colossal political victories, and done so remarkably quickly. This political triumph of transforming AIDS into a medically related malady best addressed by immediate, vigorous government intervention was *not* pre-ordained. Recall that not every ailment automatically elicits a government sponsored "war." Hepatitis B and hepatitis C are far deadlier worldwide than AIDS and continue to rise, but perhaps due to their link to the drug culture, are seemingly invisible in the public's imagination (Ocama and Lee 2003). Obesity is even more serious measured by soaring incidence and cost to the healthcare system and receives a mere pittance from NIH compared to AIDS (Sturm 2002). Indeed, obesity has increased by 70 percent since 1990, is related to 9.1 percent of all U.S. health expenditures, and in 2002 cost the Medicare and Medicaid programs some $45 billion dollars. Combating corpulence would have a major impact on reducing several cancers, heart problems, and other serious maladies (Finkelstein, Fiebelkorn and Wang 2003). One might have initially predicted otherwise regarding this drive to tackle AIDS—throughout the early 1980s when AIDS first surfaced and was closely identified with homosexuals, clear public majorities affirmed that homosexual sex was morally wrong. This moral aversion sentiment continued into the mid-1990s though somewhat diminished. Polls during this period also showed widespread resistance to the legality of homosexuality (Yang 1997).

A "Fairness" Baseline

Taxpayer bountifulness aside, the case for relentless anti-AIDS spending vis-à-vis rival illnesses can be challenged on purely cold-hearted financial grounds. Equally deadly illnesses abound, and since resources are always constrained, the pro-AIDS argument cannot be just that "people are dying." That simple mortality standard makes old age (or physical inactivity) our chief public health priority. Assessing the impact of political activism on funding levels thus requires hard benchmarks regarding "too much" or "too little" spending. The value of combating AIDS is undisputable. Our aim is aligning spending with a "fair share" standard to assess political success vis-à-vis rivals also competing for federal funds.

How might this objective baseline "fair share" be computed? Letting the public directly carve up health care budgets is one possible solution. That is, via a poll people would allocate funds to various diseases, and this would be the public budgetary mandate. If a majority wanted, say, $5 billion spent on AIDS, and only $2 billion were committed, it might be assumed that "politics" explained the discrepancy. Leaving aside the public's considerable medical ignorance and vulnerability to scare stories, the technical obstacles to extracting this guidance are overwhelming. Even if the public were familiar with AIDS, the average citizen is scarcely in a position to weigh the benefits of various treatments, their costs, and what additional expenditures might produce.

Linking dollar allocations to frequency is more realistic, and can be derived according to a different formula (and may vary by illnesses classification). Thus, in 1999 there were 170,000 instances of TB reported in the U.S. and 346,000 of typhoid fever, so whatever the budget, Typhoid fever should get roughly twice the funding of TB (*US Statistical Abstract,* table 181, 2001). Unfortunately, this "one case of a disease, one allocation unit" egalitarian approach neglects seriousness—chickenpox is a widespread personal nuisance, but rarely is it fatal and it typically vanishes without treatment. Surely chickenpox and leukemia differ profoundly.

Factoring in lethalness adds seriousness to this equation. For example, in 1998 the mortality rate for cancer was 541.5 per 100,000 compared to a death rate of diabetes of 64.8 (*US Statistical Abstract,* table 105, 2001), a ratio suggesting that cancer should receive about eight times the funding of diabetes. Still, this approach may be far too unrefined. For one, crude death rates obscure changing patterns, for good or bad. Once-dreaded diseases (e.g., yellow fever, polio) are rapidly disappearing due to vaccination and better hygiene, so backing eradication programs, let alone expensive new research, may yield slight marginal benefit for soon-to-disappear maladies. Meanwhile, diabetes mortality is rising, and though still modest, now may be the opportune time for "over-kill" before matters deteriorate. The appropriate funding standard might be new cases encountered, especially deadly outbreaks of contagious sicknesses.

Lethal incidence can also be handled more sophisticatedly by calculating expected years lost to a disease. Alzheimer's, for example, characteristically strikes the elderly, so while increasingly common, the total number of years "lost" is slight compared to, say, Reye's syndrome that afflicts children. More complicated is incorporating the "social value" of who dies, with greater weight given to those more socially or economically valuable. Though morally awkward and technically arduous to calculate, such investment distinctions are commonplace in awarding scarce education or housing benefits. Hospital ethics committees frequently ration treatment based upon the recipient's personal traits. From this vantage point, a liver cirrhosis epidemic among skid row alcoholics might be judged far less worthy of expensive intervention than curing demented college professors.

Cost benefit analyses also provide multiple baselines for an optimally fair health allocation system since (a) illnesses impose variable burdens and (b) resources are always finite, so a "good" system secures the best health for the least cost. According to one study, for example, hypertension screening for men aged 45 to 54 would cost $5,200 per year per life saved. By contrast, a colonoscopy for routine colon cancer would be $90,000 for each year saved per person while the same life-saved benefit would cost $190,000 for an annual mammogram for women between 40 and 49. At the extreme is the sum of $26,000,000 per year necessary to add one year by having an extra colon cancer screening procedure (cited in Ubel 2000: 35). From this perspective, sustaining a handful of elderly patients a few months is wasteful if the same money spent for cheap vaccines might save millions of children.

Costs and benefits can also reflect treatment expenditures. Some diseases are extremely expensive to alleviate in their terminal stages, so early intervention can bring major savings. Finding cholesterol-lowering medicine is thus a superior investment to high-priced heart transplants. This logic can push the intervention back to the point where it hardly appears "medical." Government-sponsored campaigns to encourage fruit and vegetable consumption may far outshine developing costly radiation treatments to fight cancer, though this cost-effective strategy offers scant comfort to cancer patients.

There are also limits on government help, no matter how well justi-fied. Though obesity costs taxpayers billions, and is soaring, imag-ine the problems facing a government cracking down on compul-sive overeaters?

A final wrinkle in these calculations concerns the definition of "curing." Keeping a person alive who might otherwise die from an illness may be defined as a cure, but the improvement for the person saved may be more ambiguous. For example, medical progress in treating heart attacks and stroke has saved over a million lives since the 1970s (Kolata 2003). But for many of those saved due to quick medical intervention, the quality of life is sharply diminished. Life now can be compromised by frailty, dementia, and other impair-ments. Chapter 9 returns to this point by showing how medications have kept alive countless AIDS sufferers though with extremely un-pleasant (and costly) side effects. Can these disrupted lives be judged an unambiguous success since the person remains alive?

National Institutes of Health Allocations

The National Institutes of Health (NIH) comprises the health re-search arm of the federal government though actual work is often contracted to investigators in private foundations and universities. Established in 1887, with initial resources of $300, today it com-prises some twenty-three separate institutes and centers focusing on both specific illnesses and medical-related issues such as health-care for minorities. Of the utmost importance, Congress *by law* sets bud-gets for each individual research institute and center and, as with all expenditure requests, these must survive countless reviews and votes. Opportunities for political meddling flourish: there are four major congressional committees supervising this budget, and funds for specific illnesses are occasionally quietly inserted elsewhere, for example, research funding for breast cancer has been put into the defense budget. Even without specific fiscal authorization, appro-priations committees can "encourage" certain research initiatives, or call for a progress report (among other admonitions), and these are carefully heeded. Nor are champions of specific illnesses, all of whom feel neglected, shy about lobbying Congress, and legislators do regularly cater to these requests (NIH, "Congressional Role" http://bob.nap.edu/html/nih/Ch5cc,e.htm#nih). Within these specified funding levels experts have some option, but it is Congress that controls overall direction and can micromanage if it so chooses. That top NIH officials regularly testify before Congress to defend their budget choices confirms this inescapable political element (Varmus 1999, "Testimony," for a quick overview of allocation criteria).

There is no pretense that these allocations are absolutely scientifically objective. Harold Varmus, in his May 1, 1997 Senate testimony frankly admitted that all commitments are approximations based upon myriad uncertainties and informed guesses (Varmus, "Statement" http://hih.gov/about/director/testim2.htm). Over and above technical considerations, these figures reflect what emerges from consultations with patient advocacy groups, health care providers, individual legislators, executive branch officials, and whoever else can get their opinions heard. Public meetings around the country also elicit input from community leaders and citizens. An Office of Public Liaison (and something called the Director's Council of Public Representation) further helps gather public feedback. Clearly, these "disease constituencies" differ in their access and negotiating skill, and not all carry the same political clout, so legislative decision-making inevitably involves wheeling and dealing with some illnesses getting neglected.

In FY 2002 the total authorization was $17.8 billion, a figure far removed from the $9.2 billion spent in 1990. High-profile events regularly push allocations from one area to another, for example, in FY 2001 the Anthrax research allocation was $7.3 million, but this soared to (an estimated) $287.4 million in FY 2003 after the 9/11 terrorist attack in which anthrax was spread via the U.S. postal system. Even larger increases appeared for research on bio-terrorism—from $52.8 million to over $1.7 billion two years later (National Institutes of Health, http://www4.od.nih.gov/officeofbudget/FundingResearchAreas.htm). For better or worse, NIH spending serves as a fiscal portrait of our public, congressionally negotiated (and thus publicly influenced), anti-disease commitment, not some hard-edged objective formula.

A useful place to observe these politically established obligations is to examine monetary allocations according to disease. Table 7.1 tells us, for example, that in FY2001 Hepatitis C was "worth" $84.0 million but by FY 2003 its worth had grown by $19 million to $103.0 million. The NIH's financial promise to eliminate AIDS is especially noteworthy—nearly $2.3 billion in FY2001, a figure that imperfectly reflects total spending since research elsewhere, for example, vaccine development ($550.9 million in FY 2001) and autoimmune diseases (nearly half a billion in FY 2001) unquestionably have anti-AIDS applications. Equally significant has been the rapid government response to the AIDS epidemic. Unlike many diseases with deadly consequences, AIDS did not have to languish before public officials took the illness seriously, a major feat in a system mired in budgetary incrementalism. Between FY1991 and FY2000, the resources going to AIDS work doubled, a growth rate somewhat in excess of the total NIH budget, and one that far exceeded growth attributable to inflation (*Key Facts and History of Funding FY1991-FY2000,* NIH, 32).

Table 7.1 National Institutes of Health
Research Initiatives/Programs of Interest

(Dollars in Millions) Research/Disease Areas	FYI 2001 Actual $	FY 2002 Actual $	FY 2003 Estimate $
Aging Research	1,667.4	1,878.2	2,039.6
AIDS (Budget Authority)	2,247.0	2,515.0	2,770.0
Minority AIDS	439.5	487.9	535.8
Pediatric AIDS	272.8	196.8	535.8
Vaccines AIDS	269.2	339.5	422.3
ALS	27.5	30.0	32.3
Alzheimer's Disease	524.9	594.7	644.0
Anthrax Research	7.3	42.1	287.4
Arthritis Research	278.1	316.2	342.6
Asthma	208.8	233.7	255.6
Autism	55.8	65.1	70.5
Autoimmune Disease	495.1	563.4	608.6
Behavioral and Social Science	2,100.6	2364.0	2,575.2
Bioengineering	692.4	792.5	960.6
Bioterrorism*	52.8	274.5	1,747.9
Brain Disorders	3,916.5	4,437.7	4,809.1
Cancer Research	4,376.4	4,929.8	5,558.8
Breast Cancer	580.9	655.2	732.3
Lung Cancer	225.6	259.2	297.0
Ovarian Cancer	90.3	104.0	118.9
Prostate Cancer	320.1	362.1	408.3
Cardiovascular Research	1,723.1	1,920.8	2,064.6
Clinical Research	6,433.3	7,235.7	8,037.3
Complementary and Alternative Medicine	212.9	247.6	269.1

(Dollars in Millions) Research/Disease Areas	FYI 2001 Actual $	FY 2002 Actual $	FY 2003 Estimate $
Cystic Fibrosis	107.3	117.2	126.7
Diabetes Research **	688.1	781.3	845.1
Diagnostic Radiology	489.5	574.0	633.3
Emerging Infectious Diseases	222.6	382.4	1,466.6
Chronic Fatigue Syndrome	5.8	6.2	6.5
Fibromyalgia	9.5	10.6	12.3
Gene Therapy	349.4	390.1	427.4
Hepatitis C	84.0	95.2	103.0
Hypertension	277-0	307.5	329.5
Infant Mortality/(LBW)	448.8	506.8	561.3
Kidney Disease	320.7	367.1	399.1
Lupus	64.6	73.4	78.9
Mental Health	1,446.3	1,635.0	1,769.6
Multiple Sclerosis	69.8	77.5	83.9
Muscular Dystrophy	21.0	23.4	25.4
Neurosciences Research	3,800.7	4,305.7	4,665.0
Nutrition	755.7	859.2	942.7
Obesity	222.6	252.3	274.1
Osteoporosis	173.0	193.9	209.6
Parkinson's Disease	175.1	198.9	215.1
Pediatric Research	2,509.6	2,829.2	3,052.9
Polycystic Kidney Disease	18.7	21.0	22.9
Prevention	5,124.2	5,927.1	6,852.3
Sexually Transmitted Diseases/Herpes	167.8	190.0	208.6
Schizophrenia	276.1	312.4	338.4
Sickle Cell Disease	71.6	79.7	85.5
Sleep Disorders	148.1	166.0	178.8
Smoking and Health	448.3	503.7	554.9
Spinal Cord Injury	71.5	78.9	84.7
Stem Cell Research	306.0	346.0	380.2
Stroke	238.9	263.5	283.1
Sudden Infant Death Syndrome	54.2	62.0	67.5
Topical Microbicides	47.0	55.7	68.2
Transmissible Spongiform Encephalopathy (TSE)	24.0	24.3	26.4
Tuberculosis Research	87.3	99.4	108.4
Vaccine Development	550.9	704.3	1,195.7
Women's Health	2,923.1	3,390.1	4,120.4

* Amounts include $180 million appropriated to the PHS Emergency Supplemental Fund through the H& 2002 Department of Defense and Emergency Supplemental Appropriations (P.L. 107-117).
** Funds available for diabetes research (P.L. 105-33 and P.L. 106-554).

Yet, to recall our previous fairness benchmarks discussion, these figures by themselves say little about political pressure. Conceivably, lawmakers and scientists have coldly calculated just how much each disease is objectively worth according to its health seriousness, social and economic costs, and other objective measures. Perhaps chronic fatigue syndrome truly deserves $5.8 million, not a nickel more, given its miniscule impact. Fortunately, for those curious about the relationship between funding and social burdens of various illnesses, research has attempted to align NIH spending with overall harm, variously measured (Gross, Anderson, and Powe 1999). Specifically, NIH figures from 1996 were statistically compared with six burdens of disease: total mortality, years of life lost, the number of hospital days stayed in 1994 and three different indicators of disability-years lost to the illness. Note well, these measures are proxies for more subtle and complex phenomena, and apply to only a single year, but they offer systematic "bang for the buck" evaluations to assess how politics can shape medical attentiveness.

In FY1996 the total NIH research funding were $11.9 billion, of which $4.9 billion was specifically targeted for some twenty-nine diseases (representing 63 percent of all reported deaths in 1994). Analysis is further limited since estimates of incidence was unavailable for some maladies (e.g., injuries, oral and dental disorders). Overall, leaving aside certain statistical transformations of the data, neither the incidence of the malady (number of people affected) or prevalence (number of new cases recorded) predict these HIM allocations. Nor did the number of hospital days used predict spending in general, which suggests that illnesses soaking up lots of expensive care failed to be judged especially deserving of heightened outlays. There were, however, unsurprisingly strong relationships between mortality and funding; namely the "big" killers—heart disease, stroke, and lung cancer—did draw the largest financial commitments. This positive correlation also held when a measure called "disability-adjusted life-years" was the standard—this roughly captures years spent in less-than-perfect health due to the malady. For example, alcohol abuse seldom kills immediately, but it can progressively destroy life quality for decades prior to death. Nevertheless, while these illnesses generally follow a similar pattern regarding quality of life lost, AIDS is a dramatic outlier in the direction of being "over-funded." Put another way, if we based funding choices only on suffering, AIDS research would be sharply *reduced* (Gross, Anderson, and Powe 1999: figure 1).

An even sharper picture regarding AIDS generosity emerges when the relationship between years of life lost and spending is examined. This approach makes childhood mortality more "serious" than deaths among the elderly. Table 7.2 reprints these data that depict spending and three distinct measures of life lost, and while the data's coarseness deserves reiteration, the differences are huge, so different calculation formula are unlikely to sway the outcome. We can readily see that some conditions, particularly various cancers (uterine, ovarian) are under-funded while breast cancer receives generous NIH support. The government's concern with breast cancer is, however, absolute tightfistedness compared to how AIDS is treated. *Measured by either lives lost, the poorness of life's quality, or net years lost, AIDS funding is about five times more plentiful than its nearest competitor (beast cancer).*[3]

Table 7.2
Difference Between Actual and Predicted Funding by the NIH According to the Measure Used to Predict Funding*

Condition or Disease	Mortality	Disability-Adjusted Life-Years	Years of Life Lost
Chronic obstructive pulmonary disease	-83	-79	-76
Perinatal conditions	-81	-79	-109
Peptic ulcer	-79	-36	-72
Pneumonia	-79	-41	-66
Uterine cancer	-61	-23	-58
Ovarian cancer	-57	-12	-41
Stroke	-39	-95	-29
Lung cancer	-31	-36	-36
Prostate cancer	-27	25	-14
Colorectal cancer	-27	-13	-25
Otitis media	-23	-15	-25
Cervical cancer	-21	22	-28
Parkson's disease	-17	18	-1
Epilepsy	-9	-8	-17
Asthma	-2	-20	-7
Tuberculosis	-2	35	-1
Multiple sclerosis	14	41	9
Cirrhosis	53	53	40

Depression	53	-140	72
Injuries	54	-89	-4
Sexually transmitted diseases	56	46	57
Schizophrenia	61	-29	68
Ischemic heart disease	70	-24	68
Dental and oral disorders	149	105	152
Diabetes mellitus	167	155	168
Alcohol abuse	170	48	160
Dementia	185	144	207
Breast cancer	257	272	249
AIDS	1,287	1,307	1,252

* Negative numbers indicate that research on a condition was underfunded in relation to the burden of the disease and posiposition numbers that it was overfunded.
One disability-adjusted life-year is defined as the loss of one year of healthy life to disease.

*Amounts include $180 million appropriated to the PHS Emergency Supplemental Fund through the H& 2002 Department of Defense and Emergency Supplemental Appropriations (P.L. 107-117).
** Funds available for diabetes research (P.L. 105-33 and P.L. 106-554).

The decline in AIDS-related deaths and the government's contin-ued research generosity has widened this cost-benefit discrepancy. In 2002, for example, the HIH allocated $2.5 billion to AIDS re-search; in 2000 it killed 15,288 people. By contrast, heart disease received $1.9 billion while the deaths in 2000 were 709,894. In other words, heart ailments got less, but the number of people dying was forty-six times as great! Diabetes takes the lives of 193,000 Ameri-cans annually (though many actually die from diabetes-related ill-nesses), nearly thirteen times the number of people dying of AIDS, and yet its NIH funding is only about 30 percent of what AIDS re-ceives. In addition, it is exploding at an alarming 30 percent per annum rate, and soaks up 10 percent of all U.S. health care dollars, and its estimated total economic cost is about four times that of AIDS (Smith 2000). Judged by the trend in AIDS funding, these ratios will only get larger—AIDS deaths have declined dramatically since 1995 (from 51,147 to 15,288) yet funding is double the 1995 level (Price 2002).

The government's anti-AIDS bounteousness is hardy limited to NIH research. All told, according to testimony offered by NIH Di-rector Anthony Fauci, Washington in FY2000 allocated some $15 billion to research involving conquering HIV-AIDS that has gener-ated some 16 officially approved anti-HIV medications (Fauci 1999, testimony). Indeed, the secretary of the Department of Health and Human Services declared AIDS to be the number one health priority of the Public Health Service. The variety of programs absolutely confirms this heartfelt effort. The Center for Disease Control (CDC) received $762 million earmarked for prevention efforts. The Ryan White CARE Act first enacted in 1990, named after the youngster whose tragic early death due to AIDS drew immense national sympathy, entailed some $1.9 billion in FY2002 directed toward early intervention, AIDS drug assistance programs, emergency assistance, and other educational efforts. The states via block grants received some $1.67 billion in FY2001 and the little noticed "Housing Opportunities for People with AIDS" drew $258 million in government assistance in FY2001. Tens of millions were likewise targeted for minorities, women and children, and these totals are separate from more general anti-drug efforts that affect AIDS transmission. Significantly and consistent with NIH funding patterns, these budgets are generally expanding despite a notable slowing of deaths (Human Rights Campaign, News Release 2002).

A different calibration of this massive intervention effort comes from the avalanche of AIDS-related research findings that this sudden outpouring of funds produced. When AIDS initially appeared in the early 1980s it generated only a few dozen scientific publications. By 1983 this figure had reached six hundred, and by 1987 it soared to twenty-seven hundred, an enormous increase rate given that biomedical publications generally rise at only about a 3 or 4 percent annually. In 1986, there were some 2,000 scientific papers published about HIV, and this topic comprised only 37 percent of this exploding AIDS-related literature. Entire scientific journals were now devoted to HIV and AIDS (these figures are reported in Epstein 1996: 79-80). To suggest, as some activists did, that scientists "were ignoring" AIDS is a bizarre claim.

These multi-million outlays buy an incredible cornucopia of material benefits. In heavily impacted cities like San Francisco during the early 1990s the AIDS stricken could receive federally subsidized home health care, financial assistance, dental care, daycare, home delivered meals, transportation, prescription drugs, shopping assistance, psychotherapy, Chinese medicine, legal advocacy, and multiple other useful services. New York offered, among countless other benefits, AIDS assistance for the deaf, educational materials for Native Americans, even sensitivity training for prison guards. The National AIDS Clearinghouse in 1994 compiled a list of 18,402 AIDS-related service organizations virtually everywhere that, in various degrees, depended on federal largess (Burkett 1995: ch. 5).

These expenditure figures *minimize* the movement's political accomplishments. Benefits well beyond free meals or legal advice lurk below the surface. There is also a power dividend. When these programs were first being formulated it was unclear just who would control the actual administration. Numerous options were available, everything from assigning responsibilities to existing public health professionals to deeply involving charities such as the United Way. Thanks to brilliant legislative lobbying, gays themselves, particularly organizations dominated by white male homosexuals, acquired substantial control of this far-flung effort. Now activists would play a central role in guiding key health care delivery decisions. The justification was reasonable enough: homophobia might hinder program effectiveness and who better appreciated the AIDS menace than gays themselves.

Staid budgetary figures do not reflect the full impact of this newfound administrative control. Militants once relegated to raucous street theater instantly became part of a freshly fashioned "AIDS establishment." An immediate monetary advantage was now gained. Haranguing Washington could be accomplished while safely on the federal payroll with a paid staff to assist this beseeching. Advocates further enjoyed the status and access that comes from being part of "officialdom." That thousands of these assistance organizations were scattered across multiple congressional districts created a boisterous pork-barrel constituency. A powerful dynamic ensued: the more funding, the greater the number of organizations, the more resources available to pay salaries and organization overhead, the more vigorous the pleading. Success bred success; taxpayers now supported advocacy.

Conclusions

These data unambiguously show that the potential objective allocation formulas previously elucidated do *not* mechanically predict AIDS funding. To be sure, this snapshot is hardly absolutely conclusive regarding the oft-murky hand of political influence. Perhaps our calculations are misleading. Curing AIDS may be uniquely expensive and justifiable on non-traditional grounds, so financial comparisons with "traditional" killers such as cancer are deceptive. Or, a possible worldwide AIDS epidemic would be so catastrophic that an immediate "excessive" Manhattan Project-like effort is reasonable to head off catastrophe. Perchance government's immense role here merely reflects private sector insufficiency. One could further argue that many victims are among society's most creative and productive members, so the bounteousness is commendable preservation of society's resources.

These arguments may ring true, yet nearly all afflictions can be similarly defended. Narcotics addition undoubtedly ruins the lives of millions (including family members) and the criminal justice system spends billions in policing and incarceration, and these victims tend to be youngsters. Heart disease advocates might demonstrate the gigantic economic cost of incapacitating millions of potentially productive workers. The argument that we must spend until a cure is found is applicable to hundreds of deadly illnesses, not merely AIDS. Nor is it self-evident that U.S. national self-interest or humanitarian passion requires eliminating AIDS overseas. All in all, this "my illness is more deserving than yours" approach is beyond scientific resolution. Instead we offer a more political explanation of why AIDS outshines its rivals in extracting government's bigheartedness. To be blunt, AIDS activists have done masterfully, far better than adversaries advancing equally laudable cases.

Notes

1. This overview, though extensive by the standards of those reflexively calling for even greater commitment, is still superficial. For example, we have not addressed individual health care preference variability—an individual's value assigned to "being healthy" versus other benefits in a free market. Chapter 9 will show that at least some people will value immediate sexual pleasure ahead of being healthy tomorrow, and hard statistical formula cannot resolve this issue. Victor R. Fuchs, *Who Shall Live* (1974) analyzes these quandaries in detail.

2. The difficulty of establishing the exact transmission route should be noted, and this imprecision can be politically relevant. It is sometimes alleged that heterosexual transmission can disguise a homosexual path given the reluctance of many men to admit being gay (and fear of criminal sanctions, as well). These are officially reported statistics, and thus may underestimate incidence since cause of death can legitimately be listed as something other than AIDS to spare family and friends embarrassment.

3. A different way of calculating this proportionality is to assess research investment as a proportion of the total spent on patient care. According to one calculation made in 1989, cancer research expenditures equaled about 4.5 percent of total cancer patient cost. For heart disease the figure was 2.9 percent. By contrast, for AIDS this number was 230 percent! Cited in Fumento (1993: 328).

8

Assessing Impact: The Positive Side of the AIDS Activism Balance Sheet

How did gays and their allies manage to extract this federal bounteousness? And in competition with innumerable other, and better-
established, rival claimants? The gay movement's meteoric rise is
well documented (see, for example, Clendinen and Nagourney 1999)
but to explain this victory tersely with "politics did it" is insufficient.
The devil is in the details, and these must be recounted though a
step-by-step history is obviously impractical. We can only highlight
major strategies (and implementation) of this triumphant multi-front
"war." And our conclusion proposes just why it succeeded over and
above sheer mobilization. But, as the following chapter reveals, the
campaign's overall verdict is deceptively complicated and, ultimately,
ambivalent.

Built-In Advantages

Despite the alleged immorality associated with AIDS transmission and gays' ambivalent societal standing, the substantial built-in
civic advantages justified plunging into the political fray. The central, tangible goal was clear-cut and embraced a revered cultural
value, namely, a bigger slice of the health care budgetary pie to save
lives. That respected big-time science was enlisted further enhanced
legitimacy. The contrast between chasing vacuous, contentious "respect for homosexuals" versus science/healthcare budget funding is
of the essence. Measuring progress and fine-tuning tactics is also
less complicated with a dollar yardstick and new agencies or research initiatives are readily visible. Unconventional lifestyles and
episodic rowdy incidents aside, the campaign fundamentally resembled other humdrum health care forays to beseech government.

The battle also transpired in a clearly delineated, legally accessible institutional setting so prodigious effort could be (conveniently) concentrated on a few obvious targets. Millions of indifferent people did not have to be converted or energized. Within Congress this meant appropriations committees plus key party leaders. Political force could also be tightly focused within Health and Human Services or the NIH. At the state and local level, victory could come by zeroing in on a city's Department of Public Heath or a few city hospitals. Of the utmost importance, the sums requested, while substantial, hardly impoverished other laudable endeavors. Noticeable tax increases to battle AIDS or gutting well-defended budget items were unnecessary. Politics was in principle zero-sum, but not excessively so, and saving lives is far different than redistributing wealth to rectify hazy claims of injustice. In the worst case scenario, curing AIDS would still be a pittance compared to sweeping environmental cleanups or solving the nation's schooling woes. Early modest authorizations were even buried in innocuous omnibus bills to avoid controversy (Rom 2000).

Expanding government largess here *automatically* attracted useful allies, and since this fiscal escalation would (it was alleged) halt the carnage, proponents effortlessly achieved lofty moral ground. Significantly, the most unsavory AIDS sufferers, notably drug addicts (largely blacks and Hispanics) and Haitian immigrants, were scarcely welcomed into this campaign though activists periodically invoked inclusiveness. With saving lives (many being totally innocent victims) by spending more defining the crusade, millions could now jump on the anti-AIDS bandwagon. Non-gay groups traditionally endorsing gay rights, for example, the influential American Civil Liberties Union (ACLU) could also be enlisted. Ditto for pharmaceutical companies, universities, and research organizations (all with their own political muscle) likely to benefit financially as well as hospitals, clinics, and impacted cities wrestling with soaring, unreimbursed caseloads. Even condom manufactures were thrilled by the prospect of an upturn in a business that had fallen on hard times. Entire *industries* quickly materialized to goad government, including charlatans galore ever anxious for a slice of the publicly funded pie.

Within government there were highly professional (and indispensable) public health officials whose medical ethics dictated pursuing solutions, regardless of disease origins. The admired, admittedly conservative, Surgeon General, C. Everett Koop (a Reagan appointee) openly endorsed a fervent federal commitment, as did prestigious scientific commissions created to investigate the subject. Public health officials understood that effective eradication required working closely with gay organizations, so a community of concern was easily established (Rom 2000). Myriad expansion-minded bureaucrats regardless of personal feelings further welcomed this government-focused approach.

Of particular significance, opponents were weak and scattered. The most strident antagonists were religious fundamentalists far distant from power or, if situated inside (a few were in Congress, notably Senator Jesse Helms), they generally played minimal public health decision-making roles. AIDS was, moreover, usually peripheral for anti-gay forces compared to fears over teaching homosexuality in schools or same-sex "marriages" (Herman 1997 details this fundamentalist resistance). This partial non-overlap of agendas expediently permitted those morally apprehensive about homosexuality to nevertheless defend expanded health care. Nor did Bible-based doom- and gloom sodomite rhetoric attract bystanders upset over guiltless people dying. Opposition also occasionally surfaced in business-oriented groups though this usually reflected health cost issues, not homophobia.[1] The argument that since AIDS was self-inflicted gays forfeited government assistance also made little headway. For over a century public agencies had treated sexually transmitted diseases and some casualties were innocent victims. Perhaps the strongest counter-argument was that this mortality level hardly justified an all-out war, a plea increasingly irrelevant as death tolls mounted.

Gays were also resourceful adversaries vis-à-vis rivals in the quest for government funding. Though militants habitually grumbled about their "outsider" social status, they tended to be college educated, often holding prestige jobs in communications and the arts.[2] Young urban professionals abounded while gifted writers and advertising executives could easily be tapped for key organizational positions. A national association of gay and lesbian journalists also existed together with countless, and well-organized, gay lawyers. The spirit of volunteering was also strong along with a knack for raising money. Gays were prodigious consumers, and businesses selling to gays eagerly sponsored events. One 1995 community anti-AIDS fundraiser was, for example, sponsored by Tanqueray gin and this corporate link was hardly unusual. Gay-oriented media overflowed with ads from major corporations. Considerable personal wealth was also plentiful. A handful of entertainment executives like David Geffen, Barry Diller, and Fred Hockberg are extremely rich, and generously support gay causes. Fundraising banquets charging $250 per ticket had no trouble selling out (Vaid 1995: ch. 8). This was not a movement of the inarticulate, slothful downtrodden.[3]

Nor was the campaign built from scratch. Countless past homosexual rights efforts had preceded the advent of AIDS. Access to the powerful was already a fact-of-life in major cities where mayors appointed official gay community liaisons. Well-organized gay doctors and other healthcare professionals further provided credible, expert professional voices to the battle. Past movements such as the African American civil rights campaign offered abundant useful tactical lessons. Infuriating disruptions, huge Washington rallies, tales of wholesome people suffering grievous discrimination, victimization rhetoric, and cultivating mass media gatekeepers were borrowed directly from the civil rights playbook. Previous successful anti-disease battles such as the one to conquer polio likewise served as models.

Gays also enjoyed a dense network of civic-minded organizations, many with multiple chapters in every state, ready to be enlisted in the anti-AIDS battle. One observer estimated this number at "thousands" (D'Emilio 2000: 31) and they could be found in such off-the-beaten-track places as Auburn, Alabama. Little Rock, Arkansas, Belfast, Maine, and similar venues hardly famous as centers of gay life (*Gayyellow Pages* 1982). Hundreds of vocations and hobby groups, from airline pilots to rodeo performers to academics across multiple disciplines, have gay-centered links. A similar pattern applies to ethnicity—gay groups exist for blacks, Hispanics, Asians, and virtually all other demographic entities, as well as religious denominations and business associations. Dozens of anti-discrimination organizations also flourish. A robust network of gay-centered publications (including wire services) further linked this community together.

Geographical strength in New York City, San Francisco, Los Angeles, and other urban areas (plus neighborhood concentration with these locales) proved invaluable in promoting networking and mobilizations.[4] The inherent bias favoring geographically clustered interests in U.S. electoral politics typically made gays a must-be-satisfied voting bloc. That notable anti-gay forces resided outside these enclaves only strengthened potential cohesion since those seeking gays votes thus seldom worried about alienating anti-gay constituents. The upshot was a near automatic representation *within* government, a situation comparable to what senior citizens enjoy when clustering geographically but quite *unlike* those suffering from cancer, heart disease and similar competitors. California House members like Henry Waxman, Phil Burton, and Barbara Boxer (eventually a U.S. Senator) heavily relied on gay support and thus immediately embraced the fight while employing key gay staffers.

Physical proximity also grimly personalized the carnage to make indifference nearly impossible. Emaciated sickly men in wheelchairs, daily obituary notices, and dead friends were inescapable, not abstract statistics or distant TV dramas. Gays routinely told of losing countless lovers and close friends; funerals became a regular morbid social happening. Larry Kramer recounts tracking the deaths of gay acquaintances, and when the figure reached 200 in 1985, he stopped, though the numbers continued upward (Kramer 1989: 220). Compare the problems of, say, mobilizing widely scattered cancer patients, most of whom share little else in common, versus assembling protesters in San Francisco's heavily gay Castro district.

A final advantage, if it can be labeled as such, is impending death. Unlike many other illnesses, including most cancers and incapacitating heart aliments, AIDS appears to be fatal once contracted though life expectancy has increased. A more forceful impetus to militancy is unimaginable, and by the mid-1980s innumerable homosexual men were galvanized out of lethargy. One might deny life-shorting obesity or even a proclivity toward heart disease, but not AIDS. Grim reality also insured tenacity—engagement was unlike saving a personally irrelevant tropical rain forest. This fear of approaching death overwhelmed all intra-communal divisions among gays though, to be sure, tensions occasionally did surface.

Getting Public Attention

That the squeaky wheel gets the attention is a truism, and this aphorism certainly applies to federal budgeting. Though AIDS activists labored under the burden of a malady resulting from voluntary sexual contacts often viewed with revulsion by ordinary citi-

zens, the anti-AIDS quest quickly drew immense sympathetic public attention. Achieving this empathy was hardly accidental, as we
shall see below. Newspaper items especially illustrate this flattering
perspective. Theodoulou, Guvera, and Minnassians (1996) content
analyzed AIDS-related stories published in six leading newspapers
(including the nationally influential *New York Times*) between 1981
(when AIDS first appeared) to 1994 when the epidemic peaked. The
outbreak was largely ignored during the first two years, but by 1983,
about 400 AIDS-related stories had appeared in these six papers that
year. Frequency sharply rose to about 1,500 items in 1985 and 1986,
peaking at over 3,000 in 1987, and then declined steadily though
the figure did not fall below 1,000 per year until 1993. Judged by
this incidence, many readers justifiably came to view AIDS as a
mushrooming crisis.

Story content further lent a hand. Articles were classified according to fifteen categories, by time period. Significantly, the immoral
side of AIDS transmission largely escaped attention. After all, these
sleazy details—anal intercourse with countless strangers, anal-oral
sex, and marathon drug-induced orgies—are hardly mass circulation newspaper staples. Of the 17,082 articles in the six newspapers,
a mere 554 broached immorality or personal irresponsibility, and
this incidence proportionally declined with time. The overwhelming
focus was on human-interest themes, the disease's medical character (including prevention), and government policy. Readers were
regularly informed about unfair discrimination against AIDS victims, blameless children being infected, and how communities
bravely rallied to fight the dreaded illness. In a word, newspaper
accounts "mainstreamed" AIDS, implying that it resembled past illness like malaria that "just happened" to countless hapless victims.
Those who learned about the world via TV news would receive a
similar antiseptic picture. Over a five and a half month period in
1987 when AIDS received enormous media attention, televised news
ran about one AIDS-related story per day, and the homosexual element in this transmission was scarcely mentioned (data cited in
Fumento 1993: 273).

An explosive rise in books about gays, undoubtedly most of them
sympathetic, paralleled this journalism.[5] Haider-Markel's (1999)
analysis of *Books in Print*, a compilation favoring mainstream publishers, found a sharp rise in books about gays beginning during the

early 1990s. The 1995 edition, for example, listed some 150 titles, up from about fifty in 1988. And this upsurge excludes titles by small and specialty presses catering to gay audiences. Books about AIDS have emerged as a publishing staple. The 2001/2001 edition lists some 208 relevant general titles plus countless others covering specialized topics (e.g., forty-seven books with religious themes). The contrast between AIDS and diabetes, a far deadlier malady, is instructive. Total columns devoted to diabetes books ran to about twenty-six; by contrast, sixty-three and a half were devoted to AIDS books. A bookseller can literally stock his or her store with hundreds of assorted AIDS-theme books (including ones helping to educate children) with scant worry about homophobic items sneaking onto the shelves. A bookstore customer looking over shelf space could well conclude that AIDS is legitimately America's highest health priority.

Favorable selective treatment likewise infused TV portrayals. As the epidemic gathered momentum, televised accounts depicted white male heterosexuals as typical casualties, a portrait contradicted by statistical evidence. One detailed study of the 1992 TV season found that while 58 percent of all AIDS suffers were gay, only 6 percent of those depicted on TV were homosexuals. TV almost totally ignored infected intravenous drug users during this period, though addicts were 23 percent of all AIDS casualties. Blacks and Hispanics were especially ignored in TV portrayals (Goldberg 2003: 87). A $6 million government-sponsored AIDS TV campaign virtually skirted homosexuality altogether. The mass media instead become fixated on "typical" heterosexuals who contracted AIDS in ways potentially affecting everyone, for example, contaminated blood transfusion or flings with "normal"-appearing partners. The story of Kimberly Bergalis, the totally virginal young woman who contacted AIDS from her dentist made it to the *New York Times* front page plus the highly rated *60 Minutes*. The exceptionally rarity of such transmission was irrelevant—the strident message was that nobody, absolutely nobody, was safe (Fumento 1993: ch. 19).

TV's "reality" during this period reinforced the sympathetic picture that had become nearly mandatory beginning in the 1970s (Lichter, Lichter, and Rothman 1994: 93-6). Situation comedies in particular seemingly went out of their way to make homosexuality "ordinary," if not amiable. Treating the gay character as the innocent victim was commonplace. That many gays engaged in promiscuous risky (and occasionally illegal) sexual contacts went unmentioned. NBC's 1985 *Early Frost* focused on family reactions to a gay, AIDS-infected son, not how this illness might have been transmitted. Other sympathetic portrayals appeared on the Showtime network and CBS (an episode of *Trapper John, M.D.*). Equally relevant to rousing public compassion (and de-stigmatizing gays) was the mushrooming inclusion of admirable openly gay characters on *Spin City, The Larry Sanders Show, Mad About You, Frasier, Friends, Ellen,* and *Roseanne*, plus several others, all widely watched shows. The absolutely pedestrian TV hit, *Who Wants to Be a Millionaire*, had an admitted gay winner in 2000.

Several notable high-profile (and conspicuously partial) mass media accounts further sounded the shrill but highly selective alarm. In 1985 the renowned, hyper-masculine movie actor, Rock Hudson, succumbed to AIDS and this death received enormous, empathetic publicity. Though Hudson's homosexuality was known to Hollywood insiders, and was discretely acknowledged at his death, that the macho Hudson could succumb further promoted the everyone-at-risk message. Sordid details of Hudson's rapacious carnal appetites were politely left unsaid. In 1987 Oprah Winfrey on her top-rated TV showed announced that in three years one in five heterosexuals would be dead from AIDS. A 1986 book selling some 300,000 copies predicted that 64 *million* Americans would be HIV-infected by 1991. The highly praised sex researcher William Masters seconded these doomsday messages to reporters anxious to spread the dire prognosis (Rotello 1997: 164-5).

Perhaps the most far-reaching event here was the 1985 case of Ryan White, an absolutely ordinary-looking hemophiliac Indiana youngster accidentally contracting AIDS via a contaminated blood transfusion. When his Kokomo school misguidedly suspended him, the media had a feeding frenzy condemning AIDS discrimination. His untimely death at nineteen generated a groundswell of public sympathy, and the major anti-AIDS legislation law inspired by this tragedy passed with strong bipartisan support (with sixty-four Senate co-sponsors) and became the Ryan White Act. The 1991 announcement that Earvin "Magic" Johnson, the celebrated NBA all-star basketball player, was HIV-positive further promoted this sanitized image. Media coverage again stressed AIDS' universality and Johnson's "courage" for going public. Drug abuse or homosexuality never surfaced—reporters just assumed typical heterosexual activity as the culprit. Similar shallow media treatment in 1992 attended Arthur Ashe, the renowned, married tennis star when he announced his HIV infection (he died in 1993). That thousands of nondescript gays annually succumbed from infections acquired during non-stop drug-assisted anal sex was delicately, and conveniently, omitted in these prominent media accounts.

Meanwhile TV and Hollywood celebrities rushed to demonstrate compassion. Like eye-catching though incomplete newspaper accounts, this persuasively transformed AIDS from a grubby drug/gay malady occasionally transmitted in public toilets into a "respectable" disease. Heart disease may be deadlier, diabetes more escalating, but—thanks to movie star endorsements—conquering AIDS (unlike combating heart ailments) became outright fashionable. This celebrity association also generated money, which, in turn, could spawn even more money by certifying the cause as chic. Thousands of well-meaning donors could now ogle movie stars. The initial celebrity reaction was, ironically, quite different. Many entertainers panicked when AIDS first appeared given the widespread homosexuality pervading the entertainment industry. Routine kissing scenes (let alone more intimate encounters) were cut altogether, or performed delicately while some actors and actresses refused to work with gays. Hollywood social gatherings, including the restaurant business, abruptly dwindled out of fear of contamination from glassware or mere physical proximity (Fumento 1993: 220-1).

Private aversion quickly gave way to energetic outward support. On June 23, 1983 a National KS/AIDS fund-raiser in San Francisco featuring Shirley MacLaine and Debbie Reynolds, among others, kicked off this campaign before a madly enthusiastic, largely gay crowd (Shilts 1988: 331). Ted Danson of *Cheers* fame did an early public service announcement. Ronald Reagan, Jr. (the president's son), filmed a provocative video about the dangers of AIDS. Elizabeth Taylor, Carol Burnett, Sammy Davis Jr., Burt Reynolds, Barbra Streisand, Whoopi Goldberg, and dozens of famous people soon joined in. One 1985 Los Angeles "Commitment to Life" dinner hosted by Elizabeth Taylor attracted 2,500 people and raised $1.3 million for AIDS (Clendinen and Nagourney 1999: 515). Publicized Oscars, Emmys and other high-profile media events typically featured award recipients bedecked with red ribbons signifying their heartfelt concern. In 1994 the handsome matinee idol Tom Hanks received an Oscar playing a highly affable, AIDS-stricken gay lawyer in *Philadelphia* to rave reviews and box office success. A comparable legitimizing campaign transpired among the highbrow set as famed artists Christo, Robert Rauschenberg (plus many others) auctioned their creations at well-attended benefits.

A detectable counter mobilization never materialized. Nobody hinted that focusing on AIDS neglected other equally laudable maladies, or that forgoing dangerous sexual behavior, not zealous politics, was the superior cure. This silence was hardly pre-ordained. Notable conservatives such as Charlton Heston, Tom Selleck, and Bruce Willis do exist in the entertainment industry. We can only surmise that within the Hollywood mainstream, to criticize dangerous gay sexual behavior—not homosexuality itself—might endanger one's career. Millions of otherwise non-political people now heard the inescapable message disseminated via fluff mass circulation magazines such as *People* that AIDS was a baffling horrible tragedy, and endorsing massive government intervention was beyond reproach.

Businesses soon fell in step. The beauty firm Clairol in 1991 ran a promotion in which a quarter of the money spent on a certain day for haircuts and hair colorings would be donated to an AIDS charity. The trendy Benetton clothing chain's advertisements prominently featured people with AIDS while Nike commercials highlighted HIV-positive runners. The Red Ribbon Foundation permitted thousands of retail firms—including the ultra chic Tiffany's and hip art galleries—to sell a bedazzling red ribbon collection (some with rhinestones) so this newfound social awareness could be outwardly demonstrated (Burkett 1995: 135). The chasm separating seamy bathhouse anal sex and respectability outwardly vanished.

Was this deft spin on AIDS a conscious political act? Were those TV producers putting "average" blue-eyed blonds, not Hispanic drug addicts, on their programs indistinguishable from gay rights activists? What about reporters skipping over how celebrities became infected? This key question is technically unanswerable—tens of thousands of individuals independently made these choices, and knowing what, exactly, motivated each one is beyond scrutiny. Perhaps a few uncaringly following convention sans any overt political purpose; others might have pursued agendas though would conveniently deny it if pressed. That these disparate decisions did advance the activist agenda cannot in and of itself, by strict scientific standards, prove conscious intent.

Still, uncertainties aside, ample circumstantial evidence suggests that this pro-gay portrayal was at least partially (if not largely) ideologically motivated. The AIDS outbreak was certainly subject to several plausible characterizations, and that one version (a "normal" disease on the verge of a massive epidemic deserving immediate public attention) was hardly predetermined. The media enjoys enormous discretion in its gate-keeping role, and nothing prevented reporters from digging deeper into "Magic" Johnson's sexual escapades or interviewing doctors alarmed over rampant gay promiscuity, let alone reporting about other illness sufferers dying due to massive AIDS funding. A centrally directed, concerted effort to smother alternative versions was unnecessary; it occurred spontaneously.

One corroborating though indirect piece of evidence concerns the political views dominating the news media—overwhelmingly leftish compared to the general public. Embracing the gay rights agenda was not difficult for media gatekeepers. It was already accepted as part of a larger ideological embrace of those deemed "downtrodden" or oppressed. This liberal predisposition has been statistically documented repeatedly via both interviews with those in the mass media industry and content analyses of programming. Recall chapter 3's analysis of how TV portrays crime, for example, over-representing white, middle-class criminals—a view consistent with the prevailing liberal view that lower-class blacks do not disproportionately commit crimes. One 1979-80 survey of 238 journalists at such elite outlets as the *Wall Street Journal,* the *New York Times,* and *Newsweek* found that liberals out-numbered conservatives three to one, were far more likely to vote Democratic, and were quite unlike ordinary citizens in terms of income, education, and were distinctly less religious. Overwhelming support existed for affirmative action, a women's right to abortion while only a tiny few believed that homosexuality was morally wrong. Significantly, liberalism was more pervasive among younger journalists who would soon occupy key gatekeeper positions (Lichter, Rothman, and Lichter 1986: ch. 2). A 1985 *Los Angeles Times* nationwide survey of about three thousand journalists found that journalists were more than twice as likely to define themselves as liberal than the general public. Regarding abortion, school prayer, affirmative action, the death penalty and gun control, journalists were decidedly more liberal. A 1996 survey of 139 Washington and bureau chiefs and congressional correspondents found that only 7 percent of the journalists voted for George Bush in 1992 versus 37 percent of all voters. Eighty-nine percent voted for Clinton versus 43 percent of all voters. A mere 4 percent identified with the Republican Party! (cited in Goldberg 2003: 129-132). Particularly critical, as Bernard Goldberg has argued, a systematic bias toward liberalism (and this includes gay rights) infuses the prestige media such as the *New York Times,* and CBS News, a bias often trickling down to less prominent media outlets. It is not that these journalists consciously promote gay rights or increased funding for AIDS, though this is often factually correct; rather, it seems plausible they effortlessly find that pro-gay version of reality are more compelling and thus easier to pass on to their audiences.

A sympathetic media elite is only the beginning. Where interest congruence is insufficient, overt pressure is necessary, and gay activists have not been shy about coercing the media. Though not every threat may be publicly admitted, they have been periodically acknowledged, and only a few incidents may suffice to teach enduring lessons. After all, why infuriate and easy-to-anger group when repeating activist interpretations is so effortless? And the handful that might object (such as religious fundamentalists) can be safely ignored as irrelevant to one's career.

Burkett (1995: ch 1) offers a riveting first-hand account of gay activists pressuring the *Miami Herald* to steer clear of anything that organization leaders felt hindered their cause. Certain topics and words were taboo.[6] The "official" terminology to characterize those infected was PWA's—People With AIDS. This was less "discriminatory," according to militants, and implied that this condition "just happened" versus resulting from imprudent licentious sex. Even "victim" was off-limits (it evoked weakness). In this politically correct world there were no "high-risk groups," just "high-risk behavior." Paradoxically, while gay zealots became inflamed over disrespectful terminology, they vehemently (and openly) defended sexual practices such as "fisting" widely branded perverse, if not dangerous medically.

In 1988 infuriated AIDS activists belonging to ACT-UP (see below) picketed the corporate headquarters of *Cosmopolitan* over an article correctly asserting that heterosexual women had little to fear from AIDS. Chanting, "For every Cosmo lie, more women die," demonstrators blocked traffic and forcefully attempted (unsuccessfully) to enter the building to confront staffers. Unless a retraction was printed, announced the protestors, a worldwide boycott of *Cosmopolitan* and its advertisers would ensue (*Guardian* 1988). The *New York Times* in 1989 likewise drew gay outrage, including hundreds of disruptive pickets at its 42nd St. headquarters and having orange neon "Buy your lies here" stickers affixed to Manhattan newspaper boxes (Sorge 1989). Nor were openly gay newspapers immune to pressure—when several refused to endorse boycotting the Miller Brewing Company, or otherwise repeat the activist gospel, boycotts of these gays papers and their advertisers were threatened (Coleman 1990). When Lorimar Productions was filming a *The Streets of San Francisco* episode in 1988, gay activists objected to its plot as unflattering to gays and sought a rewrite. When writers demurred, activists disrupted production, and continued to do so despite a legal restraining order. The episode's finale was eventually modified to be less objectionable. The respected *Chicago Tribune* reporter, Mike Royko, was once harassed with posters denouncing him all over Chicago (among other disconcerting tactics) when he openly criticized a gay media campaign linking AIDS to corporate greed (Novak 1990). ACT-UP has a well-deserved reputation (see below) for intimidating enemies with nasty letters, threats of boycotts, disrupting newsrooms, and similar unpleasant gambits to coerce the media to follow a pro-gay stance. No doubt, the mass media realistically dreaded AIDS zealots.

An especially forceful intimidation example concerns the treatment accorded Michael Fumento's *The Myth of Heterosexual AIDS* (Introduction: 1993), a painstakingly documented book that enraged gay activists by contesting their allegation that AIDS could strike anyone. *Myth* did *not* condemn gays or demand reduced AIDS funding—it merely disputed one element of the then prevailing accepted belief regarding widespread risk. Message mildness and the careful documentation aside, finding a publisher was an ordeal, and rejections were often obviously disingenuous ("too many books already with this viewpoint"). As magazine excerpts appeared, Fumento's promised employment opportunities "mysteriously" vanished, and when the book was finally released, a concerted campaign kept it out of bookstores likely to carry it. That Basic Books, a respected HarperCollins subsidiary, published it was irrelevant. One national book chain refused to buy a single copy, a decision reversed only when Fumento exposed this cowardliness on national TV. Inquiries to dozens of stores confirmed this evasion, even in cities like San Francisco, Seattle, and Denver where information on AIDS via heterosexual contacts was timely. Reasons given for refusing to stock *Myth* verged on bizarre (e.g., the book is six months old!). Prospective buyers were often informed that the book was unavailable. When limited stock sold out, it was not reordered. Meanwhile, pro-gay agenda alternatives were widely available, even if issued by obscure publishers, and filled with preposterous, undocumented claims. British and German publishers initially avoided it like the plague though it ultimately received ample favorable press abroad. Gay activists even went so far as to remove *Myth* from library shelves and report it lost.

Messenger shooting was relentless. Countless book reviews (including some in scientific journals authored by non-scientists) unfairly savaged *Myth*, often by misrepresenting its findings and calling Fumento a racist, hate-monger, or worse. Respected TV public affairs shows would invite Fumento, tape a discussion, and then inexplicably refuse to air the interview. Magazines exhibited a similar pattern—evasion after an initial interview invitation. Fumento was fired from his regular *Rocky Mountain News* job for "making too many telephone calls" (an obviously trumped up charge), and was largely unemployed for a year-and-a-half. When *Forbes* magazine recounted Fumento's controversial thesis, ACT-UP picketers gathered outside corporate headquarters and soon barged into the building. The editor-in-chief, Malcolm Forbes, Jr., was forced to sign a statement denouncing *Myth*, a book he had not even read. The *New York Daily News* and *USA* both reported this humiliation, a tactic that probably succeeded due to threats to "out" the closeted Forbes. The reporter doing the story was meanwhile repeatedly beleaguered by telephone. The saga continued when Fumento reviewed two AIDS-related books for *Newsday,* an act that again galvanized an intimidation campaign. His experience was not unique—for those in the media to differ with AIDS activists almost inevitably invited serious trouble.

Harassing and Disrupting

Bullying people like Michael Furmento together with highly favorable media coverage provided an extremely effective pincer movement. Foremost on in this confrontational side is an organization called ACT-UP (AIDS Coalition to Unleash Power).[7] ACT-UP got underway in New York City in 1987 as a desperate reaction to apparent government indifference to an impending lethal crisis. Chapters quickly surfaced almost everywhere (including overseas) and ACT-UP became a national, and justifiably feared, force. Since inception it has adopted an avowedly militant, troublemaker image dedicated to achieving solutions, *now*. Its logo is a pink triangle (the symbol labeling gays in Nazi death camps) against a black background inscribed with "Silence = Death." The edgy, "By any means necessary," is a favored catchphrase, and one consciously borrowed from violence-prone black extremists. These activists also favored attire calculated to inspire unease among more conventional types, for example, eye-catching body piecing, bleached weirdly cut hair, full black S&M style leather regalia, and a penchant for offensive language. That some militants suffered from AIDS-induced dementia exacerbated this craziness.

Organizationally it is more an impromptu band of impulsive urban guerilla fighters than conventional lobbying group—no formal directors, no paid staff, no elected leaders beyond office administrators and, critically, near zero central control. Meetings often resembled "organized anarchy" and membership barriers were unknown though most of those affiliated were white males. Its national organization was virtually powerless, serving largely as an information-sharing mechanism. Though local chapters had specialized committees and sub-groups, these were hardly traditional bureaucratic entities. Volunteering and donated resources made a hefty budget unnecessary, and requisite funds are readily collected by individual donations plus the sale of logo tee shirts, posters, coffee mugs, and occasional art auctions. This independent, amorphous character, for better or worse, hindered restraint—barely anybody could anticipate the next outrage or its location; almost everything was spur-of-the-moment, and thus beyond "responsible" leadership. This impulsiveness was both an advantage—officialdom cannot dictate to thousands of scattered autonomous "leaders"—and a liability since it impeded overall internal coordination. "Managing" ACT-UP was like manipulating the weather.

ACT-UP attracted younger white, middle-class, better-educated men, though women frequently participate in actual demonstrations (Halchi 1999). Observers have depicted ACT-UP as a collection of militant yuppies. That many had skilled business backgrounds was invaluable in gaining access to corporate leaders. Scattered about were talented graduates of top universities preparing the detailed technical reports on neglected drugs and inefficient regulations that provided the causes' invaluable intellectual ammunition (Burkett 1995: 325). ACT-UP is *not* an organization of the unsophisticated downtrodden despite its cultivated "wild" image.

ACT-UP's effectiveness rests on two plausible assumptions. First, notoriety is the life-blood of political causes, especially those needing public acquiescence. Being ignored means defeat, and being pushed into oblivion for the AIDS-stricken means certain death. And since today's media is infatuated with novelty, catching the public eye demands never-ending ingenuity. A boisterous sit-in that garnered TV exposure on Monday is old hat by Friday, and thus ignored. Better to chain yourself to the New York Stock Exchange's balcony, blow foghorns and disrupt trading (as was done). Next week drop off a casket full of bloody chicken bones or wrap a train station in red ribbons to protest government red tape (as was done). In another instance activists discovered the Virginia residence of arch-foe Jesse Helms and blew up a giant (15ft!) condom that partially covered the house. Those protesting a U.S. Civil Rights Commission hearing once wore rubber clown masks to draw attention. This is a proven "philosophy" borrowed from commercial advertising— keep it fresh and interesting. Creativity is also necessary to get bystander interest. One Wall Street rally handed out literature resembling U.S. currency. It is, however, a deceptively demanding strategy, one alert to what draws media notice, how gatekeepers select news items, and the legal/cultural limits of confrontation. Why yet again organize an inaccessible boring march witnessed only by passing cars that only insures jail time? Crews from *60 Minutes* hardly spontaneously appear. Keeping things reasonably legal or avoiding lawsuits is daunting when causing havoc.

The second assumption is psychological: those targeted can be successfully intimidated into acquiescence by imposing unpleasantness. That ACT-UP members may be HIV-positive or actually have AIDS, and targets might reasonably dread this contact, can make encounters exceptionally discomforting. Effectiveness may only require sporadic action. If enough scientific meetings or government hearings are disrupted, a sword of Damocles becomes omnipresent. Apprehensive officials will now "spontaneously" advance the ACT-UP agenda without prodding. Synergetic opportunism also helped. Harassed bureaucrats or legislators spending taxpayer funds, and fighting AIDS is a worthy, socially acceptable cause, so why invite unnecessary (and potentially hazardous) trouble? Why should hassled scientists be upset if the disruptors demand more research funding? ACT-UP could be a useful ally in squeezing Congress. Since coerced private firms can sometimes cover these added expenses elsewhere, why risk uninvited terminally ill infected people sitting in your office? Needless to say, this logic is plausible only in a civil, highly tolerant society like the United States. ACT-UP militants in Stalin's Soviet Union would end up in a Gulag, or worse.

Cataloguing the full flavor of ACT-UP's haranguing is impossible so a few notable illustrations must suffice. One episode foreshadowing untold similar outrages occurred in 1987 when 200 protestors in West Hollywood, California, brought traffic on Sunset Boulevard to a standstill for more than two hours. One marcher occasionally "dropped dead" and his body would be immediately outlined on the pavement in chalk as if he were murdered. The precedent-setting event made all the evening news programs and the *Los Angeles Times* front page. Similar troublemaking "die-ins" soon appeared elsewhere with comparable media attention. The "phone zap" was another stock ploy—constantly calling the target's home and office to render phone lines inoperable. Constant faxes were also sometimes sent to further disrupt businesses. An especially controversial gambit was threatening to "out" public figures concealing their homosexuality. The magazine *Outweek* gladly published their names (recall the threat to Malcolm Forbes, Jr.). And like the black civil rights movement, the impending boycott was an arsenal staple. Among those pressured were Miller Brewing Company, Philip Morris (both major contributors to the hated Senator Jesse Helms), and several pharmaceutical firms, notably Bristol Meyers and Burroughs-Wellcome, for allegedly overpricing anti-AIDS drugs (Burroughs-Wellcome makes such best selling over-the-counter drugs as Actifed, Sudafed, Neosporin and Empirin).

Shocking middle class sensibilities, a tactic that fitted well with the finely honed theatrical inclination of many ACT-UP followers, was widespread. Provocative acts like holding homosexual "kiss-ins" (sometimes with gays dancing together) at bars frequented by heterosexuals or scientific meetings was one popular tactic. Dressing as a giant condom, throwing condoms at passing pedestrians, simulated sex, and countless other outrageous antics were commonplace. Terms shunned in polite company (e.g., sodomy), were sometimes conspicuously put on placards to draw attention. Activists often wore buttons inscribed with phrases like "Sister Vicious Hungry Bitch" or "It's *Mr.* Faggot to You" to further accentuate this "in-your-face" stance.

ACT-UP's list of targets was immense, and reflected the group's fluid, opportunistic line of attack. Hostile candidates for public office could acquire a retinue of annoying, chanting ACT-UP hecklers. As already noted, news media such as the *New York Times* got "hit" when they failed to report AIDS correctly, used faulty terminology, or just otherwise incensed militants. The CBS newsroom was "seized" one evening during the 1991Gulf War, and the live broadcast momentarily halted. Government offices, including the White House, were favored demonstration sites, as were the bastions of capitalism such as Wall Street and corporate headquarters. Nor could hospitals and public health agencies escape if they resisted testing or drug distributions programs. The famed Rose Bowl Parade in Pasadena, California, was once disrupted to garner publicity. Attacks were at times highly personal, for example, putting an offending New York City official's picture on a poster with the label "Pig" and plastering it all over town.

This scripted "spontaneous" mayhem involved immense expert planning, a fact seldom appreciated by non-participants. That this was achieved without a centralized, permanent organization, makes this accomplishment all that more remarkable. This skill was illustrated in ACT-UP's commotion at the Sixth International Conference on AIDS held in San Francisco in 1990 that included specialists from 121 nations. ACT-UP followers made a huge uproar in the lobby, complete with some mild same-sex lewd behavior, to demand greater organization involvement of AIDS sufferers. Despite the chaos, however, the attending international news media were painstakingly informed of ACT-UP's laudable aims. Everything was video recorded for future use and widely disseminated thanks to assembled computers, fax machines, and other sophisticated communications gear. Those fluent in half a dozen languages informed non-English speaking foreign reporters. Impact was undoubtedly multiplied a thousand-fold thanks to this meticulous planning (Burkett 1995: 316-18).

ACT-UP was far more than a bunch of clever rowdies hassling enemies and then disappearing until the next incident. Beyond public view were activities that displayed a more serious side. It published *Digest: The Treatment and Data Digest* that offered meticulous information on treatment progress (including ongoing drug trials and their locations) plus assistance hotlines for those overwhelmed by technical arcana. Its tone was professional, quite scientific, and usually skipped street theater rancor. The research undergirding demands was often prodigious, a far cry from activists elsewhere announcing fantasy-driven ultimatums. ACT-UP once sent letters to dentists to boycott Xylocaine (a popular oral anesthetic) since its maker, Astra Pharmaceutical Products, was pricing its Foscarvir, a drug that could prevent AIDS-related blindness, at an unaffordable $24,000 (wholesale cost!) a year per recipient. Rather than just implore dentists to just "do the right thing," ACT-UP's letter explained why this cost was unjustified—its key ingredient had been around since 1924, its anti-viral properties known since the 1970s, and critically, its development has been heavily government subsidized while Astra's Swedish parent company was already highly profitable. A more equitable price, said the appeal, would be $10,000 a year. To encourage this boycott, a cheaper, generic version of Xylocaine was listed, and the name/address of Astra's president was also provided for those who wished to express their displeasure with Astra's predatory pricing (ACT-UP letter of August 1992). This is a far cry from a simplistic "down with greedy drug companies!!!"

Did ACT-UP succeed? The answer obviously depends on the criteria applied. Measured by organizational vitality, it has largely faded away though its spirit apparently lives on—when Health and Human Services Secretary Thommy Thompson tried to speak at a Spanish 2002 AIDS conference, activists repeatedly chanted "murderer" and "shame" to drown him out. By the early 1990s, however, most founders had succumbed to AIDS, or were too debilitated to carry on. One compilation shows that ACT-UP declined from 113 chapters in 1991 to just eight in 1998 (Halchi 1999, 148). In some instances chapter members have veered into futile extremism, complete with bizarre conspiracy theories and arrest-provoking behavior, to harass the "AIDS establishment" itself, much to the chagrin of serious AIDS workers (*AIDS Weekly* 2002).

The everybody-is-welcome membership attitude ultimately brought irreconcilable and ultimately destructive fissures in San Francisco, Seattle, Chicago, and New York (Pepper 1990). Stridently militant anti-capitalist agendas ("people not profits") were incompatible with pragmatic discussions with pharmaceutical firms and the movement splintered. Peter Staley, an early ACT-UP leader, once candidly complained that newer recruits seemed more infatuated with social activism for its own sake than concrete results, a charge confirmed by the near fixation with direct-action in the face of diminishing returns (Staley 1991). Limits were reached on attracting media attention or threatening public officials. Counter-measures became more effective —conference organizers made admission badges counterfeit-proof thus keeping disruptors out. Reporters became blasé about receiving bags of unwelcome Christmas cards from incensed zealots. Once-exciting novelty grew tiresome, as did the never-ending meetings. And those public figures helpfully inspiring outrage, notably George H. Bush and Ronald Reagan, inconveniently disappeared.

On the other hand, the accomplishment record was substantial so, in sense, ACT-UP helped put itself out of business. In the words of Dr. Ronald Valdiserri, deputy chief of sexually transmitted diseases for the CDC, "Generally they did a very important service in terms of making mainstream American aware of prevention needs. Other patient advocacy groups, such as breast caner and Alzheimer's disease, have looked to early ACT-UP as the model" (quoted in *AIDS Weekly* 2002). By the mid-1990s several pragmatic ACT-UP activists jumped ship and joined the very policymaking establishment that they once harassed.[8] They now served as board members of government-funded organizations like the AIDS Clinical Trials Group; they consulted with Congress, the drug industry and federal regulators. If the NIH or the FDA needed a certified AIDS champion, who better than an ACT-UP representative, and these were avidly recruited. Even more important, these advocates *had* dramatically speeded the delivery of anti-AIDS drugs, lowered their cost, and assisted in disseminating innovative medical information. Former street theater types now were welcomed at medical conferences and hobnobbed with pharmaceutical executives at corporate cocktail parties. Leading researchers sought their expertise and legislators solicited their advice in drafting complicated legislation to fine-tune the war on AIDS (Burkett 1995: 320-44). Yet, when all was said and done, despite all this absorption into the establishment, gay males still died by the thousands, and nothing seemed to end this carnage once and for all. The following chapter will return to this point.

Pressuring Government

Voting and Electioneering

The role of electoral pressure in extracting government-supplied benefits is axiomatic among devotees of political activism. The logic seems incontestable: officials are more likely to bestow budgetary help if sizable voting blocs and hefty campaign contributions back requests. Yet, as chapter 6 demonstrated, this mobilization-benefit nexus can be deceptively complicated. Conceivably, government-bestowed advantages can energize the once apathetic or the relationship is spurious, for example, emergent prosperity independently increases both a group's wealth and turnout. To wit, in chronicling the gay electoral surge, it seems apparent that heightened activism generally came *after* Washington bestowed its bounteousness on the anti-AIDS war. It was not that gays disdained the electoral route prior to AIDS. The 1970s saw a major upturn in open gay activism to eliminate the most odious restraints on gay sexuality (e.g., harassing patrons in gay-oriented bars). In a handful of cities, gays finally elected openly gay local leaders or helped pass anti-discrimination ordinances. Rather, their greatest and most visible electoral triumphs occurred when the battle against AIDS-HIV was *already* sacrosanct. Indeed, today's gay leaders boasting of their increasing electoral clout scarcely mention this illness. That triumph is enshrined history.

Does this mean that electoral mobilization has become extraneous to fighting AIDS? Hardly. Civic engagement can be about protecting gains since what has been done can be undone. New budgetary rivals are always waiting (particular with illnesses), and one's public benefactors will eventually leave office or grow apathetic. Activism must sometimes be defensive—enemies must dread retribution. In the logic of social science analysis (to reiterate a point made in chapter 6), incessant mobilization (voting, campaign donations) can explain a constant, that is, the government's unswerving commitment to a all-out war on AIDS. Statistically, explaining constancy is a nightmare yet it is quite plausible politically, and thus warrants our attention if we are to understand just why Washington continues its lavish AIDS funding. Simply put, few officials want to enrage gays by announcing that AIDS money can be better spent elsewhere.

Though gays are, admittedly, a relatively small population group (usually estimated at about 2 to 3 percent) compared to, say, African Americans, this statistic generally reflects those of voting age, not total population, and thus underestimates the gay vote. Gays are also above average in education (most having some college) and (at least according to some studies) income, two factors generally promoting activism. Hertzog (1996: 2) relying on a special survey targeting gay voters asserts that in the 1992 election self-identified gay voters were as numerous as Latino voters and outnumbered those of Asian ancestry two-to-one. A 2002 Zogby midterm election poll reported that gays comprised 5 percent of the total electorate, a figure only half that of African American voters (*Financial Times Information* 2002). The youngish nature of gays indicates a growing segment of the electorate, particularly since younger gays are more inclined to include sexuality in core identities.

Further recall that many gays live in urban enclaves in Houston, Boston, Atlanta Philadelphia, Chicago, New York, Los Angeles among others, all in key presidential election states, and our electoral system rewards geographical concentration. Surveys from the 1996 and 1998 congressional elections indicate that gays make up nearly 9 percent of voters in large cities of more than a half million and 7.2 percent in cities of 50,000 to half a million (Bailey 2000: 17). When elections are close (including primaries), this sizable voting bloc can be the margin of victory.

An especially relevant mobilization facilitator is that is that "being gay" infuses most homosexuals' group consciousness though, to be sure, it typically co-exists with other traits such as race and religion (Bailey 2000: 14). This categorization is deceptively advantageous when mobilizing to boost health budgets. Potential rivals suffering from heart disease, asthma, cancer, and similar far-ranging chronic illness are unlikely to define themselves primarily by their illnesses. There is certainly no extensive geographically based "cancer culture" where the stricken daily network with fellow sufferers; at most, face-to-face support groups periodically convene to share experiences. Not even health care obsessed senior citizens describe themselves by their maladies. Few obese people with high-risk fatty diets with family histories of coronaries pester Congress to fund preventive screening programs.

Homosexual behavior by contrast typically fosters a common identity, and combating AIDS is inescapably integral to this consciousness, even to many not-at-risk-lesbians. AIDS to gays might thus be likened to Jewish support for Israel—a non-negotiable voting issue. The upshot is that while not all homosexuals may be vulnerable to AIDS, nearly all appreciate that they *could* be victimized given their distinct sexual life-style, or have friends or lovers at-risk, and are thus readily mobilized *before* it is too late. Thus, opposing the war on AIDS *automatically* makes one politically objectionable among gays. No doubt, if potential diabetes sufferers collectively defined themselves by their illness, and daily socialized with other diabetics, leaders would dread alienating this constituency.

These advantages must, however, be converted into tangible influence, a deceptively problematical task.[9] Voting turnout obviously multiplies one's presence, and gays seem notably likely to vote, especially if the choices are clear. Much depends on circumstances, and at least some data shows that gays are underrepresented in congressional elections, a phenomena probably resulting from the youthfulness of the "gay vote." But, when gay issues are on the agenda, as they were in the presidential races of 1992 and 1996, turnout among gays is much higher (cited in Baily 2000: 32). One survey conducted in 2000 using respondents participating in an on-line poll (to encourage confidentiality regarding sexual identity) found that among those identifying themselves as gay, lesbian, bisexual, or transgendered (LGBT), 92 percent were registered to vote. Not only is this figure remarkably high, but 87 percent of those registered actually when to the polls ("Out and Into the Voting Booth" 2000: 40). This survey also reported relatively high levels of other forms of activism among gays, for example, 46 percent said that they had contacted an elected officials while nearly a quarter said that they had contributed money to a candidate. ("Out and Into the Voting Booth" 2000:44).

What about actual voting itself? Does a "gay voting bloc" prompt office seekers to support gay causes such as greater AIDS funding? This question is deceptively complicated. The straightforward answer is that gays overwhelmingly identify and vote Democratic, the party closely aligned with gay concerns, though this one-sidedness varies by election (see Bailey 2000: 9). For example, in 1988 gays decisively supported Michael Dukakis, the Democratic candidate, over George H. W. Bush almost 2 to 1, the reverse of the split among heterosexuals. A similar lopsided pattern in the presidential race held in 1992; differences were somewhat less sharp in 2000 when George W. Bush managed to get 21 percent of the gay vote according to a survey conducted by the Gill Foundation (cited in Morgan 2001). Ditto for Senate and House elections—gays were Democratic stalwarts while non-gays roughly divided their choices (Hertzog 1996: 86). State and local contests reflect these national patterns. The voting-benefit relationship thus seems unambiguous: gays in the main favor Democrats, and this alliance apparently translates into greater AIDS funding.

Political calculations can, however, be devious and thus more effective. Voting flexibility is vital—to be categorized as automatic inevitably diminishes influence in spite of steadfast loyalty. Fidelity must be policy contingent and be accompanied by a credible abandonment threat. Habitual voting also invites mistakes—not every Democrat might be a friend. Whether gays vote adroitly is a tough question, but evidence hints at voting suppleness. Hertzog (1996: ch. 3), drawing upon two national surveys, concludes that the gay and lesbian vote is "up for grabs" (81). For one, those gays identifying as Republicans are more prone to cross party lines than their Democratic compatriots, a pattern hinting of policy attentiveness for those associating with a party containing sizable anti-gay elements (72). His analysis (78) further intimates that the gay vote may not be entirely demographically and ideologically driven—gays vote somewhat differently when matched with nearly identical heterosexuals, though this divergence is statistically intricate. Plausibly, gay voters are distinctly reacting to "something," and gay-related policy is this something. Bailey's analysis of congressional voting (2000: 20) similarly confirms discerning voting fluidity—gay Democrats occasionally opportunistically jump ship in the voting booth though partisan affiliation remains constant.

Hertzog (1996: 182-3) finds a disproportion surge of gay first-time presidential voters in 1992, an election pitting the frankly pro-gay Clinton against a Republican ticket overtly appealing to anti-gay social conservatives. Significantly, the senior Bush fared rather poorly among gay Republicans in 1992, most of who backed him in 1988. Congressional election data in 1992 displays similar issue sensitivity (particularly in large cities)—gay voters were now even more disproportionately Democratic as the GOP took a socially rightward turn (Bailey 2000: 22-23). President Clinton's cultivation of gays clearly had a coattail affect. The 1998 California governor's race likewise demonstrated attentiveness to key gay-related candidate differences (Bailey 2000: 37). A 2000 Harris Interactive poll reporting a majority of gays believing a candidate's stance on gay-related policies was "very important" ("Out and Into the Voting Booth" 2000: 44) also bears out willingness to put policy ahead of party. Gays are also, according to Hertzog's analysis, more inclined to embrace third party candidates despite Democratic allegiances, a proclivity unlike African Americans whose voting loyalty is unfalteringly Democratic.

Evidence for electoral suppleness also comes from the partisan endorsements of prominent gay political organizations. To repeat, to be taken seriously requires occasional unfaithfulness, and this means endorsing GOP candidates, if that is advantageous—one plays "hard to get." For example, in the hotly contested 1998 New York Senate race the Human Rights Campaign, the well-heeled national gay organization, endorsed the conservative Republican, Alphonse D'Amato, over the liberal Democrat, Charles Schumer (Dreyfuss 2000). During the 2002 mid-term national election plus countless state/local races, the prominent Gay & Lesbian Victory Fund endorsed a small number of openly gay candidates. Though most were, predictably, Democrats, several were Republicans (*U.S. Newswire* 2002). Even more indicative of their non-partisan deftness, the Victory Fund generously supported ($9,082 plus another $1,200 in "in kind" contributions) James Kolbe, a gay Republican House incumbent in 2000 despite the Democrat's fervent effort to retake the closely divided House (FEC, online). The American AIDS Political Action Committee likewise supported an occasional Republican. Senator James M. Jeffords (R-Vt) received $10,000 for his 2000 campaign (though he latter abandoned the GOP to become an independent) while Arlen Specter (R-Pa) received $5000 (FEC, online), hardly surprising since Specter has championed stepped up AIDS funding.

The "up for grabs" element is also confirmed by the apparent willingness of Republican candidates with ties to fundamentalist Christian groups to seek gay votes, or at least minimize gay animosity. One must assume, then, that Republicans believe that at least some of this vote is "available," if courted correctly. Though this wooing is often kept discreet, it does occasionally spill out into the open. Bill Simon's 2002 California governor's campaign offers a striking example of this calculating outreach. During the primary Simon made no bones about his anti-gay feelings much to the delight of social conservatives. He refused to meet with openly gay Republicans and promised to "undo" past homosexuality in the governorship. He nevertheless abruptly reversed himself in mid-campaign, perhaps owing to trailing badly in pre-election polls. Simon now claimed he favored easier gay adoptions, officially recognized gay-pride festivals, tough laws against anti-gay crimes, increased AIDS funding, a greater role for gays in the state GOP, and so on. It was a complete turnabout on homosexuality though he eventually lost the election (Moxley 2002).

Another (and more successful) outreach example was Michael Bloomberg's unexpected New York City mayoral win 2001. The Republican Bloomberg captured one-third of the gay vote by clearly appealing to gays, a tactic also adroitly used by his Republican predecessor, Rudy Giuliani. George W. Bush's 2000 presidential campaign offers an especially prominent outreach. Unlike the 1996 Dole campaign, every effort was made to sustain "Big Tent" Republicanism, including having Rep. James Kolbe (R-AZ), who is admittedly gay, address the party's national convention. While Bush did not explicitly seek gay votes, he was careful not to distance himself from activists. Meanwhile, Mary Cheney, Richard Cheney's openly lesbian daughter, campaigned among gays for the GOP ticket. In the spring of 2000 the candidate Bush met with openly gay Republicans and announced that he welcomed gays into his campaign (Marcus 2000). Not surprisingly, much to the delight of AIDS activists, following his inauguration Bush reaffirmed his commitment to combating AIDS, and his 2003 State of the Union address called for a major increase in domestic spending (and this was in addition to previous sizable boosts).

And then there is giving to campaigns, perhaps second only to mobilizing voters to garner attentiveness. As the old expression goes, money talks—a rally among skinflints demanding special treatment is far different than one offering bountiful campaign funds. Needless to say, tracking campaign contribution here, particularly when given by admitted homosexuals, is complicated. Campaign finance laws make some contributions quite visible while others are prudently hidden, and not every candidate boasts about his or her lavish gay funding. Few Federal Election Commission contributor records have "gay money" labels attached to them, and exaggerating (or minimizing) contributions is a time-honored ploy. Adroitness is also relevant here—a $1,000 contribution to a likely-to-lose gay candidate might be better classified as symbolic support, not savvy politicking. Donating to a lesser-of-two evils heterosexual in a closely fought battle might have been a wiser choice though only a pittance of all contributions.

The places to begin here are the explicitly gay campaign organizations. When "gay money" first began appearing in campaigns for national office in the late 1970s, fund-raisers were exceedingly rare and when they did occur, they were carefully hidden from public view with scant mention of funding sources. Words like "gay" or "homosexual" were unmentionable (see, for example, Clendinen and Nagourney 1999: 412). Though countless gays undoubtedly contributed to campaigns, for a candidate to publicly receive "gay money" was the kiss of death. By the early 1990s, however, some ten years after the advent of AIDS, matters have changed dramatically. Gay money is now actively sought though, of course, not by all candidates.

Several gay organizations now boast of their contributions, many of which (including donor names) are public record. One leading example is the Gay & Lesbian Victory Fund whose initial board of directors all pledged $10,000 to get the Fund off the ground (Rimmerman 2000). Since its inception in 1991, it carefully screens all potential recipients according to multiple criteria (including being openly gay), and has awarded some $3 million in campaign donations, including $300,000 in the 2002 election cycle. It claims notable success—boosting the number of openly gay office holders from 49 in 1991 to 228 by 2002, mainly at the state and local level ("Victory Fund, Bond Charting New Futures," 2002). What makes the Victory Fund unusual is its attentiveness to its 9,000+ grassroots supporters. Members receive profiles of all certified candidates, and candidates receive earmarked contributions, with the Fund bundling them and sending them onward. By design, its aim is quite narrow—electing gays, and less on the broader goal of putting sympathizers into office.

Larger and more wide-ranging is the Human Rights Campaign (HRC) that had been an active fund-raiser for over two decades, often with highly publicized, well-attended dinners with tickets costing $150 and up (Rimmerman 2000). In 1982, for example, it raised $588,000, which was then carefully dispersed to 118 House and Senate campaigns. The HRC claimed an 81 percent success rate (Clendinen and Nagourney 1999: 489). Significantly, its varied campaigns have attracted the assistance of such luminaries as a former Oregon senator and ex-presidential contender (and well-known conservative) Barry Goldwater. During the 1995-96 election cycle it contributed a little over one million dollars to gay-friendly candidates and organizations (Rimmerman 20000). In the early days of the 2000 campaign it deployed some fifty field organizers working key House and Senate races (Marcus 2000). By 2002 it had grown to some half a million members, working out of an impressive corporate-like headquarters, and operated with a $22 million dollar budget. During the 2002 election cycle HRC contributed more than $1.2 million to the 210 candidates it endorsed plus other invaluable campaign-related services, notably professional advice, activist training and other services to cash-strapped office seekers (www.hrc.org).

Like other fund-raising organizations, the HRC has carefully cultivated wealthier potential donors with numerous well-attended black tie and quite pricey dinners and functions. It has a "Federal Club" for those donating $1,200 or more which in 2000 had 3,000 plus members (Dreyfuss 2000b). The American AIDS Political Action Committee (PAC) that began in 1994 is also part of this burgeoning "inside-the Beltway" funding network. Though still favoring open gays like Tammy Baldwin (D-WI), it also contributed to prominent non-gays such as Barbara Boxer (D-CA), Hillary Clinton (D-NY) and Jesse Jackson, Jr. (D-IL). All told, in the 1998 election it contributed some $75,967 to gay rights advocates.

On the Republican side are the Log Cabin Republicans (LCR), a moderate GOP organization with 11,000 members in fifty chapters nationwide endorsing many of the same policies as Democratic-oriented gay groups. In the 2000 Republican primaries it collected some $40,000 for the avowedly pro-gay Senator John McCain's bid for the nomination (Marcus 2000). During 2002 the LCR spent some $250,000 in various electoral contests. A particularly revealing show of strength was when these gay Republicans rallied around Congresswoman Connie Morella (R-MD) in her (unsuccessful) 2002 reelection fight. The LCR co-chaired the fund-raiser, the president spoke for thirty minutes, and the event brought in nearly a half a million dollars (www.lcr.org/press/20020628.asp).[10] Interestingly, the Morella campaign put gay activists on both side of the contest.

This official record is only the tip of the proverbial iceberg though, as we admit, the final picture is incomplete since contributions are typically given directly to candidates without being labeled "gay money." This incompleteness aside, anecdotal accounts show gays to be substantial campaign donors though, as we noted earlier, this upsurge has arrived *after* AIDS first appeared. During the 1992 campaign where the partisan divide was fairly sharp, one gay fund-raiser, David B. Mixer helped raise some $3.5 million for Clinton, a far cry from 1988 when the Democratic presidential candidate (Michael Dukakis) spurned an offer by gay activists to raise $1 million dollars on his behalf. Significantly, when Clinton appeared before a gay audience in Los Angeles in 1992, an event that raised $100,000, it was covered by the prestigious *New York Times,* the *Washington Post,* and other mass circulation dailies, a far cry from the days when such appearances were strictly hush-hush and not even listed on a candidate's official itinerary (Clendinen and Nagourney 1999: 567).

By the 2000 election overt campaign fund-raising by gays had mushroomed. Years of careful groundwork had decidedly "mainstreamed" the movement. A gay organized "Salute to Tipper" (Al Gore's wife) raised some $200,000 in 1999 (Dreyfuss 2000a). The Democratic National Committee (DNC) had established a Gay and Lesbian Victory Council for those giving $10,000 or more, and by August 2000, it had almost 100 members while the even more elite Jefferson Trust for those giving $100,000 had thirteen members. One April dinner held in a Washington luxury hotel included forty prominent gays paying up to $100,000 to fête Al Gore (Dreyfuss 2000a). All told, gays had contributed some $5 million months prior to the election to the DNC, putting them in the same league as such

Democratic stalwarts as trial lawyers and unions (Marcus 2000). One high-profile gay Democratic fund-raiser even estimated that as much as 10 percent of all Democratic money came directly from gays, and even the DNC treasurer is an openly gay millionaire (Dreyfuss 2000a). Gay-sponsored fundraisers, often hosted by high-profile figures such as Hillary Clinton, were a regular feature of Al Gore's 2000 push. These included a $200,000 gala in Washington, DC, a $100,000 event in Portland, Oregon, a $75,000 event in Dallas and a $50,000 meeting in Chicago (Dreyfuss, 2000a).

Beyond these cash contributions are "in-kind" services—the donated labor and supplies absolutely vital to any successful quest for public office. Many of these are grassroots activities with volunteered labor and can range from registering voters on streetcorners to driving supporters to the polls. Placing a cash value on this resource is impossible, but judged by the hundreds of gay civic-oriented organizations (and gay-oriented newspapers) scattered almost everywhere, this is a formidable campaign resource, and one probably far exceeding officially recorded cash donations. That many gays live in close proximity to each other and regularly mingle in community gatherings (though seldom overtly political) makes this pool of potential labor almost akin to the fabled urban machine capable of galvanizing thousands of steadfast workers. The decentralized nature of U.S. party politics has also seen the emergence of distinctly gay local Democratic organizations in many urban settings, a strategy that greatly facilitates access to state and national Democratic politics (Rayside 1998: 288-89). What is critical here are not comparisons to other ethnic/racial constituency groups, but the contrast to other public health funding claimants. No other illness can credibly boast, "increase funding or on election day we'll have armies of people—all over America—working against you."

Augmenting this electoral pressure was a concerted effort to influence Congress via legislative testimony—telling the AIDS story, so to speak. Access to Congress is never automatic and thousands of other diseases (many quite deadly) and misfortunes potentially benefiting from legislative attention compete for this forum. Hearings devoted to one's own agenda bestow legitimacy and weight, both valuable assets in navigating political obstacles elsewhere ("We can speak directly to Congress" or "Here's some official testimony"). Remarkably given the voracious clamor for attention, as early as

1982, when AIDS first emerged and the death toll was still tiny, Congress conducted hearings on Karposi's sarcoma. This marked the first installment of a soon-to-come stream of AIDS-funding supplicants. The overall pattern was roughly comparable to newspaper stories—low initial incidence until about the mid-1980s, and then an enormous surge as the deadly AIDS threat entered public consciousness and then a fall-off (Haider-Markel 1999). In actual numbers, hearings went from a handful per year in the early 1980s to about thirty-eight in 1990 before declining to below thirty in 1996, still a prodigious number given numerous potential rivals.

These raw statistics tell little about what was conveyed and how. Access does not guarantee success. Orchestrating a winning "tell it directly to Congress" campaign requires more than heartfelt pleading. Securing a committee hearing and synchronizing appearances (who testifies to what, who pays witness expenses, what written statements will be offered, and so on) are organizational hurdles of the first order. If technical testimony is given, future credibility requires that it better be accurate. Securing the most advantageous forum can be critical: better to testify on medicine to save lives than defend HIV-infected gay soldiers before a military preparedness committee. Nothing is accidental or spontaneous here; things differ profoundly from come-as-you-are street rag-tag demonstrations. Those testifying have to be persuasive, attention getting, able to explain complicated issues, stay on track, and otherwise add something. Less obvious, but no less essential, savvy organizers must control the debate; opponents have to be kept away along with erstwhile but embarrassing supporters.

Though quantifying this orchestration is impossible, a sampling of these proceedings does indicate a well-run, effective campaign to get the movement's message across. And this transpired from the very beginning to years later when AIDS funding was virtually sacrosanct. Overwhelmingly, sympathetic medical experts dominated these forums together with those whose lives had been affected by AIDS. With scant exception, Congress heard an ongoing chorus of credible believers. For example, in March of 1986 Anthony Fauci, the director of the National Institutes of Allergy and Infectious Diseases testified before the Senate Committee on Appropriations. His prepared statement outlined the growing incidence of AIDS, ongoing research programs, several promising potential treatments, and the "monumental social and economic implications" of AIDS. Testimony about its origins and transmission skipped unsavory details; dangerous homosexuality and drugs were nonissues. Fauci's exchanges with committee members stressed scientific or administrative details. When disease transmission was broached, discussions focused on casual contact, AIDS viruses in saliva, and the role of STDs such as genital herpes, again, all without mentioning homosexuality or drug abuse. The testiest written question concerned what other disease programs had been "raided" to support AIDS research. Fauci diplomatically said that it was impossible to determine specific losers, but that expertise in many other medical areas was now redirected toward combating AIDS. Inquiry about treatment for black and Hispanic sufferers was similarly tactfully deflected (Senate Hearings, March 5, 1986).

A subcommittee hearing of the House Committee on Government Operations held on July 1, 1986 foretold future scenarios (Hearing 1986). The chair, Ted Weiss (D-NY) began by recounting the AIDS death toll, its tragic consequences, and how the battle was being lost despite unremitting efforts. An impressive parade of witnesses then passionately reiterated the need for yet more resources. Paul Popham, an infected New York AIDS activist, explained the obstacles to adequate treatment. John Smith, an Ohioan, echoed Popham's frustrating lament. Dr. Leonard Calabrese from Cleveland told of soaring caseloads with over-extended hospital resources. Mathilde Krim, Ph.D. and head of the American Foundation for AIDS Research, castigated existing programs as insufficient, especially lack of access to drugs. Yet another doctor (Martin S. Hirsch of Massachusetts General Hospital) characterized federal efforts as only a drop in the bucket. Experts from Burroughs Wellcome, Miles Laboratories, and Praxis Pharmaceuticals all testified that more was needed. Despite all the varying backgrounds and experiences, in essence all offered the same pessimistic message—we are not doing enough. Dissenters or even advocates of rival illnesses made no appearance.

Four years later the same House Committee did a virtual repeat performance (Hearings July 28,1989). Expert witnesses now appeared from the Albert Einstein Medical College, Harlem Hospital, San Francisco General Hospital plus several other prestigious organizations to make their appeals. Notable federal government experts and harried practitioners from around the country seconded these recommendations. The materials submitted were often dense technical reports depicting both the grimness of the disease and ongoing, though deficient, remedial steps. Witnesses might be queried about specifics, but the goal of further mobilizing government seemed irrefutable. Somebody observing just these presentations would have no inkling that AIDS could come from risky homosexual anal sex, behavior that could be voluntarily shunned or legally thwarted. The role of IV drug use was similarly a "non-issue."

A series of House hearings by the subcommittee on Health and the Environment during 1989 seemingly examined every aspect of the burgeoning AIDS crisis. Some thirty-five witnesses spoke, and many appended information-packed technical reports. They ranged from distinguished medical practitioners (including several overseas experts) to treatment specialists. Nearly every purely medical aspect of the disease was explored, including the value of needle exchange programs for IV drug users. As before, the pro-increased government-funding consensus was unmistakable. At most, a few professionals testified that other illnesses, notably, hepatitis and tuberculosis, also deserved government attentiveness but this advocacy hardly challenged AIDS funding. The outspoken conservative, Rep. William E. Dannemeyer (R-Ca.), dissented. He periodically pestered witnesses about registering those infected with HIV-AIDS. Judged by reactions, his suggestion was ignored.

By the end of the 1990s, these AIDS-related hearings had become formulaic. Interestingly, though nearly everything scientific and otherwise had already been explained via congressional testimony, and new information might be better publicized elsewhere, these performances continued onward as if they were sacred rituals. A July 1999 hearing of the Senate Subcommittee on Appropriations assembled the usual cast of characters to reiterate by-now-familiar concerns (Hearings 1999). The attending senators all took turns making heartfelt pleas for more funding while respected medical experts told of progress despite the obstacles. In February 2000 the same subcommittee did yet another a rerun, with a different cast, though with the same message. What distinguished this particular hearing was that several uninvited AIDS activists disrupted it by attacking the "AIDS establishment" those seeming to put government money ahead of real progress. Following a few terse confrontations, the disrupters were forcibly ejected, and the usual parade of "established" pro-funding witnesses continued.

Whether this well-documented testimony, repeated on countless occasions, brought greater federal munificence is difficult to say, though it does seem likely. What is apparent, however, is how these innumerable hearings *defined* AIDS within the legislative body paying the bills. The never-ending message was that AIDS was a medical, not a moral issue, best solved by hefty federal (not private) directed intervention, and intervention should begin yesterday before AIDS engulfed everyone. This sanitized message essentially resembled the one conveyed via TV and the print media—AIDS is something akin to polio or Ebola that "just happens."

Certain arguments never appeared, at least in these legitimizing forums. These are the dogs that don't bark. No skeptical economists explained that policymaking required choosing among competing illnesses, all with their worthy sufferers, and that fighting AIDS might be a relatively poor cost-benefit investment given already high spending levels. Nor did local public health experts relate that it might be easier to reduce AIDS by legally shuttering establishments facilitating disease transmission. Similarly, social conservatives could not plead their case that moral education or shaming miscreants might outshine greater NIH funding. And when those representing other illness groups did testify, they simply reiterated their own cause versus arguing that, for example, millions of dollars to combat diabetes was a superior public investment.

Was this orchestrated political activism, or, perchance, just an accident or arrangements better characterized as objective administrative proceedings? Again, as was true in assessing the media slant on AIDS, an unambiguous answer is difficult. The motives of committee members and their staffers who controlled the agenda are currently unknown. Conceivably, those who resisted the gay agenda were uninterested in testifying, even if invited. Perhaps these heretical views were better expressed elsewhere (e.g., letters, private conversations), so a hearing appearance was redundant. These are surely researchable questions. Still, the assessment is crystal clear: for two decades congressional hearings illustrated the power of AIDS activists to dominate a multitude of budgetary competitors and ideological enemies.[11]

Working with Health Care Professionals

Perhaps the least visible, but absolutely vital weapon in this vast repertory was developing close ties with health care professionals deep within the Washington bureaucracy. Plunging into administrative infighting is less fun than dressing up in weird costumes to badger city officials, but this involvement can be decisive. Countless high-profile campaigns have failed when enthusiasts found administrative details too boring or arduous. All the public support, even assistance from legislators desperately trying to please their gay constituency, will come to naught unless those professionals daily fighting the war are committed. These CDC epidemiologists, HIH administrators, FDA regulators, and dozens of similar relatively obscure public servants are the indispensable officer corps of the anti-AIDS war. They must be swayed: a huge difference exists between just "doing one's job" versus working extra-long hours in labs or endlessly pestering superiors for increased funding.

This is the unexciting engagement of favorably settling technical detail and occurs in committee meetings, comments on research reports, esoteric technical conferences, and everywhere else key AIDS-related choices are made, all far removed from the public eye. This is not a task for badly informed dilettantes with short attention spans. Nor was a frenzied, in-your-face stance about to convince technocrats and independent-minded scientists who could choose to avoid confrontations. Prodigious homework was regularly required. Much of this labor is frustrating and wasteful and entails conferring with people with disliked political views. Moreover, the First Amendment does not guarantee access, and even the most heartfelt pleading of impending death cannot persuade a virologist to put in sixty-hour workweeks.

There are no statistics or even methodical accounts of gay activists "meddling" in these myriad political health bureaucracies, let alone outcome evaluations, but AIDS battle reports are replete with anecdotal evidence. This intervention was a movement staple though hardly headline-grabbing. And this includes discussions with high-ranking political appointees—even under the Reagan administration—whose cooperation was absolutely essential. The opposite observation—that gay activists were systematically excluded from the administrative inner sanctum—is never alleged, even among those damning government responsiveness. Historical narratives like Randy Shilts' *And the Band Played On* routinely describes cordial though not always successful lobbying between activists and a Who's Who of the scientific/bureaucratic establishment from the onset of AIDS. It was here that gay activists, sometimes doctors or scientists themselves, argued for more funding or rapid distribution of promising drugs.

To appreciate the adroit and typically time-consuming nature of this "insider" political maneuvering, consider one episode—getting FDA "fast-track" approval for uncertain experimental anti-AIDS drugs. One prominent leader in this endeavor was Martin Delaney, the founder of a San Francisco-based AIDS treatment group called Project Inform. Though he had initially started politicking as a rank outsider, including smuggling illegal alleged AIDS cures into the country, he eventually worked himself into an accomplished "insider" enjoying close ties to the FDA, the HIH, and top pharmaceutical industry executives. He had cultivated the friendship of the world-renowned Robert Gallo at the National Cancer Institute and Anthony Fauci, the head AIDS researcher at NIH. Despite a knack for befriending influentials, Delaney was a relentless and much-feared advocate quick to berate those standing in his way.

The value of this skilled doggedness on behalf of AIDS sufferers was manifest when the FDA in the late 1980s contemplated speeding up the distribution of several experimental anti-AIDS drugs (so-called "fast-tracking"). Strict consumer protection law regarding unproven medications made this a huge uphill battle (marketing then required nearly ten years of research and testing). Also opposing fast-tracking were influential consumer advocates apprehensive about toxic side effects plus much of the scientific establishment alarmed that unsupervised proliferation would undercut careful scientific testing. Quite a few major AIDS activist groups also foresaw deadly quackery. That these reputed wonder drug claims often relied on subjective personal stories, not clinical trials, further exacerbated the quest to loosen regulations.

Delaney bitterly and relentlessly castigated those advising caution, impugning their expertise, and accusing them of needlessly endangering countless lives. He respectably (always dressed conservatively) pushed his case in highly rated mainstream TV news-type programs and, most critically, joined with anti-regulation conservatives who long insisted that excessive bureaucratic red tape choked economic innovation. In an instant, he acquired powerful establishment allies (and insider information) who saw the mounting AIDS crisis, with its lurid tales of innocent Indiana boys dying of AIDS, as facilitating their own pro-business agenda.

The relentless haranguing and alliance building among insiders soon paid off. With the help of then Vice President (and soon to be President) George Bush, Delaney successfully won over the FDA to speed up approval for drugs for several life-threatening diseases. Nevertheless, even this moderate fast-track accomplishment still came up short, at least for Delaney. An estimated two-year wait for FDA approval was still excessive for those on death's doorstep. Delaney wanted virtually instant approval for experimental medications, a policy eschewed even by drug companies fearing lawsuits and helter-skelter research.

Delaney vigorously battled on, often assisted by leading scientists such as Samuel Broder, head of the National Cancer Institute. In 1990, a blizzard of letters was sent to AIDS activists, drug company executives, members of Congress, and consumer advocates imploring them to save lives by allowing untried but promising drugs to be prescribed. Leading scientists received urgent calls soliciting support while Project Inform members bombarded the FDA with letters. Simultaneous press conferences were held in eight cities during December 1990 to push the FDA along. Meanwhile, an arch foe within the FDA who had successfully resisted early drug release, tired of being vilified by Delaney, now resigned and was replaced by a more pliable appointee.

Even ACT-UP temporarily suspended its brash confrontational style on this issue and grew more accommodationist when privately dealing with FDA officials. Following a series of raucous Washington, DC demonstrations in the fall of 1988, a handful of now subdued activists quietly met with FDA officials at their Rockville, Maryland headquarters. Rather than push the usual laundry list of unmeetable demands, activists sought to develop working relationships with these experts, not vilify them. These once rambunctious street theater types now took a keen interest in FDA policy, for example, how it actually approved drugs and what, exactly, comprised legitimate science. Meanwhile other ACT-UP members—many of whom had zero technical background—made concerted efforts to learn the scientific vocabulary and otherwise become capable of intelligently talking with health care researchers (Epstein 1996: 225-32).

In November 1991, Vice President Dan Quayle announced a sweeping FDA overhaul that would save millions, if not billions, while rushing newly discovered drugs to desperate patients, provided these drugs might save lives immediately. Other AIDS militants, plus Republican regulation foes (assisted by Washington-based conservative think tanks) now joined forces, and by 1992 the FDA was approving several dozen iffy drugs in record time, often with the most cursory scientific review. The battle continued on for years with AIDS activists on both sides, but the FDA abandoned the old system of long, excruciatingly careful (and expensive) scrutiny for many new nostrums. Interestingly, AIDS sufferers themselves had organized unofficial clinical trials for a non-FDA approved medications called Compound Q. When the FDA threatened criminal prosecution, political mobilization (led by Delaney) garnered official approval for this do-it-yourself approach though professionals complained that the whole thing was amateurish (Wachter 1991: 210-11). The "Drugs into Bodies" campaign had been a resounding success. Whether this shift hurt or benefited those with AIDS is difficult to say, especially since the demanding, time-consuming science was seldom executed. Nevertheless, as far as Martin Delaney and his many varied allies were concerned, the paramount issue was AIDS patient choice; the quality of scientific evidence was irrelevant with the prospect of death imminent (this account is drawn from Burkett 1995: 263-275).

This battle over fast-tracking AIDS-related drugs was hardly atypical. On repeated occasions the movement adapted to the totally different "insider" strategy. Here, mastering arcane detail and building alliances across divergent perspectives was the required currency. This skilled resourcefulness was hardly unexpected though not every encounter was a resounding success. As we noted in our catalogue of initial advantages, many gays already occupied prominent positions in business and communications, and this was easily converted into political expertise. Mastering complicated subjects under pressure was a familiar task. It also helped that the gay movement could draw on an ample supply of gay doctors and other health care professionals who could converse with their government counterparts.

Conclusion: Skillfully Transforming Resources into Victories

All in all, though precisely aligning specific funding increases with particular mobilizations is impossible, the overall correlation between politicking and government generosity is self-evident: by any yardstick the war on AIDS was, and continues to be, exceedingly well funded. Many, in fact, would say over-funded given hard statistical evidence regarding competing claimants. This munificence sustains thousands of programs designed to help those with AIDS, myriad research projects, and a budding menu of prescription drugs. AIDS activists have likewise altered the way medicines are tested and marketed. Fervent militancy worked here, just as gay activists (and other participation devotees) insisted. What might this accomplishment reveal more generally about an effective recipe?

Analysis began by cataloguing the ample politically relevant resources enjoyed by gays, and all have been utilized. Foremost was having a clear and politically feasible goal—government money (and the requisite bureaucratic entities) to cure a disease, not some grandiose pie-in-the-sky anti-homophobia agenda. The tens of billions allocated is a prodigious sum, but not excessive by overall federal health care budget standards, especially when government-supported science, yet one more time, might save lives. Gays are also generally well educated, often conveniently concentrated in urban areas, not society's invisible downtrodden seeking a sweeping egalitarianism. The anti-AIDS campaign further promised material rewards galore, all for a noble cause, and this lure attracted indispensable allies. Whether intentional or not, this broad constituency-based politics was a traditional, time-tested formula for success.

Nevertheless, as in military conflicts, victories are never automatic. Assets require skilled utilization and liabilities must be surmounted. Just keeping the anti-AIDS campaign generally on track for over two decades was one such notable accomplishment, and this taxing job is seldom fully appreciated. Untold other struggles have failed in this regard and thus vanished or limp along in name only. Politics may require alliances, but not every union is happily productive, and a few should quickly end in divorce. Well-meaning individuals were forever pushing potential add-ons, and at any moment the campaign could splinter into a plethora of boutique distractions. Some lesbians sought to interject abortion and gender inequality; African-American gays periodically wanted to fight racism and press multiculturalism. A few feminists condemned drug trials for neglecting women. Various egalitarians promoted economic equality—not medical research—as the principal goal. Even drug legalization and animal rights were occasional thrown into the debate. Many Democratic activists meanwhile envisioned the anti-AIDS campaign as a vehicle to recruit gay voters. And this hardly exhausts the expansionistic urges.

This rampant opportunism is to be expected, but succumbing to these lures inevitably fragments resources while exacerbating internal divisions. Somebody had to say, "no," and this deft exclusion was usually—though not always—successful (the next chapter elaborates on this centrifugal impulse). Not every cause has been so fortunate. In retrospect, the civil rights movement offers examples of costly dissipated efforts. Little (other than internal divisiveness) was gained when activist supporters mixed in anti-Vietnam war oratory, economic inequality, cultural validation ("Ebonics") and sundry other distractions (e.g., "eco-racism"). The women's movement has also had its share of quarrelsome fragmentation. The prospect of impending death evidently focused the movement though side issues do occasionally intrude.

A particularly dexterous accomplishment was keeping illness competitors at bay. This is the politics of non-events—dogs that don't bark. It was not that rivals openly downgraded the AIDS crisis. Rather, "AIDS, Inc." has so successfully acquired the status of a sacred, "untouchable" cause, advanced by a quick-to-anger energetic constituency, that potential adversaries risked appearing homophobic, if not inviting (at least initially) a devastating worldwide plague. Moreover, who wants to contest a relatively small slice of a multibillion dollar, ever-expanding budget? Though these "too much on AIDS" voices periodically gained entrance to Congress, and even possessed hard scientific ammunition (see Gross, Anderson, and Powe 1999, above), critics of generous AIDS funding remained silent, as our overview of congressional hearings showed. Meanwhile AIDS activists themselves relentlessly pleaded human tragedy, not hard-headed economics (Wachter 1991: 85). No doubt, open dissenters were intimidated—recall the onslaught against Michael Fumento, Mike Royko and other doubters when they defied activists. Nobody, not even other illness groups, wants to tackle the AIDS lobby, and this surely stands as a monument to its dexterity.

Prodigious negotiating talent kept the disparate anti-AIDS coalition moving forward though not always uniformly. It is insufficient to inveigh, "We are dying by the thousands, so everybody should pitch in and help us, *please!*" If this were the sole standard, government would be hard at work developing a cure for smoking-induced lung cancer. Millions of grueling "i's" must be dotted and "t's" crossed to turn sympathy into productive, synergistic action, let alone organizations funded and staffed. While the potential profits from an anti-AIDS drug may be immense, pharmaceutical firms seldom commit fortunes for uncertain scientific ventures without some prodding. Neither private businesses nor university-based scientists can be commanded; cajoling and pressuring are the necessary tactics. Working with inside-the-Beltway civil service protected health care bureaucrats was especially vital both for their technical expertise and sway over lawmakers. As the fast-tracking battle illustrated, assembling an alliance of bureaucrats, free-market conservatives, drug company executives, Republican legislators, and assorted AIDS militants was a colossal tour de force against formidable opponents. This mobilization of allies, many of which were hardly natural partners, was commonplace. Recall the initial reaction of Hollywood celebrities to AIDS—panicky aversion. Public health officials repeatedly had to be won over to making AIDS (versus other public health issues) a high priority. Without these brokering and persuasion skills the movement would have surely collapsed.

The electoral ingredient in this mix was adroitly executed. Though gays remain a loyal Democratic coalition element, they still are a "must-court" constituency. It is an "up for grabs" voting bloc since millions of gay voters are quick to reward friends and punish enemies. Republicans appealing to gays can make sizable inroads, and the strategic location of gays makes these gains especially valuable. Gays also financially support friends and possess an extensive organization network easily mobilized for electoral purposes. That heightened AIDS funding has become part of the standing consensus on health care undoubtedly reflects this clout—opposition can mean electoral suicide. No national candidate can afford to alienate gay voters—even George W. Bush has joined this bandwagon despite his Christian fundamentalist constituency.

Securing unchallengeable social legitimacy for an illness typically contracted via homosexual anal intercourse or IV drug use was likewise an extraordinary accomplishment, and hardly pre-ordained. AIDS came to be viewed as a bona fide "normal" medical crisis, not nature's payback for dissolution, and even better, combating it grew fashionable among well-connected civic influentials and media celebrities. Somebody had to insure that victims highlighted on TV shows were guiltless, ordinary people, not aficionados of anonymous kinky bathhouse sex. Somebody had to give journalists digestible, accurate, and flattering AIDS-related information. That this debatable problem definition was swiftly imposed with scant opposition only adds to the accomplishment record. Alcoholism and mental illness, by contrast, have struggled to be "respectable" afflictions deserving public attention. Compare AIDS with diabetes, a far worse killer seemingly unnoticed among Hollywood and mass media denizens, and one that scarcely motivates parades of attention-getting notables testifying before congressional committees.

Similarly easy to overlook was the adroit balancing of multi-front, inside and outside strategies, a critical knack in today's political environment. A singular focus would have probably failed. Imagine if the entire campaign consisted entirely of ACT-UP protests or voter mobilization drives? Under such circumstances AIDS would have resembled today's animal rights or anti-globalization crusades—periodic provocations safely ignored by officialdom though these protestors might congratulate themselves for "making a difference." In a few years AIDS might have vanished into history's dustbin as yet one more potentially deadly STD affecting only a sliver of the population. This is hardly unimaginable—lots of far deadlier illnesses barely receive attention.

Getting the FDA to fast-track anti-AIDS drugs perfectly illustrated this synergy. Here cementing opportunistic bureaucratic alliances might have been unwelcome without the prior raucous street demonstrations. Along the way the heat was put on government via conventional electoral politics and relentlessly taking the message to Congress itself. Civil servants listen better when legislators with oversight responsibility are rewarded by donations from gay organizations or hear advocates convincingly tell their dramatic stories directly. And, of the utmost important, this was done doggedly, and with grim statistical evidence, despite feeble initial success. The movement repeatedly adjusted and abandoned unproductive dead ends. There was a learning curve. Again, the prospect of impending death sufficiently kept activists on track. This multifaceted pragmatism offers a useful message for activists hoping that a single, one-shot high-profile tactic (e.g., electing a sympathetic office-holder) can galvanize a politics mired in inertia.

Directing the right personnel to the right job was indispensable though it is unlikely that some hidden central command orchestrated it. A vast repertoire of available talent is insufficient by itself, and obstacles galore impeded sensible personnel choices. Again, this is the politics of non-events, the people *not* put into power. Person-job alignment is especially taxing in "movement politics" where it is impractical to impose formal job qualifications (see, for example, Wachter 1991: ch. 5). After all, who can dictate that "the crazies" must be excluded when beseeching bureaucrats? Pressures to fill positions by non-merit criteria were commonplace. Yet, with notable exceptions aside, this personnel alignment was adroitly executed; the stakes were too high to indulge dangerous idealism or caving into ideological pressure. The critical task of fund-raising shifted from amateurs passing the hat to professionals running well-attended black-tie formal dinners, art auctions, film benefits and the like, and the prodigious sums raised speak for themselves. One historical overview (Clendinen and Nagourney 1999: ch. 25) depicts how gays in Los Angeles meticulously arranged lucrative fund-raisers incorporating years of experience from soliciting money for Jewish causes. Affairs were expertly choreographed down to researching each potential donor and just how to make the request. To avoid embarrassing wealthy contributors paying by check, the organization's name was kept totally innocuous.

Details are critical: if selling tee shirts or coffee mugs provided the money, they must be expertly merchandised. This adroit coordination could also be negative, and, again, was often unappreciated. Imagine if a few mentally deranged ACT-UP types conferred with CDC experts to develop HIV reporting protocols? Or, conversely, if early efforts to energize an uncaring mass media were led by shy gay doctors more at ease with arcane statistical reports? Flamboyant homosexuality may be cherished in San Francisco's annual Gay Pride parade, or even handy at a medical conference to garner publicity, but dispatching glitzy drag queens to testify in Congress invites disaster. Better to have these queens (who are organized into The Imperial Court of America) stick to soliciting the appreciative faithful. Recall how ACT-UP eschewed criminal vandalism that might risk arrest and incur costly legal bills, and how it went "normal" when pushing fast-track drug distribution with FDA officials.

Capability informs every aspect of the quest. Speaking of just "being active" independent of dexterity is futile. ACT-UP protests attracted notable media coverage because they were cleverly newsworthy, and advocates knew the intricacies of getting TV exposure, not because rallies are First Amendment protected. ACT-UP manuals painstakingly explained how to generate interesting "sound bites," how to maximize visual impact (e.g., always stand closely together for photos) and other key publicizing tricks. AIDS benefit galas raised millions because these events were deftly planned. Immense boredom must sometimes be accepted. Building an effective computerized mailing list is drudgery; records of campaign contributions must be carefully kept to avoid criminal violations. Assuredly, mastering never-ending technical detail hardly guarantees success, and one's opponents may be equally well versed, but ineptitude and sloppy organization guarantees failure. Why should legislative committees heed manic anti-globalization enthusiasts clueless on tariff policy?

A Cautionary Postscript on Gay Activism

This analysis has depicted how civic engagement has promoted government generosity towards conquering AIDS. In some instances this was direct, for example, harassing public officials. In other instances, action was less noticeable, more defensive, as in the case of mobilizing gay voters (and campaign contributions) to make AIDS funding reductions absolutely beyond the pale. This account does *not* assert that this well-organized effort can be extended to win victories elsewhere though it gains strength yearly. It remains to be seen how the contemporary gay political agenda will play out— laws outlawing discrimination based upon sexual orientation, same-sex marriages, health insurance for same-sex domestic partners, and the like. The obstacles here are profoundly different from those impeding boosting health care budgets. Allies here are few and far between. Many of these desires touch deeply held moral convictions and are hardly life or death crises requiring immediate attention. And religious conservatives find these demands abhorrent, and many elected officials depend on these hostile voters. Not surprisingly, many activists now lament slowing progress despite having entered the establishment's inner sanctum. Nothing counsels that success in one policy domain increases the likelihood of victory elsewhere. Past experience hints at the opposite: early victories are typically the easiest, and with time, achieving political aims becomes increasingly arduous. This analysis is not an encomium to civic engagement; it only tells of one particular success story, and even that, as we shall soon see, is ambiguous.

Notes

1. Logically, if the government were to shoulder the AIDS burden this would *benefit* some firms by shifting extra health insurance costs to the public. Government intervention would also remove some contentious benefit issues from employer discretion and thus simplify health care choices.

2. Disputes surround the relative affluence of gays compared to heterosexuals. According to marketing survey data (cited in Wald 2000) gays are better off economically. Moreover, a 1993 *USA Today* survey (cited in Vaid 1995: 249) put the average gay male household income at $51,624 vs. the U.S. average of $37,922. Also, 58 percent of gay men were college graduates. Vaid (1995: 251) also cites data showing the average African-American household income at this time to be a mere $12,166. Other data (see Vaid 1995: 253-55) paints a contrary picture. Hertzog (1996: ch. 6) reports survey data showing that gays are relatively poorer than non-gays but are far better educated. Bailey (2000: 14) indicates that on the basis of five national surveys that there are only small sizable income differences with gays tending to be somewhat less affluent. Conflicts may, however, partially rest on differing definitions of "gay" and data collection methodology. Some of this gap may also be due to younger gays, who generally have less income, being more willing to openly identify as gay. But, just examining raw income data may be misleading and understate politically available resources. For one, most gays seldom have expenses such as children that burden heterosexuals. Second, gay male "couples" may have greater disposable incomes than married couples. The upshot is that gays probably have greater discretionary income than non-gays with identical incomes. Assessing income is also quite contentious, regardless of the sexual preference element.

3. Sherrill (1996) in an oft-cited essay reaches a contradictory conclusion, even asserting that gays during the 1990s resembled pre-civil rights southern blacks. His evidence for this powerlessness includes anti-gay violence, failure to enact anti-discrimination legislation, geographical dispersion, lower incomes, and anti-gay popular sentiment. It would be inappropriate to discuss these findings in detail; we can only say that they are either factually incorrect (e.g., geographical dispersion, surging anti-gay violence) or irrelevant (e.g., a lack of an anti-discrimination ordinance hardly shows wide-ranging weakness). Sherrill's points are more fully rebutted in Weissberg (1998: 117-29, 155-174).

4. Though census data on these concentrations do not exist, the proliferation of gay-centered businesses (depicted in compendiums such as the years *Gay Yellow Pages* plus local gay newspapers) strongly indicates this density. Sustaining all these bars, bookstores, clothing shops and the like without a large, nearby clientele would clearly be financially impossible.

5. This pro-gay stance derives from a general impression, not systematic investigation. In preparing this chapter I scanned dozens of books (plus several unpublished theses and dissertation), and the single critical book I encountered was Fumento's *The Myth of Heterosexual AIDS* (see below). "Anti-gay" tomes undoubtedly exist, but these are probably issued by obscure publishers and are beyond conventional

bibliographical searches. This one-sidedness is predictable given the liberal nature of publishing and the academy, a point documented below.

6.   While initial efforts at language "policing" came from the left, by 2003 conservatives had followed suit. Under George W. Bush, who has openly reached out to gays and upped AIDS funding, those who apply for government grants to study AIDS have been strongly advised by CDC officials to avoid such terms as "anal sex" and "men who sleep with men" (Goode 2003). This "sensitivity" might well reflect the electoral support Bush has received from Christian fundamentalists uncomfortable with explicit terminology.

7.   ACT-UP was not the only highly militant gay organization in this campaign. Others include the Lavender Hill Mob, Queer Nation, Radical Faeries, Lesbian Avengers, the Sisters of Perpetual Indulgence, among myriad others, but these are quite small and transitory. ACT-UP is also the most studied of this genre.

8.   Technically, this within-the-establishment group was an ACT-UP spin-off. Nevertheless it greatly differed from ACT-UP since membership was by (revocable) invitation only and the group employed a paid staff. Instead of selling tee shirts, funds now came from drug firms (Burkett 1995: 339).

9.   To repeat, sheer mobilization is not tantamount to influence. For example, the 1984 presidential race initially seemed a great gay victory as judged by Democratic candidate appeals and planks in the party's platform. Yet, this newfound gay presence was subsequently judged a reason for Mondale's defeat, so gays may have been better off by being "less successful" in their involvement (see Clendinen and Nagourney 1999: 510).

10.   This account is not exhaustive. Among other gay-oriented campaign organizations are The Republican Unity Coalition, ANGLE (Access Now for Gay and Lesbian Equality), and the National Stonewall Democratic Foundation.

11.   A confirming piece of evidence concerning agenda control occurred in 2003 when a Christian conservative active in combating AIDS withdrew his nomination from the Presidential Advisory Council on HIV and AIDS under intense pressure from Democrats and "mainstream" gay AIDS activists. Though he, his wife and one of his children were HIV-positive, he was unacceptable since he advanced abstinence to fight AIDS and took a dim view of sexual promiscuity. President Bush's other nominees did, however, include a board member of the Human Rights Campaign, a prominent gay activist group (Bumiller 2003).

9

Assessing Impact: The Negative Side
of the AIDS Activism Balance Sheet

Political activism is never guaranteed. Even worse than dissipating time and energy, however, is to pursue aims counter-productively. No matter how many successes are heralded, these must be balanced against losses. One-sided analyses ultimately invite disappointment. Recall travails drawn from black politics—electing an African-American mayor could plausibly precipitate an economic downturn if white-owned businesses flee the city, a situation hardly desired by blacks seeking one of their own as mayor. A clear (and ironic) downside applies to gay activism: the very political forcefulness instigating government bountifulness *also* exacerbated the epidemic. Ultimately, thanks to these occasional "victories," untold homosexuals, drug addicts, and others contracted AIDS and died. In retrospect, apathy or even failure would have proven far more beneficial and, fortunately, this militancy periodically did fall short.

The Gay Sexual Revolution

Understanding this "success brings deadly failure" requires some brief background regarding shifting gay male sexual behavior over past decades (Rotello 1997a: ch. 2 describes this change). Until the 1970s, overt male homosexuality was generally restrained. The dangers—blackmail, arrest (many homosexual acts were illegal), social stigma, and an embarrassed family—all counseled restraint. Though a few Turkish baths, bars, and similar businesses catering to male homosexuals subsisted in major cities, these operated quietly, largely by word of mouth. In New York State during the 1950s, it was even illegal for bartenders to serve homosexuals. At best, public officials ignored places were gays congregated for sexual liaisons; at other times, particularly during the 1950s, heavy-handed legal persecution was the norm. Necessity limited public sexual encounters to toilets (so-called "tearooms" in gay argot), parks, YMCAs and similar chancy venues (Bérubé 1996). Nearly every gay was in "the closet," so to speak, or risked arrest. In general, multiple same-sex liaisons were rare.

By the 1970s, this self-effacing mentality had nearly vanished. Society's more general sexual revolution hit with a special force among gay males (and lesbians, too). A no-excuse, unguarded, rampant promiscuity quickly defined contemporary gayness though, to be sure, ample exceptions existed. Once offensive, impolite terms such as queer and dyke evolved into proud badges of passionate sexuality. Beginning in the late 1960s, erotic bookstores, pornographic movie theaters, and other commercial sex establishments became commonplace in gay neighborhoods to serve as rendezvous points for amorous liaisons. A gay-oriented travel industry providing excursions to meet other gays boomed. The once-discrete Turkish baths were replaced with gay-owned pleasure palaces advertising orgy rooms, dance floors, snack bars, and other spa-like amenities designed to facilitate nonstop sex with dozens of partners. Meanwhile the more opulent venues offered entertainment by such luminaries as Bette Midler, Barry Manilow, and the comedian Dick Gregory, plus gay-oriented movies and elaborate festive theme nights.

Any gay could now almost instantly escape celibacy. One 1996-estimate put the number of gay bathhouses in the U.S. at approximately 200, including places far removed from urban gay enclaves (Bérubé 1996). A major study of gay sex habits found that 43 percent claimed to have had more than 500 partners over their lifetime; nearly one-third claimed a thousand-plus partners (cited in Rotello 1997a: 172). Among those initially infected with AIDS, on average, had eleven hundred sexual partners over their lifetime. NIH definitions of somebody with "multiple sex partners" soon came to mean 500 or more partners per year (cited in Rotello 1997a: 62-3). Readily available stamina-enhancing drugs amplified this hedonistic inclination. Among gays themselves (and their heterosexual defenders) this shift was frequently portrayed as "liberating," a new honesty about one's formerly repressed sexuality. To indulge one's carnal appetites was to resist oppression. Entire urban neighborhoods—the Castro district in San Francisco, Coconut Grove in Florida, the West

Village in New York City, among others—became thriving gay enclaves awash in overt sexuality.

Critically from a health standpoint, this swelling erotic life regularly entailed anal intercourse (particularly passive intercourse), a practice not previously unknown among gays but now, like promiscuity itself, deemed an almost ideological affirmation of gayness (Rotello 1997a: 101-2). During this liberating period several states (including California) repealed their sodomy laws to legalize this practice. Among those at this new freedom's cutting edge, passive anal sex might be experienced with multiple partners over a single evening, and with hundreds of men annually. Oral-anal sex was similarly commonplace, and these encounters often resulted in parasitic infections strenuously taxing immunity systems. In short, the post-1970s sexual culture possessed all the ingredients for a potential public health nightmare.

The Politics of Sexual Revolution Meets Infirmity

The dire health consequences of this unchecked sexuality soon arrived. Promiscuity with all populations, regardless of sexually identity, race, or creed, inevitably multiplies infections, and by the late 1970s gays were increasingly visiting clinics for various sexual transmitted diseases (STDs) such as rectal gonorrhea, chlamydia, herpes, venereal warts, and syphilis. These illnesses were not, however, especially deadly, and momentary discomfort cured by inexpensive antibiotics was judged a small price to pay for unbridled eroticism. Still, despite successfully controlling these outbreaks, several doctors and gay activists themselves grew gradually more apprehensive. If a new sexually transmitted illness did emerge, they suspected, it could rapidly reach epidemic proportions before a cure could be found. The outbreak of AIDS (depicted in chapter 7) eventually confirmed this grim speculation.

The AIDS explosion of the early 1980s presented a stark personal choice to those enjoying this newfound freedom: continue pursing dangerous gratification and risk a near certain death, or alter behavior and perhaps happily die of old age. The latter option necessitated abandoning rampant promiscuity, or at least behaving more cautiously. Economic costs also attended this return to the staid 1950s since bathhouses, bars, erotic bookstores, sex clubs, and other businesses facilitating unbridled sexual encounters (and the media advertising them) had become major industries in gay communities. That these places catered to once difficult-to-satisfy esoteric tastes (e.g., sado-masochism, non-stop orgies, and bisexuality) only increased this allure. Provided diseases were non-fatal and curable like gonorrhea or syphilis, this option was an easy one.

The mounting AIDS-related death tolls beginning in the mid-1980s sharply upped the stakes. Shigellosis (a parasitic infection often associated with anal-oral sex) did not bring death; AIDS did. What road was taken? Exceptions aside, countless gays, especially younger urbanites, generally opted for promiscuous sexual freedom over returning to an earlier more circumspect era. Sexual liberation could not be reversed, or so many decided. Dire warnings offered in widely circulated gay newspapers like the *Advocate* fell on deaf ears (Clendinen and Nagourney 1999: 467). Those who became infected were actually celebrated as advancing sexual liberation, not stigmatized and avoided as carriers of death (Rotello 1997a: 86). Even international AIDS conferences with their grim portrayals of gay mortality became venues for bacchanalian gay sex. The conquering of AIDS was thus first and foremost a way of preserving sexual liberation, not primarily a public health issue (Rotello 1997a: 111). Critically for our analysis, *this embrace of all those pleasure-providing emporiums and the accompanying behavior was sustained by political activism.* Without fervent mobilization by gays and their allies, the sexual revolution would have come to a virtual halt. Put bluntly, politics permitted a medical version of Russian roulette.

Only a tiny minority of gay activists resisted equating promiscuity with gay culture when lives were at stake. Opposing forces were just too strong. The mounting medical evidence could easily be brushed aside as inconclusive or too bothersome to digest. Abandoning bathhouse sex was a tough, if not impossible, sell to eager patrons waiting in line for their turn. Who wanted to be a killjoy? Those genuinely concerned souls, many gay themselves, who did strongly speak up were repeatedly labeled "anti-sex brown shirts" or "internalized homophobes" out to annihilate the gay community. Gay leaders even denounced early medical investigations as homophobic, and advised gays to refuse cooperation with these studies (Rotello 1997a: 72-3). Randy Shilts, the admittedly gay newspaper journalist who refused to sugarcoat the irresponsible spread of AIDS was often treated as a pariah, an "Uncle Tom," even spat upon when walking through San Francisco's Castro district (Burkett, 1995: 6). The famed author and playwright, Larry Kramer, who relentlessly screamed the grim truth was similarly ostracized and kicked off the boards of gay organizations he helped create. Promiscuous, dangerous sex was soon elevated to a human right or sacred freedom of association, not testosterone-driven self-indulgence. Choices were to be made in the context of what some called "sex positive" ethics. A huge chorus of militants equated endless unprotected anal sex as the very essence of "gay culture."

Politics and commercial greed were often comfortably though furtively co-mingled. In Miami, Chicago, and elsewhere, prominent gay leaders owned these lucrative sex-oriented hotspots, and savvy politicians feared that the slightest hint of reining in these hotspots would enrage gay organizations. Nor were gay-oriented newspapers about to banish major advertisers from their pages. In San Francisco, bathhouse owners and gay activists, in a peculiar twist of logic, agreed that these establishments should "not be singled out during this crisis." Though most of these early sex emporiums did eventually disappear (in part due to a decimated clientele), many hung on and soon were re-vitalized as a new generation of gays discovered them (see below regarding adaptation). When the Department of Public Health did require innocuous warning posted in bathhouses, Alice B. Toklas Democratic Club leaders complained that this was a "direct attack on the social and economic viability of our community" (Shilts 1988: 306-17). Militants routinely denounced urgent warnings from anxious experts as merely the first step in forcibly interning all homosexuals. In another peculiar twist of logic, the San Francisco Public Health Director (Mervyn Silverman) resisted closing the baths on the feeble grounds that they could expediently educate gays about dangerous sex, a line of reasoning that soon proliferated as a morally harmless justification for lethargy among those intimidated by pleasure-seeking gays. That these posted warnings were usually hidden or unreadable was irrelevant.

These trepidations similarly inhibited initial education efforts. Gay physicians who daily witnessed the suffering seldom spoke forcefully regarding their fears. A New York City gay doctor who early on warned of dangerous promiscuity went out of his way to recount his own pro-sex, loose behavior and advised restraint only as a practical survival tactic, not a moral virtue (Epstein 1996: 63). When the

San Francisco Department of Public Health in 1983 sought to warn gays, announcements were purposely kept wishy-washy, a policy that became standard. Nobody wanted to appear "homophobic," anti-sex or offend homosexual sensibilities. Notices just advised bath-house patron to "reduce" unprotected casual sex and recreational drug use, worthless advice given the already high incidence of these practices. Politically correct euphuisms further permitted escape from harsh reality. Openly mentioning anal intercourse was absolutely *verboten*; guidelines only vaguely referred to sharing bodily fluids (Shilts 1988: ch. 31). Even this elusiveness enraged some status quo defenders who insisted these announcements were futile since sex-hungry gays would seek outlets elsewhere, venues such park bushes or darkened movie theaters. One prominent San Francisco gay ac-tivist denounced condoms use and safe sex in general. Others ac-cepted the idea of condoms while viewing admonitions to use condoms as "too judgmental" (Rotello 1997a: 101).

Concerted gay outrage was so feared that in 1983 public health officials in both San Francisco and Los Angeles assured gay leaders that they would *never* close their beloved bathhouses (Shilts 1988: 318). New York's Governor Mario Cuomo in 1985 repeated this pledge. In 1986 and 1988 California voters voted on two initiatives (Proposition 69 and Proposition 101) that called for coercive public health measures to stop the spread of HIV-AIDS (including the track-ing of all HIV infections). Both were opposed by the state's leading public health organizations and were rejected by voters (Vaid 1995: 227-8). This fear of offending gay militants by raising awkward trans-mission issues, even by gays themselves, seems endemic. When the most prominent Los Angeles gay fund-raising organization suggested that bathhouses voluntarily close during the AIDS epidemic, this meek suggestion was strongly denounced by members of the Gay Liberation Front (Clendinen and Nagourney 1999: 522-3). Gabriel Rotello (1997a: 149-52) describes a 1994 AIDS prevention confer-ence of prominent specialists. Virtually every nostrum imaginable was proposed, but the actual process by which AIDS is transmitted was a non-issue, an oddity that Rotello attributes to the political might of sexual liberation-oriented gay zealots. In fact, Rotello suggests that the movement's liberationist wing dominates the AIDS preven-tion establishment, even seeing their role as politically defending promiscuity from the puritans.

Consistent with strong civil libertarian views, militants often defined illness transmission as "informed choice," so just alerting people
to impending death via unprotected sex sufficed. Anything stronger,
these spokesmen asserted, comprised a homophobic assault on gay
life, even if gays themselves sounded the alarm. Countless gay-oriented magazines repeated this defense and further warned that to
attack a promiscuous lifestyle was an attempt to label gays "sick"
and "perverse" (Epstein 1996: 64-66). Innocuous non-coercive
education projects advanced by sympathetic professionals were denounced in one gay newspaper as "Behavior Modification for Tricking
Gays" (Shilts 1988: 453). One gay-sympathetic *Miami Herald* reporter claims that even publicly revealing precisely how AIDS was
transmitted, let alone its disconcerting moral and legal overtones,
risked disruptive militant demonstrations (Burkett 1995: 6-7).

Misguided political zeal also zeroed in on AIDS-tainted blood.
By 1983, medical experts had observed growing mortality among
transfusion recipients, and while the precise blood and AIDS link
was imprecise, Center for Disease Control professionals desperately
wanted to screen out admitted male homosexuals. Gay militants
blithely ignored these admonitions and were more upset that screening scapegoated gays, and returned collection to the days when blood
was racially classified. Their expensive and impractical alternative
was for all blood to be tested for hepatitis antibodies. Even here,
however, one belligerent militant differed, insisting that blood testing would mark gay men with a "biological pink triangle." Another
prominent gay spokesman implored gays to lie if blood banks attempted to screen donors by sexual orientation, a position soon publicly endorsed by the National Gay Rights Task Force (Shilts 1988:
220-38).

Infusing the entire debate was the touchy confidentiality issue.
Historically, public health officials have tracked sexual contacts to
both monitor contagion and treat the infected before they unknowingly contaminate others. For these sound reasons national regis-
tries of hepatitis B and syphilis sufferers (among other illnesses) are
kept. Involuntary testing of suspected disease carriers is also relevant here and, in fact, many states routinely and forcibly test arrested prostitutes for sexually transmitted diseases. Degrees of confidentiality exist, ranging from virtual anonymity to posting lists of
those infected accessible to health officials. Despite the benefits of

professionals sharing information, let alone mandatory testing, many leading gay organizations—especially at the onset of AIDS—fiercely resisted standard public health procedures fearing possible embarrassment to transmitters and their partners and, imaginably, criminal prosecution where sodomy remains illegal (Bayer 1991). When the FDA approved a test to detect HTLV-III (as HIV was then known), the test was denounced by leading gay heath organizations as an "unprecedented threat" and gays were told not to take it. Leading gay legal groups went to court to prevent the FDA from licensing the test since it might be used to pressure gays to reveal their sex partners (Clendinen and Nagourney 1999: 517-8).

In 1983, New York City AIDS activists compelled public health officials to take a confidentiality stance that rendered information sharing almost impossible. Meanwhile well-meaning gay doctors worried over privacy shielded victims by refusing to report AIDS cases to authorities. When David Dinkins was elected mayor of New York City in 1989, one payback to gay supporters was forbidding reporting by name of AIDS carriers. Now the long-term health benefits of experts knowing just who had AIDS (and its origins) were subordinated to strict secrecy. When the New York City commissioner of public health (Stephen Joseph) in 1989 suggested a central registry of the HIV-positive, 200 demonstrators blocked the Brooklyn Bridge and shut down the city health department. The mayor and the state health commissioner quickly distanced themselves from this sensible proposal. After all, they themselves were not at risk, so why invite avoidable trouble. In 1991, ACT-UP organized a "phone zap" of the respected American Medical Association when it agreed to classify AIDS as a sexually transmitted diseases, a decision that would have applied standard STD reporting procedures to AIDS. This tracking, it was alleged, would "...only contribute to AIDS hysteria" (Chicago ACT-UP memo, January 23, 1991). Only when the true AIDS devastation become apparent did many states impose tracking the infected by name.[1]

An especially lethal example of this misguided strict AIDS-related confidentiality impulse occurred in New York during the early 1990s. Under state law, newborns are tested for hepatitis, syphilis, plus assorted other infections potentially passed on by mothers. Parents are then notified of the results, an essential step in providing professional care since the mother may be unaware of her illness.

Though babies were tested for HIV, the reasonable practice of parental notification was legally *prohibited*. Now infected babies could go entirely untreated until they died. The reckoning was that parental notification would also inform the mother of her condition, and this was unacceptable unless the mother requested this information. Apparently, at least to AIDS zealots, the same logic is irrelevant when other serious medical conditions are detected.

When a New York State legislator, known for her passionate support of women's issues, introduced legislation requiring parental notification, the state's AIDS lobby (together with militant women's organizations) branded her a fascist, a racist, homophobic, a woman hater, and baby killer. The bill was attacked as a violation of civil liberties. Some eighty-two activist groups spent a quarter of a million dollars opposing this well-meaning measure. The state's medical society, though initially favorable, was reluctant to antagonize gays and backed off despite an overwhelming medical justification for parental notification. Notification opponents favored counseling, a solution of dubious efficacy that sidestepped grim reality. In the end, the proposal died, just like many of the HIV-infected infants (Burkett 1995: 237-41).

The extreme delicacy of mandatory testing continues even as the cost of uncovering HIV infections has dropped to a mere $12 thanks to a test called OraQuick (and this can be quickly administered outside of hospitals and clinics). In April 2003, the CDC *recommended* (not legally demanded) that those at risk, including pregnant women, newborn infants, and those practicing unsafe sex, be screened, a reasonable step given that it is estimated that some 30 percent of the 850,000 to 950,000 HIV carriers in the U.S. are unaware of their condition and thus can unknowingly pass on the disease to others. That this life-saving initiative would be relatively cheap and quick and comes at a time when HIV seems to be growing is still insufficient given the politics surrounding mandatory testing (Reuters 2003).

Compounding these misguided battles were activist miscalculations regarding how the national AIDS alarm should be sounded. As chapter 8 described, in the late 1980s the media "democratized" the disease—everyone, it was said, regardless of sexual orientation, age, income, or race, was equally vulnerable. This frightening perspective contradicted statistical evidence[2] but it greatly appealed to gays (and sympathizers) since this misinformation would, allegedly (a)

scare up greater federal funding and (b) minimize the stigma attached to homosexuality (Fumento 1990: 146, 200). This everyone-
can-get-it campaign quickly triumphed, and thousands with scant
chance of infection became hyper-cautious or abstained from sex
altogether. If this democratization tactic were insufficient, the horrific specter of an epidemic soon arriving from AIDS-infested Africa
was also raised (Fumento 1990: 153).

Though this better-safe-than-sorry alarmism might have been
warranted when AIDS was imperfectly understood, and may have
temporarily boosted research funds, it eventually proved a costly
miscalculation. Precious resources were now squandered "educating" risk-free populations while those truly vulnerable were slighted.
Pointlessly distributing free condoms to nervous heterosexual college students only misspent money. Worse, millions of drug users
and gay men were lured into a false sense of complacency by transforming a well-understood transmission into uncontrollable happen-
stance—an ill-advised kiss or handshake. In addition, since the deadly
epidemic might suddenly explode "everywhere," existing sexually
transmitted disease (STDs) interventions were hurriedly cannibal-
ized to fight AIDS. Not only did this re-direction physically harm
thousands of VD sufferers (disproportionately black and Hispanics), but these untreated STDs would eventually exacerbate matters
by increasing vulnerability to AIDS (Fumento 1990: 140). Money
that could have been spent targeting intravenous drug users was
meanwhile aimed at terrifying married heterosexuals, a population
nearly risk free. In retrospect the best anti-AIDS advice was for affected populations to cease their dangerous behaviors. Denying this
harsh reality may have shielded political sensitivities and avoided
stigmatizing the culprits, but it hardly stopped the death toll.

A more contemporary AIDS activist objective has also been proven
of debatable value. Specifically, ACT-UP militants and their organizational descendants have unremittingly pressured pharmaceutical
firms to cut drug prices and permit cheap generic versions to be
manufactured in poorer nations. This seems good-hearted enough—
why should people die solely because they cannot afford available
medicines? After brief holdouts, these harassed companies bowed
to activist pressure and, it would seem, a mighty victory has been
won. But, and this is critical, these cheaper medicines still do not
cure AIDS *and*, as a result of shrinking profits, drug companies are

abandoning research that could, ultimately, provide cures. Not only will third-world victims still die (though a bit later in life), but sufferers everywhere may be deprived of scientific breakthroughs thanks to this militancy (Bate 2002). Brilliant activism cannot overturn the laws of economics.

Mixing political activism with medicine may even hinder the ultimate anti-AIDS weapon—a vaccine against contracting the illness. Experts agree that overcoming huge technical obstacles will require more than a quarter of a billion dollars and take over a decade, if success is even possible (Schoofs 1996). Still, in light of the millions of potential lives saved, a vaccine should be among the highest, if not the highest, priority. The quest has, however, attracted only modest private and government investment. Washington has largely pushed it to the back burner compared to curing those already infected. In FY 2000, for example, the NIH spent nearly 200 million on an anti-AIDS vaccine out of a $2.2 billion total budget (Fauci 1999: testimony). Several major pharmaceutical firms, (e.g., Bistol-Meyers Squibb, Merck and Genentech) have sharply reduced their vaccine-related research while start-up firms devoted to finding a vaccine now attract little investor interest.

Much of this neglect—over and above the formidable technical obstacles—is traceable to misguided political pressures, not an evil conspiracy. For one, why should the drug companies invest billions in a risky venture if activists will inevitably demand that this miracle drug be under-priced to save lives in third world nations?[3] Or given away to America's poor? Surely stockholders will rightly reject multi-billion dollar charity work when acceptable profit can be made by curing sexual dysfunction or controlling diabetes, two easier, more lucrative projects. Politics also hinders development since even the smallest accidental infection can result in huge, court-ordered liability judgments (this is an inherent risk in any vaccine). Litigation could easily wipe out the paltry profits imposed by political pressure. Under existing law, it is far better for a firm *not* to develop a vaccine that saves millions but accidentally infects a few dozen innocent victims. Only a special congressional liability waiver would offer protection (as was done with a smallpox vaccine as part of Homeland security legislation), and enacting this provision is uncertain. Finally, the bulk of AIDS-related political pressure understandably comes from those *already* infected. For them, obviously, a vaccine is pointless and it appears that those who *might* be infected have yet to coalesce politically (Schoofs 1996). Few gays or drug users are willing to tell government that they anticipate risky behavior in a few years, so officialdom better get busy.

The potentially deadly result of political "successes" is hardly limited to vaccines against AIDS. The 2003 flu outbreak has brought to light a potentially dangerous situation regarding the vaccine supply for various serious illnesses, for example, diphtheria, tetanus, and flu, among others. Heavy-handed regulation plus political pressure for cheap prices has reduced the number of U.S. firms producing these vaccines from twenty-five in the 1970s to just five in 2003. In some instances, there is only a single vaccine producer, and limited production capacity can cause havoc during an outbreak. Even when manufactures do secure a litigation exemption, clever lawyers can often defeat it (Wysocki 2003).

Economics Defeats Politics

Our account thus far depicts how AIDS militants sustained a sexual "lifestyle" that ultimately proved deadly. Though Randy Shilts, Larry Kramer, and a few others initially pleaded for restraint, they went largely unheeded. However, by the 1990s with the death toll now over a quarter of a million, a stronger gay-lead "counter-revolution" had surfaced. They contended that gays were killing themselves via unprotected sex in commercial establishments, and, critically, it was the government's legal duty to prevent this carnage. Their tactics largely mirrored those of their opponents—riveting media hype, coalition building, pestering officials, and the like. Nevertheless, reasonableness and disquieting evidence aside, this campaign largely came up short. The chief culprit was not the other side's superior political firepower, though that was considerable. Rather, these counter-revolutionaries under-estimated the opportunities provided by a freewheeling market economy. Simply put, even brilliant politics cannot always overcome the capitalist spirit. A parallel exists here between those AIDS activists coercing government to redirect gays away from dangerous sex and civil rights groups (described in chapter 4) compelling government to impose unpopular school integration. Recall how private schools and home instruction availability often reversed outcomes heralded as political triumphs.

The AIDS-related battles in New York City during the mid-1990s perfectly demonstrate how politics can be circumvented. Here, public officials, vigorously assisted by some gay activists, notably a group called GALPHA (Gay and Lesbian HIV Prevention Activists), yet one more time sought to shutter those sex establishments that these alarmed activists called "killing fields." GALPHA demanded strict enforcement of existing health code regulations express prohibiting sexual contacts, regardless of condom use plus removing cubicle doors in bathhouses so that "private" behavior could be monitored. GALPHA was joined by other anxious anti-AIDS activists such as APAL (AIDS Prevention League) and CAPA (Community AIDS Prevention Activists), though those two organizations were decidedly less draconian than those demanding that *all* public sex be banned. The chances of success were initially quite reasonable since: (1) laws prohibiting public sex are absolutely unambiguous[4] and (2) enforcement has been long standing (though erratic), and while occasionally troublesome, it is feasible. In fact, some of the most notorious sex venues had been shuttered during the mid 1980s.

Superficially this alliance had some notable victories, especially under the administration of Mayor Rudy Giuliani who was determined to eradicate virtually the entire sex industry from New York. GALPHA members and journalist sympathizers such as Gabriel Rotello and Michelangelo Signorile successfully promoted their tough message in the city's leading newspapers, including the *Daily News, Newsday, Village Voice,* and the *New York Times* (plus various gay-oriented papers). Graphic, first-hand accounts told that how unprotected anal sex still flourished were splashed about. Muckraking local TV reporters went undercover with hidden cameras and broadcast revealing, if not titillating (though evidently censored) videos of bathhouse orgies, despite safe-sex posters (Redick 1996). Under mounting public pressure city inspectors raided notorious clubs, bathhouses and porn movie houses; owners were taken to court and fined, and dozens of these establishments were permanently closed. Infamous, long-established gathering spots such as the S&M oriented Mineshaft and the New David Cinema became history. Where sex businesses remained open, owners became more careful, for example, providing condoms gratis or hiring bouncer-like employees armed with flashlights to toss out code offenders. All in all, a preliminary accounting would suggest that the GALPHA-assisted counter-attack on rampant, unsafe sex had accomplished something. Score one for political activism.

Reality was quite different and, once more, illustrates how financial incentives in the private sector can almost invisibly undermine the most "successful" political crusade. The ample profits from catering to gays plus entrepreneurial savvy in a free-market economy made a mockery of this crackdown. This moneymaking industry with an eager clientele was not about to die quietly, and survival tactics abounded. Hiring veteran "sex war" lawyers and escaping punishment by manipulating the legal system by requesting never-ending delays or claiming entrapment were standard practices. When the police raided the West Side Club in 1995, its owner declared that his establishment was merely a "meeting place" for gays interested in physical fitness, despite the presence of cubicles designed for sexual encounters and a well-deserved reputation for debauchery. After enough legal wrangling, the Club re-opened for its awaiting, old clientele (Blotcher 1996). An arrested owner might also dodge punishment with a "good faith" demonstration that restrictive rules were being enforced (however carelessly) and that repeat offenders were barred from returning. That these chronic lawbreakers could then immediately visit another sex venue, again perform dicey sex, night after night in dozens of nominally compliant establishments, was legally irrelevant. A popular subterfuge was reorganizing as a private membership club to escape legal surveillance entirely. Clever managers devised stratagems to detect city inspectors (who refused to disrobe or engage in sexual activities), and re-directed them away from hidden, action-packed backrooms.

Far more efficient was to adapt, much like bars became speakeasies during Prohibition. Dangerous sex simply went underground as far as the public and officialdom were concerned. This was remarkably uncomplicated provided one eschewed a liquor license or disdained expensive steam rooms or swimming pools. These freewheeling "anything goes" establishments also enjoyed a marketing edge over businesses strictly enforcing rules unwelcome to many gays. A shuttered establishment could adopt a new name, inconspicuously rent cheap loft space convenient to gay enclaves, decorate with black paint and plywood, advertise in gay publications or handbills, and be up and running in a few weeks. With a minimal staff and overhead, twenty to thirty customers per day paying $30 for admission could credibly generate $10,000 a month (or more) in pure profit, and much of it in untaxed cash. Overhead (and visibility) could be cut even further by subletting legitimate daytime businesses like dance studios for nighttime sex clubs. As one might expect, the city and its counter-revolutionary gay allies had about as much success in banishing these mushrooming venues as the police had in cracking down on narcotics—the huge profits are just too tempting for potential lawbreakers.

If near invisibility coupled with legal acumen were insufficient for survival, sex entrepreneurs could usually elicit help from well-known gay organizations dedicated to protecting what they defined as the gay culture. When police raided the West Side Club in 1995, the Gay Men's Health Crisis, Lambda Legal Defense and the Gay and Lesbian Community Services Center, all venerable, respected gay organizations, arrived in court to defend the arrested owner (Blotcher 1996). In another instance, the highly regarded Gay Men's Health Crisis lent their protective authority to a sex establishment by providing twice-a-week lectures on safe sex (Rotello 1995a). These displays of gay solidarity (plus legal shrewdness) were typical—the criminalization of gay sexuality, regardless of motive or demonstrated illegality, let along health dangers, almost automatically energizes gay rights organizations who equated sexual promiscuity with gayness itself. Politicians nervous about alienating potential voters undoubtedly pay attention to such hair-trigger mobilization. This obliviousness is reasonable: why should politicians invite trouble if gays want to kill each other?

Over and above the doubtful civil libertarian arguments about permitting public sex, sexual liberation defenders made two more practical claims against closure. First, closure would be pointless since sexual liaisons would remain undiminished, only shifting to more personally precarious settings elsewhere, for example, public toilets. At least the bathhouses were secure. Second, these central, gay-administered sites offer splendid educational opportunities—places to post warnings, hold safe-sex workshops, etc. The upshot, then, was that tolerating public sex was sound policy regardless of potential health hazards.

The statistical evidence paints a contrary picture. Two studies of San Francisco gay men from the 1980s showed that when these venues were (temporarily) shut, transmitted infections leveled off and, according to one study, declined to zero. A nearly identical pattern was found in New York City when officials did, briefly, manage to end the gay sex industry in the mid-1980s—transmission rates dropped to near negligible and stabilized for several years before soaring again when gay life returned to "normal." The explanation is pretty uncomplicated: bathhouses and the like are much more inviting than unreliable park bushes or back alleys. Sexual encounters are ruled by the same cost-benefit calculations guiding all behavior—"cruising" outdoors on a dreary evening for a partner may be too bothersome vis-à-vis visiting an amenities-filled club with a choice of countless potential lovers (and far riskier given criminal predators and the police). Better to stay at home and watch TV. Recall that HIV infections may require multiple exposures, so going from a few different partners a month to a half dozen liaisons per night makes a huge difference in risk (studies are cited in Rotello 1995b).

The Wages of Hyper-Activism

A further and related cautionary point regarding activism is especially ironic given nonstop calls for "more engagement" by those actually affected by AIDS. Recall our previous discussion of how gays themselves, and politically savvy white male homosexuals in particular, came to dominate federal health service outlays. This inclusiveness push initially made perfect sense since it was widely agreed that successful intervention would have to be community based, and gays themselves had unique knowledge of the epidemic's impact. In fact, this element was a key ACT-UP aim, and its achievement as official policy was heralded as proof that in-your-face harassment works. Unfortunately, this noble intent to let every voice be heard quickly encouraged immense trouble. It was not that this inclusiveness lacked benefits—these varied contributions were occasionally substantial and, as chapter 8 pointed out, the movement did generally stay on track. Rather, given that the "gay community" itself was quite culturally heterogeneous, even laced with antagonisms, and because no "one-size-fits-all" medical solution existed, seeking multiple accommodations also imposed some serious liabilities. With ample money available, armies of petitioners, true to form, arrived to stake their claims, and they scarcely spoke with a unified voice. Unfortunately, this cacophony could not always be surmounted by those determined to keep the movement focused. At a minimum, valuable energy was dissipated.

Randy Shilts (1988: 376) early on foretold the problematic outcome when *too* many energized cooks meddle in the political kitchen. Specifically, when San Francisco in 1983 created the AIDS Activities Office to coordinate city programs, myriad gay political factions, all advancing dissimilar viewpoints and financial aims, overwhelmed the office. Bickering participants often only vaguely appreciated arcane medical issues, standard public health practices, or mandatory municipal legal procedures. Group "membership" was often informal and sometimes only required appearing to make demands, so agendas shifted from meeting to meeting, and varied according to who momentarily spoke the loudest. Responsible officials feared sabotage if they ignored some strong-headed advocate or tiny sect. Better to placate everyone. Coordinating this boisterous multitude, let alone taking decisive, wise action, predictably pushed everything toward a hazy consensus and vague rhetoric. This democratic widening of participation, good intentions aside, probably *impeded* determined measures to slow down an ever-mounting death toll.

This early, disconcerting lesson went unappreciated, and this "more the merrier" fiasco was soon played out on a national scale. The wide dispersal of funds coupled with the imperative to satisfy a plethora of divergent constituencies soon brought a feeding frenzy. "Inclusiveness" inevitably mandated proliferating specialized agencies, many unable to afford professional, competent staffs necessary to coordinate efficient outreach programs. Hurried efforts to save those on death's doorstep and placate vociferous activist-minded constituencies created organizational problems galore. Minuscule organizations claiming a few clients were often so internally disorganized that funds remained unspent or were dissipated altogether. Cases of serious embezzlement and fraud soon appeared. Impending gridlock repeatedly forced judges or mayors to impose priorities against the wishes of enraged militants. Entire boards of "community advisors" were sometimes fired over policy squabbles. Delays were common until turf battles could be resolved (if ever). Well-intended hyper-proliferation also meant financial inefficiencies in rents, staff, equipment, and all else necessary to run an agency, funds that could have been better spent elsewhere.

Enduring acrimonious racial/cultural divisions over priorities were especially distracting. That deep-seated, society-wide conflicts intruded when government spent billions to assist "people" was predictable in a society increasingly attentive to group differences. After all, why should white males arrange health care for transsexual Asians?[5] African Americans frequently worried that white middle-class gays didn't particularly sympathize with black drug addicts. Militant lesbians, perhaps feeling invisible despite their contribution to movement politics, soon demanded a "piece of the AIDS action" though countless reputable scientific experts assured them that they were absolutely risk-free unless they used intravenous drugs or had heterosexual contacts. When socially conservative religious groups like the Nation of Islam or Catholic agencies sought funding from gay-controlled service organizations, liberal gays suspected ingrained homophobia and tried to deny requests. Meanwhile many black churches saw the crisis as one of homosexuality itself, not comforting the ill, a dispute that could make education nearly impossible. That slighted groups galore could rally allies within government further aggravated this squabbling. One account depicted events as "a war zone" (Burkett 1995: 147-55).

An Unbridled Faith in Science and Education

Recall that the movement's chief focus was on government-funded science and education as *the* efficacious solution. This choice, as we also noted, not only left gay sexual liberation unchallenged, but also greatly simplified the battle—just coerce those guarding the treasury and science will surely produce a cure. This focus represented an enormous competitive political advantage in marshalling the troops—House Appropriation Committee members and public health departments are easy, vulnerable targets, quite willing to award tax-payer money to fight laudable battles. This tactically inspired stratagem, however, reflects enormous confidence in modern science and the power of education to impede sexual desire. Faith in both may have been misplaced, regardless of how astute the political force.

The record clearly shows that educational efforts repeatedly fell short within at-risk groups. A huge gap separates getting a message out versus modifying behavior. Attempts to glamorize safe sex, for example, brightly colored fruit-flavored condoms, even X-rated movies demonstrating safe practices, generally failed. Research indicates that even at the height of the AIDS epidemic, no more than half of gay men consistently used condoms. Another condom-use study in the mid-1990s found that even those gays educating other gays about sex often shunned condoms. Such behavior by "those who know better" is understandable in settings where excessive alcohol or drug (especially D-methamphetamine or "crystal meth") use is common (Rotello 1997a: 123, 136-9).[6] Certain populations, notably African-American drug addicts, are especially difficult to reach with standard public health messages. There is also the awkwardness, particularly in popular outlets monitored by conservative religious groups, of detailing *exactly* how AIDS is acquired and recommending alternative, satisfying homosexual techniques. Federal law in fact prohibits any instruction that might be interpreted as promoting homosexuality. Persuading young, sexually charged men to take time-consuming, unerotic precautions may be asking too much, even when the Grim Reaper sits a few inches away. Keep in mind that even the mildest educational admonitions were denounced by leading gay activists, so the safe-sex message could easily be dismissed as just "an opinion." Why those familiar with sexually drenched gay culture believed that a poster could do the trick remains an unanswered question. Quite possibly this "more education" tactic permitted public officials the option of acting "positively" without angering gay militants.

As for the anticipated miracles that science would definitely deliver, this faith initially appears completely reasonable given past triumphs against far deadlier illnesses. Still, this *particular* embrace of science rests upon dogmatic conviction, not hard laboratory evidence. The laws of nature are not as malleable as anxious-to-please public officials. The common cold is virus-based, and it remains incurable despite the riches and fame awaiting those discovering an antidote. Writing in the prestigious *Proceedings of the National Academy of Sciences*, the respected Dr. Albert Sabin (discoverer of the polio vaccine) declared that finding an AIDS vaccine was a medical impossibility (cited in Burkett 1995: 125). Maurice Hillman, a famous researcher responsible for vaccines to combat measles, mumps, rubella, and hepatitis B has expressed a similar deep pessimism (Schoofs 1996). In 2003, the long awaited results from the extensive trials of vaccine, Aidvax, were announced, and while it showed some promise in slowing infection rates among blacks and Hispanics, it was generally judged a failure. Leading AIDS researchers were hardly surprised given the evolving numerous strains of HIV (Pollack with Altman 2003). Whether these gloomy assessments are correct remains to be seen, though repeated expensive failures add credence to their warning. If accurate, however, the quest's stress on the scientific route—however politically and organizationally convenient—will have proven to be a terrible bet. This infatuation may even lure those yet uninfected into a false hope of future salvation when they personally test HIV-positive.

Truth be told, many of the "miracle cures" have proven imperfect (and often very expensive) despite the initial hope. For example, various protease inhibitors initially came on to the market in the late 1990s and were hailed as revolutionary breakthroughs. While they do help, they are not a cure, and require a difficult regimen (including dietary restrictions) and produce nausea, diarrhea, and vomiting over the entire course of treatment. Others, such as non-nucleosides, can be defeated by HIV mutations and have troublesome side affects like allergic reactions. All in all, medical progress is just inching alone despite the billions spent (Horn 2002).

The belief that Mighty Big-Government Science could discover a cure *if only astutely pressured* may have also proven harmful by narrowing the range of possible solutions. A political version of the gambler's fallacy apparently infused the movement—if one noisy demonstration fails to bring progress, demonstrate louder and yet again until the laboratories win the battle. Militants—like primitive people sacrificing goats to guarantee the harvest—thus relentlessly harassed NIH officials and other scientific establishment figures as if progress only depended on commitment.[7] Perhaps investing in irrigation might prove more profitable than rounding up more goats.

Recall chapter 8's account of FDA fast-tracking as an example of activist success. There is, however, another side to this tale, one particularly evident in the premature release of AZT, a once-heralded "miracle" cure (Epstein 1996: 202-4 depicts this perilous rush-to-save). This was part of a larger "Drugs into Bodies" campaign extremely popular among zealots. Here so-called treatment activists coerced government to cease extended, though necessary, clinical trials to rescue the dying. AZT's value eventually proved to be grossly exaggerated and perhaps largely ineffective (and highly unpleasant for those taking it). The widespread use of AZT among those at risk also complicated investigations into other potential cures. Soon the very idea of placebo-controlled trials when an AIDS drug was tested came under attack. The gay press now talked of "death by placebo" (Epstein 1996: 214). This militancy, compounded by a distrust of "established medicine," fostered a treatment underground ("guerrilla clinics") in which experimental drugs were illegally distributed or imported from overseas, behaviors further undermining solid science. The unfortunate upshot of this let's-up-the-political-heat mentality until the victory is achieved was that rather than say, "politics has proven quite ineffective, perhaps we should look elsewhere," the objective became intensifying political pressure. Plausibly, greater patience and less bullying would have yielded improved outcomes. This manic, throw-everything-at-the-disease approach despite strings of failures was, however, a bonanza for drug companies who quietly encouraged activists seeking miracles.

This oft-naive embrace of a science-provided "magic bullet" also encouraged some wasteful wild goose chases that should have been quickly abandoned but nevertheless survived thanks to misguided, intense political pressure. Quackery per se is irrelevant; bogus (and expensive) cures are inevitable when frantic people seek miracles. What draws our attention is mobilizing political pressure to push quackery at public expense when the remedy's worthlessness is indisputable. This is not pursuing long shots via political pressure; this is advancing alleged cures that have *zero* chance of success. Here politics becomes a force for evil by needlessly allocating scarce resources away from fruitful endeavors while cruelly deceiving sufferers. At best, activism offers some mental health therapy.

A particularly grievous, but far from unique, example of wrongheaded politics concerns the drug Kemron. This alleged miracle palliative burst on the AIDS scene in 1990 when a Kenyan doctor claimed that it cured nearly all the symptoms of AIDS within four weeks. Kemron had been around before—it was merely an oral preparation of alpha-interferon, a naturally occurring protein previously used (unsuccessfully) to treat cancer. The dosage used in these "miracles" was, moreover, far below normal prescription levels, even less than levels normally found in one liter of blood. At best, extremely high doses might slow the growth of Kaposi's sarcoma, but multiple careful laboratory studies had already dismissed it as an AIDS therapy, or even as a way to kill HIV. Experiments conducted in African similarly rejected Kemron. Scientifically speaking, it was absolutely, positively worthless. The substance is also virtually destroyed by the digestive tract when taken orally.

Damming evidence aside, its popularity soared among those craving any prospect, no matter how faint. What transformed Kemron from yet another discarded snake oil cure into something deserving prompt government attention was its fictitious association with Africa. Kemron, in truth, lacked any connection to Africa—the oral version was U.S.-developed, perfected in Australia, and manufactured in Japan. Only the preposterous medical claim was Africa based. Nevertheless, this erroneous African link led Kemron to be widely embraced by black activists, abetted by black newspapers, as the African-invented cure for AIDS. When the (white) medical establishment dismissed it, the hot-button charge of racism erupted. According to this theory, whites refused to acknowledge black scientific acumen and, even worse activists hinted, its banishment (perhaps purposely!) condemned thousands of blacks to death. Faced with this politically sensitive accusation, repeated trials were conducted, all with identical outcomes: it just didn't work as advertised. Prestigious scientific investigatory committees were equally pessimistic. Nevertheless, black-run clinics plus the Nation of Islam still continued to sell the drug (often at inflated prices) as "the black-invented cure."

At the prodding of the National Medical Association, the national black doctors group, amid charges of racism and genocide, unfettered by reference to scientific evidence, the federal government soon launched full-blown clinical trials. The justification of this commitment was that the black community "was interested" in this remedy, rather than positive scientific evidence warranting further investigation. The trials, unlike other AIDS trials, were to concentrate on "psychological factors" such as perceived life satisfaction, as progress markers, variables notoriously hard to measure accurately versus tangible evidence like T-cell counts. Predictably, political pressure failed to make Kemron work. Burkett (1995: 178) cites one expert who priced this wastefulness at "several million dollars" but the larger price tags undoubtedly were the opportunity costs plus the immeasurable lives lost resulting from this embrace of an "African cure."

A similar substitution of objectives surrounds how "assistance" came to be defined. Faced with a mounting death toll and scientific frustration, it is tempting to focus on bureaucracy building as the key success measure. This displacement is a familiar organizational pathology: constructing imposing offices becomes proof of a more difficult to uncover financial accomplishment. Medicine is similarly vulnerable to substituting outward signs for the more difficult to discern advances. Compared to saving lives, creating new programs, expanding staff, printing up handsome brochures and otherwise showing visible "progress" is a snap, and it is all too human to equate one with the other.

This "progress" may well be delusional and counterproductive. Opportunity costs abound. The same energy aimed at, say, patrolling bathhouses to stop dangerous sex now becomes re-directed to wrangling over funding formulas or fighting off rival agency claimants. Similarly, money that could be spent by police interdicting drugs went to coalition building aimed at extracting even more administrative overhead. The means become the end. Worse, a dreary status quo becomes worth protecting and so livelihoods ultimately *depend* on the problems continuing. All in all, it is understandable why harried public officials turned a blind eye to fiscal malfeasance when militants only insisted, "spend more" without monitoring actual outcomes.

Organizational Alternatives to Big Government

The AIDS activist near obsession with government-supplied treatment initially seemed eminently sensible for two reasons. First, the federal government possessed the ample wherewithal (funds, technical expertise, legal authority) to battle AIDS. Indeed, it could wage this assault with only a tiny faction of its overall healthcare budget. Second, the potential economic return on political investment is enormous—leverage in financial parlance. A $100,000 spent to pressure public officials might eventually return tens of millions from the public treasury, so by any asset allocation formula, taking to the streets or cajoling legislators appears a superb multiplication of limited resources. That many gays were Democrats, and this party has generally favored a government interventionist problem-solving approach, undoubtedly cemented this embrace. Nevertheless, the allure of federal munificence did not dictate an exclusive government-centered strategy. Other options, singularly or in conjunction with Washington assistance, might have proven more effective.

Government bureaucracies have seldom had a monopoly on combating illnesses. Long before Washington assumed this responsibility, the public's health was guarded by countless private charities and religious organizations. These efforts frequently enjoyed remarkable success, even overcoming obstacles frustrating today's mighty federal government, despite its gigantic budgets and legal powers. During the last years of the nineteenth century, a small handful of reformers, assisted by a single wealthy philanthropist, accomplished near miracles on New York City's lower East Side. Myriad deadly illnesses resulting from poor hygiene and sanitation (including typhoid fever) plus such social pathologies as alcoholism and crime, were sharply reduced, all without the assistance of modern scientific medicine (Trachtenberg 2000). William J. Stern (2000) describes how a single individual—John Hughes, a former derelict—assisted by a few Catholic priests helped thousands of alcoholic Irish New Yorkers to abandon drink, all on a miniscule budget. Similar upbeat tales, often entailing little more than hectoring from the pre-social welfare state abound (see, for example, Olasky 1992).

Even with multi-billion-dollar budgets, the federal government's Big Science is not the exclusive health care provider. The potential mix of participants and their roles is considerable, and no single combination is preordained. Dreaded polio was largely banished during the 1950s thanks to the March of Dimes. Hundreds of disease-related charities currently exist and play a vital medical role. Consider the contemporary activities of the American Cancer Society as what *might* be accomplished outside direct government involvement. In 2001 the Society invested over $130 million in cancer research, and since its inception this figure is $2.4 billion. Research awards are given via rigorous screening, a fact attested to by the thirty-two Nobel Prize winners benefiting from Society funding. This endeavor covers basic research, prevention studies, training funds, studies of risk factors, and almost anything else relating to cancer. Education is a major focus. Besides the national organization, there are some 3,400 local units and participation from both those affected and experts is welcomed. There is also political advocacy, namely a vociferous anti-smoking campaign and lobbying government for more cancer-related funding plus access rights. In 2002 the Society raised $770 million from the public (these data come from the Society's homepage, www.cancer.org). It certainly is a model for combating AIDS.

Unsurprisingly in light of Washington's ineffectual assault, private organizations are now stepping up their anti-AIDS efforts. On December 1, 2002 ("World AIDS Day") the popular youth-oriented MTV offered two worldwide AIDS awareness concerts instructing viewers how to avoid infection, the right of women to refuse sexual advances and other useful advice. The jeans maker, Levi Strauss and Company, is one major sponsor. Private organizations such as the Kaiser Family Foundation, the Paul G. Allen Charitable Foundation, have now joined the anti-AIDS bandwagon. Foremost in this "privatization" is the Bill and Melinda Gates Foundation that, among other medical projects, has so far donated $450 million, including $100 million to fight AIDS in India and $126 million to develop an anti-AIDS vaccine. Less visible private foundations such as Doctors Without Borders and the Glaser Foundation have likewise enlisted, often favoring small but vital measures, for example, dispensing free condoms in poor nations (forty-seven of these organizations in this campaign can be found at www.interaction.org). The overall assistance menu is remarkable: using proven drugs to avoid mother-child HIV infection, providing alternative means of support to prostitutes (diary cows) who frequently spread the disease, or digging wells to supply clean water that helps immunity systems, among untold other initiatives (McNeil 2002).

Pharmaceutical companies are also multi-billion-dollar players in providing cures, and these initiatives are often free of Washington involvement. In November 2002, for example, scientists reported a possible vaccine against the virus causing cervical cancer, a disease killing 4,100 women in the U.S. each year (with some 13,000 being infected). Hopefully, this drug will prevent infection though it will not kill the virus once transmitted. Relevant for our analysis, Merck & Company funded the research and it was carried out at sixteen universities (Grady 2002). Of the sixty-four AIDS and AIDS-related drugs on the market as of early 2003, fifty-seven were the product of private pharmaceutical firms, and many small technologically oriented firms are in the forefront of innovative solutions (Glassman 2003).

The advantages provided by a non-governmental approach are substantial over and above confronting a slow-moving, compromise-based political system. Critically, the private sector is unconstrained by demands that elected officials must heed or risk outrage. Explosive moral issues such as free condoms for adolescents or instructing gays about safe sodomy are irrelevant to many foundation trustees. The local police may be powerless to harass bathhouses encouraging dangerous sex, but vigilantes can. This freedom of action is indispensable when confronting behaviors that might be legally off-limits to public officials. Indifference to political calculations also permits a focus impossible when expenditures must navigate multiple legislative and bureaucratic gauntlets. Recall how public officials often pushed scientific expertise aside to generate stopgap public relations accomplishments. Who needs the endless inter-agency rivalries and inevitable squabbles when dividing up funds? In such circumstances political necessity can easily trump solid science and wise service delivery.

Our point is not that a government-centered strategy proved to be a lethal mistake. We cannot say if a more private orientation would yield superior progress. That conclusion requires the construction of a parallel alternative universe. Perhaps the government-oriented strategy was comparatively the most effective. Nor can we conclude that the millions eventually spent on organizing rallies or "die ins" would have made a difference in the lives of the afflicted.[8] And it also must be acknowledged that some gay organizations have moved beyond government dependence, for example, the Gay Men's Health Crisis (GMHC). This tax-exempt— 501(c)(3)—charitable organization does occasionally engage in lobbying but it is largely a self-help, gay-run service organization. In fiscal year 2001, for example, it took in $22.6 million, about three-quarters of which came from non-government sources. The GMHC, like many traditional charities, offers a plethora of critical health-related services: distributing updated information to patients and medical practitioners, training volunteer to assist the AIDS afflicted (including meals), counseling, and countless educational programs. All told, these direct-to-sufferer outlays cost some $17.1 million in 2001, and this excludes the incalculable number of donated hours and services (www.gmhc.org). Still, when all is said and done, the rush to extract salvation via government largess has been the enduring theme of the anti-AIDS campaign, and judged by the paucity of genuine progress, this embrace can be challenged.

Assembling the Audit Materials

On balance, how is the anti-AIDS political campaign to be judged? Does it confirm the gospel of political participation as the great savior? Defenders of civic engagement would surely answer "yes," and argue that the data regarding AIDS mortality, government spending, and explosive AIDS-related activism clearly indicates civic engagement's role in this progress. One might further claim that without this intervention, the United States would be mired in an even greater catastrophe. Ambivalence remains, however, and much depends on what evidence is collected for the final verdict. This is comparable to a trial—guilt or innocence can rest on how witnesses testify or the relevance of physical evidence. Contrary assessments regarding mobilization utility are equally plausible without ever delving into complicated moral issues.

Exhibit A in refuting this civic-pressure-brings-success supposition is that, despite huge outlays, AIDS has *not* been cured medically, only slowed, so gays carry on a few years longer versus succumbing to old age. Calibrated by the all-important HIV infection rate, which in 2002 stood at about 35,000 for that year, matters may still be terrible given AIDS deadliness (HIV/AIDS Surveillance Report 2002). According to congressional testimony offered by Anthony Fauci, Director of NIH, between 650,000 and 900,000 people are currently living with HIV, and are therefore at risk of contracting AIDS (Fauci 1999: testimony). Endless announcements of magic bullet "miracle cures" have, as we noted, proven premature. We may even be losing ground as HIV mutates and increasingly grows resistant to attempts to kill it, a deadly evolutionary pattern found in other illnesses such as hepatitis C and antibiotic-resistant gonorrhea that may facilitate AIDS and still persists among many gays. In 2003 the CDC even reported that in at least twenty-five states the incidence of HIV has turned slightly upward after a long decline, particularly among homosexual men (Zimmerman 2003). A decline in infection rates may also be deceptive since a relatively smaller pool of infection-free gays remains to be infected. Current government munificence or organizational vitality, regardless of measurability, are thus the *in*appropriate success indicators; lives saved *ought* to be the standard, pure and simple, and to substitute the former for the latter produces a falsely optimistic picture regarding activism.

Exhibit A continues further. The "everybody-at-risk" panic infusing the late 1980s may have receded but the war is far from over, and the enemy remains resilient. Study after study confirms that since the mid-1990s the anything goes gay sex crowd has reemerged, and as the soaring rates of STDs confirm, promiscuity continues to be part of the contemporary gay identity (Rotello 1997a: Ch. 5). The well-known gay actor, Harvey Fierstein, has commented that many young gay men now see AIDS as a "gay birthright" and infection as a "coming of age" into the gay culture (Fierstein 2003). Indeed, long after the deadly epidemic's source was well understood, one gay activist blithely intoned, "Gay liberation means sexual freedom. And sexual freedom means more sex, better sex, sex in bushes, in the toilets, in the baths, sex without love, sex without harassment, sex at home and sex in the streets" (Bronski 1994).

The economic incentives continue to facilitate this inclination. In 1997 one major gay newspaper—*Home Xtra*—contained thirty-six advertisements for these emporiums together with countless ads for "models and escorts" that were evidently sexual solicitations. And this paper is only one of many tabloids reaching gays (Rotello 1997a). Nor have young gays toned down their appetites in pursing these perilous pleasures (CDC, http://www.cdc.gov/hiv/pubs/facts/msm.htm). Michelangelo Signorile (1997) writing in the gay magazine *Out* depicts fresh calamities in the making: a website (XtremeSex) romanticizing HIV transmission, web-based chat rooms facilitating dangerous sex, an unwarranted optimism in medical miracles, the popularity of sex-enhancing methamphetamine and "Esctasy" plus an alarming indifference among young homosexuals to even dying of AIDS. The CDC has explicitly singled out on-line chat rooms as burgeoning sources of AIDS infection among gay men seeking high-risk gay sex (Zimmerman 2003). Meanwhile, many of the old-guard activists are dead or have quietly retired into private pursuits.

It is hardly surprising, then, that in 2000, the CDC reported 13,562 new homosexual-related AIDS cases, infections acquired long after the transmission process was identified and publicized. The abiding ideological obstacles to impeding this contagion were ironically illustrated in a 2002 *New York Times* story telling how AIDS educators were now—almost two decades after AIDS transmission was recognized—imploring disease carriers to take personal responsibility for their potentially deadly behavior. Despite the sensibleness of this well-intentioned campaign, holdouts remain since, in their view, admitting personal responsibility scapegoats those infected (Tuller 2002). This escape from accountability theme is hardly new—when New York City in 1993 attempted to launch an anti-AIDS campaign stressing personal responsibility, political pressure from within the city's health bureaucracy killed it on the grounds that "it blamed the victim" (Rotello 1997a: 155).

This get-more-money-from-government strategy was hardly inevitable when the epidemic initially emerged, and in retrospect, it may have been a poor investment. More lives might have been saved by directing energies elsewhere and these were certainly viable. The private charity route has already been mentioned, but also consider the purely private solutions options potentially vulnerable gay men had by the mid-1980s. Even if orgiastic, anonymous sex was deemed vital to one's libido or gay identity, minimum personal prudence (e.g., shunning unprotected passive anal sex) would dramatically reduce risks. Going further, sexual escapades could exclude those practicing unsafe sex who might therefore be HIV carriers—for example, only patronize clubs strictly enforcing safe sex rules or screening out those who were HIV positive. This can also be accomplished via the net since several web-based dating services for HIV-positive people have sprung up, for example, www.HIVdate.com and www.positivepersonals.com. The promiscuous lifestyle could be abandoned altogether or, if variety still beckoned, postpone dangerous sex until after thorough medical testing of partners. Sexual appetites might also be satisfied via telephone sex, watching X-rated videos or masturbation, all behaviors absolutely AIDS-free.[9]

Politics could have been re-directed away from Washington rescues and focused on the gay community itself. Businesses permitting hazardous encounters could have been closed, if gays so desired. This is comparable to past successful campaigns to close down prostitution and, as the hard statistical evidence presented earlier demonstrated, this draconian anti-public sex measure *does* work. Where formal legal action was lacking, declining patronage would suffice. Gay organizations could publicize carriers, both as a deterrent to getting AIDS initially and to alert potential victims. Though draconian, this "Typhoid Mary" tactic is analogous to "outing" prominent gays refusing to admit openly their homosexuality, an equally privacy-invading tactic defensible as advancing gay legitimacy. Public identification scarcely imposes celibacy—the HIV positive can surely restrict contacts to similarly infected partners or practice safe sex. Meanwhile, those who financially benefited from these illness-causing behaviors, all the while pretending to be pro-gay, could be similarly exposed and harassed, a tactic akin to ACT-UP disrupting scientific conferences to, ostensibly, advance gay agendas. At a minimum, leaders could have cooperated fully with public health departments. And, if pandering politicians side-stepped AIDS dangers, fund their opponents.

The crisis could also have been exclusively defined as a crime-related epidemic and fought through a mixing of policing and aggressive (and quite traditional) public health measures. No inherent need existed to let gays themselves impose innocuous "education and safe sex" solutions, and even if this was the initial response, it could have been abandoned when it failed. Certainly many AIDS-producing behaviors are still illegal given their public (though not intrinsic) nature, or could easily been made illegal. A 1988 presidential commission dealing with AIDS did, in fact, recommend that criminal statutes for knowingly transmitting venereal diseases to be extended to AIDS, and by 1998 some twenty states had agreed. These laws brought several well-publicized prosecutions, typically for biting, blood splattering, or sexual intercourse with an unsuspecting partner, but private voluntary sexual encounters escaped law enforcement scrutiny (Bayer 1991). This criminalization is largely symbolic. Imagine the outrage if police routinely raided bathhouses, forcibly tested everyone, charged dozens of pleasure seekers with felonies, and jailed the guilty. Clearly, this solution would have required a far deeper commitment than fretful public officials were willing to make, but the bottom line remains that a far more forceful approach was legally possible.

Let us not forget that standard public health measures have repeatedly proven their effectiveness against killers such as tuberculosis, smallpox, and countless sexually transmitted diseases long before the advent of powerful modern science. Though measures such as quarantine would have been politically unpopular, they would likely have proven effective. Surely it is bizarre to insist that illnesses affecting gays and drug users are fundamentally different from equally deadly diseases contracted by heterosexuals shunning drugs.

The government's reaction to the worldwide outbreak of Severe Acute Respo Syndrome (SARS) in 2003 offers a useful contrast to how AIDS has been handled. Here the possibility of quarantine was immediately raised though experts expressed reservations about practical implementation. Nobody openly fretted that some "inalienable right" had been compromised when officials warned against travel to China or Toronto, Canada. In April of 2003 President George W. Bush, virtually without public notice, added SARS to the list of diseases under the Federal Quarantine Act that would justify prohibiting access to the U.S. or even stopping those infected from crossing state boarders (even force was authorized in handling suspected SARS carriers at international airports). In both New York City and San Francisco, AIDS hotspots, public officials without any controversy organized voluntary quarantines of likely sufferers, and when a few people refused to cooperate, compulsory measures were imposed (McNeil 2003; Chase 2003). Interestingly given the traits of those likely to be infected, nobody has yet denounced how Asians have been "unfairly" stigmatized.

And while it may be highly unfashionable to speak of rolling back the rampant sexuality defining today's gay lifestyle, monogamous relationships, if not abstinence, are virtually guaranteed to succeed where purported medical miracles fail. This is not a pie-in-the-sky nostrum or one that violates human nature given that sexual restraint has long been commonplace. Recent reports from Uganda, a desperately poor nation unable to afford condoms, let alone expensive educational programs, demonstrates that this solution is quite feasible. Here, faced with mounting mortality in neighboring nations, the government launched a major campaign to rein in sexual appetites or limit contacts to a single partner. Youngsters were encouraged to postpone sex until marriage. By 1995, both sexual activity and HIV had dropped sharply in a part of the world where it seems to be raging out of control (Green 2003).

More broadly, incorporating alternative funding allocations into this equation can also dispute the success verdict. Everything rests on whose evaluative criteria are employed, and normatively ranking these criteria is problematic. Though prodigious government funding did, unquestionably, save or prolong *some* lives, intervention elsewhere could rescue even *more* lives. Intensive targeting of gay males detracts from outreaches to other infected populations, notably the politically powerless (but quite large) intravenous drug users. Recall how the anti-AIDS crusade weakened efforts against other STDs. Calculations are purely utilitarian: the greatest good for the greatest number. Even among those between twenty-five and forty-four years old, deaths from heart disease and cancer remain substantial (see figure 7.1 above), and at least a portion of these illnesses—unlike AIDS—*are* curable. Those who died from non-AIDS illnesses might *reasonably* conclude that the gay campaign was, in its totality, a failure, a monument to narrow selfishness, a violation of government's obligation to a common interest. Going one step further, the appropriate debate may not be competition among diseases but the entire betterment menu. Given annual highway carnage, directing this AIDS money to promote child automobile seats or upgrading driver training would have generated a superior investment return. These substitutes are especially attractive since the billion-dollar AIDS initiative has largely failed while these humdrum alternatives indisputably save lives.

An immensely complicated factor in assessing ultimate pay-off concerns personally weighing benefits. A skilled defense attorney representing a sexually ravenous gay activist might make the following argument. Most fundamentally, who can conclusively say what ought to be the ultimate aim in politics? Recall how African Americans might balance a racially gerrymandered district bringing likely electoral victory versus giving the GOP a House majority. Unambiguous, morally superior options are absent in such circumstances. A comparable situation exists for gays inclined toward risky sex with multiple unscreened partners—upping federal spending while thousands ignore the message and die *might be* a success, regardless of carnage.

A gay male in the late 1980s (when AIDS transmission was recognized) might make the following *reasonable* calculation. First, steady bathhouse sex guarantees terrific pleasure. Second, an AIDS infection may occur, but then again, maybe not. The odds of contagion may be zero if there is a genetic immunity, one in a hundred, or 50-50, but who knows? Moreover, untold highly respectable scientists deny the HIV-AIDS sex link, and thousands of HIV-infected people fail to develop AIDS, so why worry (see Epstein 1996: chs. 2-4 regarding this contrary evidence and its energetic dissemination in the gay media). Third, deceptively claiming that everyone is equally at risk is preferable to stigmatizing just gays, regardless of opportunity costs. Fourth, if AIDS is contracted, a cure might be found by then, thanks to political pressure. AIDS might be comparable to such transitory "epidemics" as toxic shock syndrome or Legionnaire's Disease, both of which were quickly unraveled. Finally, even if a cure remains elusive, and death comes in five to seven years, this pleasure-seeking would, on balance, have been worth it vis-à-vis a dull sexual lifestyle. In fact, this redefinition of "survival" to a pleasurable life, not longevity, does have its gay adherents (see Odets 1995: 262-3).

From this hedonistic angle, what was previously deemed unwise political decision-making, that is, forbidding enforced safe sex procedures, now becomes eminently rational. Subjective personal utility dictates everything, and additionally, this calculation illuminates the close tie between unbridled sexuality and political activism. Dangerous hedonism and haranguing government are now inexorably linked—the more hazardous the sex, the greater the necessity for finding a government-supplied medical marvel. After a dozen sex club escapades, the dynamic is irreversible: with infection almost certain, coercing Washington (versus closing the barn door after the cows have escaped) is a life-or-death necessity. Finally, and entirely from an egoistic perspective, since multiple infections have zero downside (a single one is deadly), no personal incentive exists to abandon bathhouse sex save killing others, an option rationalized away by insisting that the uninfected surely grasp the horrendous heath risks, and thus bring misfortune upon themselves. Multiply this politically "rational" individual a thousand fold, and a perfectly reasonable (though increasingly deadly) political movement is practically inevitable.

A Final Reckoning

Having laid various pluses and minuses on the table, what can be said about specific winners and losers? Obviously, impacts varied widely: some people and interests gained immensely while others were horrendous losers. Material benefits such as higher incomes or jobs are the most conspicuous on the ledger's plus side. When Washington spends billions, tens of thousands become enriched. One account even applied "AIDS," Inc. to describe these fortunate recipients (Burkett 1995: ch. 5). This federally subsidized assistance infrastructure is substantial: hospitals, clinics, counseling agencies, university laboratories, medical specialists, research institutes and countless other services that, sadly, now have clients by the thousands. Add countless elected officials and bureaucrats at all levels (public and private) owing their careers to the AIDS outbreak. Senior AIDS administrators can now out-earn top elected officials in their jurisdiction (Turner 2001). In a few documented instances this prosperity has been acquired illegally by skimming funds intended for the sick. This is endemic to all government programs, not just AIDS. Corruption has occurred in Puerto Rico, South Dallas, Texas, Orlando, Florida, North Carolina, Los Angeles, Indiana, and elsewhere. Lavish resort outings to share information—perfectly legal—are also paid from AIDS programs (see Turner 2001 for such an account). That spending continues upward as the death rate declines may attest to these material rewards having evolved into an appropriations process sacred cow.

Political pressure has also brought riches in a more tragic way. Had draconian public health measures stopped the initial AIDS outbreak, entire industries would have forgone enormous future profits. Put bluntly, when gay militants protected their cherished bathhouses and silenced prudent public health advice, they unwittingly generated forthcoming revenues for pharmaceutical companies, condom manufacturers, hospital supply firms, and all the other commercial enterprises feeding off this illness. Perhaps even more disquieting, sex emporium entrepreneurs conscripted this activism to protect their lucrative enterprises, a tempting task since these businesspeople were often influential gay community and civic leaders. There is big money in facilitating death, as heroin dealers and gun manufacturers will attest.

And let us not forget those promiscuous gays whose sexual pleasures continued uninterrupted thanks to relentless political pressure. Those gays biologically impervious to AIDS plus those just plain lucky were the colossal winners here. This self-gratifying, libidinous dividend was virtually cost-free. Even among those whose hedonism ultimately doomed them, the hundreds of erotic encounters may added up to a net gain.

Most critically on the ledger's positive side were the untold lives saved by educational campaigns and other anti-disease measures shaped by political pressure. Add those were saved when cities did, at least momentarily, greatly restrict public sex. These numbers are unknown, and may be incalculable given HIV's long dormancy, but these fortunate souls must undoubtedly exceed tens of thousands. These gays heeded the posters, visited safe sex workshops, and otherwise took the dire warnings to heart. They can honestly say, "If not for politics, I would be dead." Further, add to the balance sheet the infected whose lives have been extended by AZT, ddI, 3TC, protease inhibitors and other medications that otherwise might not exist or be available, save relentless activist pressuring and government-sponsored science. Individuals here might declare, "I may prematurely die in five years, but I'm okay today, so bless the movement." Of all the rewards of political activism, these outshine all others.

Moving beyond material benefits into the intangible realm, we find multitudes whose activism fulfilled myriad psychological needs. Their enlistment was independent of tangible outcome though, at least hopefully, a cure would have brought even greater joy. These range from celebrities ever anxious to "do good" by wearing ribbons or attending benefits, to bystanders amused by ACT-UP's rambunctious street theater. Some movement participants such as the gay Lavender Hill Mob, a compulsive meeting disruptor targeting even fellow gay groups, conceivably found engagement exhilarating, regardless of accomplishment. For others politics was a useful, even therapeutic, vehicle to channel pent-up rage or lessen tragic grief against opportune targets. Endless far-flung agendas were fulfilled here beyond merely saving those succumbing to AIDS. Even Marxists lacking any principled reason to champion gay rights joined the AIDS bandwagon for their own capitalist-bashing purposes. Ditto for those wanting to loosen restrictive drug laws or champions of government-paid national health care. Frankly acknowledging this non-instrumental or cooptive aim hardly impugns motives or otherwise damns activists gratifying idiosyncratic private needs. We only recognize that even the noblest cause draws varied adherents. Self-esteem building charity work can certainly assist the recipient, regardless of impure motive.

The ledger's negative side is equally substantial, if not more so. First and foremost are all the deceased who might otherwise be alive, save for misguided militancy. This paradoxical saga has been recounted many times. Candid critics like Larry Kramer and Randy Shilts would certainly agree: *at least some activists have blood on*

their hands. This carnage is minimally a quarter of a million, perhaps higher if we include women, drug users and all other victims
who took their counsel from activists promising a politically manufactured solution when such a way out was iffy, at best. Nor is this
epidemic finished—deaths will undeniably rise as infections contracted years back eventually appear as full-blown AIDS. To be sure,
early deaths were misdiagnosed and unpreventable, so this horrific
figure of unnecessary killing might be reduced. Still, by the early
1990s the science was unambiguous, and so every death resulting
from an encounter in places deserving closure, or undertaken thanks
to misleading militant-issued propaganda portraying unprotected sex
as an unalienable civil right must be chalked up to the deadly siren
song of activism.

Confrontational fund-raising rhetoric aside, these fatalities were
not due to President Reagan's silence, the obstructionist Jesse Helms,
public homophobia, drug company greed, scientific ineptitude, or
any other standard movement-provided excuse. This blame-some-
body-else litany may make for excellent therapy and mitigate trauma,
but it only sidesteps a grim reality of personal irresponsibility. Nobody coerced gullible men into unprotected risky sex, drugs, or other
behaviors destroying their immunity systems. Conversely, somebody
prevented public health officials from taking prudent action that fell
within their legal prerogatives. There were innocent victims, especially
those who unknowingly contracted AIDS from blood transfusions,
but this number is relatively small and grew even smaller with time.

Furthermore, in retrospect it is clear that an early Manhattan
Project-like anti-AIDS crusade would have failed, and drug firms
and scientists would surely have welcomed a cure. Guaranteed Nobel
Prizes and huge profits awaited these saviors. Enduring efforts to
extract government bounteousness to better serve the ill or promote
research does not eliminate the debits. Great medical care cannot
substitute for longevity and the NIH cannot be held accountable for
instant medical miracles. Brilliantly executed demonstrations do not
kill viruses, and many of these gatherings may have even worsened
matters by providing fresh sexual opportunities. To inform those
about to enter a bathhouse in 1990, "don't worry, we'll force government to find a cure, so go ahead and indulge" might now be
judged a criminal act.

These needless quarter-of-a-million deaths hardly end the grim accounting. Permanently extracting thousands of young, often gifted people out of the economy plus debilitating an even larger number adds to the liability. Again it is nearly impossible to calibrate this price tag, but it must be immense, especially in those industries distinguished by a strong gay presence. The publicly reported deaths of famous fashion designers, actors, and untold other creative people represent only the tiny tip of a vast iceberg of destroyed talent. Further add the time and energy spent caring for the ill, let alone the grief of loved ones. Here losers must exceed millions, and this loss is beyond compensation; replacing people is not comparable to replacing stolen furniture.

Finally, there are horrendous opportunity costs. The hundreds of billions of taxpayer money spent on AIDS plus the millions of hours devoted to prevention were not pre-determined government outlays akin to education or maintaining highways. Make no mistake—once the epidemic erupted officials were obligated to wage war. But, and this is critical, the AIDS catastrophe was preventable, or could have been minimized at the onset. These expensive anti-AIDS efforts, then, could have been redirected elsewhere, and perhaps with improved results. Just how many people dying of cancer, heart ailments, accidents, and dozens of other treatable conditions would now be alive is impossible to estimate, but it may well exceed the human benefits of the AIDS campaign. Lacking these figures, our conclusion can only be approximate but it is undeniable: AIDS activists did win some mighty victories, but to celebrate their accomplishments as proof that political participation "works" is a gross, and potentially disingenuous, misstatement. Tomorrow's cure will not resurrect the dead.

Notes

1. Tracking also assumed that the infected could name sex partners, an untenable assumption since many gay relationships were anonymous. Hundreds of unidentified yearly contacts made the situation especially futile. This unsavory element of gay life is seldom publicized but is important in understanding the epidemic.
2. This misleading democratization argument was also buttressed with misleading statistics, for example, including lesbians among homosexuals to reduce the incidence of AIDS among gays or (falsely) claiming that up to one-third of heterosexual men have had a homosexual experience and are thus potential AIDS carriers. Another scare tactic is exaggerating estimates of future deaths, sometimes running into the millions (Fumento 1990: ch. 14).
3. The argument that wealthier consumers might subsidize those in poorer nations makes sense abstractly but is ultimately specious. Recent border interdictions in

Europe confirm what skeptics had anticipated—cheap anti-AIDS drugs are diverted from African nations to Europe where they enter the black market at much higher mark-ups though still at levels below prices in legitimate channels.

4.   The New York State Sanitary Code, Section 24-2.2 (as amended in 1993) states: No establishment shall make facilities available for the purpose of sexual activities where anal intercourse, vaginal intercourse, or fellatio take place. Such facilities shall constitute a threat to the public health.

5.   That these community-based organizations often functioned successfully prior to federal funding suggests that the prospect of these newfound funds might have detracted energy away from core purposes. This acrimony is in addition to the requisite bureaucratic burdens, everything from strict accounting rules to monitoring non-discrimination in employment. In fact, turning volunteers into paid employees invites employment discrimination lawsuits. Conceivably, these organizations might have been more efficient had they raised funds privately.

6.   Rotello (1997a: ch. 6) outlines some recent safe-sex education strategies, and all suggest a losing battle. In some instances professionals sought minimal compulsion and stressed reducing homophobia as the solution; elsewhere gays themselves have invented "folk remedies" better understood as pseudo-education. Most important, a sizable element of those at risk simply rejected safe sex as unacceptable.

7.   The gay activist stance toward science was often ambivalent. Scientific research was supposed to be all-powerful, but when careful investigation produced unwelcome results, it was roundly castigated as craven politics. A fair number of the AIDSinfected also distrusted science and relied on alternative folk remedies. Misgivings were particularly evident in estimates of the HIV infected—militants typically accept quite high figures as truthful, perhaps eager that these terrifying statistics would energize officials.

8.   These publicity-gaining enterprises are seldom cheap. When activists disrupted an international conference in 1990, this cost $83,000 for such things as photocopying, phone lines, and all else that could not be absorbed by volunteer labor (Burkett 1995: 318).

9.   In fact, gay sex clubs featuring group-based masturbation did eventually spring up and did become popular among many gays. Though this practice is entirely safe, it is impossible to say whether this alternative successfully stopped HIV transmission since nobody can be sure of what actually transpired in these settings or whether participants exclusively practiced self-stimulation. More on this type of sexual outlet can be found in Thomas (1996).

10

Conclusions: Advice and Puzzles

We began by observing that civic engagement is often preached as the grand problem solver, and endless admonitions "to get involved" are offered with scant proof of effectiveness. Far worse, accounts stress successes as if disasters were inconceivable. With much of this advice emanating from the academy and lectured to the naïve, it is no accident that activism has evolved into a creed effortlessly applied to almost every imaginable problem. Chapter 2 argued that today's scholarship pushes consequentiality away from empirical scrutiny—recall the tale of the drunk and the lost keys. Research recipes ignore such central issues as impending obstacles, available resources, and institutional barriers, among multiple factors warranting serious attention. This overview concluded that a far superior analytical pathway would be to commence with objectives (however defined). We repeatedly drew a parallel with evaluating businesses—the primary question concerns achieving profitability, not just engaging in business.

Chapter 6, drawing heavily from the literature on African-American politics, explored various conceptual issues embedded in assessing impact. We showed that political activism has had incalculable benefits for African Americans, everything from eliminating odious Jim Crow segregation to upgrading municipal services and securing better treatment from the police. Massive voter mobilizations have produced stunning political victories at all levels, including electing black mayors in virtually every major U.S. city. Tens of thousands of black municipal employees undoubtedly can thank politics for their personal betterment. African Americans are now political "players" of the first rank, white candidates of both parties routinely seek their support, and it is unthinkable that this progress will be reversed.

Yet, when shortfalls are added to the ledger's positive side, the picture is less bright. African Americans still have yet to achieve proportionality in elected office and past accomplishments in securing anti-discrimination and voting rights protection may have peaked. More important, early progress has slowed considerably and major goals, particularly closing socio-economic gaps, continue to be elusive despite massive political pressure. Even the affirmative action victories achieved years back are now being challenged, often successfully. That protest marches and voting campaigns can improve city services does not mean that these tactics can be effective in securing decent private sector jobs. Likewise, litigation proved invaluable in ending school segregation but it has proven less effective in boosting student academic performance. Some outcomes are quite mixed—gaining municipal jobs may assist many of those previously excluded but the price paid may be a general decline in services rendered. There is also a downside to this picture, for example, achieving greater African-American congressional representation at the expense of giving Republicans control of the House, an outcome often inimical to the civil rights agenda.

Remarkably absent from these typically triumphal accounts is how many of these efforts have been blocked or even reserved by below-the-radar private efforts. As chapter 4 showed, whites opposing forced integration are far more likely to just move or seek non-public schools than form anti-civil rights organizations. Outsourcing production overseas is often far easier than battling costly anti-discrimination lawsuits. These possibilities, moreover, only skim the surface. The upshot, then, is that any account of civil rights political progress is grossly incomplete if limited to the battle's public side. Worse, this one-sidedness further encourages the risky belief that political solutions are the superior pathway to progress and the disappointments come only from political insufficiency. To the extent that African Americans wish to better themselves, embracing this partial picture is a serious liability insofar as it exaggerates gains.

Chapters 7-9 pursued this results-oriented strategy concretely using the battle against HIV-AIDS. Chapter 7 showed that the war on AIDS is exceedingly well funded, regardless of the allocation criteria employed. Politics best explains this bounteousness—AIDS activists are just more dexterous at extracting government largess compared to rivals such as heart illness or diabetes. Chapter 8 carefully demonstrated how gays enjoyed substantial initial political resources and then artfully converted these advantages into compelling pressure. Within two decades the massive, publicly funded anti-AIDS campaign has become sacrosanct, even under the Republican, George W. Bush. But, budgetary munificence is only one possible success measure—plausibly, the primary criterion should be lives saved, not dollars spent. Chapter 9 grimly illustrated how pressure *im*mobilized life-saving efforts, and, credibly, thousands would be alive today had this politics failed. Still, this immobilization is precisely what some gays preferred though the lethal downside was well recognized. This ambiguous assessment is probably standard across other topics—political aims are typical multi-faceted, miscalculations are commonplace, and triumph in one setting can invite failures elsewhere. It is idealistic to insist that every political venture yields a net gain.

Compared to conventional treatments, this objective-centered strategy has been quite laborious, and the battle against AIDS is only one small outcropping in a civic landscape overflowing with even larger struggles. If our approach were made the model, general knowledge would probably proceed at a snail's pace as countless case studies would have to be assembled and broadly interpreted. We further admit that this lengthy investigation is cursory, and key details remain unexplored. Omitted were the efforts of disease rivals—we just depicted the skillfulness of AIDS activists without examining other budgetary claimants. A full picture must examine these rivalries—perhaps the triumph of AIDS activists relied less on movement adroitness than competitor ineptitude. Three chapters are obviously insufficient but, we suspect, fleshing out these vital details are unlikely to alter our main conclusions.

There is a different perspective, however, that justifies this more microscopic approach. Imagine auditing an enterprise that had flourished for two decades, was widely scattered geographically with countless "branches," and had consumed some $100 billion dollars in taxpayer money. The audit's purpose was, simply, "Did the huge investment deliver as intended?" These auditors would also probe if these resources might be allocated elsewhere and whether enterprise participants maximize their ample assets, among other germane queries. This task would probably employ armies of experts, require millions of dollars, and might last a year or more. This is, admittedly, a far cry from the standard political science perfunctory treatment of political activism, but it is a worthy model. Politics is not business but practices from one might usefully be applied to the other.

Lessons to the Would-Be Activist

If the war on AIDS is representative of political campaigns, what can we advise those about to plunge into the fray? Our most sage piece of advice is that not every quest will succumb to political pressure, no matter how brilliant the strategy or bountiful the committed resources. Goals differ profoundly in amenability to political solutions, and some absolutely admirable crusades are hopeless. It is a matter of calculating the odds, not applying abstract principles. The dissimilarity between extracting government largess versus saving lives via medical cures perfectly illustrated this distinction. The pursuit of the former—money—was relatively easy though still not a snap. By contrast, science cannot be commanded to crack Mother Nature's secrets, no matter how intense the hue and cry. This civic-centered strategy rested on optimism, an uncertain estimation of what can be realized overnight by the best and the brightest, if only generously financed. To be sure, when the malady was imperfectly understood a comparison between AIDS and, say, polio or smallpox might appear plausible. By the early 1990s, however, it was evident that a cure, let alone a vaccine, was frustratingly elusive. As in gambling, one must learn when to quit the game or try one's luck elsewhere.

A far-sighted, would-be activist might have thus asked, "Is politics still the most efficacious route?" The lure of countless millions in government assistance can be intoxicating and easily cloud judgment. Yet, that we live in a system of limited government often mired in gridlock should counsel against an over-reliance on government intervention. Chapter 4 explicated this point—almost every agenda item has a non-government option, and this certainly applied to the war on AIDS. The Gay Men's Health Crisis (GMHC) among other private charities certainly proved that non-government options existed and these may ultimately outshine Washington-provided remedies. The energy spent disrupting FDA meetings for yet one more (uncertain) government program might be used to counsel young men about the stark consequences of unprotected anal sex.

Perhaps the greatest impetus to overvaluing public engagement is the effortless extrapolation of past triumphs into the future. A disconcerting, all-too-familiar pattern often applies: early efforts return substantial benefits on a modest civic investment, so the political pathway evolves into a fixation despite diminishing results. Chapter 6's overview of black politics strongly hinted that monumental past accomplishments do not foretell present-day or future success. Washington's growing commitment to fund the battle against AIDS likewise shows a diminishing pay-off—funds have soared but HIV infections continue onward. A $100 billion-plus effort has not proven sufficient. One can only be reminded of the gambler's fallacy in which bets are constantly doubled in the hope that a single win will cover all previous losses.

The limiting impact of rules and institutional arrangements shaping any political battle is another caution easily disregarded by those rushing to agitate. The plusses and minuses of the playing field can be ignored; it is delusional, however, to dismiss them as a nefarious conspiracy. We argued that the geographical concentration of gays was fundamental for transforming votes into political influence by "automatically" producing allies *within* Congress while permitting a dense network of helpful organizations. Not all illness sufferers enjoyed that advantage. That national healthcare budgets permit focusing on a few identifiable legislative committees and agencies likewise proved invaluable. Of the utmost importance, enhanced funding did not have to reverse long-standing laws, achieve favorable court rulings, or overturn cultural norms defended by well-ensconced competitors. Compare this narrow quest to far more ambitious efforts to convert urban voting power into zero-sum economic transformations that require formal acquiescence from officials (and private firms) well beyond political reach. In these circumstances, the difficult-to-change rules of the game (e.g., limits on city taxing authority, fragmented power, civil service regulations) can severely impede progress regardless of the expended efforts.

Moreover, as chapter 8 noted, what applies for one agenda item need not pertain universally. A case-by-case determination is required. The same institutional factors facilitating burgeoning NIH programs are less applicable to legalizing homosexual unions ("gay marriage") or same-sex partner government-supplied medical benefits. The pathway here is far more arduous and can be readily resisted. Legalizing same-sex unions is not as obscure as a Senate sub-committee passed omnibus spending bill boosting earmarked NIH funds. In addition, unlike combating contagious diseases, government lacks an enduring obligation to recognize non-traditional family arrangements. Nor can gays expect a parade of scientific experts to vouch that without this morally laden legal redefinition, millions of innocent people might be endangered or otherwise suffer grievous harm. The "game" here is entirely different despite the identical institutional framework. It is indeed ironic that labors that resulted in government spending tens of billions will likely fall short in achieving an aim costing zero.

A further absolutely vital lesson concerns the inconclusiveness of political victories. Democratic politics virtually guarantees that losers can fight another day, and even laws set into stone can be silently circumvented. Call to mind how soaring tax bites have been defeated by ingenious tax dodges and hiding assets offshore. Crackdowns on immoral behavior can be reversed by bribery. Chapter 9's account of clever entrepreneurs sabotaging municipal efforts to close places facilitating unsafe sex clearly demonstrated this option. New sex clubs immediately materialized beyond the knowledge of local authorities, and beleaguered inspected managed only minimal enforcement. Incessant pleas for government-promoted "more education" similarly came to naught in private, unsupervised sexual behavior. Posted warnings are not victory regardless of contrary claims, and it is debatable whether a lasting success is even possible in these circumstances. The opportunities for comparable self-inflicted delusion are abundant—just recall the "success" of Prohibition despite a Constitutional amendment and millions spent on enforcement.

Activist admonitions to "get involved and make a difference" seem especially neglectful of enemies. Chapter 2 bemoaned the fact that scholarly investigations never ask about who did, or might, resist, as if conquest was only a matter of mobilizing one's followers. This indifference reflects a serious disconnect from reality. Any decent game plan should tally up all possible adversaries and their strengths. This is commonplace in military engagements, business, and sports. Why hazard certain defeat or triumphs were costs outweigh benefits? In the case of securing increased AIDS funding it was apparent that the most serious obstacles where surmountable—Washington routinely awards funds to conquer deadly illnesses, so success just meant getting heeded. Government inertia, not pro-AIDS forces or hysterical homophobia, had to be defeated.

If there were entrenched adversaries committed to sustaining this growing death toll they were in the gay movement itself. Make no mistake, those profiting from dangerous sex hardly wanted to see their clientele decimated. Many in fact generously sponsored movement politics and were devastated when friends and lovers succumbed. Yet, when it became clear that these enterprises (including those accepting advertising) prolonged the epidemic, they frequently applied their considerable clout to sustain a perilous status quo. For these undoubtedly well-meaning culprits, the slogan was "keep sexual liberation going," not "let's kill gays." That being understood, a rational AIDS activist circa early 1980s might have concluded that it would be difficult to stop AIDS from spreading given the enormous profits accruing to countless businesses promoting risky sexual contacts.

Our account also reiterates that the activist menu far exceeds the handful of acts offered by scholarly treatments of "political participation." To update the existing compendium with a few handy innovations is pointless and can only make the picture backward looking. Technological changes, the human imagination plus enemy resourcefulness will quickly make such a compendium obsolete. Who would have ever guessed that relentless telephoning and faxing can be potent political weapons? Or that threatening to publicly reveal closeted homosexuality or embarrassing scientific conference attendees with same-sex dancing might achieve one's aims? And these only barely highlight the ingenuity. The would-be activist should ask, "How can I accomplish my goal?" and not, "Which familiar tactic should we utilize?"

The value of a wide-ranging campaign should also be obvious—exclusively working from the outside or the inside is seldom sufficient; both are required in our multi-access point political system. Compounding this quandary is that the necessary cast of characters can require prodigious cleverness. The FDA agreed to "fast-track" iffy AIDS drugs through a combination of pressures from street protestors, doctors, government scientists, pharmaceutical executives, and free-market think tank-based economists. Each element in this coalition was essential and participants were hardly "natural" allies. The most brilliantly executed harassment campaign will come to naught once officials realize that the momentary irritation will soon vanish. Conversely, quiet consultations with those in power may yield better results if movers and shakers know that thousands of zealots can be energized if negotiations fall short. This advice may seem obvious, almost trite, but those seeking political change routinely ignore it—if a public meeting fails to bring the desired policy, just organize a better, more boisterous event while neglecting putting pressure elsewhere.

Our analysis repeatedly stressed skill—being active is not the same as being proficiently engaged. This is a deceptively complicated subject for "political skill" is not a single attribute applicable across every situation and cause. The fullness of this proficiency was repeatedly demonstrated over the evolving course of the AIDS movement. In the beginning the goal was generating public awareness and galvanizing medical research. Judged by public opinion polls, getting the message out, and in the correct context (a dreaded unfortunate disease just somehow transmitted, not payback for immoral behavior) was speedily achieved—not only did polls now include AIDS items (no small matter given costs), but public support for increased funding was fervent from the onset. Graphic accounts of seamy non-stop bathhouse anal sex were kept from public awareness. The ability to mobilize celebrities was particularly notable in light of Hollywood's initial fear of infection from casual contact. By the late 1980s joining the anti-AIDS battle had become fashionable while the mass media overflowed with sympathetic accounts and Washington's duty to do ever more. This was not accidental or preordained. AIDS is certainly not an out-of-control pandemic potentially affecting millions of innocent victims; other illnesses (e.g., diabetes) can make an even more forceful case for rapid government intervention.

The careful cultivation of science professionals within government and the medical profession was extraordinary, a feat made possible when AIDS activists familiarized themselves with this science. This heartfelt promotion was most evident in the countless legislative hearings that we highlighted. Impressive highly credentialed witnesses all agreed: AIDS was not to be cured by reversing gay liberation, but by upping government commitment to expensive science. Potential dissenting voices—Christian fundamentalists, other illness advocates worried over budgetary inattention—were adroitly relegated to the sidelines. Religious opponents were further demonized into mean-spirited ignorant bigots, not providers of traditional sagacious counsel. Combating AIDS via sexual restraint or even abstinence was made to appear homophobic. Talent was even more abundant when former outsiders joined the decision-making inner sanctum. Now ACT-UP members expertly discussed intricate treatment plans with leading drug manufactures.

The implications of this "assemble the necessary skill" recommendation is deceptively far-reaching. As in military planning, there must be congruence between the battle plan and the inventory of available resources. The same logic applies to those demanding government improve education, end poverty, provide affordable healthcare or any other objective, for that matter. It is one thing to coerce officialdom's commitment, quite another to help supply the necessary blueprint, including how these betterments are to be financed. Upping the pressure via vague-sounding, boisterous rhetoric or threats of impending litigation is *not* a recipe for success unless one assumes that those in charge possess the answers (and resources) but balk at implementing feasible solutions. Offering viable options may not assure success but the opposite guarantees failure.

The needed dexterity across innumerable circumstances sets powerful (though seldom acknowledged) limits on advancing up the first rungs of the socio-economic ladder via politics. Numbers by themselves are useless without substantial talent relevant to our highly complicated political arrangement, and it is difficult to envision how this groundwork endowment can be achieved *politically*. The skills necessary to play politics successfully cannot be successfully demanded from government, though, to be sure, officialdom can facilitate innumerable (though hardly guaranteed) educational opportunities. Imagine insurgents demanding that government teach them how to raise funds or communicate their ideas? And the more ambitious the agenda, the greater is the required capacity. Protestations to "give us proficiency" will likely be inept and fall short. Gay activists did not need government assistance to help them articulate their needs—they already enjoyed a knack for self-expression. Ditto for lending a hand to get them organized—gay communities spontaneously overflowed with groups easily harnessed to join the political fray. This is a paradox of the first order, a situation reminiscent of the old joke that getting two million dollars is easily accomplished once one has already secured the first million.

The observation we offered about the table scraps received by IV drug users afflicted with AIDS bears repeating: tragic suffering does not guarantee access to benefits even when government is waging a holy war on one's behalf. Critically, admonitions for these addicts "to get involved" to extract their share of the grand prize is probably pointless Utopianism. Their enduring debilitation—drug abuse and chaotic lives—renders them unfit soldiers in present-day complicated political campaigns. Imagine attempting to gather hundreds of addicts for a march, or bringing a delegation to Congress to explain their plight? This can be done, but the addicts themselves will undoubtedly not do it. More likely, proficient sympathizers will shoulder these responsibilities and likely orchestrate events to appear spontaneous. And who can guarantee that what is requested is, indeed, what these IV addicts truly desire or that it will be successful? This suggests a political version of the old adage that "the rich get richer."

Unresolved Problems of Analysis

Our primary analytical goal has been to formulate a way of judging the value of political activism—return on investment (ROI) in business parlance. Though this exercise has examined one conflict (the battle over AIDS funding) in considerable detail, and periodically delved into African-American politics, we admit that our framework remain relatively primitive while scarcely meeting strict scientific standards. Progress obviously requires that formidable analytical vexations must be addressed. With this inadequacy in mind, let us offer some puzzles that might profitably be addressed in subsequent endeavors.

The current approach to "political participation" infusing conventional research obviously requires rethinking. Chapter 2 outlined how investigators select a few readily ascertained behaviors to serve as the entire available menu to those operating outside this listing, or pursing objectives non-politically, are classified as "apathetic." This strategy greatly simplifies inquiry, especially in survey research, but it totally misrepresents reality. That being said, how then do we capture this vast terrain in a way that permits scientific rigor? What questions might we ask those involved in the battle for AIDS funding? Do we simply ascertain what people did, regardless of political content? Given that this far-ranging inquiry will doubtless generate an unwieldy plethora of results, especially given the disputatious nature of "political," can these be reduced to something more manageable?

Going one step further, is the random sample survey, a technique now often favored by those investigating civic engagement, the most useful vehicle when attempting to calculate ROI? Might not this tactic generate information about so many causes, pursued in so many ways, that reaching a firm conclusion about any one campaign is impossible? Or, are we to embrace the venerable case study of a single quest (as we did) as the most efficacious path to understanding? Plausibly, multiple approaches are vital, but the precise formula remains to be determined. There is also the matter of how the quest shall be defined. It is far from self-evident whether broad or narrow problem definitions are the most useful. For example, would our analysis of AIDS funding have been more insightful if we cast it as competition for all government medical funding? Or, might knowledge be better served if we had instead focused on, say, an effort to get a neighborhood AIDS clinic? This quandary is no different from the one faced in business analysis—in attempting to measure success, do we focus on the entire industry, the individual firm, a single merchant, or some combination of them all?

A deceptively complicated question may seem largely technical— the appropriate units of analysis in calibrating civic accomplishment. Chapters 8 and 9 spoke about "activists," "the anti-AIDS campaign," and similar terms denoting imprecise collectivities. References were also made to groups such as ACT-UP or the government agencies such as the NIH. Only periodically did individuals enter this account, people like Larry Kramer or Michael Fumento. This mixture of "players" is quite conventional in accounts of far-ranging political campaigns. Indeed, it is difficult to imagine executing this panoramic task without this constant switching back and forth from groups to individuals to government agencies and institutions.

Yet, if net pay-off from political action is the appropriate yardstick of success, what is this measuring instrument to be applied to? Conceivably, this could be done entirely on an individual basis, one act at a time. For example, we could ask each ACT-UP member about to launch a die-in what he or she seeks to accomplish in that event, and then align effort with outcome. If the objective was "get publicity" we might track down generated newscasts and magazine stories or just elicit reactions from those witnessing the event. The participant might then decide that the die-in was "profitable" if, for example, a thousand people ultimately saw the incident, and 60 percent reacted positively. Score one for activism—mission accomplished given net gain. Calibrating movement success here just sums individual accomplishment though, to be sure, precisely aggregating overall improvement may be arduous.

But, what if this activist quite reasonably said, "Get government to approve effective medicines and then distribute them for free"? By this far stricter benchmark, this single die-in was an abject failure—even months afterward this progress was not forthcoming and, alas, many ill participants soon succumbed. Score zero for return on investment. And the "free" element was absolute fantasy. Nevertheless, as the years rolled by, officials became more attentive to die-ins and slowly responded and then, after the 101st die-in, the FDA agreed to release certain drugs and the pharmaceutical companies priced them cheaply. ACT-UP immediately, and correctly so, claims credit for this achievement though hundreds of past die-in participants had already passed on with zero to show for their efforts. The balance sheet would be a complicated one: "the movement" had succeeded yet thousands of its members never received the hoped-for drugs and thousands of non-ACT-UP members now enjoyed the rewards of these demonstrations with zero personal engagement cost. And the drugs were still only partially effective.

Nevertheless, sorting out the winners and losers is not especially difficult here—those receiving the drugs clearly won something (measured strictly by this aim) regardless of effort. Rather, it is the aligning of personal effort and benefit that is so vexatious—some beneficiaries expended zero effort while untold losers were frantic activists who died before help arrived. Again, is profit and loss to be calculated simply by summing across all individuals or do we look at what ACT-UP, a collectivity, accomplished?

A different assessment formula is to skip individuals and groups altogether and simply focus on "the movement." This is essentially what our analysis of AIDS did though we periodically mentioned its key figures and organizational components. This is the standard procedure in business—profitability comes from the firm, not each employee or administrative unit though it is possible to calculate what each of these contributes to the bottom line. This macro approach infuses today's political activism—we speak of successes or failures of "the environmental movement" or the "civil rights movement" and so on. Here the individual's "profit" from civic engagement is collectively beside the point though, no doubt, rightfully a matter of personal concern. Quite possibly it is irrelevant that untold demonstrations were ineptly organized or pursued whimsically while leaving activists disappointed; the movement triumphed if, eventually, something valuable appeared though the precise connection is incredibly tangled.

Infusing this "profit" calculation is the vexing issue of choosing aims. In principle, the researcher can settle matters independently of activist motives. It might be asserted, for example, that AIDS activists primarily wanted effective drugs, a vaccine and similar medical advancements so as to live normal lives while pursing sexual gratification. This taking a movement's aim directly from what it openly advocates certainly simplifies analysis. Yet, as we readily concede, more may be sought than what may meet the eye or is candidly admitted. Politics draws people for multiple reasons, everything from the action's ostensible purpose to more personal incentives such as social camaraderie or economic gains, and these can be ever shifting and idiosyncratic. Compounding this mixture is that "true" motives may be less than altruistic and thus hidden—perhaps the ACT-UP participant attended meetings to acquire new sexual partners or just vent rage. Establishing which aims are primary and which are secondary can also be daunting—recall the problem of separating the desire to cure AIDS with the quest for sexual excitement.

Tallying up gains and losses is complicated under these murky circumstances. What appears a failure may, indeed, be a success for some and vice versa. Participants are certainly free to shift goals as situations evolve—what was originally purely a quest for socializing may become a passion for altering public policy, and both may co-exist in varying proportions. Such shifting can certainly be retroactive so as to make the best of a bad situation. Pushed to its limits, fluidity of aims can render a judgment of gains and losses pointless since the standard so easily fluctuates. Everything for everyone becomes—by declaration—a resounding success, and there is no way that goals can be rejected as inauthentic.

If this make-it-up-as-you-go-along standard prevails, then our discussions of dexterous activism, let alone gains and losses, are beside the point. Even catastrophes can be certified as authentic victories though according to some convoluted individual criteria. This quandary is clearly unsolvable, so imposing judgments invites contentiousness. If activists are judged by standards they themselves reject, they certainly can dispute what comprised success or failure. Consider the following quite distinct assessment: (1) AIDS activists won their battle since the campaign was *really* about sustaining sexual liberation and legitimizing homosexuality, and the tens of thousands who died from AIDS were merely (regrettable) battlefield casualties; (2) the battle against AIDS was a defeat since thousands needlessly died due to government lethargy; or (3) the war on AIDS essentially had a mixed outcome since untold lives were saved via education and publicity while others died due to insufficient pressure on drug firms and researchers. All are correct to some participants, no doubt, and these three assessments hardly exhaust the possibilities.

Further complicating this picture is how to assess losses. Just as we must calculate gain, the losses must also be tallied up to reach a net benefit figure. What makes this calculation element especially troublesome is that debits (like benefits) can be exceedingly extensive and ongoing to the point of being almost incalculable. Chapter 9 showed how a few activists during the mid-1980s kept bathhouses and other venues permitting dangerous sex open against the wishes of public health officials. The negative upshot of this political "success" was substantial loss of life, emotional bereavement among survivors, and, no doubt, extensive economic dislocation. The "collateral damage" here may still be occurring as HIV acquired in these settings continues for decades to come. It is also likely that many of today's losers have no idea that their harm is traceable to successful political agitation decades ago.

And how is one to decide whether the *net* return on investment is satisfactory? This is a familiar problem in business and, fortunately, standards do exist here. A potential investor might insist that he or she must receive at least 5 percent above inflation before putting a nickel into the enterprise. Others may want more (or take less) but all apply some yardstick before taking the plunge. There are standard formulas in planning investments that permit these issues to be plainly stated. Obviously, this prior calculation, no matter how meticulous, hardly guarantees outcome—even "safe" ventures may prove catastrophic and investors routinely differ in their judgments regarding risk assessment.

If these calculations are somewhat uncertain in business, they are exceedingly thorny in politics. Of special relevance to would-be participants is the expected utility of a given engagement vis-à-vis alternatives, both civic and private. A rational AIDS activist in the mid-1980s might reason as follows. Stressing a government-only "big science" strategy has a 50 percent likelihood of future success, and a success likelihood of 20 percent for those currently infected. A total private vigilantism solution (e.g., forcibly closing a few un-safe sex venues) will have an even lower overall rate of return but, critically, it can be more easily achieved and it's more certain given what we know of AIDS transmission. Or, alternatively, I personally can avoid these venues and HIV-infected partners and thus achieve my goal with 100 percent certainty though I will lose many friends to AIDS. Which pathway offers the most productive use of resources? Recalculating these figures will undoubtedly yield quite different rates of return. Those activists insisting that massive government intervention was virtually a sure bet vis-à-vis private restraint prob-ably misjudged the odds.

The availability of these divergent formulae can cast decisions into an entirely different light. Chapter 6 mentioned the difficulty that African Americans face in seeking substantial economic progress via the political route. From our historical vantage point this strategy now looks inefficient given the inherent obstacles and diminishing returns. Inefficiency, however, does not preclude pursuit: compared to any other alternative, it may still be the most productive option. Everything is relative—a 5 percent return is fantastic during defla-tion; it is a disaster when inflation exceeds 15 percent. Judgment ultimately depends on assessing non-political alternative options. Forgoing politics altogether and entering the private sector could conceivably offer even *worse* pay-offs. The sensible advice is that so long as ROI is positive and private options will yield negative outcomes, pursue a political strategy no matter how feeble the pay-off.

Such messy indeterminacy is frustrating but this should not pre-clude *some* judgment. Murkiness is inevitable when appraising all large-scale enterprises. Statements on the order of "the civil rights movement was a great success" or "the women's movement gener-ally improved the lives of Americans" are commonplace though each of these movements abounds with ambiguities and complexities. Only glibness (or ideological devotion) hides a fuller accounting of these (and all other) civic crusades. Judgments regarding success or failure *can* be made, and disputes over standards or ambivalent outcomes should not preclude a verdict. Perhaps we should take heart that it took centuries for businesses to achieve comparable profit-loss standards. Surely those who disagree with a finding may freely offer a contrary assessment. Disagreements are surely preferable to declaring, "Who can say exactly what the evidence means, so let us just celebrate civic engagement?"

This tangled web of costs and benefits inescapably leads us to the question of causality, a topic we broached in chapter 6. Our analysis of AIDS is filled with murky cause and effects dilemmas and, like so many treatments of activism, these have been conveniently slighted. If pay-off from engagement is to be calibrated, however, this linkage must be explicit. To ignore them would be the equivalent of accepting the rooster's claim that he, and he alone, was responsible for the sun rising. Matters are complicated since it is customary for organizations to claim credit for triumphs (regardless of their role) and to deny parenthood with failures.

The paradox of burgeoning gay electoral campaign clout *after* the government's generous commitment to fight AIDS illustrates one causality-related puzzle. It is naive to insist that this mobilization that essentially began in the mid-1990s "caused" a government intervention that started in the early 1980s. Initial federal government effort obviously did not depend on electoral mobilization. A more reasonable assertion is that growing voting strength made the campaign politically sacrosanct and, conceivability, led George W. Bush to increase funding after his 2000 election. In other words, voting turnout and other electoral efforts sustained the effort but did not instigate it. Though quite intuitively plausible, the role of voting is difficult to establish statistically—a surging "gay vote" will only be weakly correlated to far slower AIDS budget increases, and this suggests a minor contributing role. On the other hand, it is likely that these mobilizations *may* be decisive in protecting existing gains, statistical indeterminacy aside. Obviously a gap exists between available statistical techniques and plausible reality.

Using civic engagement on behalf of the status quo might also be applied to contemporary black activism. Chapter 6 demonstrated that African-American efforts from the early 1970s onward seemingly had only modest (at best) impact on contemporary aims stressing economic advancement and permanently closing racial gaps in education. This stands in contrast to earlier effort-benefit relationships—civic engagement in the 1950s and 1960s dramatically ended state-enforced segregation, achieved voting equality, and promoted countless other tangible gains. Nevertheless, it is credible that today's "ineffective" activism prevents backsliding though those pursuing today's quite different goals may not embrace this protective purpose. In social science language, a non-event (reversing progress) is the outcome of these demonstrations, boycotts, voter registrations drives, and the like. A rally to extend affirmative action in municipal employment may be an utter failure, but this show of strength may strongly caution city officials from disenfranchising potential black voters. How this type of relationship can be addressed scientifically is a major analytical dilemma.

The multi-front, multi-year nature of the anti-AIDS campaign further complicates demonstrating causal links. The overall battle involved tens of thousands of separate incidents, dozens of varied tactics, and these all had multiple, far-reaching outcomes. Connecting activities with profit is routine in businesses though arduous. For example, General Electric might calculate what each of its many divisions added to the total corporate bottom line, and then decide whether to keep each enterprise given alternative uses of precious capital. Thus, a few years back GE decided that its small appliance business was under-performing the company generally, so it was sold off and the proceeds invested elsewhere. If the AIDS campaign were run along comparable lines, somebody might say, die-ins are no longer effective, let's take the resources and re-allocate them to getting IV drug addicts to vote. What is critical in this calculation is showing the link between multiple activities on multiple benefits. Needless to say, this is a Herculean task and one well beyond current social science capacity.

The possible (and unknown) shape of this A-brings-B relationship only adds yet more complexity when establishing causality. Nothing suggests a continuous linear relationship, and threshold or ceiling affects can readily disguise causal impact by showing zero covariation. Much depends on where analysis begins and ends. Conceivably, the early efforts had a dramatic across-the-board impact with each additional exertion bringing diminishing returns. That is, the first few die-ins and celebrity galas dramatically boosted public awareness and brought forth government funding though by the 1990s this was old hat and thus ignored. Or, the earliest efforts made a near-zero impact until one day, government officials suddenly acquiesced—a sort of the straw the broke the camel's back scenario. A third possibility is that the impact was initially positive, then flat, and then became negative due to a public backlash at being annoyed.

Though exceedingly arduous to establish, this ratio of effort to outcome over the flow of the campaign is of the utmost importance to those seeking guidance. Would-be activists certainly want to know when tactics have reached their maximum impact levels or, conversely, when thresholds are being approached. Why schedule yet one more die-in when the return on investment has become negative? This difficult quandary must be established empirically and, to be frank, it is quite unclear how this task can be realized. After all, who can predict the future—a series of acts may seem absolutely futile, but unbeknownst to anybody, success is just around the corner. Our discussion of black politics in chapter 6 highlighted how many items on the black agenda once seemed hopeless and that it was only their dogged pursuit after countless failures that brought fruition.

And speaking of offering wise counsel to those contemplating civic engagement, the difficulties surrounding assessing proficiency deserve special mention. Chapter 5 wrestled with this problem at length and only offered the most cursory advice, for example, aims such be legally obtainable and within range given available resources. This insufficiency is in stark contrast to the standards available to those mulling business ventures. Here guidelines explicitly address such mattes as necessary starting capital, market size, competition, required personnel, and similar pre-requisites. Formulating such a checklist would surely be a boon for those seeking political solutions. At a minimum, we should be able to warn would-be activists against charlatans offering utopian schemes or causes likely to exacerbate matters. Sad to say, this evaluative capacity is presently severely under developed.

These are formidable research agenda items and we further admit that few investigators are likely to delve into them. Disentangling political activism is certainly not like conquering AIDS—nobody dies if academics fail to demonstrate the cost/benefit ratio of peace marches. The disciplinary incentives actually point in the opposite direction—better to tackle easy, at-hand problems and then move on as bafflements mount. Nevertheless, their resolution is essential if political activism is to progress beyond being a faith unanchored in factual calculations. One can only imagine if those about to start a restaurant told their bankers that they lacked any idea of how to measure their progress since investors had sharply different views of what comprised "a success." Or that the enterprise might become profitable only after everyone had passed on, if ever.

The Value of Civic Engagement: A Cautionary Postscript

Compared to conventional treatments of "political participation" our analysis has been cautionary; some might even say negative. A more accurate depiction would be balanced and encompassing. It is "negative" only in the sense that past accounts are so entirely one-sided. Moreover, we argued that "political apathy" might mean only a choice of weapons—inner-city parents moving to escape terrible schools are not lethargic; they are merely pursuing their objectives privately. Let us not forget that substantial economic progress among African Americans during the twentieth century occurred when they left the South and migrated northward. Today, countless other African Americans improve educational prospects for their children by abandoning terrible schools, not demanding government relief. Our point of departure is that aims are funda-mental, and the political pathway is only one of several choices, and nothing demands that civic engagement be the default option. This is especially true in our constitutional system of limited govern-ment where a capitalist economy offers alternatives to govern-ment-provided services. Better to ship UPS than hassle the Post Office for quicker delivery.

We will admit, however, that this utilitarian framework is hardly the last word. That collective engagement, totally apart from its in-strumental utility, can occasionally improve civic life is beyond dis-pute. Human beings are, after all, social animals, not cost-calculat-ing hermits. It may be deeply satisfying to vote or attend city coun-cil meetings even when the effort is futile and time could be more wisely invested elsewhere. Even voting in a one-sided election may have its rewards. Our cautions regarding political solution are not an encomium for libertarianism; civil society is worth preserving, and this demands civic engagement apart from tangible pay-offs.

No less important, a profoundly practical justification exists for this engagement: all the escapes we catalogue *presuppose* sustaining the existing political framework. The sequence is politics *then* a choice of further engagement, not politics *or* private action. Shoring up the status quo via obeying the law, paying taxes, voting, keeping leaders accountable, and the like are not options in our cosmology. Many non-political choices exist precisely *because* politics permits them to flourish. Freedom of movement, one of the great alternatives to politics, ultimately rests on a sustained civil society. Those avoiding taxes by sending money abroad could not do so without FCC regulation. Civic engagement is absolutely inescapable though there is no reason to seek political solutions in all instances. Our counsel concerns how to play politics adroitly (if necessary), not abandoning civic life as a shoddy investment.

Even the flawed "just get involved" dogma so favored by countless academics is useful though hardly in the ways they intend. From the perspective of preserving a commendable status quo, it is expedient to advise the disgruntled to embrace conventional civic strategies regardless of advice worthiness. Things can be worse than wasted effort. These incomplete academic-dispensed lessons with their heavy stress on election-related options redirect potentially aggressive acts into more manageable, peaceful channels. Petitioning school officials over dismal pupil performances may be inefficacious vis-à-vis more private or other political options, but this humdrum pathway outshines assassinating teachers or sabotage. The tumultuous though pointless march may even be healthy, readily available therapy when circumstances more realistically suggest futility. A parallel exists with religious devotion—prayer may be of psychological assistance in absolutely hopeless situations by offering a glimmer of hope. Wasteful ineptitude outshines desperate craziness in protecting a peaceful democratic society.

Nevertheless, the benefits of moderating conflict aside, imploring those in need to seek exclusive political solutions may be hazardous for those preferring moderate, democratic politics. It is not a question of restraining appetites to preserve an unequal status quo. We can hardly counsel those in need to abandon political fixes at the first sign of failure. Nor do we wish to impose legal "off-limits" signs on anybody's agenda. Far more perilous is forcing a system committed to limited, gridlock-mired government to extend its domain to meet a desperate clamor for unobtainable results. Hibbing and Theiss-Morse (2002: ch. 8) review numerous studies on the personal impact of political participation, and their conclusion is quite cautionary. Activism, benefits aside, can also engender frustration, diminish tolerance, undermine effective decision-making, and otherwise be disruptive to democratic politics. Instigating "more input" can be risky. At some point, these escalating—if not insatiable—demands forwarded to anxious-to-please leaders may engender a cure far worse than the disease, even if the remedy is feasible (and it may not be possible). Our constitutional system is not designed to alleviate the world's problems regardless of how skillfully pressured.

The war on AIDS illustrates such potential dangers. Imagine that champions of a rival illness suddenly realized that they had been short-changed by the extravagant war on AIDS and now wanted that campaign dramatically scaled back. Moreover, these newly aroused advocates plausibly insisted that since big government sponsored science had failed, containment should be pursued via the criminal code and draconian public health measures. The agenda would now consist of stamping out dangerous sex in private, closing down each and every venue facilitating these liaisons, or even quarantining chronic offenders. Here the potential mischief from a political strategy is far greater, especially given that light-handed initial efforts are likely to fail. This might well become a world of dreaded "sex police" willing to violate personal privacy to root out a deadly exploding epidemic. And if plainclothes police and surprise midnight bathhouse raids come up short, perhaps full-time electronic surveillance or entrapment is necessary. If that draconian approach fails as well, instigate even more totalitarian measures such as mandatory therapy, drugs to inhibit carnal desires, and similar nostrums now beyond the pale. Never underestimate what may transpire with the combination of public hysteria and an all-powerful government committed to "solutions" by any means necessary.

This is not a bizarre, unlikely-to-happen example of government overstepping its legitimate boundaries thanks to incessant popular outcry. Other illustrations of this pernicious tendency abound though advocates can scarcely be accused of evil intent. Civil rights activists have for years demanded government close racial gaps in educational performance (and income, too), and failure has only strengthened this fervor. The upshot has been a level of federal government educational involvement heretofore unimaginable—Department of Justice attorneys negotiating grade school boundaries, judge-imposed higher local property taxes, lawsuits contesting classroom disciplinary procedures, meticulous state textbook edicts, and countless other expansions of national authority that, ultimately, failed to close these gaps. A roughly similar progression has occurred in the quest for sexual equality—early victories eliminating blatant sexual discrimination have now evolved into ever-escalating demands to micro-manage society. At the outer edge of this movement are calls for even more government intervention into family life, for example, mandating federally funded daycare to eliminate aggressive behavior among boys to promote true gender equality.

Lest we be misunderstood, we are not defending racial gaps in education, sexual inequality, or any other defects judged intolerable by today's activists. These examples may be ideologically colored but the dangers know no ideological boundaries. Social conservatives are often just as guilty in reflexively aggrandizing government power—public school abstinence instruction can be just as invasive of personal privacy as celebrating alternative sexual lifestyles. Ditto for government guidelines to ensure "pro-family" messages on TV and other forms of censorship. The deeper question concerns enlarging government's scope to achieve iffy objectives subverting individual liberty and autonomy. The operative term here is risk. Today's political activists, on both sides of the ideological divide, seldom want less government; those wanting less often find ways to escape it, as chapter 4 showed. This expansion may be a precarious bargain, for who can guarantee that today's sympathetic office holders will not be replaced by adversaries now armed with expanded power. Those same Department of Justice lawyers who once unsuccessfully coerced local school districts to promote racial integration may tomorrow be worried over insufficient patriotism and perfunctory religious devotion.

A special problem awaits the unsophisticated recruited into activism. These are the poorly educated, often recent immigrants, who are told that mobilization is the superior pathway to moving up the socio-economic ladder. If only city government were in their hands they are told, life would abruptly improve—crime would vanish, children would learn their school lessons, and well-paying jobs would be forthcoming. No doubt, for those residing far outside the areas of power, this upbeat "get-the-power" scenario appears intoxicating. This is especially true if these novices are (falsely) told that those who have already climbed up the ladder got there via political acumen and now it is their turn to seize the levers of power. That a political strategy seems far less personally demanding than time-consuming, tedious alternatives (for example, acquiring marketable skills) only add to the attraction.

Impulsively embracing political solutions can effortlessly engender an unfortunate dependency that may be far worse than forgone opportunities. What begins as a tactical choice evolves into an all-consuming, faith-based passion in which once promising non-political alternatives recede into dimly remembered history. Politics soon comes to resemble a South Seas cargo cult—islanders faithfully assemble by water's edge expecting the immanent return of goodies-laden Americans decades after war's end. This is the world of demanded sure-fire government programs for all ailments. Such easy ritualism may well outshine learning how to alleviate one's misfortune. To wit, for parents alarmed about excessive TV violence political action becomes a consuming way of life with victory "just around the corner." Even if this victory were achieved, this might end the quest—what if these TV-less children are still violent? Might government-supplied psychiatric counseling or drugs comprise the next demand?

Relentlessly attempting to extract government benefits is a two-way street, and a recipe for enduring dependency. At best, this relationship engenders paternalism; at worst, a flight from personal responsibility. Expeditious politics may not produce the most preferred personal outcome. Government, unlike private firms, do not collapse if they ineptly supply goods and services. Disbelievers might wish to purchase Soviet-built automobiles. Officialdom may even flourish if it lurches from disaster to disaster. Perhaps AIDS sufferers would prefer other options than those that have survived the political gauntlet or are easily supplied by constrained government bureaucracies. This is hardly hypothetical—chapter 8 noted that many AIDS activists sought medicines abroad beyond the FDA's regulatory power or alternative cures here at home. Remember, programs such as large-scale public housing and easy-to-obtain welfare were once stridently demanded and judged marvelous additions to the public good. Today, of course, new programs exist to assist these past beneficiaries to escape public housing and welfare.

The burgeoning conflation of heightened activism with "democracy," especially the notion that apathy among those near the bottom of the socio-economic hierarchy blemishes democracy also deserves mention. This is nonsense. Surely it is debatable that democracy, by definition, requires being active over and above having the right to participate. As the dreary turnout in countless local elections will attest, American democracy will not collapse if poor people disdain voting or the wealthy flock to the polls. This is a theoretically odd spin on "democracy" apparently popular only among those academics uneasy about government's alleged middle-class tilt. Moreover, as chapter 3 made abundantly clear, activism is hardly limited to the conventional researcher-supplied, electoral conflict centered menu. Those at the bottom can readily express themselves via violence, avoiding taxes, and otherwise making their dissatisfaction felt. Opportunities abound for political self-expression via the marketplace. More important, the non-political options may be far superior compared to lengthy struggles in a system mired in gridlock.

Invigorating those now apathetic will not level existing inequalities; surging mobilization may well exacerbate them. Democracy will not be "perfected" if only the lethargic downtrodden were galvanized to counterbalance the wealthier. Differences in proficiency do not vanish with equal engagement. We saw this when the federal government sought to involve AIDS sufferers themselves in actual administration. In principle, no one group had any initial special claim on resources—inner-city Hispanic drug addicts began on an equal footing with better-educated middle-class whites. In practice, the bulk of these resources soon came under the control of those already advantaged, namely middle-class white homosexuals. This should hardly be surprising. When funds were specifically earmarked for disadvantaged groups (as was occasionally done), administrative ineptitude often impeded effectiveness and in all likelihood also discouraged future allocations. Remember from chapter 9 how organizations to assist the less fortunate often became mired in corruption and inefficiency as those with limited aptitude struggled with tasks that would overwhelm even skilled bureaucrats.

It is not as if the pathways to greater engagement are being blocked. For decades Washington has sought to promote access via tactics such as easier voting registration and has regularly intervened when access have been impeded. Privately funded efforts such as MTV's "Rock the Vote" has similarly become ubiquitous. There is no evil-doing here; as Hibbing and Theiss-Morse (2002: Ch.5) make abundantly clear; abstention is purely voluntary. One can only speculate why so many academics bemoan apathy when this is what people themselves desire. Perhaps a hidden agenda exists, conceivably these professors hope that an influx of new players will shift policies in directions more favorable to their own preferences. Put another way, if these academics themselves are incapable of imposing their political will, this might be more easily achieved by getting the now apathetic to do it for them.

All in all, then, political activism should be understood as one avenue of betterment, not *the* pathway toward success. It is not for everyone despite its ready accessibility. This advice is no different from the counsel one might give to those about to found a business: a few became very rich, many more make decent livelihoods, and countless others go bankrupt. Be careful before taking the plunge.

Bibliography

"ACT-UP letter to Dentists or Physicians," August 1992.

Adams, Charles. *Those Dirty Rotten Taxes: The Tax Revolts that Built America.* New York: The Free Press, 1998.

Adelman, Carol. "America's Helping Hand." *Wall Street Journal,* August 21, 2002, A12.

Adler, Jeffrey S. "Introduction." In *African American Mayors: Race, Politics and the American City.* Edited by Colburn, David R. and Jerry S. Adler. Urbana and Chicago: University of Illinois Press, 2001.

"AIDS 'dissidents' target health officials, other activists." *AIDS Weekly,* May 13, 2002.

Armor, David J. *Forced Justice: School Desegregation and the Law.* New York: Oxford, 1995.

Associated Press. "Klan Group Plans Rally to Support Augusta Club." *New York Times,* March 2, 2003. Online version.

Bailey, Robert W. *Out and Voting II: The Gay, Lesbian, and Bisexual Vote in Congressional Elections, 1990-1998.* New York: The Policy Institute of NGLFT, 2000.

Barker, Lucius J., Mack H. Jones, and Katherine Tate. *African Americans and the American Political System,* fourth edition. Upper Saddle River, NJ: Prentice-Hall, 1999.

Barlett, Donald J. and James B. Steele. *The Great American Tax Dodge: How Spiraling Fraud and Avoidance are Killing Fairness, Destroying the Income Tax, and Costing You.* Boston: Little Brown and Company, 2000.

Bartlett, Bruce "Unpaid Taxes," National Center for Policy Analysis, Idea House. April 16, 2001. Online at www.nepa.org/oped/bartlett/

Bate, Roger. "AIDS Activists Hinder Their Cause." *Health Care News,* November 2, 2002, 1, 7.

Bayer, Ronald. "The Politics of Prevention and Neglect." *Health Affairs* (Spring) 87-97. Reprinted in *AIDS: The Politics and Policy of Diseases,* edited by Theodouou, Stella Z. Upper Saddle River, NJ: Prentice-Hall, 1991.

Bayor, Ronald. "African-American Mayors and Governance in Atlanta." In *African American Mayors: Race, Politics and the American City,* edited by Colburn, David R. and Jerry S. Adler. Urbana and Chicago: University of Illinois Press, 2001.

Beinart, Peter, "The Rise of Jewish Schools." October 1999. *Atlantic Online.*

Bell, Allison, "Social Funds Post Socially Acceptable Returns." *National Underwriter,* March 22, 1999, 18, 20.

Berman, Richard. "Animal Groups callous, not cute." *USA Today*, April 16, 2003, 15A.

Bernstein, Robert, Anita Chada, and Robert Montjoy. "Overreporting Voting: Why It Happens and Why it Matters." *Public Opinion Quarterly* 65 (2001): 22-44.

Bérubé, Allen. "The History of Gay Bathhouses." In *Policing Public Sex: Queer Politics and the Future of AIDS Activism* edited by Dangerous Bedfellows (Colter, Ephen Glenn, Wayne Hoffman, Eva Pendleton, Alison Redick, and David Serlin). Boston: South End Press, 1996.

Best, Joel. "Promoting Bad Statistics." *Society,* March/April, 2001, 10-15.

Bickel, Alexander M. *The Supreme Court and the Idea of Progress.* New York: Harper and Row, 1970.

Birnbaum, Jeffrey H. "Fat and Happy in D.C." *Fortune,* May 26, 2001, 95-100.

Blotcher, Jay. Sex Club Owners: The ~~Fuck Suck~~ Buck Stops Here." In *Policing Public Sex: Queer Politics and the Future of AIDS Activism,* edited by Dangerous Bedfellows (Colter, Ephen Glenn, Wayne Hoffman, Eva Pendleton, Alison Redick, and David Serlin). Boston: South End Press, 1996.

Bositis, David A. "Black Elected Officials: A Statistical Analysis 2001." Joint Center for Political and Economic Studies, 2001. Online version at www.jointcenter.org.

Braybrooke, David. "The Meaning of Participation and of Demands for It: A Preliminary Survey of Conceptual Issues." In *Participation in Politics,* edited by J. Roland Pennock and John W. Chapman New York: Lieber-Atherton, 1975.

Brisbin, Richard A., Jr. "The Politics of Private Rights of Action." *Whittier Law Review,* 11 (189): 111-170.

Bronski, Michael. "Sex in the '90s: The Problems of Pleasure." *Steam,* Summer, 1994, 132-4.

Browning, Rufus P., Dale Rogers Marshall, and David H. Tabb. "Has Political Incorporation Been Achieved? Is It Enough?" In *Racial Politics in American Cities,* edited by Browning, Rufus P., Dale Rogers Marshall, and David H. Tabb, second edition. New York: Longman, 1997.

Bullock, Charles III. "Congressional Voting and the Mobilization of a Black Electorate in the South." *Journal of Politics* 43 (1981): 662-682.

Bumiller, Elizabeth. "Under Fire, Conservative Withdraws From AIDS Council." *New York Times,* January 24, 2003. Online version.

Burkett, Elinor. *The Gravest Show on Earth: America in the Age of AIDS.* Boston: Houghton Mifflin, 1995.

Burton, Thomas M. "Test for Aneurysms Might a Lot of Lives, Some Say." *Wall Street Journal,* January 13, 2003, A1, A6.

Business Week. "Can Anything Rise From Ashes?" May 18, 1992, 42.

Button, James W. *Black Violence: Political Impact of the 1960s Riots.* Princeton, NJ: Princeton University Press. 1977.

———. "Southern Black Elected Officials: Impact on Socioeconomic Change." *Review of Black Political Economy* 12 (1982): 29-45.

——. *Blacks and Social Change: Impact of the Civil Rights Movement in Southern Communities.* Princeton, NJ: Princeton University Press, 1989.

Callahan, David. "$1 Billion for Ideas: Conservative Think Tanks in the 1990s." Washington, DC: National Committee for Responsive Philanthropy, 1999.

Cameron, Charles, David Epstein, and Sharyn O'Halloran. "Do Majority-Minority Districts Maximize Substantive Representation in Congress?" *American Political Science Review* 90 (1996): 794-812.

Canedy, Dana. "Critics of Graduation Exam Threaten Boycott of Florida." *New York Times,* May 13, 2003. Online version.

Canon, David T. *Race, Redistricting and Representation: The Unintended Consequences of Black Majority Districts.* Chicago: The University of Chicago Press, 1999.

Carey, Susan. "A City-Slicker CEO Finds Fun and Profit At Home on the Range." *Wall Street Journal,* April 10, 2000, A1, A17.

Carlson, Tucker. "D.C. Blues: The rap sheet on the Washington police." *Policy Review* (Winter) 26-33.

Carlton, Jim. "Tech Executives Devote Energy to Green Causes." *Wall Street Journal,* December 27, 2000, B1.

Carnahan, Ira. "Asylum for the Insane." *Forbes,* January 21, 2002, 33-34.

Chase, Marilyn. "With Few Cases in U.S., Patients Accept Isolation and Quarantine." *Wall Street Journal,* April 30, 2003, A13.

Cleeland, Nancy. "Off-the-Books Jobs Growing in Region." *Los Angeles Times,* May 7, 2002, Online version.

Clemetson, Lynette 2003. "Protest Groups Using Updated Tactics to Spread Antiwar Message." *New York Times,* January 15. Online version.

Clendinen, Dudley and Adam Nagourney. *Out for Good: The Struggle to Build a Gay Rights Movement in America.* New York: Simon and Schuster, 1999.

Clotfelter, Charles T. "Are Whites Still Fleeing? Racial Patterns and Enrollment Shifts in Urban Public Schools, 1987-1966." *Journal of Policy Analysis and Managemen,* 20 (2001): 199-223.

Cloud, David S. "Virginian Fights for International Tax Havens." *Wall Street Journal,* July 30, 2001. A20.

Cohen, Debra N. "$18 million pledged for Jewish day schools." *Jewish News of Greater Phoenix,* nd. Online version.

Colburn, David R. and Jerry S. Adler, eds. *African American Mayors: Race, Politics and the American City.* Urbana and Chicago: University of Illinois Press, 2001.

Cole, Robert E. and Donald R. Deskins, Jr. "Racial Factors in Site Location and Employment Patterns of Japanese Auto Firms in America." *California Management Review* (1988) 31:9-22.

Coleman, Paul Rykoff. "ACT-UP takes on the Gay Press." *Outweek,* August 22, 1990, 16, 30-1.

Colfax, J. David. "How Effective is the Protest Advertisement?" *Journalism Quarterly* 43 (1966): 697-702.

Combs, James. *Polpopp2: Politics and Popular Culture in America Today.* Bowling Green, KY: Bowling Green State University Popular Press, 1991.

Conge, Patrick J. "The Concept of Political Participation." *Comparative Politics* 20 (1988): 241-249.

Conway, M. Margaret. *Political Participation in the United States,* third edition. Washington, DC: CQ Press, 2000.

Coombs, David W., H. M. C. Alsikafi, Bryan Hobson, and Irving I. Webber. "Black Political Control in Green County, Alabama." *Rural Sociology* 42 (1977): 398-406.

Coulson, Andrew J. *Market Education: The Unknown History.* New Brunswick, NJ: Transaction Publishers, 1999.

Crotty, William. "Political Participation: Mapping the Terrain." In *Political Participation and American Democracy,* edited by Crotty, William. New York: Greenwood Press, 1991.

D'Emilio, John. "Cycles of Change, Questions of Strategy: The Gay and Lesbian Movement After 50 Years." In *The Politics of Gay Rights* edited by Rimmerman, Craig A., Kenneth D. Wald, and Clyde Wilcox. Chicago: University of Chicago Press, 2000.

Deane, Claudia. "Computer-Assisted Influence?" *Washington Post,* April 19, 2002.

deGale, Anabelle "Coalition vows legal fight over FCAT." *Miami Herald,* May 18, 2003. Online version.

Denn, Rebekah. "NAACP considers lawsuit against school districts." *Seattle Post-Intelligence Reporter,* September 28, 2001. Online version.

Donohue, John J. III and James Heckman. "Continuous Versus Episodic Change: The Impact of Civil Rights Policy on Economic Status of Blacks." Working Paper 3894 Cambridge, MA: National Bureau of Economics, 1989.

Dooren, Jennifer Corbett and Mark H. Anderson. "IRS Says Cost of Tax Scams is Getting Higher." *Wall Street Journal,* April 12, 2002, A4.

Dreyfuss, Robert "The Double-Edged Wedge." *American Prospect.* August 28, 2000a, 25-27.

——. "Pride and Prejudice: The State of Gay Politics." *Rolling Stone,* May 25, 2000b, 39-41.

Dunham, Martin. "Preparing for Armageddon: Citizen Militias, the Patriot Movement and the Oklahoma City Bombing." *Terrorism and Political Violence* 8 (1996): 65-79.

Dye, Thomas R. and James Rennick. "Political Power and City Jobs: Determinants of Minority Employment." *Social Science Quarterly* 62 (1981): 475-486.

Edds, Margaret. *Free at Last: What Really Happened When Civil Rights Came to Southern Politics.* Bethesda, MD: Adler and Adler, 1987.

Eisinger, Peter K. "Black Employment in Municipal Jobs: The Impact of Black Political Power." *American Political Science Review* 76 (1982): 380-392.

Encyclopedia of Associations: An Association Unlimited Reference. Edited by Hedblad, Alan, 39th edition. Detroit, MI: Thomson-Gale, 2003.

Epstein, Richard A. "Equal Opportunity or More Opportunity: the Good Thing About Discrimination." *Civitas: The Institute for the Study of Civil Society*, March, 2002.

Epstein, Steven. *Impure Science: AIDS, Activism, and the Politics of Knowledge.* Berkeley: University of California Press, 1996.

Fainstein, Norman and Susan Fainstein. "Urban Regimes and Black Citizens: The Economic and Social Impacts of Black Political Incorporation in US Cities." *International Journal of Urban and Regional Research* 20 (1997): 22-37.

Fears, Darryl. "Disparity Marks Black Ethnic Groups, Report Says." *Washington Post,* March 9, 2003. Online version.

Fernández-Morera, Dario. *American Academia and the Survival of Marxist Ideas.* Westport, CT: Praeger, 1996.

Fierstein, Harvey. "The Culture of Disease." *New York Times,* July 31, 2003.

Finkelstein, Eric A., Ian C. Fiebelkorn, and Gujing Wang. "National Medical Spending Attributable To Overweight and Obesity: How Much And Who's Paying?" *Health Affairs* May 14, 2003. Online at http://healthaffairs.org/WebExclusives/Finkelstein_Web_Excel-051403.htm.

Foer, Franklin "Meet the New Left: Bold, Fun and Stupid: Protest Too Much." *New Republic,* May 1, 2000, 21 Online version.

Forelle, Charles and Daniel Golden. "Responding to Iraq, Hackers Shut Web Sites, Post Graffiti." *Wall Street Journal,* March 28, 2003, B1.

Fox News, "Berkeley Club Holds Anti-Affirmative Action Bake Sale." February 27, 2003. Online version.

Fuaci, Anthony S. "Testimony." *Hearings before a Subcommittee of the Committee on Appropriations, United States Senate,* 106th Congress, first session. Washington, DC: U.S. Government Printing Office, 1999.

Fuchs, Victor R. *Who Shall Live?: Health, Economics, and Social Choice.* New York: Basic Books, 1974.

Fumento, Michael. *The Myth of Heterosexual AIDS.* Washington, DC: Regnery Gateway, 1993.

Gavin, Robert. "The Rockies Emerge As Pocket of Prosperity In a Slowing Economy," *Wall Street Journal*, June 6, 2001.

"Gay & Lesbian Victory Fund Endorses Five More in 2002 Election Cycle." *US Newswire,* April 26, 2002. Online.

"Gays Comprise 5 Percent of Electorate in 2002, New Poll Finds." *Financial Times Information,* November 21, 2002.

Gayellow Pages, The National Edition. New York: Renaissance House, 1982.

Gill, Dee. "Want to Put Your Money Where Your Conscious Is" (edited by Amy Duncan). *Business Week,* September 8, 1997, 134-135.

Ginsberg, Benjamin and Martin Shefter. *Politics by Other Means,* revised and updated version. New York: W. W. Norton & Co, 1999.

Glassman, James K. "A Different High-Tech War," Tech Central Station, 2003. www.techcentralstation.com.

Goldberg, Bernard. *Bias: A CBS Insider Exposes How the Media Distorts the News.* New York: Perennial, 2003.

Goldberg, Robert A. *Grassroots Resistance: Social Movements in Twentieth Century America.* Belmont, CA: Wadsworth, 1991.

Golden, Daniel "Home Schoolers Learn How to Gain Clout in the Beltway." *Wall Street Journal,* April 24, 2000, A1, A6.

Goode, Erica. "Certain Words Can Trip Up AIDS Grants, Scientists Say." *New York Times,* April 18, 2003. Online version.

"GOP Visa Card? Party Study Sees Profit in Affinity." *Wall Street Journal,* January 17, 2001, B1.

Gore, Al. *Earth in the Balance: Ecology and the Human Spirit.* Boston: Houghton Mifflin, 1992.

Grady, Denis. "Vaccine Appears to Prevent Cervical Cancer." *New York Times,* November 21, 2002. Online version.

Graff, Garrett M. "Program Encourages New Civil Rights Leaders." *Harvard Crimson,* Friday, July 6, 2001. Online version (www.thecrimson.harvard.edu/news/articles.asp?ref=13407).

Green, Edward C. "A Plan as Simple as ABC." *New York Times,* March 1, 2003. Online version.

Gross, Cary P., Gerald F. Anderson, and Neil R. Powe. "The Relation Between Funding by the National Institutes of Health and the Burden of Disease." *New England Journal of Medicine* 340 (1999): 1881-1887.

Gross, Paul R. and Norman Levitt. *Higher Superstitions: The Academic Left and Its Quarrel with Science.* Baltimore, MD: Johns Hopkins University Press, 1994.

Guzzardi, Joe. "Why The Black Caucus Looks The Other Way On Immigration." May 9, 2003. VDARE.com.

Haider-Markel, Donald P. "Creating Change—Holding the Line: Agenda Setting on Lesbian and Gay Issues at the National Level." In *Gays and Lesbians in the Democratic Process* edited by Riggle, Ellen, D. B. and Barry L. Tadlock. New York: Columbia University Press, 1999.

Halchi, Abigail. "AIDS, Anger, and Activism: ACT-UP As a Social Movement Organization." In *Waves of Protest: Social Movements Since the Sixties,* edited by Freeman, Jo and Victoria Johnson. Lanham, MD: Rowman & Littlefield, 1999.

Hayashi, Yuka 2003. "'Peace Funds' Are in Awkward Spot." *Wall Street Journal,* April 9, D9.

Health Care News, vol. 1, August 2001.

Hearing before a Subcommittee of the Committee of the Committee on Government Operations, House of Representatives, 99th Congress, second session. July 1, 1986. Washington, DC: U.S. Government Printing Office.

Hearing before a Subcommittee of the Committee on Appropriations, United States Senate, 106th Congress, first session, July 9, 1999. Washington, DC: U.S. Government Printing Office.

Hearing before a Subcommittee of the Committee on Appropriations, United States Senate, 106th Congress, second session, February 14, 2000. Washington, DC: U.S. Government Printing Office.

Hearings before the Human Resources and Intergovernmental Relations Subcommittee of the Committee on Government Operations, House of Representatives, 101st Congress, first session. July 28, 1989. Washington, DC: U.S. Government Printing Office.

Hearings before the Subcommittee on Health and the Environment of the Committee on Energy and Commerce, House of Representatives, 101st Congress, first session, April 4, 1989, April 5, 1989, April 24th, and July 19th, 1989. Washington, DC: U.S. Government Printing Office.

Henry, Tarma. "NCAAP issues a call to end inequality in USA's Schools." *USA Today,* May 16, 2001, 3A.

Herman, Didi. *The Antigay Agenda.* Chicago: University of Chicago Press, 1997.

Herrenstein, Richard J. and Charles Murray. *The Bell Curve: Intelligence and Class Structure in American Life.* New York: Free Press, 1994.

Herring, Mary. "Legislative Responsiveness to Black Constituents in Three Deep South States." *Journal of Politics* 52 (1990): 740-758.

Hershey-Webb, David. "Number One with a Bullet: Songs of Violence Are Part of America's Folk Tradition." In *Mass Politics: The Politics of Popular Culture,* edited by Shea, Daniel M. New York: Worth Publishing, 1999.

Herszenhorn, David M. "Bounded by Gates, Over a Toll Bridge." *New York Times,* June 18, 2001, B5.

Hibberd, James. "Trumped Up Eco Terrorism: An Arsonist Tale." *New York Times,* February 12, 2002. Online version.

Hibbing, John R. and Elizabeth Theiss-Morse. *Stealth Democracy: Americans' Beliefs about How Government Should Work.* Cambridge, UK: Cambridge University Press, 2002.

Hill, Kevin A. "Does the Creation of Majority Black Districts Aid Republicans? An Analysis of the 1992 Congressional Elections in Eight Southern States." *Journal of Politics.* 57 (1995): 384-401.

HIV/AIDS Surveillance Report: Cases of HIV Infection and AIDS in the United States, 2002, Addendum. Department of Health and Human Services, Public Health Service, Centers for Disease Control and Prevention, Atlanta, GA. Online version.

Hoerder, Dirk. *Protest Direct Action Repression: Dissent in American Society from Colonial Times to the Present.* München: Verlag Dokumentation, 1977.

Holcombe, Randell G. *Writing Off Ideas: Taxation, Foundations, and Philanthropy in America.* New Brunswick, NJ: Transaction Publishers, 2000.

"An hourly fee buys White House banner," *USA Today,* August 15, 2001, 3D.

Horn, Tim. "Meet Your Meds: Hooking Up With the Right Drug Regimen." *POZ* Spring, 2002, 9.

Horowitz, Donald L. *The Courts and Social Policy.* Washington, DC: The Brookings Institution, 1977.

Hough, Jerry F. "Political Participation in the Soviet Union." *Soviet Studies* (1976) 28: 3-20.

Human Rights Campaign 2002. "Federal Funding FY2001-AIDS/HIV-Related Programs." www.hrc.org/newsreleases/2000/001218fy2001aids.asp.

Johnson, David Cay. "The High Price of Estate-Tax Cheating." *New York Times,* December 17, 2000, Online version.

——. "U.S. Companies File in Bermuda to Slash Tax Bills." February 18, 2002a. Online version.

——. "I.R.S. Says Offshore Tax Evasion is Widespread." *New York Times,* March 26, 2002b. Online version.

——."Affluent Avoid Scrutiny on Taxes Even as I.R.S. Warns of Cheating." *New York Times,* April 7, 2002c. Online version.

——. "Cuts in Tax Enforcement Cost the States Billions." *New York Times,* April 12, 2002d. Online version.

——. "U.S. Discloses That Use of Tax Evasion Plans is Extensive." *New York Times,* May 22, 2002e. Online version.

——. "Haunting Tax Cheats, I.R.S. Vows to Focus More Effort on the Rich." *New York Times,* September 13, 2002f. Online version.

——. "Departing Chief Says I.R.S. is Losing War on Tax Cheats." *New York Times,* November 5, 2002g. Online version.

——. "Crackdown on Tax Cheats Not Working, Panel Says." *New York Times,* October 20, 2003. Online version.

Jonsson, Patrik. "The new face of home schooling." *Christian Science Monitor,* April 29, 2003. Online version.

Joulfaian, David and Mark Rider. "Tax Evasion by Small Business." Office of Tax Analysis, U.S. Department of the Treasury, Washington, DC, 1998.

Keech, William R. *The Impact of Negro Voting: The Role of the Vote in the Quest for Equality.* Chicago: Rand McNally, 1968.

Keim, Donald W. "Participation in Contemporary Democratic Theory." In *Participation in Politics.* edited by J. Roland Pennock and John W. Chapman. New York: Lieber-Atherton, 1975.

Keller, Edmond J. "The Impact of Black Mayors on Urban Policy." *Annals of the American Academy of Political and Social Sciences.* 439 (1978): 40-52.

Kelley, Tina. "From Ancient Greece, a Weapon for Peace." *New York Times,* March 4, 2003. Online version.

Kelly, William R. and David Snyder. "Racial Violence and Socioeconomic Changes Among Blacks in the United States." *Social Forces* (1980) 53:739-760.

Kern-Foxworth, Marilyn. "Aunt Jemima, the Frito Bandito, and Crazy Horse: Selling Stereotypes American Style." In *Mass Politics: The Politics of Popular Culture,* edited by Shea, Daniel M. New York: Worth Publishing, 1999.

Kerr, Brinck and Kenneth R. Mladenka. "Does Politics Matter?: A Time Series Analysis of Minority Employment Patterns." *American Journal of Political Science* (1994) 38:918-43.

Kleinfeld, Judith. "Exposing Junk Science in Cyberspace." *Society,* March/April, 2001, 16-22.

Koch, Stephen. *Double Lives: Spies and Writers in the Secret Soviet War of Ideas Against the West.* New York: The Free Press, 1994.

Kolata, Gina "Gains on Heart Disease Leave More Survivors, and Questions." *New York Times,* January 19, 2003. Online version.

Kotkin, Joel. "White Flight to the Fringes." *Washington Post*, March 10, 1996, Online version.

Kramer, Larry. *Reports from the Holocaust: The Making of an AIDS Activist.* New York: St. Martin's, 1989.

Kristof, Kathy M. "Truth or Dare?; It's a Fine Line Between Legal Tax Avoidance and Larceny." *Los Angeles Times* February 26, 1995. Online version.

Kurian, George Thomas and Jeffrey D. Schultz. *Political Marketplace USA.* Phoenix, AZ: Oryx Press, 1999.

Lavin, Douglas. "Globalization Goes Upscale." *Wall Street Journal,* February 1, 2002. Online version.

Lee, Martha F. "Violence and the Environment: The Case of 'Earth First!'" *Terrorism and Political Violence.* 7 (1995): 109-127.

Leighley, Jan E. "Attitudes, Opportunities and Incentives: A Field Essay on Political Participation." *Political Research Quarterly* 48 (1995): 181-209.

——. *Strength in Numbers? The Political Mobilization of Racial and Ethnic Minorities.* Princeton, NJ: Princeton University Press, 2001.

Levine, Arthur, "American Education: Still Separate, Still Unequal." *Los Angeles Times,* February 2, 2003. Online version.

Lichter, Linda S. and Robert S. Lichter. *Prime Time Crime.* Washington, DC: The Media Institute, 1983.

——, with the assistance of Daniel Amundson. *Prime Time: How TV Portrays American Culture.* Washington, DC: Regnery Publishing, 1994.

Lichter, S. Robert, Stanley Rothman, and Linda A. Lichter. *The Media Elite.* Bethesda, MD: Adler & Adler, 1986.

Lijphart, Arend. "Unequal Participation: Democracy's Unresolved Dilemma." *American Political Science Review* (1997) 91: 1-14.

Lott, John R. Jr. "Does A Helping Hand Put Others At Risk? Affirmative Action, Police Departments and Crime." *Economic Inquiry* 38 (2000): 239-277.

Lowenstein, Gaither. "Black Elected and Appointed Officials: Black Mayors and the Urban Black Underclass." *Western Journal of Black Studies.* 5 (1981): 278-284.

Lubin, David. *The Paradox of Representation: Racial Gerrymandering and Minority Interests in Congress.* Princeton, NJ: Princeton University Press, 1997.

Luo, Michael. "Taking Lessons From Another Culture." *New York Times* October 20, 2003. Online version.

Magnet, Myron, editor. *What Makes Charity Work? A Century of Public and Private Philanthropy* Chicago: Ivan R. Dee, 2000.

Malkin, Michelle. "Hostile Fire from Eco-Extremists." *Washington Times*, December 11, 2001. Online version.

Marcus, Ruth. "'Pink Money' Flowing to Democrats; Gay Contributors Now Major Source." *Washington Post,* April 18, 2000. Online version.

Matthews, Anna Wilde and Eduardo Porter. "Radio Stations Turn Back Clock for Songs to Capture Nation's Mood After Attacks." *Wall Street Journal,* September 23, 2001, B13.

Maxwell, Bill. "Black families open up, cram education in." *St. Petersburg Times,* October 22, 2003. Online version.

McGinn, Daniel. "Trying to Outfox Uncle Sam." *Newsweek,* April 16, 2001, 42-44.

McKinnon, John D. "US Taxpayers Often Fail to Tell Of Overseas Finances, Report Says." *Wall Street Journal,* July 18, 2001, A2.

McNeil, Donald G. Jr. "One by One, Charities Attack the AIDS Juggernaut." *New York Times,* November 18, 2002. Online version.

——, 2003. "Wielding a Big Stick, Carefully Against SARS." *New York Times,* April 20, 2003. Online version.

McWhirter, Cameron. "State posts are few for blacks." *Detroit News,* February 14, 2000, Online version.

Meeks, Annette. "Planning A Successful Event in Eight Weeks." *Insider,* March, 2003, 11-13.

Milbrath, Lester W. *Political Participation: How and Why People Get Involved in Politics.* Chicago: Rand McNally & Co., 1965.

——. "Political Participation." In *The Handbook of Political Behavior,* vol. 4. edited by Long, Samuel L. New York: Plenum Press, 1981.

——. and M. L. Goel. *Political Participation: How and Why People Get Involved in Politics,* second edition. Chicago: Rand McNally College Publishing, 1977.

Mladenka, Kenneth R. "Blacks and Hispanics in Urban Politics." *American Political Science Review* 83 (1989): 165-191.

Morgan, Ryan. "Gay, lesbian coalition gaining political clout." *Denver Post,* February 16, 2001, B-6.

Morris, Bonnie Rothman. "Teach Your Child, Virtually." *New York Times,* May 29, 2003, E1, E4.

Moxley, R. Scott. "Simon Flip-flops, Woos Gays." *OC Weekly.* April, 2002, 23.

Murray, Charles. *Losing Ground: American Social Policy 1950-1980.* New York: Basic Books, 1984.

Murray, David, Joel Schwartz, and S. Robert Lichter. *It Ain't Necessarily So: How Media Make and Unmake the Scientific Picture of Reality.* Lanham, MD: Rowman & Littlefield, 2001.

Nagel, Jack H. *Participation.* Englewood Cliffs, NJ: Prentice-Hall, 1987.

National Catholic Education Association, "United States Catholic Elementary and Secondary School Statistics," 2000-2001. Online version.

National Center for Educational Statistics. "Use of School Choice." June 1995. Online version.

National Center for Educational Statistics, Quick Tables and Figures, Common Core of Data, Local Education Agency Universe Survey, 1997-98. Online version.

Nelson, Beryl and others. "The State of Charter Schools 2000." Washington, DC: Office of Educational Research and Improvement, U.S. Department of Education, 2000.

Nelson, Joan M. *Access to Power: Politics and the Urban Poor in Developing Nations.* Princeton, NJ: Princeton University Press, 1979.

Nelson, William E., Jr. and Philip J. Meranto. *Electing Black Mayors: Political Action in the Black Community.* Columbus: Ohio State University Press, 1977.

Norris, Pippa. *Democratic Phoenix: Reinventing Political Activism.* Cambridge, UK: Cambridge University Press, 2002.

Novack, Janet. "Are You A Chump?" *Forbes,* March 5, 2001, 122-129.

Novak, Genyphyr. "AIDSphobia communist blasted in Chicago." *Gay Community News,* August 12-18, 1990, 3.

Ocama, Ponsiano and William M. Lee. "Don't Forget This Infection Killer." *New York Times,* March 1, 2003. Online version.

Odets, Walt. *In the Shadow of the Epidemic: Being HIV-Negative in the Age of AIDS.* Durham, NC: Duke University Press, 1995.

Olasky, Marvin. *The Tragedy of American Compassion.* Washington, DC: Regnery Gateway, 1992.

Ollman, Bertram and Edward Veroff, editors. *The Left Academy: Marxist Scholarship on American Campuses* (vol. 1). New York: McGraw-Hill, 1982.

Ollman, Bertram and Edward Veroff, editors. *The Left Academy: Marxist Scholarship on American Campuses* (vol. 2). New York: Praeger, 1984.

Onishi, Noirimitsu. "Nongovernmental Organizations Show Their Growing Power." *New York Times,* March 22, 2002, A10.

"Out and into the Voting Booth." Denver, CO: The Gill Foundation, 2000.

Overby, L. Marvin and Kenneth M. Cosgrove. "Unintended Consequences?: Racial Redistricting and the Representation of Minority Interests." *Journal of Politics* (1996) 58:540-550.

Oyer, Paul and Scott Schaffer. "The Unintended Consequences of the '91 Civil Rights Act." *Regulation,* (Summer), 2003, 42-47.

Palmeri, Christopher. "Politicians Should Butt Out of Pension Funds." *Business Week*, June 11, 2001.

Parker, Frank R. *Black Votes Count: Political Empowerment in Mississippi After 1965.* Chapel Hill: University of North Carolina Press, 1990.

Parry, Geraint. "The Idea of Political Participation." In *Participation in Politics,* edited by Anderson, Bryce and others. Manchester, UK: Manchester University Press, 1972.

Patai, Daphne and Noretta Koertge. *Professing Feminism.* New York: Basic Books, 1994.

Peper, Rachel. "Schism Slices ACT-Up in Two." *Outweek,* October 10, 1990, 12-14.

Perry, Huey L. "The Socioeconomic Impact of Black Political Empowerment in a Rural Southern Locality." *Rural Sociology* (1980) 45:207-222.

"Policy: AIDS Activists 'dissidents' target health officials, other activists." *AIDS Weekly.* May 13, 2002.

Pollack, Andrew with Lawrence K. Altman. "Large Trial Finds AIDS Vaccine Fails to Stop Infections." *New York Times,* February 24, 2003. Online version.

Pranger, Robert J. *The Eclipse of Citizenship: Power and Participation in Contemporary Politics.* New York: Holt Rinehart and Winston, 1968.

Price, Joyce Howard. "Mortality Risk Seen Best for Funding." *Washington Times*, April 22, 2002. Online version.

"The Professor." *Time,* December 16, 2002, 33.

"The Promise of Solidarity." *Black Enterprise,* 32, September 2001, 14, Online version.

Pruitt, Kathey and Rhonda Cook. "GBI reviews state flag threats: Lawmakers who favored the new banner receive rubber snakes, letters." *Atlanta Journal-Constitution,* April 14, 2001. Online version.

"Race in the Voting Booth." *American Enterprise*, January 2001, 10, Online version.

Ravitch, Diane. *The Language Police: How Pressure Groups Restrict What Students Learn.* New York: Alfred A. Knopf, 2003.

Rayside, David. *On the Fringe: Gays and Lesbians in Politics.* Ithaca, NY: Cornell University Press, 1998.

Redick, Alison. "Dangerous Practices: Ideological Uses of the 'Second Wave.'" In *Policing Public Sex: Queer Politics and the Future of AIDS Activism.* edited by Dangerous Bedfellows (Colter, Ephen Glenn, Wayne Hoffman, Eva Pendleton, Alison Redick, and David Serlin). Boston: South End Press, 1996.

Reed, Ralph Jr. "Casting a Wider Net." *Policy Review.* (1993) Summer, 31-35.

Reeves, Hope. "Read Their Lips: No Taxes (Period.)." *New York Times,* July 8, 2002, Online version.

Reuters. "Some Routine AIDS Screening is Advised." *New York Times,* April 18, 2003. Online version.

Rogers, Jimmie N and Stephen A. Smith. "Popular Populism: Political Messages in Country Music Lyrics." In *Mass Politics: The Politics of Popular Culture.* Edited by Shea, Daniel M. New York: Worth Publishing, 1999.

Rom, Mark Carl. "Gays and AIDS: Democratizing Disease?" In *The Politics of Gay Rights* edited by Rimmerman, Craig A., Kenneth D.Wald, and Clyde Wilcox. Chicago: University of Chicago Press, 2000.

Rosenstone, Steven J. and John Mark Hansen. *Mobilization, Participation, and Democracy in America.* New York: Macmillan, 1993.

Rotello, Gabriel. "For Sale: State-of-the-Art Unsafe." *New York Newsday* January 26, 1995a.

——. "What Happens When Baths are Closed?" *New York Newsday,* May 11, 1995b.

——. *Sexual Ecology: AIDS and the Destiny of Gay Men.* New York: Dutton. 1997a.

——. "An Open Letter to Sex Panic." July 25, 1997b, Online version at http://www.grd.org/grd/media/print/gabr.../1997/open.letter.to.sex.panic.-07.25.97

Rothchild, John. "Why I Invest With Sinners." *Fortune,* May 13, 1996, 197.

Rowe, David. *Popular Cultures: Rock Music, Sport and the Politics of Pleasure.* London: Sage, 1995.

Rubin, Barry R. *A Citizen's Guide to Politics in America: How the System Works and How to Work the System.* Expanded edition. Armonk, NY: M.E. Sharpe, 2000.

Rusk, Jerrold G. "Political Participation in America: A Review Essay." *American Political Science Review* 70 (1976): 583-591.

Salholz, Eloise with Patricia King, Clara Bingham and Nonny De La Pena. "The Right-to-Lifers' New Tactics." *Newsweek,* July 9, 2000, 23.

Salisbury, Robert H. "Research on Political Participation." *American Journal of Political Science* 19 (1975): 323-341.

Santoro, Wayne A. "Black Politics and Employment Policies: The Determinants of Local Government Affirmative Action." *Social Science Quarterly* (1995) 76:794-808.

Scherreik, Susan. "A Conscience Doesn't Have to Make You Poor." *Business Week,* May 1, 2000. 204-207.

School Reform News. "Survey: 850,000 Students Homeschooled." October 2001, 1.

Segal, David. "Main Street America Has Advocates Aplenty; On the Hill, Lobbyists for All." *Washington Post,* July 10, 1995. Online version.

Senate Hearings before the Committee on Appropriations, Labor, Departments of Health and Human Services, Education and Related Agencies Appropriations, 99th Congress, second session March 5, 1986. Washington, DC: US Government Printing Office.

Sewell, Gilbert T. "History Textbooks At The New Century." New York: American Textbook Council, 2000.

Sewell, Gilbert T. and Stapley W. Emberling. "A New Generation of History Textbooks." *Society,* Nov./Dec., 1998, 78-82.

Shales, Amity. "Voucher Program Passes a Test." *Wall Street Journal,* October 30, 1998.

Shapiro, Robert Y. and John T. Young. "The Polls: Medical Care in the United States." *Public Opinion Quarterly,* 50 (1986): 418-28.

Shaw, Randy. *The Activist Handbook: A Primer for the 1990s and Beyond.* Berkeley: University of California Press, 1996.

Sheehan, James M. "Socially Irresponsible Investing." *Free Market,* May 2002, 3-6.

Sherrill, Kenneth. "The Political Power of Lesbians, Gays and Bisexuals." *PS: Political Science and Politics.* 29 (1996): 469-73.

Shilts, Randy. *And The Band Played On: Politics, People and the AIDS Epidemic.* New York: Penguin Books. 1988.

Shoofs, Mark 1996. "An AIDS Vaccine: It's Possible. So Why Isn't It Being Done?" In *Policing Public Sex: Queer Politics and the Future of AIDS Activism,* edited by Dangerous Bedfellows (Colter, Ephen Glenn, Wayne Hoffman, Eva Pendleton, Alison Redick, and David Serlin). Boston: South End Press, 1996.

Silverstein, Ken. "Trillion-Dollar Hideaway." *Mother Jones* November/ December, 2000 38-45, 94-96.

Simon, Julian. *Hoodwinking the Nation.* New Brunswick, NJ: Transaction Publishers, 1999.

Simpson, Glenn R. "U.S. to Crack Down on Violations of Laws on Offshore Bank Accounts." *Wall Street Journal,* April 30, 2002. A6.

Skolnick, Jerome. *The Politics of Protest.* New York: Ballantine Books, 1969.

Smith, Daniel, A. *Tax Crusaders and the Politics of Direct Democracy.* New York: Routledge, 1998.

Smith, Stephen H. "Testimony." U.S. Senate, Subcommittee on Labor, Health and Human Services, and Education, and Related Agencies, Committee on Appropriations, Department of Health and Human Services, National Institutes of Health, May 6, 1999. Washington, DC: U.S. Government Printing Office, 2000.

Sorge, Rod. "ACT-UP/New York blasts the 'Times." *Gay Community News,* August 13-19, 1989, 1

Sorokin, Ellen "No Founding Fathers? That's Our New History." *Washington Times*, January 28, 2002. Online version.

Sorokin, Ellen. "Blacks turn to home-schooling." *Washington Times,* February 9, 2003. Online version.

"The Species Litigation Act." *Wall Street Journal,* April 20, 2001, A14.

Staley, Peter, "Has the Direct-Action Group ACT-UP Gone Astray?" *Advocate,* July 30, 1991.

Stern, William J. "How Dagger John Saved New York's Irish." In *What Makes Charity Work?: A Century of Public and Private Philanthropy* edited by Magnet, Myron. Chicago: Ivan R. Dee, 2000.

Stille, Alexander. "Textbook Publishers Learn to Avoid Messing with Texas." *New York Times,* June 29, 2002. Online version.

Stout, David. "Tab for Washington Lobbying: $1.42 Billion." *New York Times,* July 29, 1999, A15.

Strassel, Kimberly A. "Done Him Wrong: Ms. Maines Regrets Anti-Bush Remark." *Wall Street Journal,* March 20, 2003, D8.

Strom, Stephanie. "Gifts to Charity in 2002 Stayed Unexpectedly High." *New York Times,* June 23, 2003. A14.

Sturm, Roland. "The Effects of Obesity, Smoking, and Health Problems on Chronic Medical Problems and Health Care Costs." *Health Affairs* 21 (2002): 245-53.

Tate, Katherine. "Black Opinion on the Legitimacy of Racial Redistricting and Minority-Majority Districts." *American Political Science Review* (2003) 97:45-56.

Temple, Johnny. "Noise From Underground." *Nation,* October 18, 1999.

The Heartlander, November 2002.

The Left Guide: A Guide to Left-of-Center Organizations, edited by Wilcox, Derk Arend. Ann Arbor, MI: Economics America, Inc, 1996.

The Right Guide: A Guide to Conservative, Free Market and Right-of-Center Organizations, fourth edition, Edited by Wilcox, Derk Arend. Ann Arbor, MI: Economics America, Inc, 2000.

Theodoulou, Stella Z. "AIDS Equals Politics." In *AIDS: The Politics and Policy of Disease* edited by Theodoulou, Stella Z. Upper Saddle River, NJ: Prentice-Hall, 1996.

——. Gloria Y. Guevara, and Henrik Minnassians. "Myths and Illusions: The Media and AIDS Policy." In *AIDS: The Politics and Policy of Disease,* edited by Theodoulou, Stella Z. Upper Saddle River, NJ: Prentice-Hall, 1996.

Thernstrom, Abigail and Stephen Thernstrom. *No Excuses: Closing the Racial Gap in Learning.* New York: Simon and Schuster, 2003.

Thomas, Kendall. "Going Public: A Conversation with Lidell Jackson and Jocelyn Taylor." In *Policing Public Sex: Queer Politics and the Future of AIDS Activism.* Edited by Dangerous Bedfellows (Colter, Ephen Glenn, Wayne Hoffman, Eva Pendleton, Alison Redick, and David Serlin). Boston: South End Press, 1996.

Tilove, Jonathan "2000 Census Finds America's New Mayberry Is Exurban, and Overwhelmingly White, *Newhouse News Service,* Online version. www.newhouse.com/archive/story1a051001.html.

Tomsho, Robert "Controversy Flares Over Public Funding of 'Cyber Schools." *Wall Street Journal,* April 5, 2002, A1.

——. "Charter-School Movement Sputters." *Wall Street Journal,* January 21, 2003, A3.

Trachtenberg, Leo. "Philanthropy that Worked" In *What Makes Charity Work?:A Century of Public and Private Philanthropy,* edited by Myron, Magnet. Chicago: Ivan R. Dee, 2000.

Trend, David. *Cultural Democracy: Politics, Media, New Technology.* Albany: State University Press of New York, 1997.

Tucker, Neely. "Report Say Youth Violence Overplayed." *Washington Post,* April 10, 2001. Online version.

Tucker, William. "Overregulation and the Black Market." *Consumers Research* 74 (1991): 32-34.

Tuller, David. "New Tactic to Prevent AIDS Spread." *New York Times,* August 13, 2002. Online version.

Turner, Wayne. "AIDS Incorporated: How federal AIDS money ended up funding psychic hotlines, Neiman Marcus, and flirting classes." *Washington Monthly,* 33, April, 2001, 17-21.

U.S. Bureau of the Census, *Statistical Abstract of the United States: 2001.* Washington, DC.

U.S. Department of Health and Human Services. *Physical Activity and Health: A Report of the Surgeon General.* Atlanta, GA: Center for Disease Control and Prevention, 1996.

Ubel. Peter A. *Pricing Life: Why It's Time for Health Care Rationing.* Cambridge, MA: MIT Press, 2000.

Uchitelle, Louis. "Blacks Lose Better Jobs as Middle-Class Work Drops." *New York Times,* July 12, 2003. Online version.

US News, "The New Education Bazaar." April 27, 1998. Online version. www.usnews.com

Vaid, Urashi. *Virtual Equality: The Mainstreaming of Gay and Lesbian Liberation.* New York: Anchor Books, 1995.

VandeHei, Jim. "Mississippi's Choctaw Find an Unlikely Ally in a GOP Stalwart." *Wall Street Journal,* July 3, 2000, A1.

Varmus, Harold. "Testimony." U.S. Senate, Subcommittee on Labor, Health and Human Services, and Education, and Related Agencies, Committee on Appropriations, Department of Health and Human Services, National Institutes of Health, May 6, 1999. Washington, DC: U.S. Government Printing Office: 2000.

Verba, Sidney, Key Lehman Schlozman, and Henry E. Brady. *Voice and Equity: Civic Voluntarism in American Politics.* Cambridge, MA: Harvard University Press, 1995.

Verba, Sidney and Norman H. Nie. *Participation in America: Political Democracy and Social Equality.* New York: Harper & Row, 1972.

——. and Jae-on Kim. *Participation and Political Equality: A Seven Nation Comparison.* Chicago: University of Chicago Press, 1978.

Verba, Sidney, Key Lehman Schlozman, and Henry E. Brady. "The Big Tilt: Participatory Inequality in America." *American Prospect* (1997) May-June, 74-80.

"Victory Fund, Bond Charting New Futures." *US Newswire,* October 4, 2000. Online version.

Wachter, Robert M. *The Fragile Coalition: Scientists, Activists and AIDS.* New York: St. Martin's, 1991.

Wald, Kenneth D. "The Context of Gay Politics." In *The Politics of Gay Rights* edited by Rimmerman, Craig A., Kenneth D. Wald, and Clyde Wilcox. Chicago: University of Chicago Press, 2000.

Wall Street Journal, November 30, 2001, W19. Also see their website: www.WalkForCapitalism.org

Wall Street Journal, June 6, 2001.

Washington Information Directory 2002-2003. Washington, DC: CQ Press, 2003.

Weissberg, Robert. *Political Tolerance: Balancing Community and Diversity.* Thousand Oaks, CA: Sage, 1998.

Weissberg, Robert. *The Politics of Empowerment.* Westport, CT: Praeger, 1999.

Whitby, Kenny J. and Gilliam, Franklin D. Jr. "A Longitudinal Analysis of Competing Explanations of the Transformation of Southern Congressional Politics." *Journal of Politics* (1991) 53:504-518.

Whittlsey, Frances Cerra. "Mutual Funds That Match Your Beliefs." *Nation's Business,* December 1998, 23.

Williams, John. "Minorities compete on political field." *Houston Chronicle,* April 23, 2003. Online version.

Williamsom, Christine. "Religious Funds Find a Following." *Pensions & Investments,* May 1999, 3, 26.

Wittenberg, Ernest and Elizabeth Wittenberg. *How to Win in Washington: Very Practical Advice About Lobbying The Grassroots and The Media,* second edition. Cambridge: Blackwell, 1994.

"Women Picket Cosmopolitan Magazine." *Guardian,* January 27, 1988, 4.

Wysocki, Bernard Jr. "The Lack of Vaccines Goes Beyond Flu Inoculations." *Wall Street Journal,* December. 8, 2003, A1, A8.

Yang, Alan S. "The Polls—Trends Towards Homosexuality." *Public Opinion Quarterly* 61 (1997): 477-507.

Zimmerman, Rachel. "AIDS-Virus Cases Rise in 25 States." *Wall Street Journal* February 12, 2003, D2.

Zipser, Andy. "Abhorring a Vacuum." *Baron's,* January 12, 1998, F18-F19.

Zweig, Jason . "Why 'Socially Responsible' Investing Isn't Quite As Heavenly As It Might Sound." *Money,* June 1996, 64.

Index